Inside the United Nations

In A Leaderless World

Samir Sanbar

Table of Contents

Contents

CHAPTER I:

CROSSING FIRST AVENUE

It took me 26 years of working in Manhattan before I was able to fully enjoy living there. Not that I resided too far from work – to get to my office, it took me six minutes every morning door to door. I made a special effort to explore the city's uniquely vibrant pulse at a time when Bob Dylan and Joan Baez drew crowds in Washington Square; Ray Charles rhythmically proclaimed he was busted; an emerging Carole King confirmed, "you've got a friend," though you're far away; aspiring actors bided their time as waiters in select restaurants; brilliant intellectuals fervently debated pressing issues; key universities held internationally interesting seminars; New Yorkers were open to eye contact, particularly as they heard Stephen Stills, suggesting, "If you are not with the one you love, love the one you are with." Actually, weeks after my arrival, I went with my direct UN boss, Under-Secretary-General Gabriel d'Arboussier, a French-Senegalese marquis to watch the fight between rising star Cassius Clay and world champion Sonny Liston. Minutes into the match, I bent to light a cigarette. When everyone stood up with roaring astonishment; I had just missed the historical knockout that launched Muhammad Ali into world space. Immediately after that, I stopped smoking. My continued determination to keep in touch was limited by UN calling duties, but once I crossed those security-guarded gates of the United Nations compound, my only image of Manhattan consisted of a partial view of the East River. Like any true believer, I went home merely to sleep and returned the following morning ready to contact any envoy, speak any language and listen to any speech in order to promote the cause.

I served five UN Secretaries-General – U Thant, Kurt Waldheim, Javier Perez de Cuellar, Boutros Boutros-Ghali and Kofi Annan – in a variety of positions, including as Special Representative of the UN Secretary-General and Head of the UN Department of Public Information and Communications. My commitment was fueled by the issues we faced daily and stimulated by the people I met, within an engaging, almost contagious atmosphere. The United Nations is a perpetual university on the human condition.

There is so much more to the United Nations than meets the lens of a camera. And what we see through limited media coverage is less than what one learns from the briefest assignment. The complex's corridors, gardens, lobbies, lounges, entrances and exits display a unique cultural blend of history, politics and art. These objects range from carvings of the first peace treaty signed 3,000 years ago to modern works by Pablo Picasso, Marc Chagall, Henri Matisse, Salvador Dali, Henry Moore and Norman Rockwell. Since its founding days of the 1940s, United Nations member governments and newly anointed leaders from newly created states have come bearing offerings as if in dedication to a new shrine of hope.

Still, it's the people who inhabit the building – the diplomats, staff, peacemakers, humanitarian workers, and representatives from many non-governmental organizations (NGOs) – who offer the most precious experiences and inspiration. The first lesson, if you have any sense, is in modesty. Whatever you think of yourself, you soon discover that there's always someone more important; whatever you think of your achievement, you're bound to meet someone better accomplished. If you feel that an ambassador looked too distinguished, you have only to wait to see him with his Foreign Minister. And the same applies to the Foreign Minister when his or respective President would arrive. As to that President, simply watch when he or she meets their counterpart from a Big Power.

Within the Secretariat, the most modest were often the most important, starting with the Secretaries-General: U Thant, listening intently to views of junior staff while awaiting WQXR radio news on the hour; Javier Perez de Cuellar, phoning to ensure the safety of a staff member on a risky mission; or Boutros Boutros-Ghali enjoying an argument over one of his favorite UN "Blue Books", an edition on anti-apartheid that he wanted to present to Nelson Mandela. And then there were the prominent cast of characters: "Madiba", the affectionate nickname of Mr. Mandela himself, a shining tower of modesty who appreciated the slightest of services, with gracious comments like "First class, first class," or Under-Secretary-General Ralph Bunche, Nobel Peace Laureate and civil rights activist, asking for a briefing on an upcoming meeting while wondering whether the shaky elevator would actually get us to our destination.

Dr. Bunche relished telling a story about one of the first astronauts in space. Upon returning to Earth, the newest world hero went on an international tour. In Moscow, Soviet leader Nikita Khrushchev took him aside to ask whether he saw signs that God above existed. When the astronaut was affirmative, the General Secretary of the Communist Party whispered, "I thought so. But please do not say so in public." In Italy, the president asked the same question, but the distinguished visitor shifted his impressions, saying he was not sure. The Catholic leader then whispered, "I also had my doubts, but please do not inform the public." Upon return to the United States, the Governor of Alabama, George Wallace, rushed to his side. Did he see God? Yes, was the answer. "Wasn't he such a glorious white man?" asked the segregationist politician. The astronaut paused for effect, then coolly responded, "She was black."

The UN system is the most open university in the world. Everyone is a student and teacher at the same time. If thoughtfully kept, valuable contacts made there would remain forever. Alumni remain in touch wherever they are. They feel a special bond whenever they meet again elsewhere. Personalities and nationalities mingled within agreed lines, learning not only from other people's experience but also from exploring unprecedented paths. A collective wisdom, enriched by diverse cultures, made its way gradually into a staff member's mind and spirit, as a remarkable number of other varied personalities equally learned and taught. Many unforgettable, yet some easily forgotten, appeared in major or minor instructive roles. The world, literally, was our stage.

A related lesson learned through the UN experience is that we are all human. A king anxiously awaits his son's return while overseeing a crucial meeting. Another king, from a much smaller country, without missing a beat, awaits alternative transportation in lieu of stepping

3

regally into his vehicle. Argentine President Carlos Menem handles Security Council matters but longs for a "cafetito". Czech President Vaclav Havel wonders whether there was a way to find some time to eventually visit a jazz club downtown. A surprised and annoyed 'Mr. Nyet", Soviet Foreign Minister Andrei Gromyko, draws the media behind him as he leaves a crisis meeting for the bathroom. An Asian Prime Minister is frustratingly fascinated by a disinterested UN guide from his region. The Ambassador of a superpower is infatuated with a female UN press officer. To handle these correctly, discreetly - indeed, cheerfully and in stride – is part of a full day's work.

While learning to distinguish English accents of various nationalities, you also recognize not to evaluate people by them. To begin with, it would be useful to ascertain the accent in question. My first secretary, a young graduate from Hicksville, Long Island, broke into tears once during a dictation by one of the most senior British civil servants. She couldn't "stayend" his "aqccent". In a cool voice and understated tone, the offending - and offended - Oxford graduate responded: "Let's get one thing straight, young lady: it is you who has the accent."

The terms "developed" and "developing" may apply to countries, but not necessarily to their citizens. In addition to the Secretaries-General, ambassadors such as Tommy Koh of Singapore, Juan Somavia of Chile (later to become head of the International Labour Organization), Brazil's Celso Amorim (later to become Foreign Minister), Chief Simeon Adebo and Ibrahim Gambari of Nigeria, Carlos Romulo of Philippines, Paolo Fulci of Italy, Louise Fréchette of Canada (a good Ambassador but poor Deputy Secretary-General), Marjetta Rasi of Finland, and before her, Martti Ahtisaari, who became President of that country and later also won a Nobel Prize for Peace, are just a few names that would stand out in any nationality and whatever their accent.

Big Powers, or to be accurate, the five permanent members of the Security Council, naturally had their large shares of impressive and instructive representatives. A special curriculum could be drawn from observing the Hamlet-like style of Adlai E. Stevenson, the judicious approach of Justice Arthur Goldberg or the sharp operational talents of Vernon Walters; the Cold War interventions of Nikolai Fedorenko or the post-cold-war negotiating tactics of Sergey Lavrov, later to become Russia's Foreign Minister; the outstanding maneuvers of Sir David Hannay or the biting wit of Lord Caradon; the careful far-sighted approach of Huang Hua, who led the "restoration of China's rights" that brought the People's Republic to the UN, or the discreet charm of Ambassadors Jhi and Jin; the analytical minds of François Gazier of the École Nationale d'Administration, the easy, meticulous, handiwork of France's Alain Dejammet and the discreet peacemaking of Bernard Millet.

Lord Caradon, who hailed from a Scottish glen, used to refer to his bow-tied, aristocratic-looking Soviet counterpart as the "Laird of Glen Cove", the Long Island town where the Soviet staff had a large, restricted colony compound. A favorite among Anglophile staff of the time, Lord Caradon's actual name was Hugh Foot. His brother, Michael Foot, was prominent on the left of the Labour Party; and another brother, Dingle, was also prominent, but at the center. "In our family," he would quip, "the right Foot does not know what the left Foot is doing". Presumably, all was well, as long as the family put the right foot forward at the right time.

With such instructors, one eventually develops a nose for the scent of power. Over time, some learn to separate the real from the pretentious and sense the source of power: who has it, where and how it is exercised. Experience indicates that power needs no introduction; it gives its own signals.

It is therefore also unwise to underestimate the fellow seated nearby. While some transient players insist on inflating their role, there were many unassuming staff members who had played very important historic roles, yet each with casual dignity. At one of my meetups, a guest colleague of the U.N. World Food Programme listened attentively and gave me valuable advice. It turned out that Raymond Aubrac was not only a French resistance hero, but he was also one of the very few individuals to have the respect and admiration of Vietnamese leader Ho Chi Minh – which allowed him to play a vital mediation role. Another, a modest talking diplomat, had headed military intelligence in his country giving him easy access to almost every source of information, yet he rarely displayed his influence, except when wrongly exposed.

You also find out that you get better results working as a team. It is more effective when everyone strives to advance on one issue in a joint effort. Obviously, there are national interests to be represented and points of view to be expressed, but being human usually works in both directions. Initial suspicion, shyness, even arrogance are overcome through daily doses of human warmth and shared concern. Thus, a corps- a body - of varied people, drawn from different countries, is reshaped flexibly and regularly to face different situations. Whether on the specific questions of the eradication of smallpox or the general matter of sustainable development, there is always some joint group preparing a "non-paper" for the consensus support of the international community.

And the international community is inclusively, universally represented by the United Nations, east of First Avenue, on the site of a former slaughterhouse in Turtle Bay. It could have been in San Francisco, where its Charter was signed, or in Lake Success, Long Island, where its Secretariat started. But the Rockefeller family made an offer that the international community could not refuse. Diplomatic gossip had it that the purpose was to raise the value of the vast adjacent property stretching from the East River to Rockefeller Center on Fifth Avenue. But what was good for Rockefeller at the time was good for America, and indeed, good for the world. When the rectangular glass tower was ready for occupancy, there were fewer than 60 member countries, served by fewer than 1,000 staff members, led by Norwegian Secretary-General Trygve Lie. When designing the General Assembly Hall, architects believed they were optimistic in visualizing an expansion of the membership to 100 by the year 2000. Today there are 193 countries; the relatively young United Nations is older than two-thirds of its members.

Everyone has a human interest story. One of my first culture shocks – a pleasant one – was to see a fierce looking Gurkha standing up to read his poetry. During a visit to a commanding officer, it was touching to find out that among his notes on war and conflict he had jotted down a poem picked up from somewhere that day: "I sent you a rose in a glass of champagne while the Gypsies played as Gypsies do. Then you turned to the man you were with and said: You see his eyes? He's in love with me too."

For years, most visitors, particularly Americans, wanted to see where Soviet leader Khrushchev had banged his shoe. A more enduring spot of puzzlement, though, might be the modernistic mural on the interior wall of the Assembly Hall. When inaugurating the Hall, President Eisenhower reportedly gazed at the mural in utter silence, shaking his head. He then picked a quarter out of his pocket and handed it to Dag Hammarskjold, saying, "Secretary-General, I'll give you this quarter if you can tell me what the thing on the wall means." Though a modern art enthusiast, Mr. Hammarskjold pulled out a dollar and responded, "Mr. President, please take this dollar and spare me that task." Secretary-General Hammarskjold used to enjoy standing in the garden next to the Assembly Hall and contemplating the beauty of the water fountain at the Secretariat entrance.

Dag Hammarskjold died a martyr for peace, instilling a profound sense of international civil service in generations like ours that followed. You objectively and faithfully acted for the whole world. You worked closely with Member States, but never took instructions from any Government, especially not your own. Each staff member even signed an oath to this effect under the heading, "I solemnly swear." You took instructions only from the Secretary-General. We needed to work with the Big Powers for the world to survive, but we needed to work with the small Powers for humanity to succeed.

Clearly, as anywhere else, there are a few, very few, who may spend time not working but networking. There are always those who, in their rush to exploit their fleeting authority, tend to forget who they should work for and are visible enough to provide a negative example for use by the adversaries of the Organization. These exceptions do a terrible disservice to the tens of thousands of unknown, unseen and unheralded staff around the world who exert their utmost to uphold the objectives of the Charter, sometimes at risk to their own lives.

Drastic changes were injected in the appointments and promotions exercise in order to allow politically appointed "managers" – Under-Secretaries-General, heads of departments and offices, aides to the Secretary-General – to make appointments on his behalf with impunity, shortening the contract cycle to generally make it not very tempting for those looking for a career in the international field, plus the predominant influence of a very few powerful countries regarding appointments in key and senior-level posts – all these actions have eroded the spirit and corps of the international civil service as envisaged by the UN's founding fathers.

Besides active members of non-governmental organizations, a number of what could be described as "UN groupies" evolved; individuals or couples, who were hoping to receive reciprocation by calling people "honorable." They may have been perceived as social ego tippers, though others could have been exploring opportunities. For example, one shopkeeper of Italian-sounding men's apparel offered special discounts in return for national day events, on which he would proudly report. Another prodded diplomatic couples to spend time in Iceland, though he was not from there, urging investment in its banks before they were reported bankrupt. Again, these are exceptional, eventually discredited cases.

With the "end of history" at the UN, the classification of the staff within the Secretariat seems to be between the majority who were working and a minority that was not working, but networking. The workers promoted the UN, the networkers promoted themselves. And while devoted staff upheld faithfully the oath of international civil service, the networkers boasted about their keen interest in following instructions from influential governments. Instead of faithfully serving the Secretary-General, they used his name and office to connect, get on the invitation circuit and pontificate on any question except pressing UN issues.

An unprecedented state of confusion and lack of focus eroding the international civil service has given rise to new characters, which are almost a modern version of the Beatles' "Nowhere Man," making nowhere plans for nobody. They were never concerned or preoccupied except for a politically correct minute about a politically correct topic du jour.

There was a time when staff came to work with great joy. Now, regretfully, a politically expedient few have been allowed to "de-inspire," and to train the name of the dedicated majority. That must change.

Will the international civil service survive? Can it be resuscitated? And if it can be given a lease on life, will the new Secretary-General be the right person to do it? Will they be able to revive the spirit of the international service, or will political demands and daily pressures divert their attention from their closest and most readily available resource – their staff?

The morale of the UN's personnel used to receive an annual boost on Staff Day. For years, almost everyone would participate in colorful performances, friendly competitions and the normal exchange of brief speeches. Although those celebrations have ceased, UN Day is still widely commemorated at Headquarters and beyond every October 24th with a free musical concert open to staff and diplomats alike.

Like the wooden, nesting *matryoshka* dolls, the international diplomatic community is composed mainly of three groups: governments, non-governmental organizations and executive civil servants. That is the simple part. The more complex aspect is the consensual structure of civil service that covers every aspect of human life. Here again there are primarily three categories: the Secretariat in New York with regional offices; related programs and funds, such as UNICEF for children and UNDP for development; specialized agencies, such as the United Nations Educational, Scientific and Cultural Organization (UNESCO) in Paris, the Food and Agriculture Organization (FAO) in Rome, the World Health Organization (WHO) in Geneva, and the World Bank group (IBRD, IMF) in Washington. Some agencies, such as the Universal Postal Union in Bern, Switzerland, had existed before the creation of the UN. Others, such as the banking institutions known as the Bretton Woods group, developed a partnership through a negotiated arrangement that they established around the same time the UN was born.

The chiefs of this international mosaic used to meet under the unassuming name of the Administrative Committee on Coordination, and now as the United Nations System Chief Executives Board for Coordination. The names change, yet the older body's acronym, ACC, gave rise to alphabet soup riddles. An original dozen grew to over 30 "bodies and organs", from WIPO, which deals with intellectual property, to UNWTO, which handles tourism. As in the Security Council, however, where five permanent members have veto power, a more discreet group of five has always been predominant internally: UNESCO, ILO, FAO and the World Bank. The Secretary-General, who chairs the meeting, is, of course, first among equals. Yet, he (or perhaps in the future she) has to tread very carefully between the political and the pragmatic, the effective and the feasible.

During my first ACC meeting in 1965, I took notes sitting attentively behind U Thant when a thorny item was raised: a General Assembly resolution to boycott completely the apartheid regime of South Africa. After a concise presentation by the Secretary-General and supportive remarks by some program managers, the World Bank chief explained politely that banking transactions could not be interrupted except at great risk to the entire currency system. A Canadian-based United Nations International Civil Aviation (ICAO) chief emphasized his political support for the proposal but added that in practical terms South

African Airlines had connections around the world and partnerships with other airlines. A boycott directive from his office might not make it to Montreal's airport. To avert an open rift, a suggestion was made that another day of private consultations could help to reach a politically correct and practical outcome. Rene Maheu, the French Director-General of UNESCO, then intervened and announced: "I will not be with you tomorrow due to an urgent appointment in Paris. Therefore, I regret that I will not be able to add to the confusion." It took some time, as usual, for everyone to get on board. But, in a major victory for human dignity, the UN system rallied beyond the boycott and was instrumental in first establishing the State of Namibia out of what had been known as apartheid-dominated South-West Africa, thus opening the gateway to the first fully democratic UN-sponsored election of Nelson Mandela as President of South Africa.

The process can be painstakingly slow. Occasionally, an argument about placing a sentence between brackets or lifting a comma may take days. A definition of the "least developed of developing countries" took a decade to finalize. But patience is a virtue, although, as one of our colleagues often repeated, it should not become a policy. As long as the objective is truly shared and the political will to back it persists, an eventual consensus will be achieved.

Those on the west side of First Avenue who are not familiar with the complexities of the UN galaxy are not alone. Most of those on the inside are so preoccupied with their own assignments that they might only understand what directly involves them. It is like the proverbial reference to missing a forest and seeing only the trees. It may also seem like an organizational jungle, or mostly lions resting with lambs; but there's also a limited number of wolves and vultures who tend to prey on their unsuspecting colleagues. Much depends on the leadership from above. There are always the occasional opportunists on the fringe of even the most dedicated civil service in the world. A limited few manage to continue their own interest with their government's influence or other people's money. Yet, there are always legitimate causes that yield exceptionally pleasant results. Helping displaced people through disaster relief, intervening between obstinate parties to a conflict, combating poverty and promoting human development are some typical examples. Some less taxing posts are at times devised by an enterprising official to accommodate a diplomat in need. No example will be given here; most are known through the grapevine. There is one very interesting task, however - a very legitimate, yet pleasant one dealing with our beloved

Mediterranean Sea. Based in Athens, the Director of the Environmental Regional Programme (Mediterranean Action Plan) is responsible for persuading countries like France, Greece, Italy, and Monaco to protect the maritime atmosphere – it entails only inspection of their exquisite beaches – an assignment most of us would readily perform for free.

One of the greatest attributes of the United Nations during its first 60 years is that it nurtured a generally harmonious group of talented international civil servants drawn from a wide cultural and geographical balance, who patiently dedicated their lives – and sometimes sacrificed them – for international peace and human development.

As a mirror of an imperfect world, however, it was inevitable for the United Nations to get caught partially – though not exclusively – in diplomatic adversities and political conflicts, mostly during periods of the Cold War – and cold peace.

Most insiders at Headquarters generally knew who's who. Those of us in the field had a notion about the main figures but not the full picture.

Clearly, as both the U.S. and U.S.S.R. commanded the two political departments, it was generally assumed that some of their close assistants were advancing their country's agendas. Amazingly, even amusingly, these agendas were not always conflicting. Sometimes, an agreed framework seemed to be tacitly drawn between them on their UN "modus operandi." Sometimes, that most exclusive "club of two" seemed jointly determined to lay down the rules that everyone else will have to follow. The French and British would then make some noises and the Chinese would bargain on something totally unrelated to UN work, most likely some point on Taiwan, Hong Kong, or world trade. Influential developing countries like Brazil, Egypt, India, Nigeria, Mexico, Senegal and Tanzania would go back to the drawing board to ascertain what was going on and arrange for a face-saving compromise.

Working within the UN premises is conveniently addictive. As an international meeting place, conference rooms abound. When active, they beam varied vibrations of controversy or consensus. When empty, the spaces may seem overwhelmingly depressing. Once, while taking the late Mother Teresa on a tour during a slow period, I recall her bemused comment at the sight of the eerily empty halls: "Could you imagine how many homeless could find refuge there?" Well, in a way, they did. Some of the most desperate causes of our time, like the fight against apartheid, the claims for self-determination and affirmation of human rights started there; within 50 years they became uncontested facts of international life. Admittedly, it is almost impossible to have a full house for every meeting. Many delegates float around outside the General Assembly during a long speech. They would time their movements, however, to allow for a profuse handshake as the concluding orator stepped into the nearby "Indonesian Lounge" to receive well-wishers. It would take a Nelson Mandela or another remarkable figure to draw the full membership. Otherwise, the Assembly is often half full, or half empty, depending on the leader. An impressive achievement was credited to Ambassador Paolo Fulci when he pulled in a massive attendance during a visit by the then Italian President Scalfaro during the slowest period in August. Mobilizing the large Italian-American community in New York, he not only managed to get a full house, but he also succeeded in ensuring that in the absence of the Assembly President on his usual leave, the Vice-President who was chairing the gathering spoke in fluent Italian!

Office space is certainly less contentious than in the private sector. Nonetheless, there are specific indications of status. Except for the Secretary-General's floor, where the smallest corner is a declaration of bureaucratic achievement, higher rank was generally noted by the number of windows in an office. The most senior professional, a General Director (D-2), for example, would have four windows and a sofa; a Principal Officer (D-1), three windows and some armchairs. A Head of Department - an Assistant Secretary-General or Under-Secretary-General -- could have six windows, a carpet, sofa, leather chair and walk-in closet. There is also selectivity between a view looking out over Manhattan and the exclusive view of the East River. A unique thrill for a dedicated internationalist is to go from no window at all to the full treatment.

Since the massive renovation of the United Nations Headquarters campus known as the "Capital Master Plan" in 2012, all directors have offices with doors, while most other staff have cubicles. The stated reasons are better air circulation and energy efficiency, as well as the nebulous "synergies" that are supposed to result from this lack of privacy for most staff. Clearly, separating senior and junior staff within departments is not conducive to effective teamwork. Placing them in a strictly business-like atmosphere will not create the sense of camaraderie and commitment, particularly in an organization based not on revenue and profit but on universal principles. While installed with the rationale that this "open plan" approach was the latest rage, management psychologists, before staff even moved back in, had widely refuted the view that such a total lack of privacy was conducive to work and, indeed, affirmed that more productive results come from better conditions. Instead of this productivity, the general staff, boxed in like sardines, take mini-breaks to visit each other, while the higher-ups seem like penguins hopping around in their own areas to gather with one another or consult about what's going on.

In addition, access by elevator to the 38th floor, the location of the Secretary-General, has been deleted, even for Permanent Representatives. With immediate effect, all visitors must stop at the 37th floor and buzz, to be welcomed by one or more security officers, who will escort them upstairs. That puts more stress on the sardines to be alert to whatever diplomatic officialdom is arriving. It also put more security officials in the position of administrative receptionists. Several delegations consider it quite bothersome if not dismissive. The rest of the staff don't even try as the distance has grown way beyond floors. There were several other unintended consequences to that arbitrary decision to keep the 38th floor completely off-limits to all but a selected few who work there. Was this a wise step?

A blend of Secretariat staff, diplomats, journalists, non-governmental groups and interested visitors circulate in this self-sufficient compound. On a daily basis, and often on weekends, they share meeting rooms, restaurants, banks, bookshops, newspaper stands and, more importantly, human contact. Occasionally, special lunches may require strolling across to one of six or seven convenient restaurants nearby. But, in particular on rainy days, the Delegates' Dining Room provided acceptable nourishment with diplomatic showmanship: who is having lunch with whom and at which table. Lunches start at 1:15; cocktails or receptions marking national days, bidding farewells or extending welcomes - all are held between 6:15 and 8:15 in the evening; working dinners start at 8:15. Why diplomats added an extra 15 minutes to the hour I often wondered but never asked.

The Delegates' Lounge was for a long while one of the rare places in New York to share a Cuban cigar. President Fidel Castro habitually brought along prized gifts to counterparts attending the General Assembly opening session while the Cuban mission distributed similar presents during the annual holiday season. With the predominance of smoking-free public space in New York, the lounge remained one of the few areas where it was comfortably allowed. When a politically correct Kofi Annan announced a ban throughout the UN premises, certain delegates protested, indicating that only they had the authority over their congregating venues. For example, Russia's Permanent Representative, Sergey Lavrov, made a point of smoking with friends there. During a visit by Lebanese publisher of the daily newspaper As-Safir, Talal Salman, who was yearning to puff, had a welcome introduction to Mr. Lavrov, as they shared adjoining seats in the Lounge.

High season usually starts every year around the third week of September with the opening of a new General Assembly "general debate". Particularly on milestone anniversary years, heads of State take the opportunity to officially make policy statements yet practically hold discreet meetings. The international glass house turns into a vivid theatre of political bargaining unobserved by the outside world. If each one of the visiting dignitaries extended at least one obligatory invitation to lunch or dinner, you could actually leave home for one week without your credit card. A British delegate was widely admired for going through an average of three obligatory dinners an evening, maintaining the traditional stiff upper lip. The 50th anniversary of the UN in 1995 was a special learning experience. As Head of the Department for Public Information, I had a unique opportunity to deal with almost every one of the more than 150 Heads of State from varied cultures and political systems. One of the most instructive moments was when the Heads of State posed alone for a commemorative photograph. Looking into the eyes of a lonesome ruler separated from his personal entourage was worth 30 years of service.

While certain delegates seek the limelight, others prefer to be left alone at least for a brief period where they can get a quiet nap before returning to the monitored conference chambers. One of the most sought after papers among Security Council members in the year 2000 was a secret map left by departing French ambassador mamet about where to sleep uninterrupted in the busy sprawling compound on the East River. A workaholic tough negotiator with a stern gaze and a warm heart, Dejamet had offered it along with other more serious briefings to his successor, Jean-David Levitte, who did not seem to have done the same when he left to become ambassador in Washington DC. The list included the Indonesian Lounge, next to the General Assembly hall, when there are no meetings and the x-press bar when there are no parties. There are those delegates, however, who do not shy away from a public nod, not realizing that U.N. cameras have caught up with the age of technology. The Japanese in particular seem to unabashedly fall asleep, but once you assume the delegate is out of it, he would suddenly open his eyes to ask a very pertinent question. By the time you start to answer he would doze off again. Diplomats from a certain region who habitually sleep late at their hotels would tip toe softly to their seat before they realized that they had not yet read their local newspaper.

While certain delegates compete to obtain prominent seating in the conference rooms or in the Assembly, others explore ways to locate a back seat. At the early days of the Organization for example, a usual listing in alphabetical order placed Afghanistan at the forefront of any gathering. At the time, representing a country that had never been occupied throughout its long history, the delegate from Kabul did not wish to take sides. He was partly suspicious of what the big powers were up to and he was keen on avoiding any potential controversy which would undercut his King Zahir Shah's smooth relations with all sides. So when Afghanistan was called to cast the first vote its delegate habitually abstained to the point of being dubbed "Abstainistan". Later, a different seating formula was agreed upon based on a lottery. Each year the Secretary-General in a procedural ceremony will pick a random name out of a box and the selected country will take the first seat in the General Assembly to be followed by alphabetical order.

Although printed press were assigned seats with pad holders, no media were allowed for the first four years except for specific events. The meetings were still held at Lake Success, Long Island, when General Assembly president of 1949 general Carlos Romulo, former Philippine aid to US. General Douglas McArthur agreed with Frank Stanton of CBS "to bring the UN. to the living rooms of thousands" who would not find their way to our meetings. In his book "A Third World Soldier at the U.N.," the General known in his country as "Mr. U.N." found the exposure very valuable despite initial tension by delegates as the cameras focused on them. It personalized the U.N. beyond the course of newspapers, he said. There were however some awkward moments, like when the French Foreign Minister George Bidault after a wine tasting lunch slipped under his chair when he was called upon to be the first speaker, or when the Shah of Iran pulled the wrong speech from his imperial pocket then explaining after an awkward pause "This is the one for the Council of Foreign Relations".

A Security Council summit in 1992 was another special occasion - there the power was more concentrated and the focus clearer. My fortunate assignment was to accompany King Hassan II of Morocco. As royalty, he was to be among the last to arrive. So I had a chance to see all of the leaders at close range. British Prime Minister John Major, who held the rotating presidency of the Security Council for that month, President Francois Mitterrand of France, President Boris Yeltsin of Russia, China's President Jiang Zemin, Prime Minister Kiichi Miyazawa of Japan, President Carlos Menem of Argentina - all started arriving minutes after one another in their heavily guarded limousines. There was a point of protocol as to who would arrive last. As head of the host country, US President George Bush was expected to conclude the list of visitors. Yet, the Head of State of Morocco was a King, and as such should arrive last, according to traditional protocol. Whether by coincidence or design, one minute after President Bush arrived, King Hassan smoothly dropped in, wearing a white national robe, referring with a soft smile to the delay in the traffic that, in fact, had been totally cleared off First Avenue. His Majesty then sailed through, beaming, embracing and saluting the Heads of State assembled in a curtained VIP room. Never have I seen so much power in such a tiny space. It was elbow-room only. I had received and met with several Heads of State repeatedly in small rooms. But those 15 together in one spot radiated immense power. What struck me was the reassuring ease I felt – if they were all together here, our world was fairly safe.

One of the benefits of attending key meetings is the opportunity to occasionally hear impressive speakers. This, however, may turn into an endurance test when the odd delegate wanders into dubious oratory in desperate need of an elusive conclusion. A speaker in London's Hyde Park Corner used to entertain listeners by never finishing a sentence he had started 15 years earlier. A limited minority of representatives who see a captive audience in their obliging staff take their incoherence more seriously and would even insist on having it reflected in a press release.

While ensuring the success of continuous special events, we had to deliver a daily program of pressing activities. Some of us felt the only period to concentrate on urgent business was between closing hours and dinnertime. Weekends and holidays were merely opportunities to work without interruption. Even then, there were a number of exhibits to open or a flow of specific occasions when a political diva was determined to have a word with the world.

And the world for years used to be actually right here at the United Nations in Manhattan, New York. Yet, New Yorkers mainly know about special events through traffic jams. Otherwise, most would not care to know what is going on there, and many UN officials have little time to find out what was really happening in New York. Still, New Yorkers are generally impressed by the United Nations, and most UN people are in awe of New York. But there is something about that tiny wall with 193 flags flying on the East Side of First Avenue between 42nd and 49th streets; like a trip around the world every morning and then a return around sunset to New York when the national flags of its Member States are ceremoniously taken down, only to be raised again at sunrise the following day. Thousands of dedicated people, from various cultural and geographical backgrounds, promote causes shared by New Yorkers within these walls. When they exit the UN building and cross First Avenue, they enter a totally different world, with its own totally different perceptions. I recall once leaving at about nine in the evening when I saw Richard Butler, then head of UNSCOM, the commission dealing the elusive weapons of mass destruction in Iraq. He had spent the day talking to foreign ministers on the phone, with Security Council members and the UN Secretary-General, as well as having a telephone conversation with the President of the United States, giving a press briefing and being the subject of a special CNN interview. He was indeed a prominent, though controversial, person of that day. Yet, as he went out of the gates opening to First Avenue, he was looking for public transportation. To the young lady across the street dressed for a date, he appeared to be merely another competitor for a taxicab. On another occasion, the then-President of the UN General Assembly during the 40th anniversary, Jaime de Pinies, who was Ambassador of Spain, could not even cross the street because of a barricade put up by New York's finest. When he insisted on passing, the policeman responded firmly that he could do so only "after the show inside the UN building was over around noon". The president then advised the puzzled policeman that there would certainly be no "show" unless he was allowed to cross the street to start it. Since we habitually figure that our own perceptions are shared by everyone else, the distinguished Spaniard assumed that a uniformed policeman in the neighborhood would be fully aware of His Excellency's leadership role in presiding over all attending Heads of State. The policeman's top priority, however, was to ensure that law and order were kept at both sides of those wooden horses marked 'Do Not Cross".

Some years ago there was a political storm about parking

between diplomats accredited to the UN and the Mayor of New York City. Each had different priorities; each had different constituencies. The Mayor was mainly thinking of his position in New York City, and the diplomats were clearly thinking of the special parking allowed by binding agreement on privileges and immunities. Caught in between was the New York City Commissioner to the UN at the time. The helpful lady thought she had managed to bridge the gap, until she was alerted otherwise through a small incident. She had invited the wives of ambassadors to her home mainly to celebrate renewed close relations after assuring everyone that diplomatic cars would never be ticketed anymore. As the ladies left the celebratory luncheon, they found that each of the diplomatic cars had been given parking tickets. The Commissioner left her assignment soon afterward.

Having worked closely with five Secretaries-General from different backgrounds and with varied styles, I eventually felt it was time for me to stroll back across First Avenue. Diplomatic status was a welcome privilege, but I hardly violated traffic rules, because I rarely drove my car. I had resided in New York longer than in any other city. Why not become a full-time New Yorker and help to bridge the perception gap between my home of commitment and my city of choice?

It is a two-way street. As international officials will need to appreciate more the unique character of their metropolis, New Yorkers will need to know more about how the UN presence is helpful to their city. Take, for example, the fact that through its staff, its expenditures and the diplomatic missions, the UN pumps more money into New York annually than the United States Government contributes (when it does) to the UN budget. Diplomats may need to overcome adverse perceptions about their presence, but New Yorkers will have to know that most diplomats accomplish serious work and are not obsessed with double parking along Fifth Avenue. Upset as some New Yorkers may be with occasional traffic jams, they recognize that the UN presence confirms their city as the diplomatic capital of the world. Most international officials share with New Yorkers their countries of origin, their feelings and their beliefs.

Indeed, during the UN's 50th anniversary celebrations, Mayor Rudolph Giuliani made the point that every Member State could find at least one of its compatriots in New York. Rudolph Giuliani was still Mayor on September 11th. 2001. At that devastating moment, every New Yorker found a supporter at the United Nations.

As host and hosted, New York City and the UN have always thrived on one another. They've worked closely together when their priorities have converged - safety of diplomats and dignified security of visitors - despite mounting challenges. Other priorities may not be far apart in a city with a multinational structure and multicultural predominance. Quite possibly, there lies a bigger role for a strengthened UN public information culture. Its staff everywhere may need to go the extra mile to keep more closely in touch with their living environment, despite mounting work. They could explain its everyday work to everyday people through everyday contact in everyday language. Then the relevance of the UN will become clearer, while perceptions and realities grow closer.

Officials around current U.N. Secretary-General Ban Ki-moon must have discovered during Hurricane Sandy in 2012 that the Vienna Convention on Privileges and Immunities did not stop Mother Nature. No diplomatic immunity prevented the wind from whistling its way through Turtle Bay nor stopped the water flooding to submerge its basement. While some bewildered U.N. officials were debating whether to turn on or off electric engines, the storm couldn't read their minds. U.N. Headquarters suffered like the rest of New York.Besides the obvious teardown of the dome on top of the General Assembly Building, the flooding, the electric shortage, and the disabled computers, there were angry delegations that felt no serious prevention had been taken, despite days of warnings.

Meetings slowly picked up in the aftermath, only to have questions raised not only by delegates, but by some staff and - to a degree - by some supportive New Yorkers: Why didn't the U.N. Secretary-General reach out to New Yorkers -- publicly through the media and through visits with Mayor Bloomberg and Governor Cuomo -- to the most distressed areas? No, he would not be injecting himself in an internal national issue. The U.N. is involved in Emergency Relief all over the world. The Secretary-General visited stricken areas in several countries - more than twice to Haiti for example. What about his host town?

Particularly after the General Debate of September, when New Yorkers mainly witness traffic jams, blocked streets, and tripled parking lanes, New Yorkers would have felt better if senior U.N. officials rushed out publicly to identify with the human suffering and metropolitan hardships. There was a statement issued on 1 November "attributable to the Spokesman of the Secretary-General offering condolences to millions who suffered across a wide arc of destruction." He reportedly "intended to speak" with the Mayor and Governors of New York and New Jersey. He rightly pointed out that U.N. staff had been affected in minor ways. The Staff Union, supported by the Secretariat, also took the initiative of establishing a Relief Fund and encouraged voluntary work by the staff with relief organizations.

Those were very positive steps. But they should have been known outside U.N. circles and beyond overlooked press releases. Secretary-General Ban Ki-moon has been most effective when he spoke from the heart. He would have made a much-needed impact had he found his way through the media to a wider public.

A forceful appearance was missed -- one more erosion to the U.N. image among the ordinary people of its host city. After all, the most beautiful views of New York are from the UN.

For the first time in U.N. history, its New York Headquarters was closed officially on Wednesday, 10 February 2010, due to a projected snowstorm. An unprecedented announcement was made a day earlier. By that date, the staff was already dispersed between 2nd Avenue and Madison from 42nd to 48th Streets. Even the Secretary-General - like the famous Elvis announcement - had left the building. He and about 200 others were located in a pre-fabricated 3-floor site in the Garden area, dubbed Bantenamo by an irreverent reporter. In case of an emergency elsewhere in the world, desperate callers will have to have the home or cellular number of staff concerned, except if one is counting on a central operator, an automatic recording even in normal days. General Dallaire, when fighting his demons in Rwanda, used to complain that there was no one at Headquarters to receive his phone calls on weekend evenings. That was when Peacekeeping Chief Kofi Annan at least showed up - with an elegant turtleneck dark blue sweater - at the Security Council Chambers. Now, try a snowy day in New York.

Perhaps a better feedback about public perception would help keep in touch with the real world outside the U.N. tower. Although internal communications among staff was introduced, a mechanism built gradually over the years to keep the Secretary-General and other officials abreast with media reporting and U.N.-related issues in member states was gradually dismantled. A vital network of Information Centres staffed by professionals in 90 key countries to cover the whole membership was in effect crippled. An office that was created for a while to report daily on developing issues was eventually closed. A daily briefing, "U.N. in the News", which was circulated twice a day stopped. The Spokesman's Office, with limited staff, is overwhelmed with immediate daily requirements mostly by accredited reporters in the building. The Secretary-General and his senior staff are now left to their own devices, personal connections or allowed contacts when facing major headlines with direct impact on U.N. work when they would have been able to prepare better for it if duly alerted ahead of time.

The US-UN Relationship

Partnership – and the need for an ever-improved partnership – may be a keyword in describing the relationship between the US and the UN.

A *New York Times* correspondent summarized a discussion among a group of ambassadors in the UN Delegates' Lounge, as follows: "Americans perceive a crisis of confidence. Canadians say the UN is drowning in words and suffocating in documents. The Europeans feel there is a crisis of apathy. Developing countries feel there is a crisis of irrelevance, that is, they are becoming irrelevant because nobody cares for them. Experienced diplomats say, however, that what the UN really needs is a crisis, a real crisis, in which it will move in, diffuse the explosive situation, and not have the big powers directly involved but supporting it with their political will. It will then regain confidence and overcome a crisis." This was written by Kathleen Teltsch of the *New York Times* in 1970 – close to 50 years ago.

When I joined the UN in 1965, the main concern at the time was a financial crisis. If that sounds familiar today, it could be added that the effect of evoking Article 19, suspending voting rights against a permanent member, was so close that the General Assembly President Alex Quaison-Sackey of Ghana had to gallop through the proceedings to avoid the vote. The position formulated by then US Ambassador Adlai Stevenson remains one of the most eloquent statments on the need for member states to pay their dues in full and on time.

If financial crisis and reform have long been with us, does it mean that the UN should continue doing what it does? *"Plus ça change,"* as the French say, and the rest remains the same?

By virtue of its name, the United States of America represents a nation of unified citizens who come from varied cultures and backgrounds. The human ties to Americans through relatives and nationalities represents an additional reason why the rest of the world responded with visible solidarity on Sept. 11, 2001. Reports that victims from 62 countries perished in the World Trade Center reflected the fact that almost every one of the 191 UN members could find a compatriot in New York City alone. A colossal terrorist challenge to one country instantly became a multilateral cause.

An appropriate conclusion may be to quote the UN Charter's preamble, which is very similar to the Constitution of the US: "We the Peoples of the UN determined to save succeeding generations from the scourge of war, which twice in our lifetime has brought untold sorrow to mankind, and to reaffirm faith in fundamental human rights, in the dignity and worth of the human person, in the equal rights of men and women and of nations large and small, and to establish conditions under which justice and respect for the obligations arising from treaties and other sources of international law can be maintained, and to promote social progress and better standards of life in larger freedom, and for these ends to practice tolerance and live together in peace with one another as good neighbors, and to unite our strength to maintain international peace and security, and to ensure, by the acceptance of principles and the institution of methods, that armed force shall not be used, save in the common interest, and to employ international machinery for the promotion of the economic and social advancement of all peoples, have resolved to combine our efforts to accomplish these aims."

Republican or Democrat, there is a consistent American position of supporting the UN, while also encouraging more reform. Even the language used by various US presidents sounded similar. President Nixon said in 1972: "We can easily undermine the UN by asking too much of it." A quarter of a century later, in 1997, President Clinton told the General Assembly: "In order for the US always to say 'yes' to the UN, the UN sometimes has to say 'no.'"

The UN Secretaries-General have consistently urged reform.

U Thant thought the UN had only 10 years to reform or perish. Perez de Cuellar formed a team that introduced basic changes in to the UN structure. Dr. Boutros Boutros-Ghali cut the number of senior posts from 52 USGs to 12. The number was slightly increased by Kofi Annan, who accommodated former senior officials seeking international refuge by designating over 70 of them as special envoys on a per diem basis. Disagreements that did occur were mainly of a political nature. Otherwise, even major housekeeping ventures were jointly discussed. Kofi Annan's "quiet revolution" was clearly coordinated with the US administration as well as with other members of the international community. In time the US recognized that the UN couldn't solve every fundamental dispute, especially when big powers were involved.

Perhaps US Delegate James Woodworth put it best years ago when he said, "The UN is not good enough, but it is the best we have. The UN is the latest stop along the road from caveman to the ideal state of affairs." A key answer was once given by Secretary-General Hammarskjold. Using a French expression, he stressed "*Le courage de nos différences.*" Although it translates as "the courage of our differences," it means to accept creatively what divides us with humility and courage. A veteran internationalist would be inspired by the belief that far from being separated by our differences, we could be enriched by our diversity.

To use a health term, the relationship is organic. The US influence on the UN is deeper than generally recognized or acknowledged. As a host country, whatever Americans think of the good city of New York, UN diplomats and UN staff, who are making decisions and proposing ideas, are actually living in American society. Their main media link is with the American media. Their families are educated in US schools and in an American atmosphere. Indeed, the UN spends more in the city of New York than the entire US contribution to the UN. In political matters, the UN would seem to be a convenient scapegoat.

The US representation at the UN has been mostly of the highest quality, from Adlai Stevenson, a presidential candidate, to George H.W. Bush, who was of course later elected president. They are always supported by a representative team of professionals, covering not only questions of peace and security but every aspect of human endeavor, from human rights to the environment to administration and management. In terminology, the UN and the US are so close that even the most professional officials seem to confuse the names on various occasions. Reportedly, the name United Nations was offered by President Franklin D. Roosevelt after discussing it with Prime Minister Winston Churchill. I recall that Dr. Boutros Boutros-Ghali, when he was swearing his oath of office as the fifth UN Secretary-General, had an apparent slip of the tongue and pledged allegiance to the US instead. Little did he realize that four years later the US would be the member to block his second term.

The American public has greater knowledge of the UN than most other people. Visits by American schoolchildren have been a tradition now for generations. While the UN remains a lofty organization in the opinion of a large number of American people, they also want it to work. They support the UN generally. They may criticize it, but they would like it to work. As an indication of how close the UN and the US were in a previous period, one should be reminded that during the first 24 years of its existence, the US did not once use its Security Council veto power. The first time the veto was used was on March 17, 1970, when there was a Security Council resolution condemning Rhodesia. The US later relented and supported the independence of Zimbabwe, the successor to Rhodesia.

Our swiftly changing world with its shifts in borders, social fabric and communication leaves no other option for the UN but to reflect the dynamics of its membership and look forward. That would mean a participatory operation with a sharpened focus on current issues and other partnerships. This may require, among other things, a strengthening of internal public information capable of highlighting the UN's relevance to everyday people in everyday language.

A credible relationship would have to be based on performance, commitment and relevance. The media could provide an indispensable link, particularly in exploring common ground and mobilizing public support. The UN needs the US to survive, as it needs the rest of the world to succeed. The US needs to survive with the rest of the world, and it needs the UN to succeed.

The UN is not merely an international island floating on the Manhattan East River. It is a shared commitment by people worldwide from various backgrounds, including those sharing its host city and country.

CHAPTER II:

ABSOLUTE POWER, ABSOLUTELY

While working at the Palais des Nations in Geneva, I noticed that a man in a nearby building displayed contradictory signs of health. Similar-looking buildings at the Petit-Sacconex, behind the Hotel Intercontinental, shared large green gardens with narrow paths. Sometimes I saw the distinguished African gentleman walking briskly, beaming with health, nodding his high head politely, yet firmly, to neighbors encountered along the way - *bonjour* or *bonsoir* - as the case may be. At other times, he was carted dejectedly in a wheelchair by a Swiss nurse wearing a uniform. He would confuse his *bonjours* with *bonsoirs*, although he would strive to maintain his gracious manners - a prerequisite to a peaceful life in Geneva.

Puzzled and curious, I approached a British journalist after I saw her greet him profusely. She said the gentleman was the heir to the Abyssinian throne of the aging Haile Selassie in Ethiopia, and he was recuperating from a chronic weakness. Apparently, and subconsciously, whenever he heard that His Imperial Majesty, The Negashi, was ailing and verging on death, and as the throne approached, he could feel a surge of health and strength that would parade him through the neighborhood. But when he was advised otherwise, and the throne seemed a distant prospect, he would feel ill and weak again!

When elected President of Lebanon, Camille Chamoun had a

chronic heart problem. His doctor, a relative of mine, was concerned that the demanding duties of running a dynamic country of creative, yet individualistic and argumentative citizens, would take its toll on his rebellious heart. However, throughout a six-year period, Mr. Chamoun did not have a single serious heart crisis, although the neighborhood got increasingly rougher - with a revolution in Iraq, attempts in Jordan and Syria, and a mini-revolution in Lebanon itself. Only after he left office did he need the services of his doctor.

In an abuse of power, the corrupt become absolutely corrupted. But those with the qualifying talent could use power effectively, as if effortlessly, even without any indication of their real authority. The powerful, in politics and elsewhere, do not noisily seek attention or remind anyone of their importance. As David Rockefeller reportedly responded to a decorator who had suggested a pompous office: "Whom do I need to impress?"

Having known Pierre Trudeau before Canada's Trudeaumania first crowned him Prime Minister in 1968, I used to see him after he took office during private weekends in New York. Never changing his attitude, always casually pleasant, always attentive to new ideas, always bored with a mediocre approach, he carried an enormous sense of inner power. Soft-spoken, unless insulted, he would hardly speak about himself, more often listening to others. My neighbors at the time, three Pan Am stewardesses, were obviously thrilled. He was single then, and each of them felt she might have had a shot because "he was shining with power, yet quietly paid full attention." Once, when we went around the corner on First Avenue to have a casual Sunday meal, Pierre Trudeau insisted on paying the bill. He only had travellers' cheques, which he countersigned. The cashier refused them in disbelief until he noted that the secret service agents were discreetly waiting outside.

Mostly, it is the *nouveau riche* who abuse power long enough to hurt innocent bystanders before they depart in good riddance. Actually, power can bring wonderful aspects to life - health, wealth, focus, respect, creativity and commitment. Some, like Dr. Henry Kissinger, and possibly Ms. Barbra Streisand, would claim it could also be an aphrodisiac, but then that is a part-time bonus. This is neither a scientific fact nor a philosophical conclusion. It is merely a reflection of the human condition. *"La Dolce Vita"* Director, Federico Fellini, who made his career by watching people, had his own interpretation: "You know what ages people?" he would ask; and then would respond: "Boredom." When he was working in a youthful environment, travelling and moving around he felt like a lion; staying bored at home: "I feel eighty."

Not a single United Nations Secretary-General had a health crisis while in office, despite the pressure of work and the demands of member states. Most of these men were older than 60 years of age. Mr. Boutros-Ghali was officially 69 when he took over, and he challenged a correspondent who questioned his health to a track run outside the Foreign Ministry in Cairo. Mr. Perez de Cuellar chose to undergo a heart operation and returned to serve a second term by unanimous choice.

Some UN colleagues used to tease Dr. Ingrid Laux, Director of the UN Medical Service, that she had a unique advantage in having seen more than one Secretary-General with no clothes. Perhaps, as his doctor, she may have seen more of Kofi Annan than the others. In addition to being her immediate boss when heading the Personnel Office, he had a record of continued hard service in different positions. Anyway, every Secretary-General, whatever his immediate health status before taking over, once elected, displayed exceptional stamina, energy and staying power.

Drawing on a theory that power corrupts, a New York weekly had a cartoon of a crowned monarch responding to a telephone call, saying: "Absolutely corrupt, how about you?" In fact, most current-day kings and queens (princes and princesses) hardly have absolute power, would rarely be accused of corruption and are far less presumptuous than most of their official underlings. Even those who do have tremendous political power, like a President or Prime Minister, are more polite. Many diplomats or journalists who met King Hussein of Jordan, who dominated his country's politics for over three decades, would recall his polite baritone voice addressing them as Sir. King Juan Carlos of Spain, too, was an easygoing and a brilliant conversationalist with a unique sense of humor.

During the United Nations 40th anniversary celebrations, which the King attended with his wife, Queen Sofia, he was leaving his hotel on Park Avenue and 65th Street, where we were about to enter an adjacent restaurant. With us was "King" Simeon of Bulgaria, who left his country as a two-year old. A close friend of the Spanish monarch, he urged him to join company after his official function at the Spanish Mission was over. Just before midnight, when there were very few patrons left at the old Le Cirque, the King walked in graciously and joined an expanded table. Reviewing the events of the day at the United Nations, he spoke in clear, concise language about Spain's role as a veritable Mediterranean, European, Iberian country with unique cultural links and political potential. That was just before Madrid hosted the first International Conference to settle the Arab-Israeli conflict and before Spain was elected as a member of the Security Council. When a Spanish officer professing loyalty to the King attempted a coup by interrupting a parliamentary meeting, it was King Juan Carlos who intervened firmly, forcefully and effectively to ensure the survival of democracy. One would add that Queen Sofia was equally impressive in her casual, gracious charm and devotion to issues of human dignity.

Queen Sofia, who is the sister of King Constantine of Greece, was once visiting New York. Avoiding official attention, she took a taxi. The driver was apparently ready for dinner, because he phoned home and told his wife in Greek to get it ready. As the Queen mentioned the Hotel Pierre to be her destination, the driver told her knowingly that the hotel actually belonged to King Constantine, former monarch of Greece. Not wanting to expose her identity, yet anxious to defend her brother, she interjected politely that Constantine had no property in Manhattan. Feeling challenged, the driver insisted vehemently on his very accurate uncontested information from very reliable sources. Angry, yet cool, his passenger pointedly told him: "I think I ought to know if my brother owns the hotel where I am staying."

Brakes squealed, the car ground to a halt. The driver turned around and broke out into an emotional welcome. "So you are Queen Sofia. Yes, you are," he repeated, as he started dialing all his Greek relatives in Astoria, Queens. There was no way she could leave, he insisted, except after having a "real Greek dinner" with his extended family. She eventually did, and was of course treated royally. She not only made a point, but also gained more friends. Incidentally, a real royal (in Spanish, real is royal) will make a point, if necessary, without making an enemy. Unassuming casualness, even personal warmth, will put you at ease, particularly in public; but almost always they have to be treated with due regal deference. Some miscalculating socialites discovered their swift exile after attempting to publicly show off their majestic connections, confusing them with those on the social-climbing periphery.

Whether the King of Norway rides a bicycle to work, or the King of Sweden jokingly repeats "Bubilibubb," when you deal with a king, you have to see his "majesty." A modest Danish King Christian once telephoned a German occupying officer requesting to take down a German flag just placed over an official Danish Government building. The confident German officer refused firmly. The King then said that a Danish soldier had volunteered to take it down. "He will be shot at once," the occupation officer warned. "I doubt it," the King then said, "for I shall be that soldier." Within minutes, that flag went down.

In certain cases, rulers with undisputed authority tend to lose their balance particularly when they feel threatened. The Shah of Iran approved a ban preventing theatres from playing Shakespeare's "Hamlet" because it depicted a pandering prince in a conspiracy to murder a king. Ottoman Sultan Hamid II, sensing unrest, prohibited the teaching of chemistry in the Turkish Empire because the formula for water, H_2O, might have been interpreted by disloyal citizens as having indicated that his initials equaled zero.

A confident leader does not need to make an impression. Leadership exudes itself through behavior and style. It may have been Plato who said that excellence is not a special occasion, but rather a pattern of achievement. Excellence, therefore, is not an occasional claim; it is a habit.

On the occasion of the 50th anniversary of the United Nations, the most challenging ordeal was a group photo of more than 150 heads of state. It also afforded one of the most interesting experiences of UN life: seeing the subtle reactions of Heads of State when they realized they were alone. All these leaders had been assigned numbered spots, according to protocol. Each of them had to enter the chambers alone. King Hussein of Jordan, who had reigned longest, entered first. Without special assistants, personal security, a foreign minister or ambassador, the demeanor of the most powerful men and women in the world underwent a sudden transformation. Most of them seemed more at ease, warmer and happier. Some seemed nervously uncertain.

The King of Morocco, the late Hassan II, whom I had escorted on earlier occasions, arrived accompanied by his Crown prince - then Sidi Mohammed, now King Mohammed VI. United Nations Security, following strict instructions, objected. Seeing a familiar face, the King said that while he alone would be in the portrait, he wished his crown prince to be in the room. Although no one could have guessed the King's motive at the time, Sidi Mohammed was invited to join in supervising the operation from the UN's side - which he graciously did. Two hours after the group photograph, the King of Morocco was rushed to a New York hospital in a medical emergency. One of the last serving monarchs, he had been scheduled to open the afternoon session of the Assembly. In a protocol shift, the crown prince spoke two hours later. It may have been his first address to such an audience. With such pressures as his father's deteriorating health and an unprecedented audience, he made an unanticipated presentation with clarity and poise.

Without the cover of attendants, the body language of these world leaders was on display. Jiang Zemin walked forward purposefully, arms folded in front of him, while Bill Clinton smiled easily, shoulders back, arms at his sides. It was equally interesting to see the looks on the faces of ambassadors suddenly separated from their heads of state as they entered the isolated chamber. The most powerful of diplomats could not but betray slight concern that something might go wrong, and they would be called to answer for it.

Who stood next to whom was the least of the UN's worries. That was already fixed through Protocol. Assembled shoulder to shoulder in front of a gigantic gold reflector painted with a happy face, the veneer of diplomacy between the world leaders thinned. To get these busiest of people not just to stand still in one place without being bored for 30 minutes, yet actually pause for a photo, was the most formidable task. To have them follow the directions of a photographer, when they were accustomed to always giving orders themselves, was equally challenging. In addition to the official UN photographers, that event was immortalized as a "Kodak moment." A photographer from that company, with his very South American accent, firmly and joyfully requested "my beloved President, please move a step to the right," or a Vatican cardinal "to shuffle upward," or the French President to "show us his smiling side." Most of them took it in stride. Initially, nervous laughter rippled through the hall when the photographer, standing several feet below them, introduced himself with honest-to-goodness American sincerity, and proceeded to wave the most powerful men and women in the world back and forth in a mincing shuffle to position them for the camera. Kodak had set up a huge framework to support lighting and the camera, which would look down on the 150 heads packed together at the back of the Economic and Social Council chamber. Some covered their unease with grimaces or nonchalant shifts. Most glanced sideways to see what those around them were doing. Without simultaneous translation, some were slower than others to discard their name tags at the photographer's cheerful command. There was a noticeable ripple of relief when the photographer finally announced, "Thank you, the world thanks you, and now put your name tags back on and go back to your meetings." Obligingly, the 150 heads of state filed out, chatting jovially, and scuttled back into the waiting privacy of their black automobiles via armed guards.

After the photo was taken, it was another task to identify the 150 dignitaries. There was close work with Protocol on this. A diligent photo librarian, Joyce Rosenblum, managed to peg most of them, with the exception of one. After identifying the country, she needed the name of its head of state. Trying to nail it down in record time, she went to the General Assembly hall, where the special session was being held. She approached a man sitting alone in one of the seats allocated for that country and asked him the name of his President.

The man casually responded that they had no president. "What do they have?" she asked. "We do have a King," he answered, agreeably and patiently. When she asked for the name of the king, he spelled it out for her. She asked if he was still in New York. He responded that indeed he was, and indeed, she was facing him.

Experience shows that the more senior are the more modest. It is those around them who spin an air of importance around themselves. Actually, most ambassadors arrive at their posts through hard work and serious competition. Very few could hold onto their posts if they were not fairly competent. United Nations work is transparent for all to see - like the UN glass house itself.

Unlike bilateral relations, where matters are mostly quietly handled between officials of two countries, working in a multinational arena like the UN requires not mere competence, but also visible advocacy and a dynamic capacity to deal with more than one country or one issue at a time. Several accomplished UN diplomats or secretariat staff return home for more senior posts. For example, the President of Finland, Martti Ahtisaari, was UN Under-Secretary-General for Administration; the president of Sierra Leone, Ahmed Tejan Kabbah, worked in the UN Development Programme. Many became Ministers of Foreign Affairs in their respective countries. Egypt's Foreign Minister, Amr Moussa, Slovakia's Edouard Kucan, Ecuador's Diego Cordovez and Mexico's Rosario Green are noted examples. Obviously self-confident, they are all easy-going and pleasant, unless if crossed or double-crossed.

By sheer power of personality and effort, some ambassadors have stood out, regardless of the country's size. Ambassador Tommy Koh, who for years chaired the Law of the Sea Conference, was by far more influential than his country; in fact, many did not even know he was from Singapore. The Italian Ambassador Paolo Fulci never lost an election to any Committee and was a powerhouse in the Security Council. He initiated a coffee club of like-minded diplomats and laid claim to a permanent seat in that Council, effectively blocking powerful Germany and Japan for years. "If the criterion for winning permanent membership is losing the Second World War, then Italy also lost the war," he would quip. Ambassadors Zenon Rossides of Cyprus, Ghassan Tueni of Lebanon, Jamil Baroody of Saudi Arabia, and U Thant of Burma (who later became Secretary-General) played much wider roles than what their foreign ministries' instructions set forth. All were easily accessible, helpful diplomats.

Big powers were no different. My first lesson in modesty was when I saw US Secretary of State Cyrus Vance carrying his own coffee tray at the Delegates' Lounge. Years later, the greatest inspiration was Nelson Mandela, whose gracious modesty was truly regal.

But there are also the politically *nouveau riche*, the very few who are so full of their fleeting moment of power that they hasten its departure.

One ambassador once came to protest the quality of his photograph. According to practice, whenever a new ambassador is appointed, a portrait is made for the record. It is normally placed on the media's third floor showcase and sent to Protocol and Security for identification. In this case, a courtesy copy was sent, as usual, to the Ambassador whom I had met when he was a Third Secretary. He requested an immediate meeting because, he said, the current portrait of him as Ambassador wasn't as good as the one taken of him 15 years ago when he first came to New York. He was astonished, he added, because it happened to be the same photographer who took the two disparate portraits. The first, he said, looked "more impressive" than the second – "more youthful, more dynamic, more presentable." He regretted to say that he had expected more at this time of his re-entry as Ambassador, Envoy Plenipotentiary and Permanent Representative to the UN. When the photographer, an established professional from Japan, was called in, he was obviously shaken by the Ambassador's complaint. He had won several photography prizes for his work; and, although he had photographed most of the ambassadors, he never had experienced such a meeting with any of them. In a very cool, polite, yet somewhat sarcastic tone, the photographer responded: "Fifteen years ago, Your Excellency, you say fifteen years ago. At that time, my hands were much stronger handling the camera than they are today." There was obviously more to the Ambassador than met the eye of the camera. He extended his hand to the photographer, saying, "Maybe we should exchange places."

He continued: "But since that does not seem practical, could we exchange first names and become friends?" Weeks later at a lunch, the Ambassador cheerfully told the story and, commenting on recurring assignments, added another quip about a diplomat who was posted to Paris at three stages of his professional career, always finding it wonderful for his differing needs. As a young Second Secretary, he was thrilled that on any street he could meet beautiful women. Years later, as an elevated Counsellor, he enjoyed finding excellent restaurants in every quartier. When he returned, after two decades, as Ambassador Plenipotentiary, he was pleased to find that at almost any corner there was a pharmacy.

To be sure, there are still some wives who refer to their husbands by their official title: "The Ambassador will be sending me the official car to join him for dinner" could be occasionally but not usually heard. A loving mother, however surprised, will certainly announce to the world her son's diplomatic stature. My mother pre-appointed me UN Assistant Secretary-General 20 years before the fact, when I first travelled with my boss to the Middle East.

There are also some bodyguards who insist on confirming the absolute need for their presence. They seem to have a professional knack to get into photographs, always with a hawkish, alert demeanor and a twisted neck, looking just to the right of the camera for an impressive profile. Some of them take themselves more seriously than the body they guard.

At an Islamic summit meeting in Saudi Arabia, heads of State were invited to pray in Mecca. While two antagonistic leaders of Syria and Iraq were bowing in prayer, their guards nearby almost caused a massacre, were it not for a firm yet subtle intervention of the hosts. During the fighting in Lebanon, some self-styled leaders were more afraid of their over-armed bodyguards than they were of their adversaries.

An ambassador of Norway was fond of telling how his King had dispensed with car and driver during the oil crisis of the seventies and had resorted to public transportation like any common citizen. Once, while admiring compatriots swarmed around him in a bus, a young journalist asked whether His Majesty was not afraid for his personal safety without a protective escort. The confident King replied: "No fear. I have four million bodyguards."

It was instructive to observe the amusing shifts in reaction to a mid-level colleague's change of position from a press officer to ambassador. After an election in his country, one former press officer was offered the opportunity to become its Permanent Representative to the United Nations. One of his supervisors immediately turned very respectful, leading "His Excellency" around the various floors, with an appropriate pronouncement. A few days later, the man changed his mind. His international job was more secure. Governments in that part of the world tended to change without much notice, so he returned quietly to his desk, sharing an office with the now-disappointed, almost vengeful, supervisor. Yet again, within weeks, he felt like trying his luck in the diplomatic national lottery. Indeed, he eventually became a senior official making policy statements on UN-related issues, including, of course, staff reform. Two years after that posting, he returned, like a disarmed soldier, quietly seeking a post commensurate with his high-level functions. None was available, except at his previous level - and not in New York, but in the field. He readily agreed; his hosts were happy to receive a former Deputy Foreign Minister of a neighboring country.

It was also interesting to watch two former UN tour guides make it as their countries' ambassadors to the United Nations. Both handled it smoothly, in their own way. One, from a struggling country, continued to act like the part-time model he was in New York before his country's independence. The other, from a Scandinavian country, maintained a helpful, positive interest in the work of the Visitors Service while, of course, following up other pressing issues like peacekeeping. By the way, when Bob Dole was unfairly hammering the UN in his political campaign, one felt like calling him to say that he should know better that his claims were untrue. He could ask his wife, the charming Elizabeth Dole. After all, she had started as a UN guide.

Absolute Power, Absolutely

Throughout history, power has fascinated the weak, the meek and the powerful. It is agreed that absolute power corrupts absolutely. That is why Roman Emperors had a member of the staff behind them during ceremonial adulations to whisper in their ears and remind them that they were human. The powerful were entitled to enjoy it as long as they handled it well. They were expected to train and prepare hard to well deserve it. Otherwise, as the Latin saying went: "An illiterate King is a crowned ass" (*Rex illiteratus, Asinus coronatus*). Even when the great Julius Caesar seemed to mishandle power, he was ousted, Roman-style, stabbed by his best friend, Brutus. A more peaceful exit would lie in an open system of checks and balances. The ancient Greeks called it democracy. At any rate, every Secretary-General - or President - found out that they had much less power than they were led to believe. Even in an imperfect organization reflecting an imperfect world, established roles and inherent interests provide unforeseen limitations. A creative assistant may gain valuable recognition when cutting through the red tape. *Trova l'inganno*, find the loophole, is helpful Italian advice. Otherwise, the permanent staff, those who remain, regardless of who is appointed to lead them for five years. those who reflect cultural and geographic interests, may make a point of indicating the limits of power.

Once a newly appointed very senior official was asked by a reporter how many people worked at the United Nations. Asserting his new power and seeking a soundbyte, he responded sarcastically: "About 30 per cent." He hardly survived later, but did so only by regretting his quip. In time, he was reminded of a statement by an American admiral: "If you are going to sin, sin against God - not against the bureaucracy. God will forgive you - the bureaucrat won't." Many senior officials, assumed by the public to be most powerful, would complain discreetly that they can't even appoint their own staff. Even in autocratic regimes, the increasing role of the revolutionary media injects restrictions, however limited, on power. In such regimes people respond with subtle humor. Egypt's President Nasser reportedly used to collect, through the secret service, all the jokes about him.

An old Arabic story recounts that an autocratic ruler felt so powerful that he appointed his favorite donkey as special consultant. Thus, all officials and dignitaries had to pass by a nearby office to nod their tribute to the influential consultant whenever they sought a favor from the ruler. Satisfied with uncovering the frailty of human nature, the ruler called in a reclusive poet - an intellectual who had not participated in the tribute. Pushing for loyalty, the ruler asked what the people thought of him. The poet answered in one line: "The people's view of you is the same as your view of the donkey."

Whatever the form of government in today's world, power can only be effectively maintained by public support enjoyed by popular consensus and relayed in a smooth transition. At the entrance to the palace of the Emir of Kuwait, an inscription states: "If authority had been permanent for your predecessors, it would not have reached you." It is a daily reminder, particularly in trying times, which the Kuwaiti ruler indeed faced during an invasion of his country. The inscription tells visitors and occupants alike that power is transitory for any human and should be wisely deployed. You are most vulnerable when you believe you are invincible. That means you are in real trouble when you think you'll never get into trouble, so you go ahead and make your adversary's day.

Among Arab States, Kuwait was recognized for decades as playing a dynamic international role, including a two-year membership on the Security Council under the highly regarded leadership of its Minister for Foreign Affairs, Sheikh Sabah Al-Ahmad, who is currently the Emir of that state. Ironically that role drastically diminished. Hardly anyone at the UN would recognize the name of its current foreign minister, let alone the face of its official UN representative.

Photographer Helmut Newton once said that he had always wanted to portray Margaret Thatcher. The more she acquired authority as Britain's Prime Minister, the sexier she looked. France's Charles de Gaulle acted almost majestic when he was a lonely exiled officer in London during the Second World War - and got away with it. Before and after his presidency, his self-anointed authority travelled with him.

Many cultures express the same meaning about the presence or "halo" of someone with authority, even without any of its visible trappings. A military coup in Morocco succeeded until its leader met King Hassan II to inform him that his rule would be over. Alone and unarmed except for his wit and authoritative *haiba*, the King easily disarmed the senior officer who found himself down on his knees kissing his Monarch's hand.

A similar incident occurred with King Hussein of Jordan. Informed that senior army officers had announced a coup, he went alone to their barracks. After a brief speech in which he offered himself as sacrifice if that could help Jordan, the soldiers turned against the leading officers, who then had to be protected by the King. He took them back to Amman in his own car.

On the other hand, Suharto, Indonesia's strongman for over 30 years, lost his *awehoo* among his crowd when he was seen in all newspapers bowing to sign an agreement setting the conditions of the International Monetary Fund with its Executive Director, Michael Camdessus, looking down on him. Of course, there are always other forces at play in historical changes, but a person's space, feel, charisma or whatever else it is named, is integral to the scent of power.

Boutros Boutros-Ghali had a theory that crowds felt your status before you said a word. If you are apprehensive, uncertain or unconfident, the audience could easily sense it and respond accordingly. Incidentally, one of his closest Under-Secretaries-General, Ambassador Joseph Verner Reed, had that amazing talent of transforming any occasion into an impressive event. Once, as President of the Staff Committee, I approached him to oversee a lunch break performance by the UN Singers, a homegrown talent with no resources and a limited following. He managed to transform the entrance of the Assembly building into an auditorium, with microphones and speakers spread out, garnering the participation of the widest number of distinguished Permanent Representatives and dignitaries. The pleasantly surprised singers were so inspired that they gave their best performance to an equally inspired crowd. A routine occasion turned out to be one of the season's most popular events.

The presence of certain discreet powers behind any officer or ruler is an understood point of governance. The powers that be was always a safe reference. A description by the French of their Cardinal Richelieu's influence in the court of their King, *éminence grise* (the grey eminence), has become part of the political dictionary. The term originally referred to the Secretary who wore grey robes in contrast to his immediate boss, the Cardinal, who formally dressed in red. He was perceived as the man behind the man behind the throne. Apparently, his eminence was also a proponent of the grey position - somewhere between black and white. Since he only whispered his advice quietly, little is publicly known of his wisdom except for the view that anyone's greatest tragedy could be the gap between his own ambition and his talent. Clearly, the Cardinal was not referring to himself, but more likely to King Louis, who fancied describing himself as The Sun King and enjoyed an elaborate waking up ceremony, *le reveil*, where admiring assistants tended his bed and alternated between undressing and redressing him. His intoxication with their verbal incense may have indicated the beginning of royalty's end on the guillotine.

When asked what weapons he feared most, Napoleon replied: "Incense by admirers." In an age of increasingly sophisticated media spin, the risk to world leaders from opportunistic incense burners is even greater today. Although he left thousands of dead bodies strewn along the battlefield, that military commander refused to accept a bottle of excellent wine because he had to pay for it. A master of reflective accountability, he preferred lucky officers to efficient ones. He felt that too much intricate assessment by too many advisers would deflect from the target of power.

During constantly shifting times, regular government staff have more power than changeable politicians. Authority is mainly handled through professional civil servants experienced in drafting rules and knowing their loopholes.

An "old boy" network of Oxford and Cambridge (Oxbridge) graduates in England, products of l'École Nationale d'Administration (ENA) in France, those linked to the Salotto Buono (Good Background) in Italy, like the Japanese who occupy their influential posts through "a descent from heaven," – all of them in their own cultural way would politely put up with a transient Cabinet Minister but, if necessary, will make the point as to who exactly runs the show.

Not all power is political, though. In a dawning era of converging technologies and disciplines, power is generated through a blend of creative, professional and accidental convergence from every aspect of human interest. Whether it is power, synergy or "where the action is," dynamic cities may eventually outpower even national governments in making future leadership decisions. Hence, New York, San Paulo or Rio de Janeiro in Brazil, Sydney in Australia, Milan in Italy, or Lagos in Nigeria may not be capitals, but they have *the Capital* - the tools of power and influence. The main risk is that a great number of citizens elsewhere could be unfairly marginalized. Therein lies the balancing role of a responsible power at the center; and therein lies the crucial source of that power: an open democratic system where everyone matters, everyone counts and everyone votes.

Diplomats Awaiting Leadership

Politicians tend to think that they have to be seen to be believed. Most of their international travels are attuned to national consumption. Their media groupies are carefully selected to accommodate their home audience. A featured theatre for many is the opening week of the General Assembly session which occurs every September. The first prime-time appearance is reserved for the President of the United States, the host country, with a traditional warm-up act by Brazil. With different time-zones, and possibly to avert further competition in the US media, the other four permanent members of the Security Council choose another of the slots that corresponds to their capital's primetime news hours.

Other members have to fend for themselves, although over the years enterprising delegates managed to know who to reach within the UN Secretariat to ensure a prized spot, particularly if their head of State was in a rush or angling to court another visiting dignitary. Ambassadors - with their career in mind - tend to fight for a podium appearance more ferociously, for example, than for a resolution on climate change. Some would bargain to trade slots for future favors. For years, one of the most influential officials during the "General Debate" period was a general service staffer who prepared the final list of speakers. Somehow her favorite Foreign Minister of Egypt spoke regularly on the first day. When he changed, and she did not like his successor, Egypt was moved subtly to two days later.

Although several Foreign Ministers appeal directly to the Secretary-General to ensure a desired appearance, he would rarely intervene. His hands were tied by an elaborately drawn list of competing demands by equally influential Member States. The most he could do was to literally hold their hand and shake it during a photo opportunity. The distinguished visitor could then spin his own story upon his return home. It is striking to note the difference between facts and fiction when reading feedback from local press after a visit to the UN Headquarters. Having attended some of these meetings, I was later amazed to read that a certain country's cabinet met to review the implications to their national strategy. Equally interesting was the seemingly casual manner with which key players handled the more delicate issues. Still, a joint effort by delegates and Secretariat staff helps to maintain global follow-up action throughout the year.

Recognizing the local impact of a UN appearance, some politicians even attempt to undercut their national competitors. For example, during a Summit where Lebanon was represented by its Deputy Prime Minister, Issem Fares, another upset yet influential Lebanese official tried from Beirut to have the speech delayed by a couple of days after the opening so it would be timed too late for live evening local coverage. Perceiving a slight to the country rather than a political squabble, a Lebanese insider placed Mr. Fares prominently on the first day.

After the 1990-1991 "Desert Storm" Gulf war, sanctioned by the United Nations Security Council, it was decided to send envoys to explore the aftermath in the field of operations. Two experienced former senior Secretariat officers were selected: Abdel Rahin Abi Farah of Somalia and Martti Ahtisaari of Finland. Both had worked closely together under Secretary-General Javier Perez de Cuellar, but they could not have been more different in style. The former Finish President wrote a brief straightforward report describing the military area of operations as "apocalyptic." That did not sit well with certain influential member states. His Somali colleague, who never travelled without his own pillow, used the longer route. A graduate of Balliol Oxford, he dwelt on the intricacies of human nature and lessons of history. Shifting "from one hand to the other" he left "no stone unturned" in mapping the area. The unassuming Ahtisaari then went off to his favorite Russian sauna spot on the Lower East Side of Manhattan, while Abi Farah fascinated curious members with his high-English stuttered tales.

Delegates chairing meetings risk being carried away by their transient function. Repeated appeals to "Mr. Chairman" and diplomatic reference to their special qualifications could lead some to presume that they were indeed unique. Secretariat staff take no chances however. For example, they prepare every pronouncement uttered by the General Assembly President and chairmen of main committees almost to the word. "I thank the distinguished speaker for his statement and his kind words addressed to me" is often written down before or after parentheses on actions taken. Very rarely would a presiding officer venture outside the drafted text - except to exchange it with an updated one slipped in front of him or her by an alert staffer. "I note that the distinguished delegate from Burkina Faso is asking for a vote. In that regard, I would point out that the Assembly will have first to exhaust the list of speakers before we are able to proceed with conducting his request" could be a sample of a desired change if more time was needed. Another shift would indicate that there was a request "on a point of order," which takes precedence over other proceedings. Smaller committees could be less structured and its chairmen would have more leeway, like addressing a beautiful female delegate as "the gracious lady from Finland." During one of the Economic and Social Council sessions, a Canadian chairman wanted to get on with a long pending vote when a Commonwealth colleague - a newcomer - wondered what was the point in question. The Canadian went ahead anyway announcing: "Those in favor vote yes; those against vote no; those confused could abstain".

Arafat – the Value of Symbols

When Palestine Liberation Organization (PLO) Chairman Yasser Arafat arrived in New York for the first time in 1974 to address the General Assembly, crowds of demonstrators who had gathered to protest his visit carried signs saying "Arafat Go Home." He responded by saying that was exactly what he was seeking.

Mr. Arafat's first visit to UN Headquarters in 1974 raised a number of unprecedented questions. The first concerned where he would stay, as hotels in New York were reluctant to host him, citing security concerns and claiming that it would neither be safe for them nor for the PLO Chairman. It was suggested that the Secretary-General would host him in the clinic on the fifth floor of the UN Secretariat building. As a proclaimed revolutionary, Arafat did not care where he slept, whether in a fancy hotel or a simple bunk; what mattered was the symbolic value of being invited to speak at the UN. As a gesture he gratefully accepted, a helicopter picked him up at the airport, brought him straight to the UN garden where the Secretary-General greeted him and escorted him through the basement of the UN Secretariat up to the fifth floor.

A pragmatic issue arose when Mr. Arafat refused to take off his gun before addressing the General Assembly. As a leader of a revolution, there was symbolic value in him carrying his gun at all times; however, with a number of heads of State, foreign ministers and diplomats gathered in the Assembly, he could not be allowed to keep the weapon inside the Hall under any circumstances. Arafat was known to be a master of brinksmanship and after a night of negotiations, he finally agreed to a mediation proposal that he would keep the holster. He eventually handed the gun over just moments before stepping into the General Assembly. Its President at the time was the Foreign Minister of

Algeria, Abdelaziz Bouteflika, who later became the country's President. Handing the gun to a representative of Algeria, another revolutionary country, would be interpreted as a show of support for Algeria's victorious struggle for freedom. Still, several newspapers noticed the holster and assumed the gun was still there. Certain commentaries criticized the UN for allowing it but because of the delicate true situation when very few knew what actually happened, no UN response was made.

A procedural issue had to do with Mr. Arafat's official status. When heads of State came to the General Assembly, a chair was placed near the podium in which they were seated when introduced before making their speech. Again as a symbolic gesture, Arafat, as PLO Chairman, wanted similar seating. After elaborate discussions, a compromise was reached. It was agreed that a chair would be placed in its traditional spot but he would not sit on it. As he entered the Hall, the PLO Chairman went straight to the chair, symbolically put his hand on it, and posed for a bit, then continued his way to deliver his speech from the podium.

There was a view that the PLO Chairman who had gained international recognition as the representative of the Palestinian struggle could have used that unique opportunity to propose the establishment of a Palestinian State under transitional UN Trusteeship. That was what Namibia's Sam Nujoma and South Africa's Nelson Mandela eventually did. Clearly, their circumstances and personalities were different. One obstacle may have been that Mr. Arafat had not recognized yet Security Council Resolution 242, which he later hurriedly did in much weaker status and with substantially lesser reward. He may have suspected that resolution could imply the return of Israeli occupied West Bank to the authority of the Jordanian government. More practically, he may have been diverted by a swiftly growing presence in Lebanon within an exceedingly weakened State. Historic opportunities can only last when effectively explored. They tend to glimmer and then disappear quicker than generally recognized. Circumstances change. Perceived support is variable. For example, if the new government of Eritrea did not apply for UN membership through the Security Council immediately following a widespread euphoria over its Referendum in May 1994, it may have been blocked if it waited for the General Assembly review 1 September when its leadership clashed with both the U.S. Government and the UN Secretary-General. Similarly, the PLO was on its peak of UN diplomatic support roundly following its leader's landmark visit in 1974. The PLO prestige and predominance at the UN equaled that of a Security Council permanent member, as Lebanon's representative Ghassan Tueni, publisher of Beirut's influential An-Nahar Daily, told me at the time. Circumstances change, however, and opportunities that once glimmered fade ahead of being generally recognized. At any rate, an informed practical review of how the central Palestinian cause was handled through the UN since then will help shed some light on its current status.

When West Beirut, where I resided as a U.N. official, was under bombardment in the summer of 1982, and my seaside neighborhood of Manara was patrolled by gunboats, an aide to Mr. Arafat visited to take me to a meeting with him in an underground garage. He mainly wanted to know whether the Security Council would take urgent measures for a ceasefire and whether the Secretary-General, which by then had changed from Waldheim to Perez de Cuellar, was fully aware of the situation on the ground. Upon returning to my deserted office, the aide mentioned that one of those with the Palestinian leader wondered whether it was wise to trust me with his whereabouts. My angry response, having just risked my life, was that by then his whereabouts would obviously have changed, and that certain close associates of his were informing on him to every security apparatus available, including the Israelis. More importantly, my impression was that Israel would be not as interested in killing Mr. Arafat than in clipping his wings in order to get his signature on an agreement. At the time, the PLO was popularly and officially pronounced as the Resistance, or the Revolution (*Al Mukawama, Al Thawra*). Ten years later it was ceremoniously transformed into an official Administering Authority on a limited slice on the West Bank (and Gaza), in close collaboration with Israel's security overseen by a US General. No other Palestinian could have been able to achieve this much – with a victory sign.

CHAPTER III:

MISUNDERSTANDING THE WORLD

Misunderstandings are the spice of international politics. With over 193 governments, 1000 cultures, and at least as many more languages, a goodwill gesture may be interpreted as an insult to be repelled at any cost. Even in the same language a word would have different interpretations, as Commandante Che Guevara, then Cabinet Minister, pleasantly discovered at a Geneva UNCTAD conference when a young American interpreter insisted in her Catalan Spanish that he "come" with her, a word that had a more sexual connotation in Cuba.

A giggle, for example, is a Westerner's expression of partial delight. In East Asia, it reflects embarrassment. Describing someone at work as aggressive or hungry may be a prelude to a bonus on Wall Street but elsewhere a basis for exile. Similarly, the chummy American response "get out of here" may be taken literally and misunderstood by an unfamiliar visitor. In some cultures, speaking loudly with animated gestures may not be a threat but an indication of personal affection. Physical manhandling like shoving and pushing would express closer, almost brotherly, ties. The same may apply to exchange of insults. The nuance is the faint smile at the last minute.

The historic fall of the Berlin Wall was destined to occur. But it may have been accelerated through a confused slip by an East German spokesman. Under the prodding of then-Soviet *perestroika* leader

Mikhail Gorbachev, long-time leader Erich Honecker had been replaced by another Politburo member, Egon Krieg, a former Interior Minister. According to Leon Mangassarian of *Deutsche Presse Agentur* the stunning moment came shortly before 7 p.m. on November 9, 1989. Politburo member Guenter Schabowski announced that East Germans could make private trips abroad with no preconditions. The lack of freedom to travel had been a major issue angering the millions of East Germans who had joined protests against the regime. Surprised reporters questioned when the rule would come into force. With a confused look on his face, Schabowski shuffled through the papers and finally read out: "This comes into force as far as I know ...ahhh... immediately, without delay." In reality, the regulation was supposed to have been effective from 4 a.m. the next morning. Schabowski, according to Mangassarian, "misread the statement in what was probably the greatest slip of the tongue this century." Without delay, thousands started flooding the wall area on foot, in cars and in massive determination while East German soldiers were taken off guard, totally unprepared.

Diplomatic wisdom has it that if Cleopatra's nose had been slightly longer, history would have been changed. That is to say that if Mark Anthony was not seduced by her, the Roman conqueror would have taken bolder decisions. But then, beauty is in the eye of the beholder, whatever the length of the nose. A Mogul emperor would have fallen for a bulkier woman, and Alexander the Great of Macedonia, a passionate strategist, would have gone for a muscular chief of staff. UN Secretary-General U Thant was once persuaded to invite a number of correspondents at UN Headquarters for an informal briefing. By almost everyone's account, it was an unqualified success. When asked to repeat it, he declined. Much later, a young aide deciphered the reason. On reimagining the meeting, he noted that two of those invited were too informal by Asian standards: They had stretched their feet on the coffee table with their shoe soles in close proximity to the expressionless face of the Burmese Buddhist master.

Open expressions of affection among men are normal daily occurrences in the Arab world. Holding hands, sometimes engaged together while walking to a joint meeting, exchanges of kisses on the cheek as a welcome or farewell, and general utterances of personal admiration are mainly noted as confirmations of loyalty. All those gestures could be misinterpreted almost anywhere else. Many a visiting Arab official was puzzled by the reluctance of some New York-based diplomats to respond with similar warmth to his friendly approaches in public. Once, a newly married man from that region was given a badly needed job at the UN. It was a simple clerical assignment, but he was determined to keep it. A compatriot advised him to work hard and to be nice to his boss, a sensitive New Yorker. He tried in his own way to hug, touch and express admiration to his boss, who became increasingly nervous, much to the entertainment of other colleagues in the office. A breaking point came on Valentine's Day when our friend discovered that you send cards to those whom you loved. As love and affection were the same in his vocabulary, he hurriedly dispatched through office internal mail a Valentine's Day card to his boss. It read, "East is East and West is West. As to me, I love you best."

Commonly used expressions in one country could have a totally different understanding in another. Japanese telephone conversations regularly start with the expression *mushi mushi*. This, in German slang, refers to an intimate part of the female body. One could then appreciate the plight of the special-assistant to the German Ambassador in Tokyo who must reference *mushi mushi* every time her phone rings. The same country could sometimes misunderstand its own action. For decades at the entrance to the visitor's area of the UN General Assembly building stands a statue presented by Greece to the international community. For 30 years, the naked figure on a marble base was announced to belong to the great mythological god Zeus. Guides taking visitors through the halls passing by a replica of the Russian Sputnik and a Dutch magnetic circle proving the roundness of the earth would nod to the well-endowed bearded Greek as they prepared to take their group down the stairs to the gift shops. Suddenly a new Greek government decided otherwise. It sent official notice that there had been a serious mistake. The statue in fact belonged not to Zeus but to his brother Poseidon, god of the seas. What was the apparent difference, how it was discovered and by whom, no one asked and the Greeks would not say. All what was needed was to change the name and brief the puzzled guides about their new Greek god.

Canada came close to a similar incident. Four heavy bronze gates lead to the General Assembly building near the UN entrance at E. 46th Street and First Avenue. A special present from Canada, each of the gates carried a prominent imprint of the lightly covered goddesses of earth, wind, fire and water. But when the UN Postal Unit issued a reprint in a commemorative stamp to sell in Expo Montreal, the Canadian minister of posts blocked it. The concept was too mythological, the minister thought, and besides who would have the nerve to make such an obscene presentation of naked women to an international site? After due consideration, an immediate reversal of position was achieved.

Understanding where the other side was "coming from" is crucial not only among cultures but within the same culture. In a capital city of Western Asia, a distinguished politician fell into a large pit. He refused all offers by passersby who assembled round, each exclaiming "take my hand" to pull him out. Obstinate in his obvious plight, he may have felt disgrace at having other less distinguished people extend such help. Another man from his similar background came with the effective approach. "My distinguished friend," he called down, "would you please extend your hand to me?"

Sometimes a misunderstanding is a matter of mistaken identity. Dr. Henry Kissinger apparently has a habitual tactic when attending official receptions where he does not personally know most of those present. He would pick someone out of a crowd at random and engage in very pleasant banter with untypical modesty. He would conclude by introducing himself just before leaving. During a reception at the Permanent Mission of China to the UN, the very distinguished former Secretary of State engaged in a long yet general conversation with an equally distinguished looking foreign official. As he was about to leave he said: "By the way, my name is Henry Kissinger." The other man smiled, knowingly, and responded, "My name is Ali Akbar Velayati." then paused before adding, "the foreign minister of the Islamic Republic of Iran." Dr. Kissinger, as some would recall, had helped bring the deposed Shah of Iran into the US for medical treatment, indirectly sparking the taking of American hostages in Tehran. By mutual recrimination, relations between the US and Iran were cut; even non-official contact was strongly discouraged. The former US Secretary of State stopped suddenly in his tracks, then giggled, saying in his baritone accented voice: "That means, Your Excellency, that tonight we both got into trouble."

In a personal experience, I once noted a man and woman observing me as I hailed a taxicab to John F. Kennedy Airport. They took a similar cab along the same route, our cars overtaking one another. Dashing to the airline desk, I found the couple still behind me, observing me closely. The man's face looked vaguely familiar, Southern Mediterranean features, possibly an aging revolutionary or a retired agent on a voluntary assignment. As they took the seat immediately behind me on the flight to Madrid, I kept wondering what would they be seeking because my life was an open book. Convinced it was a case of mistaken identity, I almost confronted the man while he was, like me, a captive audience in an airplane cabin. Upon arrival, we both took our luggage from the same spot, still eyeing each other. Next day I saw his face in the Spanish newspapers. Gabriel Garcia Marquez, Nobel Prize Laureate, had arrived to promote his new work. I had met him briefly once in Beirut. Recalling my misperception of him en route from New York, I wondered how he would have perceived me. After all, his imagination was much greater than mine.

Then there are misinterpretations of intentions. In his journal on July 14, 1789, French King Louis XVI wrote in his diary about his plans: "*Aujourd'hui, rien.*" That day, when he felt he had nothing to do, the revolutionaries intended to send him to the guillotine. Napoleon III, who had been a guest of an English lady in his early years of exile, received her later as Emperor in Paris. Attuned to admiration of courtesans and busy with affairs of state he thought he was paying adequate attention to her when he saw her for a few cool minutes and asked how long she expected to stay in France. She perceived a condescending and ungrateful attitude. So she drew on her British sharp wit and responded: "Two months, Your Majesty – and you?"

In periods of tension, misunderstandings may mean the difference between war and peace.

Egyptian President Anwar Sadat's visit to Jerusalem was a major landmark in Middle East peace initiatives. Yet his speech to the Israeli Knesset was one of his toughest against Israel. Any Middle Eastern observer would understand that doing otherwise would have appeared like total capitulation. Reportedly, Prime Minister Menachem Begin was so upset that he attempted to respond angrily. If he did, the whole process would have taken a different turn. But in popular politics, major conciliatory stands may best be covered by a sharp political rhetoric. Astute statesmen would even allow for their counterparts to declare victory and withdraw if they obtained their objective. Italian Foreign Minister Count Sforza, recognizing that his country had lost World War II, reportedly instructed his diplomats: "Show your bravest face, make your best appearance, but make sure you give in at the right time." That is, ensure the others really understand. Otherwise, they may unduly go along with the rhetoric.

Part of the Arab-Israeli conflict may be understanding it too well; another part is misunderstanding. As if Syria and Israel needed further tension, a verbal misunderstanding occurred in April 2001 when the Security Council devoted a day to discussing the protection of civilians in areas of conflict. Given the situation in the Middle East, delegates from the region obviously participated. In his statement, Syrian ambassador Michael Wehbe referred to an April understanding sponsored several years ago by the United States and France, which pertained to Syria, Lebanon and Israel. Through that understanding, he said, Israel and Hezbollah, the movement that fought the Israelis in south Lebanon, had exchanged prisoners. However, the simultaneous interpreter heard, the Arabic word for prisoners, *asra*, as the similar sounding *asrar*, which means secrets. Hearing the English version, the Israeli delegate responded angrily: "It was Syria, not Israel, that supported Hezbollah," and went on to accuse the Syrian government of repression, which engendered another response by an enraged Syrian delegate. As the official press release about the meeting reproduced the English version, news agencies and most Arab media reported the exchange of "secrets" rather than "prisoners." Several papers obtained a vehement denial by a Hezbollah spokesman in an area where conspiracy theories abound, some suspecting a tangled web behind the confusion. Actually, it was a real misunderstanding. The interpreter involved was a qualified Arab professional with impeccable credentials.

At the opening of Camp David 2000 between Israelis and Palestinians, a widely circulated picture showed Prime Minister Ehud Barak and PLO chairman Yasser Arafat trying to urge one another to enter a cabin. Even a journalist with the experience of a New York *Times* correspondent interpreted it to mean that each was jockeying in order to push the other to enter the concessions room first. In fact, both were fervently honoring a Middle Eastern tradition. Allowing the other to enter first is a cordial sign of respect. That is why Mr. Barak appeared clearly touched by Mr. Arafat's insistence, and the Palestinian leader was pushed inside beaming. The disappointing outcome was further indication of miscalculating political realities and misread cultural signals. During the Iran-Iraq war, I travelled with Secretary-General Javier Perez de Cuellar to Baghdad and Tehran in 1985 and 1987 to reach a ceasefire. At a critical point in the negotiations, the Iranian Foreign Minister Ali Velayeti started consulting with his colleagues in Farsi. We did the same in English. Amongst themselves the Iranians repeated the word "Kabul" several times. One of our colleagues thought that the Iranians were planning to inject the Afghan situation in a deal for a wider settlement. That, he strongly felt, will complicate the issue further and suggested a firm response to that unacceptable tactic there and then. As Farsi and Arabic shared similar words, I understood *kabul* to mean "acceptance" and passed a quick note to the relieved Secretary-General.

Also in the Iran-Iraq war, some visiting firemen seemed to apply a futile logic. They kept cautioning the Iranians in particular that continued conflict will cause more young people to die. Well, young Iranians were in fact dedicated to die. To fall in battle as a *shaheed*, a martyr, was the surest way to knock on Heaven's door. Another misconception was the well-intentioned references to mediation. Whether in the American hostage crisis or the Baghdad-Tehran conflict, describing your mission as one of mediation would set the wrong tone. In Islamic history, Ali, the handsome warrior, social reformer and cousin of the Prophet Mohammed was favored, but the wily politician Muawiah eventually won through a deceptive political compromise. The partisans who stood by their popular choice were known by that name: "Shiite" in Arabic meant partisans. After Ali, his sons Hassan and Hussein died in legendary battles rather than compromise. Thus, an announcement that a foreign political visitor from New York was determined to mediate a compromise may not be enthusiastically welcome.

Often a misunderstood action could lead to an opposite and equal reaction. While working on the deployment of UN troops in Southern Lebanon in 1978, I accompanied UNWIL Commander General Emmanuel (Alex) Erskine of Ghana to meet with the Lebanese Prime Minister Salim Hoss at his office in downtown Beirut. There was a ceasefire in effect. In the middle of a productive discussion we heard first a burst of machine-gun fire followed minutes later by more bursts. Then a rocket exploded on one side followed by another in the other direction. Gradually, an artillery battle seemed to rage around and above us. The Prime Minister maintained his composure as he instructed his military adviser General Koraytem to find out what happened to the ceasefire. Within half an hour, all was quiet again as we cautiously left under heavy guard. I was reliably informed later that it all started with a pack of migrating ducks flying low in a clear September noon sky. That was too tempting for a bored gunman hunkered in his barricade. So he let out a burst. Another equally bored gunman on the other side, noting a fallen duck, was apparently challenged. He responded by hitting another duck. As the easily identifiable flying targets wisely edged their way to the Mediterranean Sea, other bursts followed. An enraged warlord awakened by the gunfire decided that the other side had deceitfully broken the ceasefire in an attempt to encroach on his territory. Rocket propelled grenades were dispatched in an expressive message. Under a similar impression, a warlord on the other side responded accordingly. Heavy fighting was about to break out again until the General contacted everyone and sorted it out. In press declarations the following day, of course, various armed factions claimed victory in repulsing an encroaching adversary. By then the duck would have reached Cyprus, possibly encountering a similar experience.

Daily customs could be understood differently. There may be as many types of coffee as there are countries; habits of offering it may also differ. My first immediate UN boss, Pier Pascal Spinelli, the Italian head of the European headquarters in Geneva, who was also assigned as Special Representative of the Secretary-General in the Middle East, loved his espresso but was reasonably tolerant about available types like a concentrated Turkish coffee. During visits to some Arab countries, Bedouin coffee was offered. It was the concentrated version, blended with cardamom. Poured into a tiny cup, one shot was enough to alert your nerves; a second kept you on edge, and a third sent demolition messages to your stomach. An unspoken understanding, therefore, was that after the first shot you shook the cup while still in your hand to signal a stop. Ambassador Spinelli was well versed in politics, and well versed in the intricacies of personalities in conflict. In fact, he had told me casually, 30 years before the famous peace ceremony in the White House Rose Garden, that then General Yitzhak Rabin would be the most likely Israeli leader to achieve a solid peace process with the Arab world. He knew about everything and everyone, except the habit of shaking the tiny cup to prevent further coffee dynamite. Only when I noticed unexpected interruptions in the midst of delicate negotiations and angered, or puzzled, glances by our hosts did I realize the agony of my admirable boss. After I told him, he started shaking his cup even with espresso.

Incidentally, U.N. European Headquarters in Geneva are highly amenable to prolonged gatherings in pristine surroundings and polite debates in quaint conference rooms where even the coffee lounge is discreetly referred to as "salle numéro six." As a proud owner of a Swiss driving license, a life-long prize, I would contest the analogy that a flawed argument would look like a Swiss cheese. The claim by a character in Graham Greene's "Third Man" that in a thousand years of peace, the Swiss could only invent the cuckoo clock is inaccurate. Some of us would point out that our Swiss entrepreneurs have creatively sold fresh mountain air to avid skiers; unheralded officials invented political neutrality and sold it to governments. It is a country of solid survivors and distinguished diplomats. Every Swiss has an unquestionable sense of time. However, regarding their U.N. membership, their timing was late. Those who have a special affection for that postcard perfect place wished it had joined when Geneva was the most prominent international capital, and Swiss Air was the only international airline to make a profit. It would have then taken a front seat in the leadership of international consensus. Its entry as number 190 was almost routine. There was only some internal excitement when special legal guidance was required in order to raise its flag. Unlike all others, it was square.

Some misunderstandings occur for purely natural reasons. Dr. Ralph Bunche used to describe the men's room on the 38th floor of the secretariat building as the most effective conference room. Its users were either very important visitors to the Secretary-General or key officials working on his floor. They were all in a rush, at least when coming in. Thus they were ready to make the briefest point or give the quickest response.

Sir Kenneth Younger, Chairman of Chatham House, the Royal Institute of International Affairs in London, recounted a story about Soviet Foreign Minister Andrei Gromyko at the signing of the UN Charter in San Francisco. In the middle of the debate on the charter, "Mr. Nyet" suddenly rose to his feet and started to exit from the conference. He seemed irritated. He found in front of him a huge contingent of international press and discovered behind him the entire Soviet delegation. To the clamoring queries by clicking photographers on the reason for the unexpected departure, the stone-faced Gromyko responded angrily: "For purrrely perrrsonal rrreasons." When these same personal reasons compelled me once to leave the General Assembly debate and dash to the nearest bathroom next to the Delegates' Lounge, I found myself politely yet firmly surrounded by extremely cautious security men as I discovered my close proximity to then Israeli Foreign Minister, General Yigal Allon.

Once in Baghdad while accompanying Secretary-General Javier Perez de Cuellar to negotiate a ceasefire between Iran and Iraq, I realized that at least three of the five members of the UN team were getting restless for the same reasons. None of us knew which way to politely exit and return. It was our first, long day at the Iraqi Foreign Ministry. Sighs of relief could almost be heard when the meeting was over, and we rushed to our cars. However, instead of making the few minutes' drive to the guesthouse, our hosts decided to extend us the courtesy of a two-hour tour. With sirens blowing at full blast we went through Baghdad, the Tigris River, a man-made island, a bazaar and a few mosques before going straight to a meeting at the headquarters of the UN Economic Commission for Western Asia, which was stationed there at the time. Don Javier must have felt totally deserted as he stood alone with more than 300 staff who were there to welcome him at the entrance of the commission. The rest of his team was already in the restrooms. As at any outpost, some started speculating about the sudden absence of the Secretary-General's accompanying staff. By the time we returned to headquarters in New York, rumors had it that we had an argument with our boss; with the Iraqis; with each other; indeed with the Executive Secretary; or all of the above.

Gifts mostly offer an abundance of pleasure but they could also cause abundant misunderstandings. The advice to beware of Greeks bearing gifts may have been linked to the giant wooden horse filled with soldiers deceptively offered in order to penetrate enemy defenses and save Helen of Troy. Though most political gifts are not Trojan Horses, sometimes the outcome is more tension than joy. In most cultures exchanging gifts is a sign of welcome or affection. In diplomatic practice a gift is a symbolic balancing act. American negotiator Averill Harriman described it like this: "If it was too good you would not have offered it, and if it was too bad I wouldn't have taken it." Yet incidents often happen. A Canadian Prime Minister took with him on a state visit to Tokyo what he thought was a typical Eskimo leather coat only to find out at the presentation ceremony a "made in Japan" label stitched prominently inside. When Iraqi troops invaded Kuwait, the ambassador of the occupied country in Washington was prominently active in defending his people. Seeking to demonstrate similar activity, the Kuwaiti ambassador to the UN, Mohammed Abul-Hassan, made diligent approaches to members of the Security Council and secretariat senior officials. Although all UN officials took their positions on principle, it occurred to the ambassador to thank some of them in his own way. Armed with specially packed Swiss watches, he made his rounds until he reached the UN Legal counsel, who had issued a firm ruling against the invasion. When the ambassador produced his token of appreciation, Professor Carl-August Fleischauer was not amused. The very polite soft-spoken German lawyer kept his cool but flatly rejected the offer. Offended, the ambassador pressed on. Equally offended, the UN legal chief rejected more vehemently.

Unknown to the ambassador was another complication. In addition to his strict ethical standards, his interlocutor was under consideration for a seat at the International Court of Justice, every international lawyer's dream. Any hint of improper conduct, however vague, might be exploited by potential detractors. Unknown to the prominent lawyer, the ambassador had no option but to return to his office literally empty-handed; that is, with all gifts distributed. Otherwise, how could he face his superiors or other gift-bearing colleagues? In a final attempt, the ambassador wondered where was the difficulty as others had already accepted his gifts. Which others, the legal counsel wanted to know? After noting the names, he fired off a memo to the Secretary-General strongly urging an immediate return of the gifts. Having to deal with an already catastrophic situation in that region, the unflappable Secretary-General did not wish to create a sideshow, nor did he overlook the valid position of our German colleague. Those involved were notified of the official position and all, except one, promptly complied.

Signals, particularly by words, could have conflicting interpretations. To show determination for hard work, the French would make the same repeated side-fist signal that an American, at least a New Yorker, would use to indicate having serious sex. In conflict situations, wrongly understood signals could easily trigger an escalating chain of events.

While visiting the Gulf region in 1985, its leaders put concerted pressure on Secretary-General Perez de Cuellar to shuttle immediately between Tehran and Baghdad to achieve at least a cease-fire. In Doha, Qatar, he finally agreed and the ruler gladly offered his plane. Although each flight took less than an hour, conveying the identity of the passengers, the route and purpose of the sudden flight in that warzone went through at least three linguistic degrees of separation. On approaching Tehran, two Iranian F- 16 jets appeared on both sides of us. With no military experience, we could not read their flight signals. Possibly imitating American movie scenes, one of our colleagues lifted his index finger in salute. It was obviously the wrong move. The jets winged away after one of the pilots showed what I thought was another finger signal. By the time the jets returned, we were ready to extend our arms at head level with palms open, an awkward yet passable rendition of a current Iranian salute. A smiling pilot tipped his wings in welcome as he led us in descent to Meherabad airport.

Attempts at pleasant repartee may sometimes backfire. Aiming to compliment UN Secretary-General Boutros-Ghali, U.S. Secretary of State Lawrence Eagleberger addressed him in what he thought was a reasonable Egyptian title: *Effendi*. Boutros-Ghali was clearly offended. That title was usually given to midlevel government officials. Before titles were discontinued in Egypt, Boutros-Ghali was a *Pascha*, a more lofty title. In fact, his father and grandfather were Paschas. When the Secretary-General corrected the Secretary of State, Mr. Eagleburger quickly responded: "In fact now you are a *Sultan*."

There may be cultural differences in discussing items on a visitor's agenda. In some cultures, like Japanese, Arab and Chinese, hosts would be restricted in raising a controversial question in order not to offend a welcome guest. Most Western cultures, to the contrary, restrict the guest. The more east you go, the more polite is the host, the more west, the more the burden shifts to the guest. Turkey, which is partly in Asia and partly in Europe, has a blunt expression using an analogy of a donkey: a gracious host could mount a grateful guest.

In politics, though, fancy fencing of cultures may be limited to public posturing because the bottom line is always a country's interest. How you convey or defend it effectively in a clearly understood manner is always the challenge. Napoleon used to say: "If you mean to take Vienna, take Vienna!" A Japanese diplomat, however, will totally disagree, of course without having to say so. An English book described at least 10 ways in which Japanese would say no. Yasushi Akashi was an accomplished internationalist who rose through the ranks and proudly maintained his Japanese cultural heritage. Almost single-handedly he introduced Japanese officialdom to the UN and popularized the Organization with the Japanese public. He later headed the UN's successful mission in Cambodia and the frustrating one in Bosnia, but never lost his cool or his agreeable smile. Firm when necessary, flexible at all times, he seemed to operate in different compartments, though the most basic one of course was Japanese.

Thérèse Paquet-Sévigny of Canada, who took over from Mr. Akashi the Department of Public Information, was equally admirable but totally different. Like a constantly revving motor, she approached issues directly, whatever the circumstances, and took immediate action whatever the outcome. When dealing with her predecessor on specific pending questions he answered in his own way, and she understood that answer in her own way too. That is differently. Having worked closely and affectionately with both, I would try to bridge the gap. For Mr. Akashi to respond that a proposal required very thorough evaluation meant to forget about it; for Mrs. Sévigny it meant finding someone to do it right.

Coming from western Asia, with slightly similar traditions, I would claim that I could mostly interpret Akashi's statements almost instantly. While I was once riding in my brother's car in London, the BBC World Service announced an interview with the UN Special Representatives in Cambodia. It was a critical stage, with violence from the Khmer Rouge, maneuvering by Prince Sihanouk, and almost chaotic conditions threatening the entire electoral process. As Akashi started responding that the situation was generally on track despite certain questions requiring attention, I attempted to interpret what he actually meant. My brother Ramzi was then amused to hear the correspondent make his own interpretation.

When Akashi was Special Representative over Bosnia, I went there on the urging of the then Under-Secretary-General for Peacekeeping Kofi Annan, who felt that we were getting a raw deal over Srebrenica and suggested a field visit by me and a TV crew to the area. Looking forward to working closely with my predecessor and former boss, even for a few days, I stopped in Zagreb on my way to a meeting in Geneva. After all courtesies were extended, Mr. Akashi, charming as usual, took me to dinner, showed me the sights and, as was our habit in New York, walked back at exercise pace. He neither mentioned his mission nor scheduled a visit to his office or a meeting with his press officers. It was a polite signal that I was welcome as a colleague but not as Head of the Public Information Department. Later, during an exchange of notes on a point of contention about the public information work of the Bosnia mission, Kofi Annan, who had received copies from both of us, called me to say: "You are using Akashi to respond to Akashi." That may have been true in one individual case. But I could never claim to fully understand the workings of a Japanese diplomat's mind, particularly when a certain ambassador is the father in law of the emperor's son.

Many soft-spoken Chinese, on the other hand, eventually tell you what they want. Not right away, but only after "confidence-building measures." They do not take kindly to a presumptuous approach and will let you know in due course, in their own way. When the People's Republic of China entered the UN or, as the General Assembly resolution stated, "restored its representation" its representatives tried to consult and make friends. Among others, a somewhat self-important mid-level European lady working in the Political Affairs Department was invited to visit Beijing, or Peking as it was still known. Asked what she would like to do on the first day of her arrival she confidently and quickly responded: "I wish to see Chairman Mao Zedong." There were polite nods all around. Later she was told to be ready at eight in the evening when she was taken to see not Chairman Mao but the Red Ballet. The same was repeated the following six days. Every day she insisted on an urgent meeting with Chairman Mao, and at eight p.m. she was again taken to the Red Ballet. At the last evening, she gave up and thought she had better see something else in the Chinese capital, so, when asked the usual question, she responded that a sightseeing tour would be welcome. Her escort paused then asked: "Didn't you wish to see Chairman Mao?" Yes indeed, she answered, her hopes rising. "Well," she was told, "he will be at the Red Ballet tonight!"

Similarly, a Minister of Foreign Affairs of a tiny, newly independent country visiting China assured its Premier Zhou Enlai at length of his country's solid support for China's territorial integrity and his nation's availability to extend political and military support whenever required at crucial times. Chou politely asked his bragging visitor: "May I know how many are you?" When the Minister said that his country's population was 60 thousand, the Chinese leader responded wryly, "And at which hotel in China are you all staying?"

For a while, when the Mao look was fashionable, all Chinese diplomats wore the same outfit and visited offices in groups of three, or later as a gang of five. Being inexperienced at the time, I sought to identify their most senior official in order to decipher precisely what the purpose of those vague and very polite visits were. I was told that the most senior wore better cloth material. Not good at cloth assessment, I gave up. So did the Chinese diplomats who started fielding Harvard graduates in Brooks Brothers suits.

Political communication through clothing was eventually utilized by Iranian politicians after the 1979 revolution. Obviously there were the robed clergy, the mullahs. Then there grew a class of lay politicians who wore trousers and jackets, sometimes even a suit, but without a necktie. Eventually the shirt became a telling symbol. As cleanliness is part of the faith, the quality of the shirt, especially of the upper buttons, indicated a certain position, status and approach. For a while political competition seemed to be perceived by local journalists as one between the turbans and the shirts. A dress code by the chief concierge of a major hotel was indicative of changing times. When visiting Tehran just after the fall of the Shah to help negotiate the hostage situation, I saw him fully dressed in a dark blue Hilton uniform, fully shaven, keys striped on his shoulders. Five years later, with the hotel named after "Independence" - *Istiglal* - he was in a regular suit, no tie, fully shaven. Two years after that, in 1987, he was still there, half bearded, in a jacket and separate trousers and an open white shirt, quality unclear. With some spare time during my first visit, I would watch from my window the halted construction cranes around Tehran mainly to see the trend of the wind. My feeling after the third visit was that you did not need the cranes or the weatherman to tell you which way the wind was blowing. Just watch the concierge.

Whether it is Japanese officials posturing through masks, American officials through the media or Europeans through a statement to a committee, it is always advisable to comprehend not only what was being said but the intended target. Often words addressed to you are messages to somewhere else.

One of my early UN experiences dealt with a study of the role of small states and territories as members of international organizations. Their voting pattern, the way they survived and their balancing act with larger countries was evaluated. It was generally a supportive study with a sympathetic approach to these countries. Some like the Maldive Islands could not afford even a full time UN representative. Others, like Singapore, Cyprus or Lebanon played through active delegates a role much wider than their country's geographical size. While an expecting enthusiastic welcome for a positive effort, I was stunned to experience a vitriolic verbal assault by the Ambassador of a European country. In fact it was the only statement made by that country in years. "My country is not an accident of history; it made history," the delegate announced. "Yes, it may be small in size, but it is great in achievement." Hearing one hour of such rhetoric, I meekly strayed into the office of a more experienced, senior colleague. "Not to worry," he calmly suggested. "Just make sure you have a full voice recording and send it to the Ambassador with compliments." His speech was intended for his country's radio. A new government was being formed, and he was a contender for the post of Minister of Foreign Affairs.

Another example at about the same period concerned South African lobsters. In a Trusteeship Committee of the General Assembly dealing with self-determination for countries under colonial rule, a delegate wanted to mobilize support against an "unacceptable position" by the UN Secretariat. As relations with delegations were an essential part of my new assignment, I was apprehensive and sought to preempt a crisis. It turned out that the delegate, who was from Ghana, as I recall, was irritated because "South African lobsters" were being served at the UN Delegates' Dining Room. How could the Secretary-General authorize the presence of such lobster when the UN should firmly boycott the condemned apartheid regime? Adding insult to injury, he felt, UN kitchen staff were providing water tanks for these lobsters and their playmates to swim in when people in South Africa were suffocated. On checking with the kitchen, it was pointed out that the misunderstanding was mainly in the name. The lobsters were as much South African as french fries were French or muffins were English. A group from the committee, drawn with "equitable geographical distribution," as usual, was taken to meet the chef and observe the lobsters should they wish. Yet the outspoken delegate did not retreat. His "campaign" was already reported in his country's newspapers. How would he look back home if it turned out to be a false alarm? A more seasoned diplomat provided the answer. The lobster's name was discreetly changed, and the delegate declaring victory at home quietly changed his position.

Often it takes a simple creative step to avert a serious obstacle to understanding. During the Egyptian-Israeli negotiations following the 1973 war, one obstacle to continued talks taking place at a point called "Kilometre 101" was due to its location on the highway to the Suez Canal. Should the discussion be handled by civilians or the military? Like the shape of the negotiating table in Paris over the Vietnam War, these questions may seem trivial to the general public but are of special symbolic significance to each side. In that case one would assume that if it were a military meeting it may be interpreted as purely technical, while a civilian one would indicate a political nature, possibly a prelude to wider peace negotiations. After days of stalemate a UN colleague present as observer thought of a helpful suggestion. The next day the Egyptian and Israeli military generals showed up in civilian clothes and resumed negotiations. Some would claim that this meeting eventually led, at a higher political level, to Camp David in 1978.

Another incident involved a military observer, a competent European officer who had to go daily from his home near the French embassy to his office near the airport. On dark, unpredictable nights, he had to cross at least three fixed checkpoints belonging to different camps and occasional "flying barricades" when three to five armed elements positioned themselves on the road checking potential victims' identities. Our colonel managed smoothly, often with ceremony reserved by the frustrated paramilitary for the real professionals. One evening he drove across with civilian attire after a dinner with personal friends. When stopped, he wanted to indicate his position in the local language. Instead of saying "senior observer" his Arabic claimed he was "the big spy." It was hours before the young zealots at the barricade were persuaded to part with their prize catch.

When speaking in English, one of the two UN working languages, each nationality has its own accent. Some may accentuate one word or soften a syllable. Most have specific letters especially pronounced. Dealing with many nationalities over a number of years would help locate their original English or, more accurately, their English of origin. The Germans (and Austrians), for example, replace "s" with "z" and "w" with "v." An internal anecdote had an American couple on a cruise to Hawaii ask Dr. Kurt Waldheim whether the name of that island was actually pronounced with a "w" or a "v". The Austrian immediately ruled that it was "Havaii of course." "Well," the lady said, "thank you Secretary-General." "You are velcome" came the response.

Misperception is an advanced stage of a misunderstanding. Miscalculation is its tragic outcome. Unfortunately, those who usually pay the price are innocent bystanders, ordinary people caught in the line of fire. As a young Lebanese man responded to his mother during the war there, "I am careful. But the fellow who plants the bomb isn't." In a tense atmosphere, even normal courtesies could be misunderstood and thus rejected.

There are always divergent perceptions between officials in the home country and a diplomat posted in New York. Even basic requirements like a certain car, communications equipment and a decent residence could be questioned by an official at home who believes that to begin with the salary of the diplomat in New York is beyond the pale. An ambassador of an Eastern European country in the 1970s lost his job when he bought a residence on Fifth Avenue for about $100,000. In that country's currency, the amount seemed scandalous. Bored competitors in their Foreign Ministry accused him of indulging his ego at the expense of his country. By New York calculations it was a steal. Fortunately, the envoy held his ground, kept the residence and delivered it intact to his successor. Now it is estimated at $10 million.

National politicians who normally set the pace in their own turf often misread the impact of their actions on other countries or responses to their role while travelling abroad. Although "all politics are local," according to former U.S. Senate Majority leader Tip O'Neill, some politicians are more local than others. A recurring example is the way in which a national leader would perceive media interest while visiting United Nations headquarters in New York to address the General Assembly. Accustomed to attentive - in many cases obedient - press at home, a head of state expecting multiple crowds of reporters could be embarrassingly disappointed. Part of my work was to moderate press conferences on UN grounds by visiting dignitaries. A practical suggestion was to hold it in the specially designated briefing-room 226 on the second floor. All requirements were there: simultaneous interpretation, a sound system and mobile television camera. But more subtle was the fact that it was large enough to accommodate accredited press corps yet small enough to look respectably packed. A reasonable timing was also suggested to allow for coverage by journalists operating on European, Asian, African or Latin American feeds. Most of the visitors with international experience made the best out of it. Yet some very few would send their agitated ambassador to insist on a huge conference room "at the level of my country's prestige and my president's popularity."

While Nelson Mandela or Vaclav Havel modestly and effectively went to the regular briefing room, a much lesser known, transient government official would insist on the biggest chamber on the premises. Otherwise, it would be part of a "plot of silence" by "international sources" determined to deprive the world of knowing about his decisive role. In one case, I had to moderate a press conference for a Latin American visitor in conference room 4, which has the capacity of a UN General Assembly, with only three individuals present: the president, his ambassador and myself. One Latin correspondent hovered around for minutes, found excuses and left. In a similar situation, an angry prime minister of an emerging Eastern European country went on for ninety minutes. His English was broken beyond comprehension, and his choice of words was utterly incoherent. There was absolutely no one in the audience. His ambassador had taken refuge on the podium, nodding agreeably with an occasional admiring smile at the subtle humor. It dawned on me that the speaker may have confused our officially recording camera for active coverage. A brief note to the technician ended my agony. But not just yet. I had then to listen to a tirade against various neighboring countries and almost all American newspapers and television stations directed of course by his hidden adversaries who conspired to undercut and humiliate him while on this crucial visit. After I explained politely and slowly that it was a Friday evening of a long American weekend called Labor Day, and that television stations may have more interest in traffic and weather, the prime minister thanked me for "an elaborate, timely and frank explanation," then turned to his ambassador, whom I never saw since.

Kofi Annan loved to learn the equivalent of hello, goodbye and thank you in as many languages as he could spring on his charmed visitors. He almost always got it right. On a visit to Cairo, the hotel manager was so impressed that he went round the lobby singing that Kofi Annan was actually an Arab who spoke the language "like a nightingale." As usual, it is the rare confusion that receives wider attention. Many officials confuse spoken Arabic and Hebrew, both Semetic languages, written the "right" way, from right to left. Almost similar sounding greetings in both languages convey peace: *Salam Aleikom* in Arabic and *Shalom Aleikhem* in Hebrew. Both repeat it on arrival and departure, when preparing for peace or angling for war. During a tense period on the verge of war or peace, with look-alike delegates saying *shalom* and *salam* as they quietly appeared and secretly left, a frustrated mediator asked: "How would they know whether they were coming or going?"

An understanding sometimes may not be actually an understanding. A dialogue may be a dual monologue at cross-purposes. After the breakup of the Soviet Union and the mushrooming of its former republics into member states, Secretary-General Boutros-Ghali decided to open new UN offices. It was an opportunity, he thought, to revolutionize UN representation by having one unified office rather than fragmented small units representing various members of the UN galaxy, all raising UN flags and enjoying ambassadorial privileges. My instructions were to work with my counterpart in the UN Development Programme dealing with Europe, Reinhardt Helmke, to establish Unified UN Offices in the newly Independent States. Traversing political minefields and dodging bureaucratic maneuvers, we established seven offices in one month.

During one visit to a former Soviet satellite, we were received warmly and billeted in a small villa within a protected compound previously reserved for the "nomenclature" - the privileged members of the former ruling class. Austere by international standards, it was comfortable and, more important, hospitable in our meetings with government officials "Transparent efforts to build a new participatory civil society" were highlighted with repeated vigor as we moved from one ministry to another. My turn came as we visited the Minister of Information. The joint resources of the UN system will be devoted to help establish free and varied media, I stressed, including professional training, regional seminars and, where appropriate, the provision of required equipment. As there were several countries interested in supporting this endeavor, the UN would channel, stimulate, and facilitate that interest. We hope to work together to avoid duplication, I continued, to sharpen the focus on issues like freedom of expression, and obtain the best results from available resources.

As the minister listened with full attention, I stressed the impact of free media on the development process. Confirming every possible collaboration, the minister walked us through the Soviet style building, showing us the printing unit, the bulletins and newspapers the government produced. In bidding farewell to us, at the exit, the minister summed up the collective mission by telling us with firm confidence: "We fully understand and share your objectives and will work with you closely. As to the press here, don't worry. They will do exactly what we tell them."

Negotiating styles differ with various cultures. Americans usually go to the point and immediately indicate priorities as forcefully as they feel appropriate. Scandinavians do the same, only more briefly and less vehemently. British diplomats are masters of the understatement. By the time they get to the point you would have already guessed it. The French share that talent only with more flowery language and indirect style. Former Soviet bloc officials, who covered their real position with clouds of rhetoric, used some key words to interpret an outcome. "Frank" discussions meant disagreement, "friendly" meant a partial bargain and "brotherly" indicated that the other party will tow their line. Latin negotiating stresses an elegant style, good appearance and a proper outcome. Asians take more time to bring up their crucial issues. A prime minister of a western Asian country, when pressed for time, used to surprise his visitors by suggesting that they skip items one (greetings) and two (general atmosphere) in order to start with the third item - the issue at hand.

At times when some country changes its habitual negotiating style, the other party gets suspicious and a misunderstanding arise. During secret negotiations between the Americans and Chinese through channels in Paris, the American ambassador was instructed to strike a personal relation with his Chinese counterpart. He started with the non-controversial question about where to find good Chinese food in the French capital. Reportedly, it took weeks of evaluation to arrive at the interpretation that it was a simple question that required a simple answer: the home of the Chinese ambassador.

As a young journalist while still a student at the American University of Beirut, I went to the home of Lebanon's Prime Minister to cover a meeting with his Pakistani counterpart. Arriving on time, that is before anyone else, including the host, I was allowed to wander around the sitting room. When the honorable guest arrived and found only me, he assumed I was his host's son. Noting gladly that I spoke English, he thoughtfully enquired about my education and spoke warmly about his family. When the Lebanese Prime Minister rushed in, and both discovered they needed interpretation, the Pakistani immediately proposed me: It was a tête-à-tête meeting, he said and there was no need for official interpreters who may record and leak the sensitive discussion. The host went along, assuming I was brought by his guest. While seasoned reporters were anxiously waiting outside, I found myself interpreting a proposal for a strategic alliance between Islamabad, Istanbul and Baghdad to confront the "emerging revolutionary trend," with Beirut as an active partner if feasible, or a silent supporter if possible. At the meeting's conclusion, after both patted me on the shoulders, I disappeared, while a general statement was made to the press. Struggling with my first professional decision, I was not sure that I could publish the real story. My doubt was because I did not get it through any journalistic effort. It was due to a misunderstanding; or indeed it was a conversation based on trust. I could claim luck, and that guardian angels offered me this gift to initiate my career. But did I wish to have my first scoop through a deceptive perception? My gut reaction was that I should build solid, ethical credentials rather than publish and be damned. Finally, I wrote a lighthearted story of how I was drawn to interpret the meeting, adding that I was not at liberty to reveal the substance. I found in my future dealings that the Prime Minister was not ungrateful.

A similar, though more deliberate, situation occurred years later during a United Nations Peace shuttle between Iran and Iraq. When we arrived in Tehran airport, an Asian looking well-dressed person in the VIP waiting room immediately welcomed Secretary-General Perez de Cuellar and engaged him in an animated discussion of his diplomatic efforts. As the Iranians allowed him in, we assumed he represented one of the several UN development or relief agencies and had dutifully made it to the airport for a courtesy call. Yet when we arrived in Baghdad airport several days later, the same man was also there. While the unassuming Secretary-General responded in the same friendly manner, he doubted that the Organization could place the same representative to two warring countries.It turned out that the man was some sort of a Japanese roving envoy dealing with the war, who sought to discover firsthand details of the negotiating process. In both airports, he told officials, through his active embassy, that he was expected to brief the UN Secretary-General immediately upon arrival to coordinate joint efforts. A warm response by an unsuspecting Secretary-General served to confirm that claim. After the two countries discovered the truth, the cunning envoy never showed up at their airports. My guess is that he must have found it advisable to steer clear of that rough neighborhood.

In matters of misunderstandings, the best and the brightest may turn out to be the worst offenders. Confident, they persist rather than reconsider.

The task of a modern ambassador, therefore, is not "to lie on behalf of his country," as some traditional skeptics claimed. With an active media as lively witnesses, the lie could not be credibly sustained for long anyway.

As much as humanly possible, any key official dealing with other countries should have the clarity of mind, if not the compassion of spirit, to explain a position carefully, and to listen - yes, listen patiently to the full position of the other side. Media posturing could be a question of shrewd politics. But good communications is a matter of survival.

CHAPTER IV:

A NAME IS JUST A NAME

New York's influential Cardinal John O'Connor used to preside each September over a prayer traditionally offered at the Holy Family Church on E. 47th Street before the start of the annual session of the United Nations General Assembly. Addressing assembled diplomats and Secretariat officials in 1997, he said in a somewhat bantering manner that he remembered the new United Nations Secretary-General's name more regularly in his prayers as he was drinking his morning coffee. It was the second year for Secretary-General Kofi Annan, whose name, particularly after a thrilling visit to Iraq, became more prominent outside the international glass house on First Avenue. As Annan responded politely, expressing thanks, some felt that his smile reflected a cool approach that grins now and repays later.

That was not the case. By then, Kofi Annan was used to variations on his name. He himself joked about Starbucks missing out on his particular brand.

Kofi in Ghanaian means Friday, and he was optimistic on Friday the 13th of December 1996 – the day he became Secretary-General fulfilling his life's dream. Although typically West African, the name could be identified by other cultures, with slight adaptations. Immediately after taking the oath of office at the General Assembly, he went to the eighth floor for his official portrait. An Arab colleague kept pronouncing his name with a deep-throated "Aaa," a family name familiar in several Arab countries like Jordan, Saudi Arabia and

Lebanon. Several Arab newspapers printed a similar version, some using his middle name "Atta" in the same manner, an equally Arab name meaning generosity. Within weeks, I received a letter addressed to him from the president of a group of Arab correspondents in Beirut, Mohammed Annan, congratulating his "cousin" and assuring him that the 5,000 members of the Annan clan in Lebanon were fully behind him. A brief, thoughtful acknowledgment was sent back to our friend, who proudly circulated it. During his first visit to Beirut in the spring of 1998, the Secretary-General's wife, Nane, went to a social event in a neighborhood where scores of Annan men and women cheered, announcing lifelong loyalty. In Jordan, the Annans were politically prominent, while the Saudi branch was rich - big time, as Vice President Cheney would say. Initially, one of them passed me the message that the latest model Mercedes would be waiting and a plane was ready to cross the Atlantic at a moment's notice if "cousin Kofi" was not given decent transportation by the cash-strapped Organization. Eventually, even his first name took on an Arab tone, indicating someone who originally came from Koufah, a Shiite city in Iraq. Ambassador Abul-Hassan of Kuwait, who was active in building New York's largest mosque, stopped to enquire: "Kofi" and "Annan" were some indications that the new Secretary-General was a brother in faith. "Ya salaam," he added. The Arab one turned out to be a Christian, but the African is Muslim. Actually, Mr. Annan is neither Moslem nor Catholic. A lesson one learns in living with different cultures is not to delve into other people's religious faith. A general guess is that he followed in the footsteps of his father.

His presumed relatives were not limited to Africa and Asia. During his first official visit to London, the new Secretary-General had a special meeting with none other than Lord Annan. Kofi Annan took it all in stride. Why should he rebuff those who wished to adopt him? Experience taught him that any name could take different turns. Around the millennium celebrations, while going to a dinner, he noticed a special security detail at the entrance of a Fifth Avenue building. When his team asked whom they were covering, they were told only it was a "Mr. Hoffmann." He proceeded to attend the function, to discover later that his own name had been New York-ized.

By nature of its work, names at the United Nations come in various accents and different meanings. Traditionally, the Secretary-General does not come from the host country, the United States, nor from any of the other four permanent member States of the Security Council.

A Name Is Just A Name

Coming from distinguished, yet specific, backgrounds, their names, like those of many internationalists, have not always been easy to grasp at first glance. To facilitate interaction, most American, European and Japanese groups resort to large name labels to identify those attending their functions. That may not work in some international gatherings. To begin with, every participant is supposed to be adequately known by the others. Mostly, they represent their countries and not themselves. Additionally, some names are not pronounced the same way they are written.

Anyone hearing the name Trygve Lie for the first time may think he was Chinese or Oriental. In fact, the first UN Secretary-General came from Norway. Despite his fame and unique role, very few UN staff could spell the full name of that great Swede, Dag Hjalmar Hammarskjold, pronounced *Hamarshuld*. U Thant, an Asian Buddhist, was hardly recognized in the host country despite 10 years of regular press coverage. In one of the first questionnaire polls taken in 1968, a majority of Americans were not clear what his name stood for. He sarcastically commented that they must have confused him with a U-boat or U-2 plane. Kurt Waldheim was pronounced with a V. The traditionally Latin name of Javier Perez de Cuellar may not be easy for the untrained ear. Upon his election, a nervous Asian delegate told me: "By the time I remember his full name, he may be gone." Yet, he stayed one more term and maintained a further successful life as Prime Minister of his country, Peru. Boutros Boutros-Ghali did become a household name in America, but not by his own design. Television show hosts and politicians were inspired to use the name for fun or electioneering. Viewers of a popular "Seinfeld" episode watched Jerry utter the name with utter amusement as he gazed upon a topless woman. David Letterman's viewers heard at least eight times more than ten ways to pronounce the name, including, "Things that sound better when sung by a barbershop quartet." "Stores not doing well" during the 1994 Holiday Season included "Boutros Boutros blouses." International insomniacs were particularly amused by Letterman's Ten BBG Pick-up Lines, including "Can I buy you a drink a drink?"; "I am so nice they named me twice!"; and "The nations are united; why not you and me?"

Some take-off names were adapted by diplomats. When the French Socialist President François Mitterrand reportedly proposed an outstanding Frenchman, Bernard Kouchner, for every vacated senior post at the United Nations, he was referred to as "Bernard Bernard." In the last year of the Secretary-General's term, after actively overseeing the first multiracial election in South Africa, a firm in that country produced Boutros Boutros Garlic. The Secretary-General's Spokesman's Office was thrilled enough to issue a statement that was equally exploited by those anxious for his departure. In an interview with Larry King, he was asked about his long name and, dressed in suspenders like his host, responded briefly that it was after his grandfather who had been Prime Minister of Egypt during the British mandate. The original family name was Ghali, one of the most prominent Coptic families. But after the grandfather was assassinated, his first name, Boutros, was attached in defiance of the forces behind his death. His eldest grandson was also given the name that he proudly carried and brought along to New York.

Again, there were varieties on the first name. Boutros is Arabic for Peter, as he was called by many American and European friends. Egypt's President Sadat, with whom he worked closely during the Camp David Egyptian-Israeli peace talks, used to indicate his attitude through the use of the first name. When satisfied with his performance, he would call him "Ya Boutros." If unhappy, he would coolly refer to him as "Peter."

The name of the United Nations itself is known as such only in English-speaking countries. UNESCO and UNICEF are known uniformly worldwide, although these terms are English-language acronyms. The UN is labeled differently in about 80 languages, from Scandinavian tongues, Flemish, Japanese, Chinese, Arabic, Hebrew, Farsi, Russian and Korean to Tagalog, Mongolian, Serbo-Croat, Turkish, Greek, Kazakh and Gyz. As its wider activities increasingly crossed national borders, its universal name recognition was blocked by linguistic barriers. The United Nations in Spanish is Las Naciones Unidas (N. U.). In French it is O.N.U. Some Francophone countries required more time to connect with the name. During the UN's first intervention in the Congo immediately following independence in the early 1960s, when Lumumba was challenged by Tschombe, observed by Kasavubu and eventually overthrown by Mobutu, some local officials had no clue what the name painted on troop vehicles and checkpoints stood for. Most mixed it up with habitual tribal politics. A concerned query was *"ONU, C'est quelle tribu?"*[1] The UN Delegates' Lounge hosts a variety of internationalists whose names are often called by a trained conference officer. Although it is mainly reserved for delegates, several Secretariat staff use it to get their daily fix at the downstairs bar, which

---

[1] "Which tribe?"

provides inexpensive liquor, or at the upstairs cafe that offers decent cappuccino. When informed of certain staff members who spent a lot of time there, U Thant dubbed them "Delegates at Lounge," a takeoff on the vague diplomatic term "Delegates at Large." For a while, an impressive-looking former Georgian princess dominated the announcements at the Lounge, pronouncing names at will, depending on her likes and dislikes. With very dark hair tightly drawn, very big black eyes and very white complexion, Nina Tessier's husky voice would resonate with determined syllables to the pride or chagrin of a nameholder. For example, a tall, elegant and very self-important-looking gentleman, Ambassador Fak of the Netherlands, winced as his name was sharply pronounced when he entered the Lounge. Mr. Fukushita of Japan received equal treatment. So did First Secretary Fukiu of the same distinguished delegation. Nina put her impressive foot down, however, when it came to perceived insults. She refused to call on African delegate Monsieur Sale Fou, which sounded very much like the French equivalent of "dirty fool". Sometimes the question was not with a delegate's name but with that of his country.

The same delegate may represent a member State after its name has changed. Son Excellence from Dahomey would have to be promptly and accurately linked with the new name of Benin. Upper Volta changed after a coup to Burkina Faso, meaning the "proud people who do not take bribes." Congo became Zaire with Mobutu's coup and then reverted to Congo and then Democratic Republic of the Congo, whereas Congo Brazzaville, formerly known as People's Republic of the Congo, is now named Congo. The Gold Coast became Ghana as it joined the world body. Bechuanaland became Botswana, and Northern Rhodesia is now Zimbabwe. Siam changed to Thailand, and Burma to Myanmar. Ivory Coast, after 20 years of international diplomatic activity, insisted on its French name in any official language: Cote d'Ivoire.

Sometimes a name change is imposed by circumstances. The Soviet Union seat was assumed by the representative of Russia. Newly independent countries like Kazakhstan, Azerbaijan and Armenia joined with new delegations bearing national names. When Yugoslavia split, some of its old delegates spread themselves between Croatia and Serbia. One of them even represented "The former Yugoslav Republic of Macedonia," which in 1993 had to accept that official name after Greece protested that Alexander the Great came from its own province of Macedonia, not to be confused with the newly established republic. A solemn gathering to commemorate the death of Mother Teresa brought about discreet maneuvers by several normally reticent delegates. While it was obvious to invite the Indian ambassador, since Mother Theresa had devoted her life to "the poorest of the poor" in Calcutta, the Macedonian wished to speak because she was born in his current capital, Skopje. But she was of Albanian descent, and the Albanian wanted to be recognized. Ah, but the country where she was born at that point in time was part of Yugoslavia; hence, a demarche by the now-isolated Yugoslav ambassador. What about Italy? inquired its formidable ambassador, Paolo Fulci - Wasn't she a nun? Wasn't the Vatican in Rome? Then came the representative of the Holy See, the official diplomatic name for the Vatican. You see, he argued, she had devoted her life to the Church, whose *nuncio* should have the concluding remarks. Ultimately, everyone joined in a harmonious ceremony.

Some names may appear under the most unusual or whimsical circumstances. A dynamic Japanese who represented the United Nations Organization in several countries was Mr. Uno. When working in Beirut during seven years of violent conflict, I once received a reassuring telephone message from a Monsieur Dieu (Mr. God). Participants in an international conference in Manila on population growth received the blessings of the Philippines' most powerful Cardinal Sin. An active member of a committee to combat racial intolerance was Monsieur Bigot. His colleague, Conseiller Billiard, handled problems of very small states in the Security Council. Among the delegates to an international anti-drug conference in Italy was Mr. Hashish of a certain Arab country, and Mr. Hashisho of another. An almost inseparable duo during one of the General Assembly Social Committee sessions were Mr. Martini of Italy and Mr. Skol of Sweden. A press officer from New York visiting Geneva for an anti-crime conference was received at the entrance by someone from Burundi who announced, "I am pleased to meet you. I am Innocent." Also in Geneva, the supervisor of the mailroom of the World Health organization was Mr. Johnny Walker.

In addition to the inevitable inherited names, there are custom-made ones. After his coup d'état, Colonel Joseph Mobutu changed his own name. He declared himself "Sese Seko Kuku Ngbendu Weza Banga," which reportedly means in Lingala "The overwhelming fighter, forever conquering, leaving fire in his wake." An informal translation indicated that he could additionally be the "cock that jumps without delay on any hen."

Some national names may not be easily handled, even by those international officials who have to deal with them regularly. Americans who had difficulty with the name of their Director of National Security under President Carter, Zbigniew Brzezinski, would appreciate the special effort made by a UN Chief of Protocol repeatedly introducing Professor Matia Mulumba Samekula Kwinuka upon presentation of his credentials in July 1996 as Ambassador Extraordinary and Plenipotentiary and Permanent Representative of Uganda to the United Nations. This, having just introduced the Deputy Permanent Representative of Madagascar, His Excellency Maslana Radafiarisoa Lea Raholinivini, as well as H.E. Subhas Chandra Mungra of Suriname and Jargalsaikhang Enkhsaikhan of Mongolia, all within the same season. A more delicate challenge is to introduce casually the President of Turkmenistan, His Excellency Gurbanguly Berdimuhamedow.

Indonesians usually refer to officials with only one name, such as Sukarno, Suharto or Bomboko. During public unrest against President Wahid in 2001, the Minister in charge of internal security and calming the tense situation was Mr. Bangbang, who indeed became President. NATO, the North Atlantic Treaty Alliance, has the same initials as the North American Tourist Association.

Peacekeepers tend to adapt quickly to the most complex variety of names. Odd Bull, the Norwegian General who once headed the Truce Supervision operation (UNTSO), moved between his headquarters in Jerusalem and the neighboring Arab countries in a specially marked airplane with customized trappings. Junior staff were unhappy with a decision that the plane's only bathroom should be reserved for his sole use. One of them painted on the door "Bullshit only." Then again, military officers could be very touchy, particularly in a rough neighborhood where there are so many generals and so little time to decide who's the real boss. A civilian UN official in the Middle East worked with five generals at once, each representing a different nationality. There were two in Jerusalem, one in Naqoura, South Lebanon, one on the Syrian-Israeli border in the Golan and a fifth holding forth in New York as military advisor to the Secretary-General. Each had short security code names like Alpha, Bravo or Romeo, however descriptive or ironic that may be. When it came to a label on their radio-equipped white cars, some suggested more descriptive nicknames. A legal adviser, Ramon Prieto, suggested simply inscribing the number of the Security Council resolution, like 242 or 425, that established each operation. Eventually, tradition won out. Each had a "Number 1" car in his area of operation. At UNIFIL headquarters in South Lebanon, the popular Italian contingent ran helicopters from

Checkpoint Pasta, where they once detained a visiting Secretary-General for a few more minutes to introduce him to their unique espresso.

Officials in some countries designate confidential nicknames for certain influential regular visitors. Jean-Christophe Mitterand, the eldest son of the late French President who was indicted for alleged commissions on arms sales in Africa, was known in the francophone region as *papa m'a dit* (my father told me). One of the most influential Frenchmen in Africa for decades was neither the Foreign Minister nor an Ambassador, but the resident manager of the French oil company ELF. Andre Tarello, who practically ran those countries between 1977 and 1993, was known as *le grand Baobab*. Any Italian will know when you refer to *l'Avocatto* that you mean Fiat's Gianni Agnelli.

Some names used proudly in one language may sound different in another. Lt-General Fahret was unhappy with the way some of his surly subordinates referred to him. The father of the Indian atomic bomb, known for his complete silence, is called Dr. Aboulkalam, which means "the one who talks too much." Indonesian Interim President Habibi, who failed to get popular support, has a name that translates into "our beloved." A German counselor who advocated harmonious diplomatic exchange is Professor Krapp. In Lebanon, the movie "Titanic" was very popular, because it translated into the clearest suggestion for having sex.

In retrospect, the Indians initiated a practical approach where you only had to refer to S.K., S.P., or C.V. for everyone in a particular circle to get it. For a wider audience, a shortened family name would be added. This need not be confused with similar British usage that indicates honors bestowed by Her Majesty the Queen. While C.M.G. may be mistaken in America for a trucking company or an Internet venture, in England it points to a proud owner of the Cross of St. Michael and George. A rank higher is K.C.M.G., which is given to a Knight of that order. The awesome ceremony with which the honors are bestowed, sought or received drove some cynics to explain them away as Call Me God and Kindly Call Me God, respectively.

MIT for most intellectuals and academicians would mean the prestigious Massachusetts Institute of Technology, yet for those closely following the conflict in Syria it would more conspicuously indicate Turkey's national intelligence service (Milli Istihbarat Teshlati). And while most MIT alumni might struggle to recall the name of their respective deans, fighters in Syria, particularly from abroad, will easily recognize the name of the other MIT's influential director in Ankara.

Countries are understandably attached to certain dates of popular significance. The Fourth of July in America and July 14 in France are uncontested examples marking truly historic change. That may not be the case in some countries looking for revolutionary legitimacy for an anniversary of taking over the Government, usually without much popular consent. Streets, schools and hospitals, and even new hotels, are given dates ranging from January to December, each indicating some miniscule turn in history's long march. Yet, visitors and aspiring politicians alike have to memorize them.

Some places acquired their interesting names through popular understanding or divine intervention. Banco de Santo Spirito, the Vatican's financial arm, may fall in between, but only God knows where the money goes. The Bridge of Sighs in Venice should be the most successful tourist trap, but it is an adorable little spot suitable for any occasion: any doctor will tell you that the best medicine cannot equal a deep sigh. Berlin's Palace of Tears, *Tramenpalast*, near Friedrichstrasse, between the former East and West sectors, is less famous, or more infamous. Then, of course, there was The Wall. But that is history.

Some acronyms may inspire unflinching loyalty by their adherents but may not be equally appreciated elsewhere. For example, the Conservative Reform Alliance Party in Canada had to eventually amend its name as it spelled CRAP. A UN relief operation in Bangladesh seeking to cut through red tape and combat disaster larceny was inadvertently titled UNROB.

Titles endure when names fade from memory. "His Excellency" may not know that his name escapes you at the time. "Our distinguished colleague" would cover one's ignorance while preserving a dignified cachet. President George W. Bush reportedly had a knack for giving an instant title to unrecalled names. Eventually, Stretch, Wide Eyes or Boots will know who they were. In various countries, some eager for wider credit in words give themselves a descriptive nickname. Examples would appear in the midst of some desperately miserable Francophone African countries, like the Congo in crisis, where a suitably dressed gentleman introduced himself as *Ambianceur*. His main purpose was to generate a required atmosphere (ambience) for the evening. Dressed completely in white and carrying an ivory stick, he would grin his way through the lobby of Kinshasa's Intercontinental Hotel, gleaning potential opportunities. He could sing softly, dance suavely or recite poetry. Above all, he could talk. And if the evening went bust, he could always produce some colorful diamonds, which were certainly "not for sale - but for you, *mon cher ami*, we can discuss." Another character used to roam the lobby of the Excelsior in Rome during Via Veneto's Dolce Vita era. Impeccably dressed with the usual Italian stress on shirt collar and shoes, he would bow profusely to English or American women of a certain age as he presented his card, conveying a promising yet carefully balanced mission: Romantic Latin lover. If vigor proved to be lacking, then there was always romance. The word "Latin" was added for mysterious charm or perhaps as an escape exit.

Then there are those descriptive names that are supposed to be understood without explanation. One story that our late senior colleague F.T. Liu was fond of telling in relaxed moments between tense peacekeeping situations was that of the "grand Tra la la." It happened when he was a young attaché at the Chinese Embassy in Paris. He was told that an important visitor was descending on the City of Lights and should be royally entertained, or at least kept preoccupied. Unclear what to do, he sought urgent advice from the seemingly experienced concierge of the prestigious nearby Hotel George V. Ah, he was told, the distinguished visitor could be shown around some interesting sights - museums, bookstores, churches - for about 1,000 francs, a big amount at the time. Reporting back to his boss, he was told that more events would be required to distract the visitor's attention and to keep him from breathing down the Ambassador's neck. This time the concierge suggested that, for 2,000 francs, a wider net could be cast to include an intimate gathering at Les Deux Magots with some first-rate intellectuals, a candlelight dinner at an exquisite restaurant with a fascinating lady and a stroll along the banks of the Seine escorted by a talented accordionist. When again informed by his superior that more, much more, was required, he went back to his newfound consultant. "Oh", responded the experienced concierge, throwing both hands in the air, "Then, *le grand Tra la la*," and THAT will come to 5,000 francs. Staggered by the amount, F.T. went straight without asking further questions to report to the Ambassador, who swiftly instructed him to forget about it. If any Chinese was to get *le grand Tra la la*, it should be the one representing his country with distinction in Paris and not a visiting fireman from back home. Ever since then, the young Chinese, who eventually became United Nations Assistant Secretary-General for peacekeeping, wanted to know what exactly was *le grand Tra la la*. He died, age 83, without finding out.

When working in a variety of countries, it could be helpful to learn descriptive expressions commonly known in some regions, but unknown in others. Working in Africa, one has to learn that an *Imbungi* is someone who literally sings other people's praises (at a price, preferably cash). *Kontarou* is Greek for a little of this and a little of that. A journalist working in Tokyo should know that *Ofuriko* is Japanese for off the record. *Onni* is Finnish for lucky; *Bubelibubb* was once a favorite, though ambiguous, expression used by the ruling monarch of Sweden, King Carl XVI Gustav.

Understanding South Africa's great leader Nelson Mandela would entail the knowledge of *ubuntu*, the principle that a person is a person because of their relationship with other people. It would have helped a peacemaker in the killing fields of the Bosnian war (or Kosovo) to know that *Jaca tlacei* is a Serbo-Croat term for "the weak are stomped by force." Joining an almost paralyzed tribunal on Rwanda, a member may wish to know of *Lagachaeha*, a form of tribal justice whereby the criminal is obliged to live in his own village, daily facing friends and family with their evaluation of his deed. Very few politicians who caucus know that it is a native American Indian word for a huddle. Someone enjoying massage therapy at a spa may have no interest in finding out that its derivation is the Latin concept *Saludis Per Aqua* - health through water. Anyone, like, moving to Brooklyn, would be well advised to learn Jimmy Durante's saying that "da nose knows."

A name could bring conflict or bear fortune. The British and Argentines went to war over whether 800 shepherds in the Southern Atlantic were living in the Falkland Islands or Las Malvinas. A flashpoint near Jerusalem that reached the United Nations Security Council was a settlement named Har Homa by the Israelis, while the Arabs were calling it Jabal Ghoneim. When Kofi Annan mentioned one name without the other, he immediately received a reminder from the aggrieved delegation. Driving in some multilingual multiethnic countries can be an instant lesson in geopolitics. While the Swiss sensibly maintained town names designated by their region, signs to Belgian villages seem to suddenly disappear, yielding to a completely different name. While confidently conducting your way to the University of Louvin, Flemish indications lead to Lueffen. Jacques Brel's "Marieke," sung in both languages, uses French for Gant, while the Flemish refer to it as Gent, which looks similar but sounds very different.

The same name can even have disparate tributaries. Giving directions to the prestigious International Institute of Strategic Studies at Arundell House in London, England, it is advisable to indicate that it is in Arundell Place. That is on the Embankment of the River Thames and happens to be across from a headquarters of the British Secret Service. A slight confusion with Arundell Gardens could mean a diversion to the trendy neighborhood of Notting Hill on the exact opposite side of that metropolis.

During a dinner by UN accredited correspondents in December 2006, the newly elected Secretary-General stood up to say with a slight smile, "My name is Ban, not Bond." And he's taking over as 007 approaches – that is, the year 2007. He may not be as agile and equipped as the famous Bond, he disarmingly confessed, but he cautioned assembled correspondents that he will elude them with similar gusto. After all, he was not nicknamed "slippery eel" by the South Korean press for nothing. (Very few present realized that at home his name sounds like Mr. "Bohn," which would sound closer to the 007 operative.)

After assuming office, the former Korean Foreign Minister made a point of pronouncing his own name in the way he desired others to announce it. His predecessor had spent 10 years suggesting through various spokesmen that his name "should rhyme with Sophie" - as if he had a choice. People thought his named looked like "coffee," and that's what they used to call him; he took it in stride, unless he felt it was used as a joke. He would then get back at the offender, one way, some time or another. No one, he thought, could humiliate you without your own consent.

The discomfort for Ban Ki-moon about pronouncing or writing his name reached a point that one year and three months after his takeover, the Secretary-General had to issue an official memorandum about it. In an unprecedented note dated 31 March 2008, Chef de Cabinet Vijay Nambiar (name pronounced as spelled) coached "All Heads of Departments, Offices and Funds and Programmes" on this "matter of some delicacy.""The Secretary-General has had to cope with the question of ensuring clarity and accuracy in the recognition of his name," the note said. That was not an unusual problem, it claimed, but it remained "a matter of frustration that despite passage of such long time, "there still remains confusion on this case." It suggested using the expression "Secretary-General BAN." It helpfully indicated in parentheses: "it may, incidentally also be noted that the surname BAN is pronounced *Baahn* as in *Autobahn*. In written communications, the surname should be typed in capitals, i.e. BAN Ki-moon. His spouse should be addressed as Mrs. BAN Soo-taek."

The "Chef" then requested all recipients to "disseminate" his guidance "appropriately and discreetly" among staff and public authorities and institutions, "so that Member States and their leaders as well as the media and other public figures are better aware of how they should address the Secretary-General accurately."

Needless to say, that supposedly discreet declaration of frustration was instantly circulated among amused diplomats and amazed staff with very little impact.

The names of countries can also give rise to misunderstandings. Guinea, a member of the Security Council in 2002, used to be a French colony. It should not be confused with Equatorial Guinea, a former possession of Spain; Guinea-Bissau, which declared its independence from Portugal, or Papua New Guinea, which had been governed by Australia. One wonders what language their ambassador would use when they meet - that of their former colonies, their indigenous lingua franca, or English.

During the Security Council meeting to adopt Resolution 1701 in August 2006, its President, the Foreign Minister of Ghana, had a hard time pronouncing the name of the Foreign Minister of Greece. When, after obvious effort, he managed to welcome and properly thank His Excellency Dora Bakoyannis, his microphone heaved a sigh of relief, and his own face beamed with a victorious smile as he exchanged a "high five" with his distinguished neighbor and compatriot, the Secretary-General. The Mediterranean lady smiled graciously after realizing that the Ghanaian Foreign Minister's name, His Excellency Hane Addo Dankwa Akufo-Addo, was more difficult to pronounce than hers. A more curious name was that of Ghana's permanent representative who chaired the rest of August meetings: Nana Effer-Apenteng.

In England, Crown Prince Charles is a convenient abbreviation for "His Royal Highness The Prince Charles Phillip Arthur George, Prince of Wales and Earl of Chester, Knight Order of the Garter, Knight Order of the Thistle, Commander Order of the British Empire, Earl of Carrick and Baron of Renfrew, Duke of Cornwall, Duke of Rothesay, Lord of the Isles, Prince and Great Steward of Scotland."

The nameless may well be in majority amongst the seven billion inhabitants of our planet Earth. In some Latin countries, parents find it more convenient to name children by order of their birth – Primo is the first, Secondo the second. In parts of Africa, birth names reflect the weekday of birth. In some rural tribal parts of Africa, like in Southern Sudan, most remain with no name until they have to answer to one when they get a job in a main city. Then they would accept or claim an acquired description of a name: Radio, Telephone and Wheels, even Police, are not uncommon names of choice.

Eulogizing Ronald Reagan, President George Bush recalled that when asked how his meeting with Bishop Tutu went, he responded "So-so." "One Man Banda" was a popular reference to Malawi's government when it was run by Dr. Hastings Banda, who ruled the country for 30 years and presumably occupied most cabinet portfolios.

What's in a name? Millions, if you ask the emerging island nation of Tuvalu. When an international committee distributed two-letter code names for territories around the world, the practice was to use an abbreviation close to the full name. Thus, the United Kingdom (England) got .uk, Germany (Deutschland) was .de, and Japan jp. Tuvalu happened to get .tv at the height of the electronic communications business frenzy. And it was glad to receive a reported minimum of $50 million in .tv fees over the first ten years of the new millennium.

A citizen of Sri Lanka drew attention not only because of his determination to travel abroad in any clandestine manner, but also due to his unusually long name: Wirasinghearashinanga.

Is one name just like any other name? A jolly British bloke, George Card, was not merely having a spot of fun when he called his February-born infant Valentine; he was also looking after his son's social future. Imagine, he told everyone, when the boy would grow old enough to date, how could women resist getting the only live Valentine Card?

CHAPTER V:

A SONG ON THE SIDE

When heads of state of the European Union, meeting in Brussels with new US President George W. Bush during the summer of 2001, paused for a group photo, they discovered that one of them was missing. Led by a francophone prime minister, they joined in singing a famous traditional folksong: *"Frère Jacques, dormez vous*?" (Are you sleeping, Brother Jacques?) French President Jacques Chirac entered hurriedly before the chorus reached "Ding, dang, dong".

Experience indicates that, given the right time, the sternest face may have the softest voice. Once, during a charity dinner in Moscow attended mainly by American actors and artists, Russian President Vladimir Putin surprised his guests by playing the piano and singing, *"I found my thrill on Blueberry Hill"*.

Everybody would like to sing to somebody, sometime - or just sing. After listening to years of public statements, I am convinced that enthusiastic speakers are closet performers, or singers in disguise. They have their captive audience at the United Nations General Assembly hall. Would anyone doubt the enthusiasm with which Fidel Castro or Bill Clinton would approach a favorite song with the right audience? The driving motto of President Clinton's election campaign may have been: "It's the economy, stupid," but the popular theme was a refrain from a song: *"Don't Stop Thinking About Tomorrow"*, performed by the candidates and their wives on every conceivable stage. And the Clintons named their only daughter the admirable Chelsea, inspired by a July Collins song. While the former US President is known to be fond of Elvis Presley, El Commandante only recently discovered British Beatle John Lennon, devoted a bench for him in Havana Square and managed to repeat: *"You may say you're a dreamer, but you're not the only one"*.

For the good cause of world refugees, former US Secretary of State Madeleine Albright swayed to the beat as she lip-synched Aretha Franklin's *"R.E.S.P.E.C.T."* Earlier, as a delegate to the UN, Ambassador Albright had readily instructed fellow Security Council members, with the help of Lesotho's Ambassador Legwaila Legwaila, how to *macarena*. She was not as successful later on when she tried to entertain the heads of ASEAN States in Kuala Lumpur. The atmosphere was not conducive, and Prime Minister Mahathir Mohammed was certainly not in the mood to grasp the nuanced fun. In a farewell review of her role as Secretary of State, the often ebullient, sometimes bullying Dr. Albright said that one of her jolliest moments was during the year 2000 celebration holiday season when former Soviet Prime Minister Primakov and current Foreign Minister Ivanov sang Merry Christmas carols to her over the phone. *"Don't cry for me, Argentina"*, attributed to Evita, the wife of President Juan Peron, was rendered in so many imitations, not by Paloma San Basilio or Madonna alone, but by diplomats and politicians worldwide in moments of self-release. African politicians often use popular songs to praise or evoke the powers of their leaders. Some singers are in the "going away business" - that is, they continue to sing loudly under the window of a leader until he pays them off to have a moment's peace.

If Imelda Marcos, former First Lady of the Philippines, is known for her shoe collection, many of her friends know her as an ardent singer. Her birthday parties were an occasion for an enthusiastic performance, mainly of soft romantic songs. Her late husband, who ruled his country for decades with an iron fist, was said to soften at her rendering of *"Because of You"*. Any visitor to Manila will discover that most every Filipino is a singer. When Parliament speaker Letitia Shahani received a World Population prize, the ceremony was graced by a Filipino choir performing the popular Freddy Aguilar song *"Anak"*. Her brother, former President Fidel Ramos, once publicly joined China's President Jiang Zemin in singing *"Love Me Tender"*. As that Elvis tune is known to be one of President Clinton's favorites, some speculated that a political message was somewhere there. Most likely, it may have been two leaders, two overstressed human beings, having a good time. Sending a message would be a bonus. Later in the summer of the year 2000, a similar duet by Presidents Fidel Castro and Hugo Chavez on the radio did not sound like the Buena Vista Social Club, but they tried. Apparently, the former Venezuelan paratrooper, who gained through popular vote what he had failed to win in a coup, made a habit of singing with visiting dignitaries. In the midst of the US-Chinese crisis over the forced landing of a surveillance plane, the Chinese leader, who symbolically carried through with a scheduled Latin American trip, enjoyed similar vocal treatment in Caracas. Only this time more professional support was secured. Spanish singer Julio Iglesias, who happened to be in town for a concert, was mobilized in a trio of assorted tunes.

At the peak of the Non-aligned Movement of the seventies, several Third World leaders nurtured their image as chess masters. Still, Egypt's President Nasser's most effective weapon was singing star Um Kulthoum, who dictated the mood of the Arab masses from the Nile to the Euphrates to the Atlantic every first Thursday of the month. Particularly in mediation of conflict resolution, those "facing the music" or "blowing their own horn" would prefer to be described not merely as astute peace negotiators but also as improvising jazz artists. Candidate Bill Clinton gained most voters when he donned dark glasses and played saxophone on Arsenio Hall's late night TV show. A problem sometimes arises not when politicians choose to make music but when singers insist on making policy. The election of President George W. Bush was perceived as a change of tune in the White House. After years of movie stars and divas like Barbra Streisand under the Clinton-Gore tenure, inaugural festivities featured country crooner Clint Black and Tennessee singer Lee Greenwood performing *"God Bless the USA"*. According to the *Financial Times*, it was the triumph of Nashville over Hollywood.

One of the most predominant personalities when I joined the UN was Secretary-General U Thant's Indian Chef de Cabinet. The name of C.V. Narasimhan, who practically ran the daily machinery, instilled fear and apprehension in some and affectionate loyalty in others. An accomplished administrator, he generally had one or two informed anchors in each department to ensure appropriate action. Yet, no private evening at his place was complete without some rendering of Indian chants. With the Beatles traveling to India, influenced by their guru's taste in music, the powerful Indian Chef de Cabinet of the Secretary-General, C.V. (as he was called by his colleagues), became bolder in showing off his musical passion. He even gave a free concert at the Dag

Hammarskjold auditorium for an amazed audience of staff and friends. Excessive zeal by some Indian underlings attempting to gain his favor was immediately curtailed as he briefly stared them down and then proceeded to demonstrate his vocal acumen. Narasimhan also had a repertoire of relevant jokes that, after a stern gaze, he regularly sprang on other senior colleagues with a flashing smile. It was that brief smile and his passion for music that gained him affection. The first non-classical musical event in the General Assembly hall was quietly arranged by him: an exquisite duo of sitar master Ravi Shankar and violin virtuoso Yehudi Menuhin performed in a memorable concert dedicated to harmony among peoples and peace among nations.

On my first peacekeeping mission, I realized how much some of the most decorated soldiers loved to sing when left alone. A small lounge in the former palace of the former Yemeni ruler, the Imam, was a regular after-dinner gathering spot for anyone willing to sing or listen. Assured that the last sitrep had been sent to New York, a somber-looking Scottish radio officer would normally occupy a central seat plucking his guitar while closely seeking inspiration from his two Scotch companions, Haig and Haig. *"Well, what's the matter with Glasgow? For it's goin' round and round"* was his opening signature song. An Indian Commanding Officer would then instruct an obliging lieutenant to belt out a *vedue* song using a nearby pot as a tabla. Yet, the most impressive of all was the fiercest-looking officer, a Gurkha soldier, who could supposedly take down a tiger with his knife. During a quiet lull, he broke out in a soft romantic song, completely at odds with his tough demeanor. His language was distant, but his tone was familiar. Could his love wait for him? He would be returning to her with all the perfumes of Arabia. That sounded like the general drift. He also seemed to be promising additional action when they met, as his voice strengthened and his eyes lit up. But that was something that our Ghurkha officer did not explain, and no one dared ask. While these clearly dedicated soldiers of peace were under persistent pressure to maintain their neutral position and hold their tongues under control, despite the daily challenges, getting together over makeshift music was one of their welcome outlets.

Experienced diplomats understand that they may have to cope with an unexpected tune every now and then. But a United Nations Security Council team visiting East Timor at the height of massacres by the pro-Jakarta militias were not exactly expecting the Indonesian Army chief of staff to personally entertain them by singing "Feelings." The polite applause he received may have encouraged him to expand his interest after leaving the army with the formation of President Wahid's government. He eventually produced a CD with his own lyrics and voice, which *Time* Magazine reportedly billed as one of the worst in the year 2000.

While accompanying Secretary-General Waldheim to some Middle Eastern countries, I could hardly notice specific musical inclinations. Like any noted Austrian, he would certainly have frequented the opera and politely applauded Mozart's *"Magic Flute"* performance. He would have certainly taken the traditional counter-clockwise walk during the intermissions, nodding in acknowledgement to those ceremoniously walking in the other direction. Otherwise, the only event I gathered from distant Beirut at the time was a performance by some pop singers in support of UNICEF. Then the future Austrian President reportedly watched in amazed silence as Rod Stewart wiggled, drizzling some Coca Cola on a makeshift stage so his sneakers wouldn't slip, then starting to twist and shout: *"If you want my body, you just come and get me"*. The successor to Dr. Waldheim, Javier Perez de Cuellar, was very reserved in expressing his feelings, even within a small circle. He loves classical music, enjoys Ravel's *"Bolero"* and admires Pablo Casals. The famous Latin cellist reciprocated by dedicating a much-overlooked *"United Nations Anthem"*. Incidentally, when that tune was performed during a millennium celebration, Ambassador Sergey Lavrov thought it reminded him of an old Russian folkloric song.

Professor Boutros Boutros-Ghali was a passionate workaholic and proponent of the stern image of authority. Entertainment was left generally to his lively, loving wife Leah. He did attend a musical once in New York upon the persistent invitation of television personality Barbara Walters, only to doze off. Yet, the Moroccans managed to have Dr. Boutros-Ghali sing, even for a minute. We were having a preparatory meeting for the 50th anniversary of the UN in 1995 at the invitation of then Crown Prince, now King, Mohammed VI. We were all guests at the Mamounia Hotel, once a favorite of Sir Winston Churchill, Malcolm Forbes, Elizabeth Taylor and almost anyone familiar with Morocco. Although its piscine lunch buffet surrounded by orange groves is a unique aesthetic and gastronomical experience, we did not have time to enjoy it. Instead, we had a working lunch next to the meeting room at a conference center in a golf club about a mile away. During the breaks, Bishop Desmond Tutu would walk around in circles under the shade of a tree, or Mrs. Susan Mubarak, First Lady of Egypt, would repair to a corner surrounded by an attentive Egyptian entourage. Mrs. Sonia

Gandhi would be suffocated by her protective Indian guards. Dr. Bernard Kouchner would continue proposing original ideas in English and French, depending on the willing listener. "Mwalimu" Julius Nyerere would stroll around listening attentively and talking passionately. The Crown Prince would discreetly ensure that all was well, and everyone was productively occupied. That evening, guests were invited to a colorful restaurant in the old casbah. While superb food being served in an exquisite setting, an orchestra started playing, first Moroccan music, then a traditional rhythm close to the Sufi spirituals, until they shifted to a popular folk song originally written in the thirties by the master of Egyptian folk music, Sayed Darwish. "Ya Salat El-Zein," an ode to elegance, is in praise of good people and a choral salute to "princes, poets and decent folks" for joining together in an evening of joy. Inhibited in the midst of such a group of unfamiliar, distinguished people, I casually started murmuring the tune - one of my late father's favorites - until I heard a voice singing loudly behind me. Encouraged, I raised my voice and turned around to find that my unknown partner was my boss, Boutros Boutros-Ghali. Until then, I had seen a Secretary-General whistle, another gently hum a tune, a third rhythmically move his hands along to a rendition of classical music. It was, however, the first time I heard a Secretary-General sing. And I felt fine.

Kofi Annan, no doubt, is at ease with any kind of music and seems to go along with artistic reflections of various cultures. During his first year as Secretary-General, the first fully rhythmic performance was held on UN Day in the General Assembly hall. It was my thrilling pleasure to arrange and introduce top musicians from Portuguese-speaking countries like Cape Verde, Brazil and Portugal performed in an unfamiliar yet hospitable setting. Kofi and Nane Annan, and Ambassadors Antonio Monteiro and Alfredo Lopes Cabral together with their wives, swayed with the rhythm like the rest of the crowd in an evening of joyous harmony. The General Assembly had not reverberated with such human warmth since Nelson Mandela was received for the first time or when Dag Hammarskjold had introduced Beethoven's Ninth Symphony.

Then there came the time Ban Ki-moon rapped to American hip-hop songs.

The UN Secretary-General tried his best at a dinner in October 2008 on the 50th anniversary of the UN Association of the UN/US, which like the UN Secretariat, benefited from funds donated by Ted Turner.

Hence, Ban Ki-Moon's line: *"UN stays on the front burner / Thanks to our champ, Ted Turner"*. Jay-Z, whose "Water for Life" venture was developed with UN/DPI, was overjoyed to hear our most senior vocal cord declare: *"With Jay-Z there's double strife / Life for children and water for life."* Certainly not very creative, but passable, considering the audience. So was a reference to the world's top search engine: *"When you put the org in Google / Partnerships go truly global"*. The puzzling line, "Global *classrooms are a cinch / With the help of Merrill Lynch"*, was followed by awkward silence. Media headlines had just reported that the investment firm was in more of a pinch than a cinch. Most likely, the lines had been drafted by a badly informed optimist, and the new international leader/ad hoc rapper read it anyway just because it rhymed.

Mr. Ban had displayed his musical acumen two years earlier at the UN Correspondents' dinner, as he obscurely bided his time to take over two weeks later. A pleasant surprise, after prizes were given and speeches were made, was a duo singing performance by Edith Lederer of the Associated Press – one of the toughest reporters and most charming individuals – and BBC's Laura Trevelyan, in an amended rendering of *"Arrivederci Kofi, Goodbye, Au Revoir"*. As most reporters forewarned the incoming Secretary-General that they will be watching him closely, the newcomer to the UN seemed undaunted. As he was about to conclude his brief appearance, he disarmingly sang a reworded Christmas jingle: *"Ban Ki-moon is coming to town"*. And for at least a few moments, the audience of journalists, diplomats and UN staffers stood up, dancing to his tune.

When over 150 Heads of State assembled for the UN 50th Anniversary and for the millennium celebrations, a ceremonial group photo was taken. They were asked to stand together for enough time to prepare the lens for an appropriate take. It occurred to some that the initial tension in the waiting time could be released if someone started a group song, like *"We Are the World"*. But then, those super-powerful participants would have to hold hands for more than an occasional moment. Some of them would wish to find out what they would be getting in return for such a conciliatory gesture, even at a house of peace. Some others, particularly those with limited English, would totally misunderstand.

If there was ping-pong diplomacy between China and the US before normalizing their relations, then fine-tuning diplomacy could sometimes come in handy. With relations between Washington and Tehran interrupted since 1980, several discreet channels were opened, including one through the UN Secretariat. The attendance of a high-level Iranian delegation at the Millennium Assembly was choreographed to coincide, or rhyme, with a special American attendance. There was even some unexpected music on the side. Entering the UN premises in the morning through the wrought-iron visitors' gate, some members of the Iranian delegation were cheerfully competing to complete a beautiful Persian song. They had good reason. Less than an hour later, after delivering an address on behalf of the host country, the President of the United States, William Jefferson Clinton, sustained by his Secretary of State, was intently listening to a speech by their chief, Iranian President Sayyed Mohammed Khatami. That was a clearly political move helped by a slight shift in speaking arrangements. It was preceded a day earlier by an intellectual approach.

At a debate on "Dialogue among Cultures," introduced by President Khatami, Dr. Albright - this time in a shift of travel schedule - attended and applauded. The intellectual dance was much subtler than political rhetoric. After all, theological culture is the acknowledged specialty of the black-turbaned Sayyed, and political thought is the passion of the former professor and US Secretary of State, whatever her brooch of the day. While some Americans - and possibly Iranians - were polishing their Rumi or Shirazi poetic chants in the closed lobbies, an open meeting was being held ostensibly for countries dealing with the situation in Afghanistan. That is known as the Six Plus Two Group, meaning the neighbors of that country plus the US and Russia. With full media coverage, or possibly because of it, there was no direct Albright-Kharrazzi meeting in tiny conference Room B. "They seemed comfortable with each other's presence," was the most that a spinner would claim. Actually, while Albright was informing the press afterwards about the non-meeting meeting, the experienced Kharrazzi, a former head of the Iranian Information Ministry, was seen slipping casually behind the crowd. The two had known each other since they served as permanent representatives of their respective countries in New York, yet, due to a habit established by envoys of the Islamic Republic of Iran about greeting women, both can credibly state that they never shook hands.

Nuances matter in politics, particularly in old cultures. What you see is not always what you get. But you will know it if you are generally on the right track. The tuning seemed to have achieved special progress, which could only be indicated through future complex moves. Yet, each additional day of such a choreographed friendly approach is a thousand times better than one day of recrimination. More fortunately in this case, Madeleine Albright decided artfully to play ballerina than dance the *macarena*.

The only UN lunch where all 18 invited officials showed up, without exception and on time, was the one given for Maestro Luciano Pavarotti. Not only did the representatives of the most powerful countries congregate around the boisterous tenor, but each of them also had an exchange on a favorite tune, with some humming it tentatively in a discreet effort to reflect extra-diplomatic interest. One distinguished ambassador went beyond to demonstrate his *fortissimo*. Secretary-General Annan, who had indicated that he would be out of town on that day, appeared unexpectedly around coffee time, with his then-representative on Iraq, Richard Butler. Held at one of the fourth-floor private dining rooms at United Nations headquarters, that lunch was just before the Soccer World Cup in Paris in 1998. As the Three Tenors were scheduled to sing at the finals of that championship, each of the ambassadors present was keen to gain an inside track on the potential winning team. The Maestro, a soccer enthusiast, proved his diplomatic skill by making a nod to the German ambassador on his right about that country's national team, while Nicoletta, the light of his life, said he obviously hoped Italy would win but that being superstitious he had named their stronger competitors in order to jinx them. It transpired that not only our ambassadors, but also their heads of state, were either aspiring tenors or soccer enthusiasts. What happened at the Soccer World Cup and the final performance of the Three Tenors was apparently a matter to be handled directly by the top boss.

President Jacques Chirac, the host, would not miss the opportunity of a sing-along, particularly as France edged its way to the championship. Chancellor Helmut Kohl befriended the coach of the national team, giving him daily advice. President Menem of Argentina was determined to play with the team and personally sing the national anthem until persuaded otherwise. During the semifinals between Germany and Bulgaria, at the previous championship games in a New Jersey stadium, the President of Bulgaria took off his jacket and jumped onto the field to argue a point with the referee. He then led his attending compatriots in inspirational songs to his team. Actually, the Italian Maestro was as thrilled with the reception of diplomats as they were with his enthusiastic presence. Despite a lifetime in New York, he had never been to the United Nations. When he told me that he was performing in the 1997 fall opera season, two ideas came to mind. The immediate one was initially to invite him to lunch at the UN alone for a "soft landing". A brief courtesy call to the Secretary-General was arranged just before lunchtime. At the Delegates Dining Room, my Special Assistant, Paula Refolo, quietly passed the word that it was the visiting Maestro's birthday. As the surprise candle-lit cake approached, the whole UN crowd stood up to sing Happy Birthday with stunning enthusiasm. The leader at our neighboring table, Peruvian Ambassador Fernando Guillen, was clearly in recital shape as he led the diplomatic chorus. It was then that Nicoletta thought I deserved two tickets for that week's performance of *Turandot*. Our Maestro shouted that his newly-found *fratello* should get a dozen – 12 – tickets. That invitation was a pleasant October surprise. A stream of official cars started pulling up to the side of Lincoln Center with a varied number of influential diplomats from around the world all singing along the same tune.

In a general comment on the bubbly nature of fashionable fame, it was sometimes said that basketball legend Michael Jordan became more famous than the River Jordan, and that a reference to Leonardo meant Di Caprio, not Da Vinci. During the summer of 1999, our famous opera star was having urgent hip surgery in Manhattan. Despite my insistence, the receptionist at Lenox Hill Hospital adamantly denied any knowledge of a patient named Luciano Pavarotti. After a long distance phone call, normal passage was granted to visit patient Giuseppe Verdi.

Another thought inspired by supportive singers was to start an international campaign entitled Voices for Peace. The UN Charter suggests mobilizing "the peoples of the United Nations," not just Governments. Performers have more of a popular following than do politicians and wider access to communications media. Selecting a specific cause of passionate interest would give each of them an opportunity to deliver it more forcefully and provide the international community with more effective advocates for that cause. Growing up in war-time Italy, Maestro Pavarotti's potential cause, for example, could be children in areas of conflict. He was ready to perform anywhere to raise funds for them. "Pavarotti and Friends" went to Sarajevo at its most difficult time to promote peace. His events in his hometown, Modena, and elsewhere had helped schools for children in former conflict areas from Guatemala to Sierra Leone. What he needed was a regular briefing, constant contact and an agreed focus. It took at least six months to have him nominated, but as a "messenger of peace" - a totally different approach that was politically abused during the Cold War years and equally exploited for individual networking when revived. Keeping in touch with him after leaving the Organization, I understand that he was gradually turned off by mishandling, and in particular by being requested to sing at certain ceremonial occasions in New York or Geneva. He did not turn up at the Millennium meeting of a somewhat puzzled and puzzling collection of "peace messengers."

Enrico Macias, the French singer born in Algeria, was proposed by the UN office in Paris. A number of other performers were proposed with a geographical balance to cover the widest membership of world states. Youssou N'dour or Ismael Lo of Senegal, Alpha Blondie of Cote d'Ivoire, King Sunny Ade from Ghana, Dame Kiri te Kanawa of New Zealand, Feyrouz of Lebanon, Los Jaivas of Chile, Richardo Arjuvana of Guatemala and Phil Collins of England were some proposed examples but were not followed up. Also, a joint performance on the green line of Nicosia, Cyprus, by Greek artist Mikis Theodurakis and Turkish singer Zulfu Livaneli, to draw hundreds of thousands of separated Greeks and Cypriots closer together, would have helped the cause of peace more than a thousand diplomatic envoys. Yet, one entrenched senior political affairs bureaucrat in Manhattan found fault with one performers' hairstyle and the other's sexual inclination.

While basically gaining wider support for the cause of human dignity, there may be some value in injecting some musical relief into the spirit of international officialdom. It may not only help our overstressed colleagues better to perform their increasingly daunting tasks, but it also could bring them closer to the peoples they are expected to help. Clearly, that does not mean that peacekeepers and development experts should go around pacifying the world merely with the sound of music. It only suggests that, while national languages might be a barrier in a swiftly changing world of varied cultures, music could be a helpful bridge. It may also confirm the simple fact that one of the best treatments of anger is a deep tuneful sigh, and one of the best responses to stress may be a favorite song on the side.

CHAPTER VI:

WATCH YOUR LANGUAGE

The Prime Minister of Namibia, Hage Geingob, was trying to open a special session of the UN General Assembly on "Women 2000." It was the largest assembly of women since the Beijing Conference held five years before.

Mr. Geingob had temporarily taken over from his country's Foreign Minister, Theo-Ben Gurirab, president of the regular General Assembly and a veteran UN hand since he had represented the national liberation movement SWAPO during the struggle for independence. Like any effective politician, he may have wanted the record to show his leadership role in support of women. When several poundings of the gavel at a particular gathering did not produce an orderly outcome, however, he turned to Secretary-General Kofi Annan on his right and observed "An unruly crowd - eh?" Unknown to him, the microphone was open, and his remarks could be heard not only in the hall but to anyone connected to the speaker system, including all senior staff, accredited media correspondents and any one in Manhattan who may have turned to TV Channel 78 showing UN events. Distinguished female representatives scrambled as graciously as feasible to assume their designated country's seats while an obviously irritated Mr. Geingob gaveled again several times, looked up from his reading glasses and sighed: "Women." A hush fell on the Hall, as he then proceeded without much ado to read a text about the inevitable and positive participation of women in shaping a new millennium.

During a gathering that afternoon of participating First Ladies, someone expressed the hope that senior male officials would close their microphones and open their minds. Another protested that when a male delegate committed an error, that delegate alone may or may not even be blamed; but if a female made a mistake then women in general were slammed. However, such comments, together with some sharp quips, remained within a closed circuit. For diplomats, mainly men, it was a trivial anecdote and a lesson to watch out for open microphones and - for the record - to watch their language.

When Italy's Foreign Minister Amentori Fanfani was elected president of the UN General Assembly's 20th session in September 1965, delegates representing all regional groups made the usual welcoming tributes. Britain's Lord Caradon, a master of understated political humor, recalled the predominance of Ancient Rome in spreading principles of peace and devotion to arts and sciences. He added, addressing the President: "It is not unsuitable that I should pay tribute, for I represent a country which greatly benefited from being colonized by yours. Fifteen hundred years of subsequent independence have not diminished our respect for Julius Caesar."

Not to be outdone by a competitive close ally, U.S. Justice Arthur Goldberg, representing the host country, a former British colony, interjected with a pointed reminder of even closer links to the newly elected President's country. "I hope you will forgive me, Mr. President, if I have a special message for Lord Caradon," he said. "If Lord Caradon takes justifiable pride in the fact that his country was colonized by Italians fifteen hundred years ago, I must remind him of that great and peaceful voyage of Christopher Columbus which opened the way for his country's colonization of my country, and the subsequent independence of my country. And, to emphasize the peaceful character of Italian colonization of the United States, I now extend a most cordial welcome to Lord Caradon to join me on the stand at the forthcoming Columbus Day Parade in New York."

Without missing a beat, Senor Fanfani, now speaking in French, thanked Justice Goldberg "on behalf of the peaceful Italian colonizers of this hospitable land." Contemporary political correctness aside, and although the President thought he had concluded a somewhat jovial diplomatic exchange, an intervention was requested by Spain under the "right of reply." Christopher Columbus was not Italian, came the forceful assertion by its Permanent Representative. He was in fact a Spanish citizen entrusted by Her Majesty Queen Isabella to take that historic voyage with a Spanish crew on a Spanish mission. No one of course reminded the distinguished gathering that Christopher Columbus was seeking a shorter navigation route to India when he was accidentally blown by fateful winds to North American shores. Before the argument on the nationality of that luckiest of explorers subsided, another right of reply was introduced. It was now the turn of Norway. That Latin claim about Columbus discovering America was totally unacceptable and scientifically unfounded, the Scandinavian weighed in. Firm archaeological evidence pointed to a Norwegian explorer who preceded everyone else to the New World. Thus a ceremonial meeting almost accidentally turned into a heated dispute over national territorial discoveries. The amused President, a former Prime Minister and later President of Italy, assured everyone that the minutes of the meetings will faithfully reflect all statements made. The session was adjourned and the matter dismissed - as long as it was on the record.

On, off or for the record are the bread and butter of diplomatic maneuverings and journalistic manipulations – who manipulates whom depends on who's involved. "Let the record show" is usually more a rhetorical tactic than a contribution to history. Most diplomats are likely to leave the records alone - as long as they were there appropriately. An enthusiastic reading of UN documents as I joined the Secretariat led me to one regularly submitted by the Secretary-General on "matters of which the Security Council is seized." Many of the over 300 items seemed outdated. A conflict between Britain and Iran over the nationalization of the oil company in the early 1950s was one example. The reason they remained "seized" was that "an item once included in the agenda thereafter remains on the list until the Council agrees to its removal." Since proposing the removal of any item would expose any diplomat's reputation for cautious farsightedness, the items remained untouched. With many additional agenda items, it was eventually agreed to allow some matters to drop with time.

Prudently, that responsibility was left to the Secretary-General; no member state wanted to be responsible for any omission. Starting in 1998, he would regularly propose an updated list of outdated matters. A summary was then issued of questions to be officially reviewed. A full list is now issued once a year. Still, the summary generally lists more than a hundred items in dozens of pages. A similar list of 32 items for 1965, 33 years earlier, contained these strikingly familiar issues: Indonesia, The Palestine Question, Cuban situation, Portugal overseas Territories (better known as East Timor), Congo, the India-Pakistan Situation, Iran-Iraq Dispute, Question relating to Cyprus, followed by an item on Relations between Greece and Turkey and the Question of Disarmament.

Clearly, the record showed that placing issues on the record did not always mean that action would be swiftly taken. It may sometimes mean that certain parties to a conflict insisted on their right to keep at each other's throat despite every conceivable peacemaking, peacekeeping or mediation. A special office is devoted to maintaining records, servicing the meetings, translation and interpretation into six official languages - Chinese, English, French, Spanish, Russian - and Arabic, which was added in the 1970s. A former head of that office, which was usually reserved for an Eastern European, delighted in producing a particular statistic once a year. The solemn Mr. Nozek, from the Czechoslovak Peoples Socialist Republic, would betray a wry smile as he announced how many times the documents would tour around the Earth if their pages were placed next to each other. He knew of course that it was better to argue in conference rooms with documents than to fight on a battlefield. Instead of escalating into wars, many conflicts were degraded to disputes and - after letting off steam - many disputes were transferred into issues for the record.

Every diplomat would complain about lengthy records, yet everyone would insist on them at a certain time. With 193 UN member-states, there is always a request for some record. Similarly, there is always a request for off the record meetings. The "non-papers" were created by inventive bureaucrats (yes they do exist) as a handle on an issue for which eventual agreement was intended. So is a CP - Conference Paper - which is normally floated to test the political trade winds. It would deal with a specific issue - kick off a discussion, summarize it or direct it. Initially, all meetings had records. All speeches were unlimited with simultaneous translation and consecutive interpretation.

In several tense cases, a long speech was used by some representatives as filibuster ploy to waste, or gain, time until instructions could be received from the home capital. Prior to 1990, international communications were by erratic phone connection or a confidential diplomatic courier. A delegate would speak at the Security Council for hours, often citing full texts of newspaper articles, and then allow for a repetitious interpretation. When in a hurry, the delegate will waive that right. When resolution 242 on the Arab-Israeli conflict was adopted in November 1967, Lord Caradon of the United Kingdom, who drafted that resolution, made a delicately balanced speech. After thanking various delegates, particularly US Ambassador Arthur Goldberg, who had extended political help, and the Eastern bloc, which agreed to a consensus, he concluded with a Scottish style limerick. It ended as follows: "Long live the Soviet delegation; I waive consecutive interpretation." So did the other delegates. At another debate, Council members were split on whether to take a vote that same day or "tomorrow." Those for the delay took their time; those in a hurry pressed for a vote. Very late in the evening, Lord Caradon made an unusually long speech and also atypically allowed for interpretation to the dismay of his hurried allies. By then it was past midnight. Referring to the dispute on the timing of the vote, the British delegate noted crisply: "Well tomorrow is already upon us - could we now proceed to a vote."

Long speeches were not always due to political expediency. It was often a matter of personal compulsion. Some people who needed no introduction hardly bothered with a conclusion. Some exhausted, often exasperated interpreters, started an internal game in which they gave prizes to the longest, shortest or most boring speeches. One of the longest belonged to Indian Foreign Minister Krishna Menon, who once fainted under the prolonged strain of his own rhetoric. Following emergency medical treatment, he got up, zoomed towards the microphone and continued. The shortest in the Assembly's General Debate at the time was by Lebanon's Foreign Minister Nicholas Salem who spoke for only 12 minutes. Later, his compatriot Phillipe Takla did not speak at all. Adapting to the inevitable, most delegates rearranged their work accordingly. If the speaker was a Foreign Minister of a neighboring, friendly or brotherly country, the seats of a delegation would be filled appropriately. Most would continue their paper work while listening to the orators. Others would find pressing reasons to have bilaterals - meeting with another delegation - at the exclusive Indonesian Lounge behind the President's office or the Chinese lounge in the back. In case the speaker was of limited impact on a country's foreign policy, one could retreat to the Delegates' Lounge and openly enjoy a cappuccino. The media accompanying visiting speakers would adapt.

Thus, a photo of the speaker at the podium would avert a show of a semi-empty hall and rather concentrate on a cluster of delegates present or perhaps focus on the attentive national delegation. Clearly, visiting stars draw their own audience. A president of the host country, the US, is a natural draw, particularly if an announcement about payment of dues was expected. Heads of states would normally fill the hall. In any official capacity, Nelson Mandela drew overwhelming attendance - even once when a tribute was paid to him while he was still in prison. At that time the main participant Stevie Wonder was two hours late, yet no one left. An audience casually hummed with the singer: "I just called to say I love you," in the most unlikely setting. Over the years, as the number of speakers grew, a time limit of 20 minutes was set. Another initiative by a senior colleague was to withdraw water jugs from all meeting rooms, leaving them only for the Chairman.

Although one purpose of public speaking is to communicate a position or promote a viewpoint, a number of speakers do not seem to recognize that media representatives are hard pressed to report news and meet deadlines. Journalists are not necessarily linguists, social scientists or historians. Prolonged speeches in foreign languages late in the evening would not make it even to the correspondent's desk. Statements may be for the record, but the record could be presented more attractively. Most governments have specialists in drafting statements for senior officials, some more talented than others. "Spinning" is a highly regarded art in many industrialized countries; in others, governments apply a more direct approach. In almost every delegation, there is someone who toiled diligently on a speech for which someone else received the accolades. During a summer lecture, an Ambassador of a European country told the World Affairs Council in Southampton, Long Island, about a new Foreign Secretary who was never appreciative. For three years, devoted and talented staff did their best to prepare lucid position papers and impressive speeches hoping for a gracious nod, however faint. It was all in vain. Eventually, at a fully attended international meeting, like a UN General Assembly, the rude minister took the podium and started with a pompous opening: "If we deal with an issue we have to be quite clear on it. When we are presenting a question we are expected to be precise. That is why I will make my point clearly and precisely." The Foreign Secretary then turned to the second page, which was blank except for the boldly handwritten words: "Now you're on your own - you s.o.b."

In delegations with limited staff, the ambassador ends up preparing most of the statements. Weekends and evenings are consumed in perfecting presentations. Some cash-rich countries usually entrust the task to a part-time journalist or discreetly request a Secretariat friend to suggest the main points. A number of these delegations unknowingly resorted to the same person. When the similarity of the public pronouncements was noted, it was attributed to the "neighborly meeting of minds." An informed ambassador thought that farming out such statements in return for a fee was business as usual. While studying in Paris, he said there were residents - not necessarily French - who made a livelihood out of drafting papers for others to obtain doctorate degrees. It was hard earned, even intellectual living; everyone was happy, "and who actually reads that stuff anyway?" Actually many did, trying to decipher a country's foreign policy. And while some wrote with clarity, and others with unintended confusion, there are many outstanding internationalists who pride themselves on their drafting excellence.

While most words are written to clarify the facts, some drafts are intended to cover the differences. When I joined the UN, almost everyone referred fondly to Martin Hill. Possibly the only one around who had served at the League of Nations before the Second World War, Martin was a charming gentleman and a scholar. He spoke the Queen's English thoughtfully, with an appropriate stutter or mumble as required. Although his general duties dealt with interdepartmental relations, his main forte was drafting. Hence, he held everyone in awe. He could draft a brief note with cutting clarity, and he could equally draft thirty pages of the most impressive language - revealing almost nothing. A master of the understatement, he once drafted a brief letter for the Secretary-General's signature to request the release of a political prisoner, a former UN official who was a cabinet member when a new military government in Caracas placed him abruptly in jail. The Secretary-General's letter to the Venezuelan President stated: "Now that you clearly do not require the services of Manuel Perez-Guerrero, I will appreciate your decision for him to resume his international civil service at the United Nations."

Drafting for the Secretary-General is an honor very few could successfully claim. Dag Hammarskjold was a poet and author. His work *Markings* became a bestseller. His major statements would have been written personally by him, with linguistic fine-tuning from some of his close assistants like George Ivan Smith. Who other than the inspiring and inspired Swedish Secretary-General could have blended the spirit of the UN charter with Beethoven's musical vision at a UN day concert? Instead of the usual admonition for peace and development, Hammarskjold opened with a few words "that may remind us of the purpose for which we have assembled." He went on:

"When the Ninth Symphony opens we enter a drama full of harsh conflict and dark threats. But the composer leads us on, and in the beginning of the last movement we hear again the various themes repeated, now as a bridge toward the final syntheses. A moment of silence and a new theme is introduced, the theme of reconciliation and joy in reconciliation. A human voice is raised in rejection of all that has preceded and we enter the dreamt kingdom of peace. New voices join the first and mix in a jubilant assertion of life and all that it gives us when we meet it joined in faith and human solidarity. On his road from conflict and emotion to reconciliation in this formal hymn of praise, Beethoven has given us a confession and a credo which we, who work within and for this Organization, may well make our own. We take part in this continuous flight between conflicting interests and ideologies which so far has marked the history of mankind, but we may never lose our faith that the first three movements one day will be followed by the fourth movement. In that faith we strive to bring order and purity into the chaos and anarchy. Inspired by that faith we try to impose the laws of the human mind and of the integrity of the human will on the dramatic evolution in which we are all engaged and carry our responsibility. The road of Beethoven in his Ninth Symphony is also the road followed by the authors of the Preamble of the Charter. It begins with the recognition of the threat under which we all live, speaking as it does of the need to save succeeding generations from the scourge of war which has brought untold sorrow to mankind. It moves on to a reaffirmation of faith in the dignity and worth of the human person. And it ends with the promise to practice tolerance and live together in peace with one another as good neighbors and to unite our strength to maintain peace. This year, the fifteenth in the life of the Organization, is putting it to new tests. Experience has shown how far we are from the end which inspired the Charter. We are indeed still in the first movements. But no matter how deep the shadows may be, how sharp the conflicts, how tense the mistrust reflected in what is said and done in our world of today as reflected in this hall and in this house, we are not permitted to forget that we have too much in common, too great a sharing of interests and too much that we might lose together for ourselves and for succeeding generations, ever to weaken our efforts to surmount the difficulties and not to turn the simple human values, which are our common heritage, into the firm foundation on which we may unite our strength and live together in peace. May this be a reminder of the significance of this day. And may now the symphony develop its themes, uniting us in its confession of faith."

U Thant, an English teacher and writer, tried to pen most of his speeches. On wider issues, possibly Dr. Ralph Bunche and Chef de Cabinet C.V. Narasimhan would supervise a concise text. Being for the most part in the field at the time, I am not sure whether anyone in particular drafted for Mr. Waldheim or whether he was keen on personalized statements. My impression was that heads of various departments would send recommended drafts to his Cabinet, headed by Pakistani diplomat Rafeuddin Ahmed, who would clear them. On regular correspondence, some young Columbia University graduates were recruited to respond to general letters in German and French. Soon enough there was an overwhelming increase in the number of occasions on which the Secretary-General was expected to speak, send a message or submit a report. Instead of one message on UN Day, scores of days, years and decades were proclaimed. From the obvious International Women's Day to the forgotten World Day for Water on March 22nd, to the totally ignored Day for Biological Diversity on December 29th, consistently meaningful messages were expected from the Secretary-General. One or two rising stars like Irish diplomat Paul Kavanagh were recruited to help. Virendra Dayal's swan song just before he retired to India was to draft the English text of Boutros-Ghali's "Agenda for Peace," requested by a Security Council summit in 1992. After that, the new Chief of Staff of Mr. Boutros-Ghali, Jean-Claude Aimé, only generally cleared the texts, drafted by two speechwriters -- one in French, another in English. Yet the new Secretary-General, a workaholic, cosmopolitan professor, never ceased redrafting his own speeches, supervising drafts and suggesting drafters for new ideas of books. When I politely suggested during a Saturday afternoon discussion that he might need a break to relax, he responded instinctively: "But writing is my relaxation."

Kofi Annan organized a special speechwriters unit in his office. With an international civil servant's background, it was professionally sensible and politically helpful to get the *Financial Times* columnist Edward Mortimer to lead that team. Gaining unprecedented coverage in one of the world's most prestigious dailies was of obvious advantage. More to the point, Mortimer would not only help with his journalistic writing skills but could also provide sound advice whenever accepted. Additionally, another resident of the 38th floor, Professor John Ruggie, provided Mr. Annan with crucial strategic thinking, blended with a talent for lucid conceptual prose and confident public speaking. Kofi Annan's acceptance speech as Secretary-General, however, was drafted by Ted Sorensen, the former Kennedy speechwriter.

Interpreters will readily explain that they do not just deal with languages but with cultures. They do not repeat content but convey context. Their difficult challenge is to balance the need to remain neutral while identifying completely with the speaker. In a feature story, an interpreter recounted her experience during the separation war of Bangladesh from Pakistan. Prime Minister Ali Bhutto, whose daughter Benazir later assumed the same post, was addressing the Security Council. At an emotional moment, he tore away his speech shouting: "This is what you are doing - you are tearing away my country." As he stormed out of the chambers crying, the interpreter felt her own tears flowing.

Drafting for the Secretary-General is different than producing reports on items for discussion. *Précis writing*, a summary of meeting, is a totally different category, while press releases require yet another kind of drafting. Although each activity has its own audience, a talented writer will come across impressively in any situation. In one case, a wasteful meeting was portrayed so well that some of the obviously bored participants protested. Press releases always had their share of headaches. They are mainly addressed to the press, yet many delegations watched them more carefully than resident media. Countries in prolonged conflicts count the space given not only to their statements but also to their adversaries. Many an early morning was initiated by an awaiting ambassador firmly demanding a correction, or a *corrigendum* in diplomatic parlance. Two of my predecessors who tried to abolish press release coverage of meetings met with strong resistance. Every meeting was important to some group, and small delegations did not have adequate staff to follow all of them. While big delegations with means for attending meetings and contacting the media thought the press releases were a wasted resource, small delegations - a majority - considered them indispensable. A heading of every release indicated that it was "not a record - only for press purposes." Yet most delegates treated it as a record. Any attempt to spice, spike or spruce it up to actively attract media attention was doomed by multilateral sensibilities.

During a visit by a Secretary-General to Stockholm, an accompanying officer sent a detailed description of the menu. A frustrated press officer in New York interjected a sentence that stated: "At such a high level visit, you would expect a serving of authentic Swedish meatballs..." That new addition passed by an inattentive supervisor and almost reached the press rack on the third floor, were it not for a vigilant (and hungry) distribution clerk. At least three different concepts of what is news would confront any UN related event: the UN concept; that of the resident reporter; and that of the editors selecting publishable reports. What the UN itself believed, or had to believe, to be news would include coverage of official meetings, pronouncements and activities by the Secretary-General and action taken by various arms of the Secretariat. Therein lies one of the biggest challenges. In a swiftly evolving communications culture, inter-governmental organizations take time to adapt as they are pulled by the slowest political boats.

Correspondents at UN headquarters are usually caught between their UN hosts and media bosses. Many live daily within self-sufficient UN premises in rent-free space, sharing most of the time with UN people. Similarly, they are professionals in close contact with their media operation interested in the big picture and addressing a much wider audience - the public. Like everywhere else, they occasionally accommodate a valuable source with a helpful reference.

One risk in official press announcements is that they may acquire their own language regardless of the situation. Favorite expressions tend to develop a life of their own, however irrelevant to an audience. In that, national government spokesmen are the worst, particularly if they believe they were spinning an international situation. No UN spokesman, for example, would dream of advising the Albanians in Kosovo "not to revisit" on the Serbs what the Serbs had "visited" on them, as a way of telling them not to resort to vengeful violence.

Too subtle verbal signals are often lost on their intended recipients, who may not pick them up or simply ignore them. After Iraq's leaders erroneously concluded that the US would not launch a substantive military strike, a variety of nuanced statements were meant as warnings. "The diplomatic string is running out," by State Department spokesman James Rubin was followed by Pentagon spokesman Ken Bacon's admonition that "The train is leaving the station." "The clock is ticking and it's getting near midnight," cautioned Florida Representative Peter Goss ominously. Windows were opening and closing, according to then-Defense Secretary William Cohen, while UN Secretary-General Kofi Annan warned "Saddam is at a precipice." Except for some diligent diplomats in Washington and New York, very few people took notice.

British Ambassador Sir John Weston recounted once that BBC Senior Foreign Correspondent John Simpson told him about a sudden revelation during his participation in the UN World Television Forum initiated in 1996. As those professional communicators from the world's continents took their seats in the chambers of the UN Economic and Social Council, he noted that they suddenly behaved like official diplomats. Eventually, like in any long relationship, a code of conduct emerges. Certain expressions would have a mutually understood meaning not necessarily shared by the rest of the world.

This was apparent, for example, again at this TV forum. One item was the relationship between settlement of conflicts and coverage of conflicts - in effect that between a mediator and a reporter. As Kofi Annan, then Under-Secretary-General for Peacekeeping and CNN Senior Correspondent Christiane Amanpour exchanged views, each seemed to make a special effort to understand the other. Had the satellite not been interrupted prematurely, they might have ended up with identical conclusions. Another risk is that you may be tempted to speak not like a correspondent but like an official UN correspondence.

An updated standard UN manual for writing letters indicates beginning with an obligatory "Excellency" if official and "My dear ambassador" if unofficial. In conclusion, everyone is asked to "accept the assurances of highest consideration." In between, a little flattery, particularly while turning down a request, would help. "Someone of your experience will appreciate the sensitive repercussions" may be enough of an opening to dissuade a delegate from pressing an issue. There is always the reference to a "new approach" - carefully avoiding "bold," as that may entail some repercussions. "Reform," of course, was "an ongoing process." "Joint consultations on matters of mutual interest" could easily be interjected without apparent harm. "We assure you that we will be making every effort" would suggest to the ambassador not to push too hard. "Looking into the matter and will advise you in due course" may mean something like don't call us, we'll call you. The bi-monthly *Secretarial News* once produced a list of useful definitions, with a helpful explanation to newcomers. For example, a matter "in process" would mean that it was smothered in red tape. "We will look into it" would assume that you would forget about it after a while. "Expedite" meant making the necessary commotion. "Under consideration" meant "thanks for reminding us." A "programme" was any assignment that could not be settled by one phone call. "Making a survey" involved a device to find more time for an acceptable answer.

Mercifully, most communications are in English and French - the two UN working languages. Some missions may insist on their official language, particularly if conveying instructions from the home office and to where a copy is dutifully sent. But in pursuing a particular appointment or a special request, the sender would wish the case to be clearly understood by the recipient. He may also want it discreetly out of the hands of translating compatriots. Thus, English is typically used and not the mother tongue. Besides, translation is the art of the impossible, and many a nuance had lost its flair in the hands of a harassed translator. There is always some linguistic fencing, which, like *van ordinaire* may strike a puzzled note. (Incidentally, a common expression, "short and sweet," was derived from Aramaic, "kario w halio").

Such is the role of language throughout the centuries. Diplomatic language during the 6th century B.C. was Aramaic, predominant during the era of Jesus Christ. Latin took over during Pax Romana, then a combination of Arabic, Persian, Turkish, German, English and French. It was not until the 20th century that diplomats settled on French, as well as English with an American accent. The latter thereafter became the world's most popular – if not diplomatic – language. Traditional members of the *Académie Française* were shocked at the widespread use by their compatriots of expressions like weekend, traffic and superstar. As the French adapted to "franglais," the British had to tolerate American spellings of "center" for centre, "program" for programme, and "visiting" the issue rather than discussing it. Would a gentleman lift his hat to a woman in an elevator, or elevate it to a lady in a lift?

A bulletin issued by an association of retired international civil servants (FISCA) is mainly devoted to straight information of logistical help to its vast membership. Once, though, it came out with a list of linguistically counter-productive expressions; that is those that not only fail to convey their messages to their intended audiences, but often end up with the opposite outcome. Hence the Nova Awards: *Nova* in Spanish means "no go."

International translators collect anecdotes about erratic translations as comic relief. One example was a note in an English translation advising Residents of a Swiss Alps hotel: "If you have any desires during the night, please ring for the chambermaid."

For a clear conscience, one could argue that international harmony is often worth occasional linguistic conformity - on or off the record.

CHAPTER VII:

UN LEADERS: A PERSONAL VIEW

"The peoples of the United Nations" named at the opening words of its Charter need leaders for the U.N., not just government representatives to jointly face shared challenges and seize potential opportunities. Leadership is a publicly sensed quality. It eludes precise identification but signals a definite presence. Unlike a chair that an official occupies, it extends beyond a prescribed occupation. Like charisma, any effort to claim it would mean that it is not there.

Historically, leadership is also reflected unity, overcoming fragmentation. Emerging from varied continents, de Gaulle in France, Tito in Yugoslavia, Nehru in India, Peron in Argentina, Trudeau in Canada, and Mandela in South Africa mobilized their peoples' overwhelming support to project a unifying perception across their national borders.

"Now, it is a different world," as Ban Ki-moon would disarmingly confide. Indeed, it is.

There is a saying in New York: You never know how many friends you have until you get a house in the Hamptons.

Boutros Boutros-Ghali never knew how many students he had

until he became United Nations Secretary-General. After him, it was Kofi Annan's turn to find out how many strategically placed supporters helped him to get his post. A gracious Javier Perez de Cuellar discovered to his discreet exasperation how many Peruvian, Spanish and other friends, and sons of friends, he had. So, many Austrians discovered links to Kurt Waldheim that some UN insiders initiated an "Austrian of the Year" award, given to the most creatively opportunistic of them. Many Buddhists discovered U Thant, who came from Burma, but they were mainly Indians. His outstanding Chef de Cabinet, C.V. Narasimhan, ran a fairly effective ship, particularly by placing a trusted colleague, usually a compatriot, in almost every department to ensure that he was always in the loop. U Thant, who completely trusted his Chef de Cabinet, was reported to have made a rare quip: "When an American leaves the United Nations, he is replaced by an Indian; when a Frenchman leaves the UN, he is also replaced by an Indian; and when an Indian leaves the UN, he is replaced by two Indians." Each Secretary-General firmly and clearly fended against these emerging claims of close friendships. Real friends kept their distance and indeed were regularly contacted by the Secretary-General himself. The newly found ones, often sensing that they had no bread to break on the 38th floor, sought out unsuspecting mid-level chiefs of units, who initially thought they were doing a discreet favor to a higher authority until they found out otherwise. Checks and balances eventually sorted matters out.

To be sure, every Secretary-General had the right to one or two compatriots as special assistants in the office. Some dealt with pending business on the home front or the international dimension of national politics and normally left with the Secretary-General. Others handled regular UN matters and, like the outstanding Alvaro de Soto of Peru, who often described himself as a "bird of passage", remained with succeeding administrations.

Managers of various departments were also introduced to the various cultural atmospheres of the various Secretaries-General. A small minority, a really small one, who spent their time not working but networking, immediately scouted out the shifting names of those they thought held the hidden keys to a new regime. Thus, during U Thant's time it was C.V., V.J., S.K. and other abbreviations of extended Indian names. Under Waldheim, Austrian names like Anton, Karl and Axel were repeatedly mentioned, while several started casually invoking Austrian habits like *gemuetlich* for easy-going. There was briefly a Hans who was banished swiftly for his posturing and an Erik who tried in vain to connect with the upper tiers where he apparently did not belong. With Javier Perez de Cuellar came Alvaro, of course, Emilio, Armando, Giandomenico (who was Italian but fluent in Spanish) and the admirable Louise-Maria, all of whom were more often approached than the Secretary-General. Boutros-Ghali had an Egyptian special assistant, the sensitive, popular and brilliant Ms. Fayza Aboul-Naga. Another Egyptian diplomat who was initially slated to join at the time had to leave town in a hurry after a reported incident in his hotel was front-paged in the New York Post. Kofi Annan, an African rising from the ranks, had a varied selection of nationalities, with only one African, the ever-loyal Wagaye, as his personal assistant for 20 years. With routine administrative matters handled by the respective cabinet staff, the strategic thinking - and writing - was handled by trusted American and British intellectuals.

During a 33-year period, I worked with five different Secretaries-General from different cultural backgrounds and with varied styles. While I can remember historic events and controversial moments handled by each one of them, I mainly recall certain personalized moments.

Dag Hammarskjold

When still a student reporter, I was told that becoming a journalist did not depend much on acquiring academic degrees, but on getting headlines. Looking in a daily paper, I noted that UN Secretary-General Dag Hammarskjold was in Beirut on a mediation mission. I went to the Saint George Hotel and explained to the concierge my purpose. He looked at the bar terrace where most of the international correspondents were waiting around, then turned his back to what was more important. The only reason he allowed me to linger was that I had a photographer with me. I stayed overnight on a lobby sofa. The next morning, Mr. Hammarskjold came down on his way to the airport. He had only one bodyguard - unarmed. He smiled amusingly when he heard what I wanted and looked at my face very kindly. Confused, I asked him about his name. He realized I was at the very beginning of my career and helped out by saying "Maybe you're asking about my first name. In my country 'Dag' means Day." I regained some of my journalistic composure, and listened attentively as he gave me a few pointers before proceeding to his car, a gray Pontiac. I told him that since he had taught me a word in Swedish, I would like to teach him one in Arabic: "*Shukran*, it means thank you," I said. He rolled down the car window and popped his head out, replying with a smile: "In Swedish, it is *Täk*".

By the time I joined the UN years later, Mr. Hammarskjold had been killed. His airplane fell near Ndola airport while on a mediation mission to the Congo. Until today, nobody knows for sure how the UN Secretary-General died. Was it a technical failure, a pilot error or a crime? Hanging a political crime on an unknown culprit has become an intercontinental habit. Still, many governments find it more convenient not to know.

When taking over the network of UN information centers, I made a point of visiting the office in Zambia, and spent an evening in the town of Ndola, where Secretary-General Hammarskjold's plane crashed in its forest, which was part of what was known as Northern Rhodesia, an Apartheid colony. Listening to older villagers and active civil groups did not yield specific secrets, yet it deepened my impression of a premeditated murder, whose "known unknowns" were obviously so predominant that even the local culprits were untouched – indeed promoted. Even Sweden, our hero's native country, trod very carefully, mainly focusing on establishing foundations and granting fellowships. As major gambling players would say, what happened in Ndola stayed in Ndola.

My architect brother Ramzi initiated a construction project of a Dag Hammarskjold tower across from UN Headquarters in New York with a penthouse lounge displaying unique photos of the former Secretary-General relaxing in his Swedish summer home, inspecting refugee camps, and welcoming visitors. In front of its entrance his bust, produced for an artistic contest, is placed and commands the corner of First Avenue and 47th Street, with an indication that his example would inspire residents and passersby.

Decades later on July 31, 2005, I found myself walking under lightning and rain in fields of southern Sweden to participate in the anniversary of the 100th birthday of the man. Here in Backåkra was his summerhouse: a few small rooms, some books and a writing desk. I knew well he once wrote: "I am being driven forward into an unknown land. The pass grows steeper, the air colder and sharper. A wind from my unknown goal stirs the string of expectation. Still the question: Shall I ever get there? There where life resounds, a clear pure note in the silence." He wrote as if knowing his final destiny. "Smiling, sincere, incorruptible – his body disciplined and limber. A man who had become what he could, and was what he was – ready at any moment to gather everything into one simple sacrifice." At 4 p.m., people parked their cars off the country roads and followed the green arrows towards the place. No cheering, no chanting, no long live or down with. Only thousands of people who joined together without any word, not even a whisper. Inspired perhaps by Hammarskjold's writings in that moment, I felt every great work is crowned by silence. Every deep relationship is converged by quiet. The King arrived with his Queen. Next to me was an opposition member of parliament. She stood up, like everyone did, with great respect until he sat. The heavy rain continued, but everyone was still, listening to the most beautiful music and the shortest statements.

When it was time for a statement by UN Secretary-General Kofi Annan, a message was read instead in which he apologized for his absence due to a "twist in his shoulder." Annan is loved in Sweden, as is everything related to the UN. Few believed the medical excuse. Some questioned why, if he was ill, did he not send his Swedish wife to participate in a once-in-a-lifetime occasion? No doubt, some of those present compared the celebrated Secretary-General who imposed respect for international legitimacy on all countries, big and small, and the current one in political limbo over Food for Oil. Many explanations were given – some psychological, other political – but none medical. Brian Urquhart, who was left to read the official UN message, interrupted himself several times, almost sarcastically, about the wet paper from which he had to read. One of the most talented, and possibly most beautiful, Swedish actresses stood to read parts of Hammarskjold's "Meditations" as if they were messages sent to more than one target. "Don't be afraid, try to be what you are. Destiny asks that you just start with the power that you have. Advance and try. Accept failure without embarrassment and success without bragging. Don't let appearances deceive you, it is just appearances. Initiate accomplishments that make us wiser than what we are. Advance with your faith. Do not hesitate, do not be afraid of being free, of standing up and ignore everything else around you. Do not turn back when you say yes."

Speakers recounted his life in brief. The son of a former Prime Minister of Sweden, he became the second Secretary-General in the most difficult time of the Cold War. He was launched on the international scene with his quiet diplomacy, which gained the release by Mao Zedong – symbolically on the SG's birthday – of American pilots held by China, not yet a UN member. Hammarskjold stood up against aggression, whether in Suez or the Soviet army's entry into Hungary; he threatened to resign until troops withdrew. He earned the respect of all member states and viewed the UN Charter as a framework through which creative solutions could be found. He defended human dignity and fought for freedom of the people to choose their destiny. He started the first military peacekeeping operation, placed between Egypt and Israel after the 1967 war. He faced the most ruthless powers in the world at the time. Not only were these a combination of big powers but multinational interests, which were reflected in the Congo. He knew he would pay the price.

After the ceremony, the King left, people dispersed, and I walked to the summerhouse. They allowed me, a wet stranger, to enter. I read one of the last points he wrote: "O God, my forgiveness is with You. My faith is in You. And my peace be to You." Among the last pages, he wrote: "Have mercy upon our efforts, that we before Thee, in love and in faith, righteousness and humility, may follow Thee, with self-denial, steadfastness, and courage, and meet Thee in silence. Give us a pure heart that we may see Thee, a humble heart that we may hear Thee, a heart of love that we may serve Thee, a heart of faith that we may live Thee. Thou, whom I do not know but Whose I am. Thou, whom I do not comprehend but who hast dedicated me to my faith. Thou."

The clouds dispersed suddenly and the rain stopped.

The setting sun shone.

Somehow, I recalled this Secretary-General's confident stride in Beirut and his smiling face. On a piece of paper I wrote only one word: *Täk*.

U Thant

Although Secretary-General Hammarskjold was my inspiration to join the U.N., my actual opportunity came when the Director General of the European office, Pier Pasqual Spinelli, who had been Mr. Hammarskjold's envoy to the Middle East, needed an Arabic-speaking press officer. I was employed for a short-term period with the intention of going back to journalism in Beirut. However, nothing is as constant as the temporary. I was offered to come and work in the office of Secretary-General U Thant with the long title of "Special Assistant to the Personal Representative of the Secretary-General". An impressive title, I thought, until realizing that the most important jobs at UN Headquarters are those with the shortest ones. The shorter title, the more authority. It was then that I discovered the magic that the two words "38th floor" - the location of the Secretary-General's office - had on others. I was overwhelmed to see the personalities I had only read about. Even the men's room on that floor was described jokingly by Dr. Ralph Bunche, the then-influential Under Secretary-General, as the most effective conference room in the building.

Dr. Bunche, a Nobel Prize winner for peace in the Middle East, sometimes wondered how one would find out whether our Secretary-General was happy or unhappy with us. U Thant, a Buddhist master, had such a cool, calm and collected aura about him that he would never betray any emotion. That was mainly due to the daily meditation he practiced every morning. It prodded me to closely observe the Secretary-General for any sign of tension. I discovered only one. When really challenged or angered, like during the Six-Day War of 1967, he would silently snap his finger and gently yet systematically pound his wrist on the table. A thoughtful and kind boss, he had his own sorrows, since he lost his only son in an accident. He would rarely go to receptions offered by member States. His wife hardly ever appeared in public after her bereavement, and if he had to entertain, his daughter Aye Aye acted as hostess. He lived in Riverdale, up in the Bronx, and would commute to Manhattan and back whenever the business of the day was over. Yet, he would invite his staff to lunches at the office and, sometimes, at the Delegates' Dining Room. At the time, that restaurant used to introduce a different national dish every day. On one occasion, when the chef knew that the Secretary-General would be in attendance, the plat du jour was intentionally Burmese. Obviously, the invited staff ordered it. U Thant read the menu, calmly and pensively, withdrew a pen from his pocket, changed the spelling and ordered a steak. He may have figured that if they couldn't spell it, they couldn't cook it right.

He had an exceptional memory for people's names, except for a dedicated French Canadian woman who he always called François, although she made the point politely and repeatedly of pronouncing her name "Françoise". People never knew what to call him, particularly in the West. He was often addressed as "Mr. U Thant", or diplomatically as "The Honorable U Thant". In fact, "U" is a Burmese word for "Mr.", and he signed his name as Maung Thant. He strengthened the Civil Service, consolidating its international character, by having as wide a geographical representation as available. He also consolidated the concept of international civil service, instilling pride in the fact that an international official served all Member States but receives instructions from no one except the Secretary-General. The "Oath of Office" was taken seriously, and any new staff member had to pledge that oath verbally in the presence of a representative of the Secretary-General, normally someone from the UN's personnel office. Most colleagues wondered how he kept his cool during all the deliberations of the General Assembly and Security Council. Some, however, pointed out that he had discovered a special way of dealing with prolonged speeches. At the time, there were five official languages - English, French, Spanish, Russian and Chinese. U Thant recognized that the Chinese delegate, at the time from Taiwan before the People's Republic of China "restored" its right to the China seat, spoke in English. Thus, the Chinese interpretation channel on the earpiece was mostly quiet, and the Secretary-General would turn to it, on channel five, for uninterrupted peace. Although sometimes furious, but never visibly angry, he valued decency, integrity and trust.

After the turmoil that rocked the Organization with the death of his predecessor, Dag Hammarskjold, U Thant's greatest achievement was calming the international waters to allow the UN to regain cruising speed. His serene approach and low-key personality were best suited for that task. Originally a teacher and writer, he developed the habit of listening to the *New YorkTimes* classical music radio station, WQXR, with its news on the hour. In his book "Thant in New York", Ramses Nassif recounts how he and the Chef de Cabinet sought to inform him appropriately about his son's accidental death before he would hear it on that station. Ramses was the first spokesman appointed by the Secretary-General for the precise purpose of "giving news" and handling correspondents' requests. He was keen on promoting the Organization, not his person. Calling the media the "Fourth Estate", he instructed the initiation of a daily noon briefing, a practice still followed in the same room, #226, though with upgraded furniture and contemporary equipment.

U Thant deeply respected his mother and made a point of visiting her whenever he had time. It was the modest appearance of him being photographed, seeking his mother's blessing, that always has remained with me. So did his silent yet forceful opposition to the military government that took over his country. He would not go there in sign of protest. He would rather have remained in exile than to have given any kind of legitimacy to the military rule and was only brought there after he died. I recall, years later, waiting in Beirut's airport after a January midnight thunderstorm where a plane carrying his casket passed through in transit to Rangoon. I stood alone in vigil, and then wrote on the accompanying travel documents, "Good-bye U Thant. Thank you, U Thant."

Kurt Waldheim

My first meeting with Dr. Waldheim was in Beirut, before my appointment there in 1975 as Director of the UN Information Centre. His spokesman, André Lewin, who later left to become a French Ambassador, wanted an Arabic-speaking colleague to join him for that visit, so I travelled ahead to make advance arrangements. At a dinner hosted by Lebanese President Suleiman Franjieh, repeated references were made to hints of peace overtures in a statement that evening by Israeli Prime Minister Yitzhak Rabin. The Secretary-General was rightly upset, because he had been publicly caught off guard while trying to project an influential role for himself in preparation for the related Geneva peace conference. Every repeated reference to the Rabin statement that evening stoked his impatience. By the time he had returned to the Phoenicia Hotel, he was clearly keen on getting his hands on the statement - if not on those who did not brief him on it. Normally, the Director of the UN Information Centre in the respective country prepares daily up-to-date briefings to keep the visiting Secretary-General abreast of political developments. The accompanying spokesman and senior political officers also listen to international news bulletins and alert the boss, if necessary. After a drink of cold water, Dr. Waldheim wanted to contact the Beirut Director. We were all expected to be on 24-hour duty, particularly when the Secretary-General was in the area. I was asked to join him and then to place the call. It was around midnight, and I could hear the director's Iraqi-accented voice responding, puzzled and irritated.

Suddenly, the Secretary-General decided that he himself wanted to talk. In a proper tone and controlled voice, he introduced himself. Apparently, our man had been the subject of recurring practical jokes by other Iraqi expatriates in Beirut. Convinced that it was yet another prank call, he responded with a tirade of abuse before I had a chance to interrupt. The Secretary-General first look astonished, then coolly placed the receiver down, saying with a low murmur, "I think he would like a transfer." I spent the rest of that evening looking for Prime Minister

Rabin's statement and reassuring my colleague, who, after the initial shock, had realized that his midnight caller was indeed no prankster.

I spent most of Dr. Waldheim's term in the Middle East, where he visited frequently. Although some colleagues at headquarters in New York fearfully reported regular bursts of temper, he was always cordial with me. At a distance, I mainly dealt with issues of special interest to him. This included his attempt to reconvene the Geneva conference on Middle East peace and relations with countries hosting the UN peacekeeping missions - UNDOF between Syria and Israel, and the establishment of UNIFIL in southern Lebanon. The situation in Lebanon, where I served until 1982, was of special interest. Initially, my assignment was to head the UN Press Office, or the UN Information Centre in Beirut, which covered Lebanon, Syria, Jordan and Kuwait. Events escalated in the region, however, and in the absence of a UN political officer I was called upon to do whatever the Secretary-General felt necessary, including the deploying of UNIFIL in South Lebanon, whereI kept in constant touch with Brian Urquhart, the Under-Secretary-General for Political Affairs.

Mr. Waldheim was the first Secretary-General to move into the new official residence offered by an American philanthropist at Three Sutton Place, on Manhattan's east side. Dag Hammarskjold almost lived in his office on the 38th floor, and the bereaved U Thant lived in Riverdale. Mrs. Waldheim, who oversaw official dinners and luncheons at the new residence, made it a point that guests were treated to the traditional Austrian protocol; waiters presented the food wearing white gloves. Meanwhile, U Thant's former cook opened a Chinese restaurant on Second Avenue that became popular with UN staff, many of who were unaware of his former UN connection. The only quip I heard about the orderly and organized Dr. Waldheim was when he walked out of his office and found a number of his staff, including a press spokesman, chatting to one another in hushed voices, and he commented that the place looked like a "cafe in the Balkans".

A main event covered by the press was Mr. Waldheim's visit to Tehran to negotiate the release of American hostages in 1980-1981. I arrived there on New Year's Day, 1980, to wait for Secretary-General Waldheim, who arrived later that afternoon from New York. The portrait of the Shah was still adorning the VIP Lounge at Meherabad Airport, where I spent my morning. Female officials were not yet used to the chador - only a scarf on the head that more often than not negligently fell around the shoulders.

There was a festive revolutionary atmosphere in Tehran in those days of January 1980, only two months after Ayatollah Khomeini took over as Supreme Leader of the country. Night gatherings with revolutionary guards carrying guns, and masses of people shouting slogans, were a regular occurrence. For me, coming from Beirut at the time, it seemed part of the scenery. It occurred to me only upon the arrival of my colleagues from New York that it looked very risky indeed. We were all invited to meet with the "revolutionary council" around midnight. Upon leaving, and facing the faithful crowds in a reconciliatory gesture to listen to their grievances, the Secretary-General whispered to me that he felt there was a gun pointed at him. Looking quickly backwards, I saw one of the guards carrying a semi-automatic, with its ammunition clip pointing towards Dr. Waldheim's back. Trying to reassure him, I said without thinking, "No, Secretary-General, it's just a machine gun." Seeing the reaction in his eyes, I added quickly that it wasn't pointed at his back, but upwards, which mainly meant his head. Gently, I pulled him slightly forward, looking discreetly at the revolutionary guard, who had a cool grin.

The following morning, the Foreign Minister, Gotbzadeh, dropped by to say that they had uncovered a plot to kill the Secretary-General, and he advised caution. There was then a controversy about whether the delegation should visit the cemetery where many of the Shah's victims were buried, to place a wreath in respect to the martyrs of the revolution. This had become a tradition for newly arrived visitors and political tourists. My view was that we should do the unavoidable and get on with our business, while other colleagues thought that we should avoid doing so. Some of us felt that if you were coming to negotiate the release of the hostages, placing a wreath was an affordable price to pay to establish some good will. Delay in making the visit emboldened the extremists, who pressured the government into refusing any contact with the UN delegation. Already, one of the main dailies had published a photo of Waldheim with the former Shah and denounced his visit. Eventually, the Secretary-General decided to go. But the timing was wrong. It was Thursday afternoon, when habitually widows and bereaved families visited their loved ones. The means of transport was also unfortunate. Because of the rumored death threat, it was suggested to go by helicopter. With two mechanical birds hovering over the cemetery, waiting to land, blowing dust around, every bereaved woman in the huge cemetery was alerted. They all converged, each with a grievance to relate. By then, Dr. Waldheim had the wreath in his hands, just outside the Mercedes provided by the Iranian Government. The UN American guard pushed him towards the car, and the Iranian guard pushed him towards the designated tombstone. Photographers were there, ready to capture the moment after he hurriedly was pushed back into the car and shuttled onto a helicopter back to the hotel, and the following day to Paris en route to New York. The Secretary-General had asked me to stay behind for a day or two more, just in case "some helpful signals" appeared. None did. In fact, my stay was slightly complicated by a statement made anonymously to the press in Paris that the UN group was very glad to get out of that "hellhole of crazies." I found an immediate exit via Kuwait. A Tehran-based Arab diplomat who seemed to have excellent connections asked me if I could do him a favor and carry a suitcase that would be picked up by a welcoming official upon arrival at the airport. When the suitcase arrived, it was loaded with expensive Persian rugs. Something seemed wrong. I felt uneasy, as if I was being set up.

Rugs were certainly a bargain in a country that produced them. Furthermore, most of the rich Tehranis who had left with the Shah had taken what was high in value and light in weight - that is, jewels and cash - and had left heavy carpets on the floors of the city. My local UN colleagues told me the new government had clamped down on the export of rugs - it was illegal in the first place. So why would a well-connected Ambassador ask me to be his courier, when his diplomatic immunity would cover any freight he wished to transport? Returning the suitcase as I left for the airport, I felt greatly relieved when the "revolutionary guards" found nothing incriminating as they went thoroughly through my luggage before ushering me politely to the plane. Weeks later, a newly recruited UN visitor from New York was stopped at the same airport while leaving with a collection of valuable rugs – causing not merely an embarrassment to the UN but an undue detriment to the negotiations on the release of hostages.

Within a month I was back. The Secretary-General instructed me to be the spokesman for a group of six international jurists "to investigate the practices" of the Shah's regime. My guess was that a negotiated package could be translated as follows: "If you wish to see the hostages, first you have to see what the Shah did to the people - as for the rest, we'll discuss." My understanding was also that the then Foreign Minister, Sadeq Gotbzadeh, was part of that package. One of our colleagues who came from New York was so optimistic that he carried -

secretly - a voice tape recording from President Carter addressing the hostages. There was everyday wrangling with the Foreign Minister, who arranged for walking tours of the vicinity, mosques, the cemetery, and again the cemetery, with accompanying demonstrations. There was one visit to President Bani-Sadr, who had with him two gentlemen posing as mediators - a French lawyer and a Latin-American businessman - both claiming to operate with the authority of U.S. President Carter's special advisor, Hamilton Jordan. The delegation of jurists saw as much of the prisons, disabled and victims of the previous regime as physically possible. Press releases documented that effort. But no hostages were seen. Once, after packing our luggage, and before getting into the cars to the airport, the group was taken to see the U.S. Chargé d'Affaires trapped in the Foreign Ministry, Bruce Laingen. The others were still held at the Embassy Compound. There was a brief discussion on if, as a press officer and not one of the jurists, I could respond informally to an invitation by the "spokesman" of the hostage-takers, a woman nick-named "Sister Mary" by reporters, who later became known as Maryam Rajavi, a leader of a militant group in exile, "Mujahideen e-Khalq." Although it entailed a risk of moving blindfolded into unpredictable territory, I felt confident the takers were not looking for an additional body - but rather how to best make a deal for the hostages on hand. I reasoned that one could find out directly, precisely and without rhetoric or diplomacy, what exactly they did want, whether a practical deal was possible. In the meantime, the hostages could be reassured that the international community cared and was working on their behalf. There were opposing factors: that the hostage-takers were not the decision-makers; that the matter fitted within a determined effort to disrupt Iran-US relations; and, more important for the jurists, that any dealings by that international group with those who took an illegal action would bestow some legitimacy on them. Our 21 days may not have produced immediate results, but it laid down specific areas of potential arrangements. My close contact with the helpful Algerian ambassador, Mohammed Gharib, continued for a while as Algeria played the final role, together with US Secretary of State Cyrus Vance, to release the hostages after 444 days of captivity.

Two personal impressions remain from that stay. One had to do with caviar. Apparently, "His Imperial Majesty" the Shah had left an endless reservoir of royal quality (and a list of its regular foreign recipients). While many other items were not readily available at our hotel, caviar was in abundance. Room service, the main restaurant and underground "bar" offered wonderful basmati rice and inspiring Persian meditational music - and caviar at an affordable price, except for the lemon. I rarely cared for that stuff since.

The other memory related to a carton box. When we definitely decided to leave Iran, a young man came up to the floor in the early morning carrying what looked like a pizza delivery box. He was looking for the group's Chairman, Mohammed Bijjaoui of Algeria. Not finding him, the man handed me the box, which seemed to be full of papers. Reaching our cars, I told Ambassador Bijjaoui, pointing to the man, who was still with me, and to the box. He yelled back not to touch it. Anything or any contact would legitimize their action. On the road to the airport, press photographers in tow, the box was in my lap, and the "revolutionary" man behind, telling me it contained very important information. Apparently, he and others had scotch-taped together the hurriedly shredded documents of the American Embassy when it was being stormed. He wanted to offer international visitors an indication about the "nest of spies." Admittedly, I was extremely curious. Again, I was a press professional, a former journalist, not a jurist. But I was an official spokesman for six distinguished legal experts, most of whom were to become members of the International Court of Justice. Ambassador Bijjaoui, who later was elected President of the Court, told me as we arrived at the airport, to return the box. The young Iranian refused to take it. Despite great temptation, I left it on the seat of the car. Since then, even decades later, whenever I see a large pizza box, I'm curious to see what's inside.

Normally, Dr. Waldheim had his own press officers. After André Lewin left, Rudolph Stajduhar, a Yugoslav who had fought during the war with Tito's partisans, was moved from his post in New Delhi to become Director of Press and Publications, effectively serving as the main spokesman. A rising star, the jovial French Corsican, François Giuliani, shared that role. An effective collaborator, and almost lethal adversary, François proved to be one of the best - if not the best - spokesman. A former journalist with Reuters in London, Francois swiftly adapted to Mr. Waldheim's style, although he seemed to blend more later on with Dr. Javier Perez de Cuellar, for whom he was the Chief Spokesman throughout his 10-year term. Whether it was Rudy or François travelling with Dr. Waldheim to the Middle East, we worked closely together, sharing assignments.

During the very few press conferences that I moderated for him, there was an expression that Dr. Waldheim repeatedly translated from

German. Instead of "the near future", he would say "the next future." He would always take the reminder just before a press interview, but then under questioning would repeat the same expression.

On a visit to Lebanon in 1976, he hoped that the war that had started a year earlier would soon end, and therefore he launched a reconstruction plan and appointed a Special Representative to oversee it. He insisted on visiting the destroyed heart of Beirut, despite opposition from security. The area was open to any of the thousands of snipers from all directions.

In order to attend a lunch given by the Lebanese President at the Palace in suburban Baabda, we flew by helicopter with Ghassan Tueni, the deputy prime minister and publisher of An Nahar newspaper. Watching the blue Mediterranean Sea and the luscious green mountains blend under a clear spring sky, Waldheim exclaimed about the magnificent view. One colleague commented that beautiful countries usually drove their people crazy. "Look at Cyprus", he said, "look at other countries on the Mediterranean." As he was bound to mention more enchanting trouble spots, an Austrian colleague turned to Rudy, the press spokesman, and said "Well, that doesn't apply to Yugoslavia. Look at Sarajevo, the most beautiful ski resort and symbol of peace."

Years later, after Mr. Waldheim had left and Mr. Stajduhar was retired, I was rushing on a Saturday to the Security Council, which was holding an emergency meeting on the escalating war in Sarajevo. Turning the corner of 46th Street and First Avenue, I bumped face-to-face into my former Yugoslav colleague. "Sarejevo", he said sadly, "Sarejevo" and, tearful, quickly walked away.

At the end of a visit to Saudi Arabia in 1975, where we met King Faisal, our hosts extended to us the usual watches with Saudi emblems as presents. While comparing notes during our internal dinner at the guesthouse, we discovered that I was the only one who had received a watch with the name of King Faisal on it. It may have been because I facilitated the dialogue between the Secretary-General and the King or because I displayed concern when he was hinting to his visitors that he was being threatened for his decisions. One of the Austrian colleagues then approached me with an appeal. Since I came from the region and I had opportunities to visit Saudi Arabia and possibly see King Faisal again, I could always get a watch with the King's name on it. He, on the other hand, made this visit only once. Could we therefore exchange watches? I felt that I was almost a host in Saudi Arabia, part of my region, and therefore I should make every effort to accommodate the other guests. Reluctantly, and with great hesitation, I agreed. A few weeks later, King Faisal was killed. The Austrian colleague returned as a diplomat accredited to Saudi Arabia, where he lived and eventually married a Saudi woman. I lost a precious watch but found my Austrian of the Year.

Soon afterward, when the Secretary-General was about to visit Beirut, all of the UN and Lebanese officials assembled in the airport to await the private UN plane that was supposed to arrive at noon. Half an hour before the scheduled time of arrival, someone mentioned that the plane was about to land, prompting a confused rush among the receiving party. The plane, however, did not appear on the tarmac until exactly noon. Officials circulated a story that Dr. Waldheim actually arrived half an hour earlier, but, considerate of the Lebanese hosts, had asked the plane to circle until the precise estimated time of arrival. I knew otherwise. The plane that had shown up earlier had carried UN senior military officers, led by General Siilasvuo, who had come from Jerusalem and discreetly parked at a distant corner at the back of the airport to join the reception. Waldheim's plane actually arrived as scheduled. But how could I deny a rumor that my Secretary-General was so polite?

As I was helping the Secretary-General in various parts of the Middle East, I once had to join him in Damascus, where he was trying to seek an extension of UNDOF, the UN Disengagement Force between Syrian and Israel. He was staying at a government guesthouse, a guarded one-story compound close to the old Presidential Compound. As there were crowds of journalists and officials at the main entrance, I slipped through one of the side doors and went straight to the sitting room, where Mr. Waldheim was alone. After his initial surprise, he sat me next to him and started debriefing me thoroughly. One of the photo reporters noticed someone talking alone at length with the UN Secretary-General. He quickly marched into the room and started flashing his camera. The more I tried to persuade him to stop, that I was not anyone worthy of such attention, the more he clicked. Later, I looked for that photographer, who worked for an American weekly, because I wanted one or two copies for my own record. He at first claimed he had no copies, then was terribly disappointed when I told him who I was - that is, a mere UN press officer.

Contact with various parties was not limited to policy issues. Inevitably, I was asked to deal with personalized events. One of them involved the case of a Swedish civilian staff member of the newly established UN Economic Commission for Western Asia, whose headquarters was near the airport, close to areas of armed conflict. He had fulfilled one of his dreams by buying a Volvo. At the beginning of the Lebanese war, there were certain cars that were targeted for daylight highway robbery. These included Honda, Mercedes, BMW and, failing to find any of the above, a Volvo. There was even a place in the mountains where people could locate their stolen cars and re-buy them at a special favored rate. Clearly, when our colleague's Volvo was stolen from him at gunpoint, he was devastated. In that almost lawless atmosphere, his friends told the peaceful-natured Swede that he had to do to others what they had done unto him. That is, if someone stole his Volvo, he should go and take someone else's Volvo. After weeks of hesitation, he became acclimatized to the militant ambience. While leaving the office one afternoon, spotting a Volvo he chased it. The more the car sped up, the more he accelerated. His prey increased its speed in a risky area around the refugee camps and went into the area of Sabra, a Palestinian stronghold. Our friend pressed on against his natural inclination, until the advancing Volvo made a quick stop. Suddenly, armed men jumped from it, and from about five other cars in front and behind. One of them approached our colleague and asked him politely but firmly to get out of the car and join them. They wanted to know who was behind his attempt to attack PLO chairman Yasser Arafat, who was in the pursued Volvo. Wrong Volvo.

Javier Perez de Cuellar

The next Secretary-General, Javier Perez de Cuellar, had the habit of referring to someone whose name he could not recall as "my friend." Once, a politician who learned we were going from Beirut to Damascus to meet the new Secretary-General, insisted on travelling with us on the claim that he was close to him. During a dinner given by the then-Syrian Foreign Minister Khaddam, the politician approached the dinner table, saluted the Secretary-General with much ado, and asked about his work, his family and his health. Don Javier turned around and asked whether we knew "my friend," who looked around and said triumphantly, "See, I told you he was my friend."

I had met Mr. Perez de Cuellar only once before his election. He was accompanying his predecessor to the Summit of Heads of Islamic States in Taif, Saudi Arabia's summer capital. The Soviet invasion of Afghanistan was the main topic at the time. It was of particular interest to the Islamic world. Don Javier came along to be introduced before an official announcement was to designate him Special Representative of the Secretary-General. He had a bad cold, made more inconvenient by the full blast of air conditioning in the brand new villa within a compound specially built for the occasion. "I know why I am here," he would respond if questions were raised about who should accompany the Secretary-General to attend meetings. He seemed to focus on his role and did not wish to inject himself in other issues. However, he graciously went along with protocol or political requirements. Since he was in my territory, I tried my best to alleviate his discomfort by providing him medicine and checking regularly on his health. About a year later, he was elected Secretary-General while vacationing in Peru, his native country. Coincidentally, I also returned to New York in October 1982 to head the network of UN Information Centres.

Every Director of a centre has to be approved by the Secretary-General and agreed by the host country. That gave me a unique opportunity to benefit from his experienced assessment of candidates. While reviewing the appointment of a Director in Buenos Aires, Argentina, I presented a shortlist of candidates. Their photos were attached in case a name had faded from a busy memory. As usual, my two-page brief listed varied evaluations and the specialties of each candidate. After we agreed on the appointment, the Secretary-General added with a smile: "Once the Argentinians see his picture, they will love him - he looks like their tango idol, Carlos Gardel."

Being a media rather than a diplomatic official, I was less fettered in my movements, undertaking special assignments the Secretary-General would request of me. Some were external, and some were what he described as internal damage control.

Impeccably dressed in tailored suits and Cartier/Hermes accessories, Mr. Perez de Cuellar moved easily, arriving with an inquisitive smile, always interested in listening, without a mean word to say about anyone. Once, during one of our visits, I burst out against someone I thought was exploiting meeting with him, describing the man as a crook. He eyed me with paternal firmness and commented, "You said that - I did not hear it." Quietly loyal to his staff, he thought of all aspects of other people's lives. We were discussing an administrative action involving a colleague, when he said, "You know, that very thing may save a marriage."

A man who notices a lot and says little, Mr. Perez de Cuellar once asked me about the difference between serving in Beirut during a war and coping with diplomatic maneuverings at UN headquarters. He smiled when I responded, "At least in Beirut, I knew who was sniping at me." His sense of humor is subtle, more of an elegant nuance than a cracking laugh. During the UN's fortieth anniversary celebrations, he gave a luncheon for attending heads of State. The King of Spain, Don Juan Carlos, was seated on his right and had spoken in the morning session. Philippine President Corazon Aquino, on his left, was scheduled to address the General Assembly in the afternoon. As the Spanish King was about to take leave, he said that he would have loved to stay and listen to Mrs. Aquino, were it not for protocol restrictions. Perez de Cuellar, in a play on words in Spanish, commented, "You may not be there personally, but you will be leaving us with a 'Corazon'".

When a film about Mother Teresa was screening to limited crowds in New York, I approached the Secretary-General about showing it at the UN. He readily agreed and decided to personally address letters inviting the diplomatic community to an unprecedented showing in the General Assembly Hall. He held Mother Teresa's hand and escorted her to the podium to give a special speech in her honor. Years later, the "Saint of Calcutta" came to visit his successor, Dr. Boutros-Ghali. After leaving his office, she thoughtfully asked where I was and took the first elevator she saw, which was the night service elevator, straight to my office. I hurriedly called on staff, who were fascinated by her modest charm. She looked you straight in the face with piercing eyes and spoke softly, firmly and to the point. Some of our staff volunteered to support her work, and all of them commemorated her visit by collecting donations from their salaries to help the neediest cases. That visit was indeed a most cherished one. A short while later, that down-to-earth angel returned home.

Javier Perez de Cuellar was a most agreeable travel companion, always considerate and courteous, with the habit of having everyone join him for lunch or dinner. A diplomat's diplomat, he would rarely express his demands as orders, but mainly as questions. He would wonder whether we could do something for someone, or whether it was too late to get out of a particular situation. He enjoyed exquisite food and appreciated good wine. His aides would gladly pass on that admirable habit to potential host countries. The French, of course, didn't have serious competition, but it was surprising how many countries produced outstanding wines.

While keeping in close touch with all world capitals, Perez de Cuellar used Paris as his main springboard for further travel. Thus, I made a point of having one of our best UN staff as Director of the Centre there. Hassan Fodha, a former Ambassador of Oman, of Tunisian citizenship, managed these visits and polished his contacts with French media so well to the point that the two succeeding Secretaries-General, Boutros Boutros-Ghali and Kofi Annan, kept him there.

For a while, Secretaries-General turned down offers of free airplane travel, lest their position be misunderstood or their integrity be compromised. The only special planes used were those available to peacekeeping operations. In specific cases where commercial flights were not available, like our trip to Iran during the war with Iraq, a chartered plane was used. The only private plane Secretary-General Perez de Cuellar used was in 1985 when it was decided suddenly while in Doha to shuttle between Tehran and Baghdad in an attempt to stop the war. The concerned Emir of Qatar offered his personal jet to bring us back to Paris, en route by commercial flight to New York. However, but the mid-1990s it became almost customary to receive plane rides from a number of rulers or even individuals. It was not clear how much money was saved, but it was more convenient. No political repayment in whatever form was apparent; perhaps it's a simple matter of prestige. It was understood that the Secretary-General, with appropriate media coverage in tow for his wider trip, would visit the offering country to pick up the plane – and whatever else came with it.

I traveled with Mr. Perez de Cuellar during the Iran-Iraq war and was part of the negotiating team he led. With a tactful approach - gentle but not weak, and strong but not overbearing - he listened to everyone, but eventually he made the decision. As always, in such cases, his gentle manner was misinterpreted as weakness by some who tried to exploit it for their own agendas. During a visit to the Gulf countries in 1985, all heads of State there urged him to mediate between Iran and Iraq. He was not necessarily prepared for such a sudden task at the time. He may have felt that the situation was not yet ripe for intervention, yet by the time we reached Qatar, he felt that as Secretary-General he should explore what Gulf leaders thought was a possible chance for peace. The Emir of Qatar, Sheikh Khalifah, offered his luxurious plane for that purpose. At dinner, someone who had received an international phone call tried to rescind the decision. Don Javier replied firmly in French: *les jeux sont faits*, an expression normally used in roulette games to indicate the bets had been made and could not be withdrawn. It was on a mission to Iran that we tried to see who among us could get the Secretary-General to hum a tune. We knew he was a lover of classical music. He was very reserved in public expression, even within a small circle. On a tense flight, we were told that there were demonstrating crowds awaiting our arrival in Tehran and suggested a delay in the hope that they would disperse after dark. The plane was leased from a Swiss company. Special Assistant Giandomenico Picco somehow produced a tape of Brahms' Hungarian dances, which was played on its public speaker. After a little while, a relaxed expression on the face of Perez de Cuellar was followed by a hum and an accompanying whistle to the tune.

Boutros Boutros-Ghali

Although we came from the same region, I had never met Mr. Boutros Boutros-Ghali before his election. His view of the Egyptian bureaucracy was very dim, and he may have wrongly confused it with UN bureaucracy - which got him into trouble. Once he felt you were doing your best, he eased up enough to expect you to work together with him on holidays and weekends. I recall that, having taken no leave throughout the year, I went to Southampton for an end of the year holiday. After tracing me one morning following Christmas, Dr. Boutros asked a few questions about one of the books we were producing, an article in an Arabic daily, and one other project he had in mind. He then said he was working happily alone in his office and asked where I was. On hearing my answer, he said casually, "Good, so we'll continue when I see you this afternoon."

For Boutros Boutros-Ghali the most beautiful noise was the sound of sea waves; most relaxing activity: work; most welcome compliment: "You've done a good job"; favorite characteristics: dialogue and courage; favorite individual: Egyptian film director Youssef Chahine; favorite food: Egyptian *mulukhiyah*; most repeated explanation for his problems with Washington: "The selection of a UN Secretary-General and a U.S. President coincide once every 20 years, and it happened on my watch."

My first official meeting with him was when I was sent as a

Special Representative to oversee the referendum in Eritrea. Half of the people there were Copts, like him. The other half spoke Arabic, as both of us do. The area was the back door to Egypt, where he had served as a Foreign Minister. Upon my return from a successful mission, he would call me more regularly to deal with several problems. As Assistant Secretary-General of the Department of Public Information I worked closely with him on media and publications, especially the "Blue Books" series, which focused on special UN achievements in Cambodia, El Salvador, Mozambique and anti-Apartheid.

He loved books. He also liked to take up media matters very late in the day, more towards dinner-time. Reading and writing was what he did for relaxation. He apparently had an addiction to the *International Herald Tribune* at the time, although he paid special attention to newspapers everywhere. A former columnist, Boutros Boutros-Ghali had a distinct view towards specific reporters, particularly those seeking interviews. A hand wave or subtle grin would be followed by a descriptive remark or welcoming response. Obviously particularly attentive to Egyptian media, he particularly liked a columnist in the European Herald Tribune, Jonathan Power, all the while, despite his closeness to France, he disdained a correspondent of a main Parisian daily, doubting her professional qualifications, assuming that she was placed to accommodate an influential visiting minister. He appreciated Abe Rosenthal, former Executive Editor of the *New York Times*, who wrote a weekly column, and welcomed Thomas Friedman while turning down a columnist in a Washington-based paper. His appreciation of the contributions by Lebanese expatriates in mainstream Egyptian newspapers helped strengthen friendly relations with the publisher of Beirut daily An Nahar, Ghassan Tueni, a former Deputy Prime Minister and Ambassador to the UN, and Samir Atallah, writer in "Ash-Sharq Al-Awsat," a pan-Arab daily, with whom he enjoyed friendly chats, calling him casually at his Beirut phone number regardless of time difference.

From *Le Monde* in Paris, to the *Japan Times*, to German papers, to press reports from our Information Centres, he would read them all and often telephone with his comments. He did that when all other business of the day was over; that often entailed some follow-up action, which meant that my social planning for any evening was too optimistic.

Anyone who worked closely with Boutros-Ghali would eventually have to come into contact with his remarkable wife, Leah. Although she made a point of not interfering in substantive UN business, she obviously loved her husband, who was always interested in his image, and she wanted the whole world to see all of his qualifications the way she did. That placed me as a regular recipient of her colorful, sharp and witty queries. With the best of intentions, she tried to help with his contacts, especially in New York, and generally around the world. While he was busy attending meetings, she was busy networking for him. During the tense controversy of the last year of Boutros-Ghali's tenure, a wave of faxes containing positive press reports about him in the world press arrived at the offices of Congress members, Senators and American personalities. Some adversaries in the US administration suspected the UN Department of Public Information of spearheading a campaign to reach out and touch everyone in Washington. Their quiet investigation led to an elegant address in Manhattan, where two socialite friends of the indefatigable Leah Boutros-Ghali were getting busy on the newest model of their fax machine, normally reserved for social invitations.

He had a razor-sharp sense of commentary. Ironically, it was sometimes not only lost but also distorted in the translation. While an expression in Egyptian Arabic could sound perfectly to the point, or would sound funny, it might not be so in English. The same would apply for translation from French, which was almost his native tongue. What he might think to be a thoughtful expression might come out sounding condescending. What he might think was a reminder might sound like a rebuke. What he might expect to be a joke could turn out to sound like an insult. His discreet Chef de Cabinet, Jean-Claude Aimé, had the creative task of deciphering whom the Secretary-General meant. His colorful reference to Madeleine Albright as the "fat lady" may have led to the immature interruption of his work when as eventual Secretary of State the "fat lady" did in fact sing.

Mr. Boutros-Ghali had a favorite story about a king who was very fond of his horse, to the point that he wanted to teach him to speak. He would invite doctors and sages of his country to ask whether they could help. Anyone who obviously said the job could not be done had his head cut off. So when it was the turn of an experienced politician, he responded that the horse could indeed be trained to speak. However, since this was not a normal occurrence, despite the special qualities of the horse, it would take some time, possibly about five years. The King happily and readily agreed, entrusting the man with the task and lavishing on him privileges and attention. When his wife asked the politician what he had done, risking his life for the impractical commitment, the man said, "In five years, either the King will die, or the horse will die, or I will die." Five years is the term of the UN Secretary-General. Boutros-Ghali had initially announced he would serve only one term. Towards the fourth year, he responded to a pressing query by a *Le Monde* correspondent that "only fools don't change their minds."

Pinned down in an emotional and personal battle between Dr. Boutros-Ghali and Dr. Albright, staff of the Department of Public Information strived with unprecedented difficulty to focus on our normal task: loyalty to the designated functions of the Secretary-General and consideration for the welcome role of the host country, a permanent member of the Security Council. There were agitators and opportunists whose main claim to authority was a display of ferocious loyalty to either side. A close associate of the US ambassador publicly threatened us, while freelancers within relentlessly pushed us towards confrontation. An Egyptian woman in Geneva, a well-meaning close friend of Mrs. Boutros-Ghali, presented a particular nuisance with counter-productive results. Her unwarranted and unwanted calls drove me – and another senior colleague at the Secretary-General's office, to an unprecedented rude response. Another staffer, also in Geneva, seemed more keen on settling scores with other colleagues than advancing any cause. Ironically, this same woman, a French national, feigned fiercer loyalty to new Secretary-General Kofi Annan. When years later there was an abrupt and ill-considered decision to close the UN Information Centres in Europe, including Paris, she volunteered a written view that there was no need for such UN presence because Annan was much more popular in European capitals than any of its leaders.

While the controversy of his fifth year over a second term would require a separate review, I recall a particular mystery. One evening in early 1996, I returned from a dinner where the diplomatic consensus was that Boutros-Ghali would be re-elected for a second term if he wished. An editor of a mainstream daily indicated they would come out soon with an editorial endorsing him. Upon opening my mail, I found a book of selections by a Greek poet, Constantine Cavafy, a favorite of Mr. Boutros-Ghali, who had enjoyed life in the Alexandria described by Lawrence Durrell in his "The Alexandria Quartet". Months earlier, the Secretary-General had visited Athens, and in an unusually emotional statement had recited Cavafy's ecstasy at beholding a Mediterranean sunset. Curious, I leafed through the book and settled on one page, as sometimes we do in whimsical search of unread sequels of destiny. The title announced: "God Abandons Anthony". It advises Caesar to maintain courage, "as if long prepared," and "bid her farewell, the Alexandria you are losing." Stunned, I continued reading: "do not moan in vain your fortune failing you now, the plans of your life that turned to be illusions. Say good-bye to her, the Alexandria that is leaving." Somehow, though hardly superstitious, a feeling engulfed me that a final chapter was being written. Months later, in April, the disagreement with Secretary of State Vance - and eventually Ambassador Albright - erupted, with the obvious result. When I looked for that book again, I could not find it. I quoted from memory the selection I used in my farewell note to Boutros Boutros-Ghali, It was three years later, as I was leaving the UN, that the new Greek Ambassador, Elias Gounaris, sent me the full text of that poem in two translations.

The day his successor was elected, he acted as if it was business as usual. He asked me matter-of-factly whether we could produce a new booklet. "An Agenda for Peace", his earliest and best-known publication, produced in more than 30 languages, had been complemented by a less impressive "Agenda for Development". With 16 days left before leaving the UN, he now wished to produce "An Agenda for Democracy", to be his farewell professional work. There was very little time available. The General Assembly was still in session, occupying most of those who would have to draft, edit and produce it. Actually, there were only five working days - the following week would be consumed by Christmas and New Year holidays, and the glass house would be almost deserted, even by workaholics like me. Aspiring staff had already started to shift their interim attention from the 38th to the 37th floor, where their newly elected future boss worked. Yet, Mr. Boutros-Ghali was still Secretary-General. Disappointed, puzzled, but not yet out or vanquished, as he announced later in his book, he prefaced his request with a special remark. An already tiny yet elegant figure, he pulled his stomach in to show his loss of weight. I promised to make every effort to produce the booklet, with the inevitable help of dedicated staff at the Publications section. And, indeed, on his last day in office, I handed the publication to him with a glossy cover. In a rare show of personal affection in his office, he suddenly and silently hugged me, turned his back and strode out.

Kofi Annan

Kofi Annan was my colleague for at least 20 years. And, as the first Secretary-General to rise from the ranks of UN staff, we were all enthusiastic about his elevation to that post, a vindication of the dedicated work by every international civil servant. Although already elected on December 13, 1996, he gave a Christmas party a few days later as the Under-Secretary-General for Peacekeeping. In his own quiet way, he is witty, with a distinct sense of humor. He told an anecdote about a Pope, who noticed that a football is left alone when deflated. But when it was inflated, passersby were always tempted to kick it. He added: "So be gentle in your kicks when I am unduly inflated." I felt encouraged to tell another Pope story. There were two Cardinals in the Vatican, who used to lunch regularly, sitting under a tree on a hill overlooking the papal office. They would talk about how the Vatican could be improved if they had more say in the affairs of state, and how certain things could be done or undone. One of them actually became Pope. After about a year, his colleague visited him and was graciously received. When he asked whether the new Pope recalled the views they had discussed, the Pope pleasantly responded that he did. However, he added, "The view from the Pope's seat is quite different from the view under the tree."

Some of the best advice I received from Kofi Annan years earlier related to human temptation. Consulting with him regularly on personnel matters, as I replaced him as Chairman of the Appointment and Promotion Board, he once recounted that it was prudent of me to turn down a specific tempting offer in a case under review. He then told a story about an African president's visit to Accra during the Nkrumah rule of his country, Ghana. Driving together in an open car, the two leaders were responding to cheers by the crowds and "pressing the flesh" when a women called the prominent visitor by his first name. Upon recognizing her, he approached and enquired about her status, reassuring her of continued support, to the admiration of the impressed crowd. When Nkrumah enquired, his guest told him that he had known the woman, in the biblical sense, about 20 years ago. Then he added, "You know, whatever you try, such a debt is never fully repaid".

Kofi Annan is an experienced navigator in international cross-currents whose performance qualified him for unanimous re-nomination for a five-year term. A patient listener with a unique memory, he would blend smoothly with any situation. He is often correctly described as soft-spoken. Yet, while very hesitant about confronting people, he is never reluctant to take on controversial issues of principle. He is an affectionate colleague and an inspiring team leader, loyal to his staff, although some of them use his authority to advance their own agendas.

For 30 years, Kofi Annan was a sensitive colleague, a friend and, at times, a brother within the intricate international mechanism. Since his 1986 days as head of Personnel, I mentioned him as a desirable Secretary-General. When he was indeed elected 10 years later, I stayed on for a while until it was the appropriate time to pay for a wish fulfilled.

While he was head of Peacekeeping, I was head of Public Information, and we worked closely together supporting each other in Headquarters committees and in field operations. Before his election, many of us felt it was about time for someone from the ranks to become Secretary-General. I could not have hoped for a better colleague to rise. When Annan was running for the post, I was caught between working for the sitting Secretary-General to whom I had taken an oath of loyalty and my personal wish to see Annan take his seat. There was a general feeling that I was close to Boutros-Ghali. Though I am proud of that relationship, we rarely had a personal link until he left office and realized the extent to which I stood by him. My relationship with Annan was much closer, which meant I had to manage a daily balancing act between my exclusive loyalty to the Secretary-General and my unhidden affection for his potential successor. Thus, I chose not to interfere in the campaign as a possibly disappointed Kofi Annan would be the first to confirm.

When a North African ambassador, very experienced and down to earth, saw how elated I was at the initial election of Kofi Annan, he suggested that I cool it. His view was that the next step was to reinvent and repackage Kofi Annan for a different UN. Those "producers" or scriptwriters would not want anyone around who knew him very well from the past, as they might see how much his image had been shaped rather than naturally formed. That caution did not bother me. My main goal and desire was to deliver an effective work program for "one of us" who had become Secretary-General. If he ascended to the highest level, I would only be too happy. My only reaction was curiosity about what kind of script was being prepared. It turned out the main problem was if you live by the media, you die by the media.

Still, I always knew there is a price to pay for a fulfilled wish. Having worked so closely, I did not expect to stay with Mr. Annan as Secretary-General for more than a year or two. Some of the forces at play that brought this new Secretary-General did indeed want to reinvent and package a new Kofi Annan. He became a cottage industry. PR firms, sharpshooting politicians, and an assortment of operators were making a business out of him. Some of us were looking for the real Annan in all this. I spotted him once during a concert to fight poverty in London. He came alone and spoke admirably from his heart. There were no handlers to milk every bit of his presence and no one to make sure he was behaving as scripted. It was then that I saw my friend, the real Kofi Annan – though for a fleeting moment. He had been made into a "diplomatic rock star" while I was hoping he would, occasionally, come down to earth.

A swift move by the Clinton administration to place Kofi Annan as the Secretary-General may have been motivated by a partnership in the failure to prevent the 1994 Rwanda massacres. Although Secretary Warren Christopher had assured African leaders that the US had no specific preference except to block an extension by the incumbent Secretary-General, it was obvious that Ambassador Madeleine Albright in New York and certain officials liaising with the White House in Washington were very keen on Mr. Annan, who was equally vulnerable to accusations of knowingly taking no action despite an urgent written alert from the UN staff in Kigali. Any other African would not be trusted to merely look back with benign dismay and eventually find a well-timed politically correct exit strategy. A Pulitzer Prize-winning book by Samantha Power provided documented details with names and dates about the "demons" that the UN Commander on the ground had to fight as the massacres were allowed to happen.

In any event, as new Secretary-General, Mr. Annan suggested I stay one more year. There was a different atmosphere in place, however, with new players. I understood later that the Japanese were pushing for my post of Under Secretary-General for the Department of Public Information. I double-checked with him, indicating my readiness to leave. He said there were "some things to balance" and that I should not make any move before he spoke to me again. However, I already felt it was time for me to go. The Japanese had given him the name of an average diplomat. I suggested he tell them that I was ready to depart, provided they brought a name of one of their accomplished communicators. But obviously, they insisted on the same name. In fact, some of the new people around the Secretary-General, in battles for their own turf, wanted an amenably accommodating head of Public Information. Already, they established a Communications Director, an independent "spokesman" office, and an Assistant Secretary-General for Public Relations, in addition to a private PR firm and a "strategic" consultant – all separate from the Department of Public Information. The first reform package of Annan in 1997 had suggested a Communications

Taskforce. Its Chairman was World Bank Vice President Mark Malloch Brown, who later became Chef de Cabinet and Deputy Secretary-General. The thrust of its proposal was that the Department of Public Information should be strengthened with authority to lead and coordinate all public information components within the UN; all related activities would fall within that context. Such proposals did not sit well with members of the newly influential "team" seeking their own space.

From December 1997 to March 1998 I was preparing to leave for a new life. I had started at the UN temporarily, convinced I would go back to media work sooner or later. Instead, I stayed for 33 years. It was time. If I had wanted to, I could have made a counterbalance to stay. On the 50th anniversary of the Human Rights convention, I invited Hillary Clinton to participate. It was her first official visit to the U.N., and the President graciously received me that evening to thank me "for looking after the First Lady."

After highlighting the role of the Human Rights Declaration committee president, Eleanor Roosevelt, I mentioned that the Rapporteur happened to be a Lebanese diplomat, Dr. Charles Malek, adding the name of another Lebanese expatriate, Khalil Gibran, who set forth in one of his essays whether you were someone who asks what your country could do for you or what you could do for your country – a thoughtful formulation adapted decades later in a speech drafted for U.S. President Kennedy.

A few days later, U.S. ambassador Bill Richardson, whom I met during a dinner at the residence of Morocco's Ambassador, Ahmad Snoussi, took me aside and asked if there was anything the U.S. could do for me. I thanked him sincerely but requested nothing. It was common knowledge that the Clinton administration was the main force behind the appointment of Annan. If it intervened on my behalf, he would have found more reasons for me to stay, perhaps in a different capacity. However, I thought that as an international civil servant, I should neither ask nor seek a government's personal support. I also figured that the new Secretary-General, who had been my friend and colleague for decades, would need to make his own institutional judgments unfettered by a personal consideration. I accompanied him on a trip to the Middle East while preparing to leave. I was the most senior Arab representative at the U.N., and several officials in the region who had heard rumors of my impending departure wanted to raise the subject, but I didn't want any problems for the Secretary-General. I joined the UN on my own –

with no government, group, or relative to push me. And so I would leave on my own.

Particularly between 2003-2004, Mr. Annan was in more trouble than most generally realized. He was almost on the brink of having to resign. Some around him who sought continuity for themselves established a Plan B, where someone they knew well would assume the functions of Acting Secretary-General before eventually taking over. However, they underestimated Annan, who pulled through. A 2005 article in the New York *Times* revealed that he was advised by a number of close personal friends to immediately replace his Chef de Cabinet. That was, however, only a diversion of reality that raised diplomatic eyebrows. It looked as if Mr. Annan's actual Board of Directors was a private group of individuals, rather than sovereign member states. More to the point, many of them were concerned about finding a way out for the Secretary-General rather than for the Organization.

The real deal was made elsewhere. It was reflected in a takeover by former UNDP administrator Mark Malloch Brown, first as Chef de Cabinet, and then as Deputy Secretary-General. In effect, the beleaguered Annan was placed under a trusteeship. The perception was that the British, who cared for him, had guaranteed the Americans, who started doubting him, that Annan would go along while the UN would be executively run by a trusted hand. Great Britain's close link to Annan was established long before Tony Blair was overheard in BBC's open microphone describing Kofi Annan to President Bush as "pure honey." The solid and capable Mark Malloch Brown, then Sir and now Lord, deserves credit for not only lifting the Secretary-General from almost certain disaster but also in helping to save the UN's reputation.

One indication that Kofi Annan was not fully in charge during his last year was the resignation of one of his closest and most loyal assistants for 25 years. Elisabeth Lindenmayer was let go without even a signal of objection from Annan. Obviously, it was not his wish. He knew he would remain graciously treated until the last minute of his term as long as he allowed his trustees to handle the matters as they saw fit. The Volcker report was part of the arrangement. As Paul Volcker himself hinted in an interview with *Los Angeles Times*, the former banker realized that the fate of the Secretary-General was in his hands and that he could have forced his resignation. It sounded like a warning signal. The report, indeed, was not an investigation. The thrust of it was generally forecast from the beginning. A veteran observer predicted a year earlier the main point: blame the system and save the man. Inflate the man, and deflate the organization. Unfortunately, he was right. The report hit the UN and created the image of an unmanageable, bureaucratic and corrupt organization, while not exactly exonerating Annan.

The U.N. leadership's main mistake was its silence. It should have defended itself better. Instead, everyone was paralyzed as if an electric shock had gone through the glass house on the East River. It was as if everybody stopped, then started moving in slow motion, almost robot style, with no coherence, while its pillars took destructive hits. Mark Malloch Brown played a crucial role in recognizing the symbolic link between the Secretary-General and the Organization. While many UN believers were angered at Mr. Annan for putting the UN in such a vulnerable corner, Malloch Brown pulled off an important accomplishment in letting Annan go out graciously. Throughout, Nane Annan, Kofi's wife, remained above it all. She stood by her husband in difficulties but never meddled in his controversies. She gained the respect of everybody as a lady, a jurist and an enlightened intellectual.

One of Annan's positive attributes was that he never played the race card. He was once married to a Nigerian, and Nane, his second wife, is Swedish. When asked by a feature reporter upon becoming Secretary-General whether he had felt any hint of discrimination while an exchange student at the University of Minnesota, he amenably responded "no" – to the pleasure of his readers. However, when he was encircled by negative reporting and the Senator of Minnesota demanded his resignation, Mr. Annan suddenly discovered the word "lynching." It was an indication of weakness where it might have been a source of strength.

A little known Kofi Annan, before his election, had potential star quality; he was inimitable, pleasant, sensitive and naturally charismatic in the media. As a sophisticated African expatriate who had lived in Europe and the US, he was a feel-good story for Western liberals. He also made many of the right moves in public relations. The main problem was that he needed others to back up this image, though he did have the intelligence to maintain it. When he took over, he wanted a review of communications and public information. He called me to discuss his objectives at length, and we agreed on a way forward. Since I would stay only one or two more years, my interest was to leave a good set-up. A taskforce was established, headed by Malloch Brown, Vice President at the World Bank at the time. Although the overall reform initiative in

1997 was overseen by Maurice Strong, Malloch Brown had a free hand. Despite internal sniping by several others, he and I worked out a joint understanding to discuss matters openly and professionally and agreed I would do my best to pass our agreements through the applicable UN bodies. The main recommendation was to combine all communication efforts under one focus to be most effective. Although the Secretary-General officially stated that he supported the "thrust" of the proposals, the practical result was further fragmentation.

A new office for public relations was added on the 38th floor to accommodate Gillian Sorensen, wife of the famed JFK speechwriter Ted. A very decent woman, one problem was that she raised her complaints and internal disagreements to the Democratic White House of President Clinton and to the US Mission to the UN. Yet another new office was created in the Secretary-General's area to provide the former special assistant of Mr. Annan in Peacekeeping the title of Communications Director, with a promotion at a D-2 level in the Office of the Secretary-General. A third branch, the Spokesperson's Office, was further split from the Department of Public Information and expanded with full authority to operate without supervision except by the Secretary-General. In a fourth change, the Chef de Cabinet and Director of the Secretary-General's office would also convey special directives in dealing with urgent communications issues. All these new offices were in addition to the head of DPI who, officially at least, was the main leader in the communications field. There were about 700 staff members under this remit in various areas, both at Headquarters and in the field, working for the UN representing the Secretary-General. Still, even more seemed to be needed on the personal side as a private PR firm was already placing Mr. Annan on its list of clients. In one case when the first announcement about reform had to be made, I received several different drafts at 11 am to be issued by noon. My easy access to the Secretary-General allowed me to go up to his office and show him. One was handed in by the private PR firm, one by someone in the Secretary-General's office, and one prepared by professionals in the press section of DPI, which would issue the release. I asked him which one to issue. Smilingly, he suggested I decide. I sided with the most accurate version, which had been drafted by the DPI professionals.

What later saddened some of us was that when the Secretary-General was in difficulty, only a limited number of those self-promoters stood up to defend him. They were all looking for the next opportunity. It was difficult to tell him that; yet, although he pretended otherwise, a perceptive man like him would certainly have noticed.

There are a number of former senior people who believe that Mr. Annan, as an ultimate insider, was brought in to destroy the UN. Who could do it better? The claim was certainly unfair. For someone who had spent his whole life at the organization, it is impossible to think for a minute that he would intentionally undermine it. More likely, showering him with exhilarating praise may have turned his gaze away from those under him who perpetrated damage. Napoleon was once asked what the most lethal weapon was. His reply was "incense burning"; when people were telling you all the time how great you are, then you cannot run the battle because you're so carried away from reality.

In retrospect, the question of what kind of Secretary-General Kofi Annan would make arose the moment he was appointed. During a dinner given by an active member of the Security Council, there was a somewhat pseudo-intellectual discussion on whether Annan would be a Becket or an Oedipus. Given that his main support came from the US administration, which had a specific list of demands, the question was would he go along and "stab his mother" (meaning the organization that raised him) or would he be a Becket rebelling against the king who put him there? An entertaining evening indeed, but they did not take into account Kofi Annan's personality. He turned out to be neither of the two – not a rebel nor a traitor. He was rather a navigator finding his way the first five years in fairly calm waters, and the second term in treacherous territory.

During the bombings by NATO of Kosovo, which were supported by the Clinton Administration, Secretary-General Kofi Annan issued a statement in March 1999 that sounded like the clearest endorsement possible by a UN official: "It is indeed tragic that diplomacy has failed, but there are times when the use of force may be legitimate in the pursuit of peace." But four years later he had a nuanced, different attitude about the invasion of Iraq by the Bush administration. Although he initially refrained from declaring a clear position, he came as close as possible to condemning it. In an interview with Al-Jazeera correspondent Abderrahim Foukera, on April 2, 2003, he stated that it was not a UN sanctioned war: "the Council did not endorse the war and I think that was clear." When asked whether he would therefore condemn the war, he responded: "The legitimacy of this action has been questioned, and widely questioned, and I myself have raised questions about it. I have raised questions about the legitimacy and whether it was in conformity with the Charter." Perhaps because the interview was mainly broadcast in its Arabic interpretation, it did not seem to irk the administration in Washington as much as a deliberately arranged interview with the BBC weeks before the close US presidential election in 2004, when he was clearer in questioning the legitimacy of the war. The remark was picked up by certain circles to brand Mr. Annan as interfering with US internal politics and in effect endorsing presidential candidate John Kerry.

After the invasion of Iraq and the swift fall of Baghdad, Secretary-General Annan had what seemed like a nervous breakdown. Those who worked closely with him over the years had come to identify specific personal stress signals. The softest was in fidgeting fingers and roaming eyes; the most telling was a break in his voice. These signals became even more visible a few months later.

Despite resources available to the UN Secretary-General, including effective legal counsel and funds at his disposal, Annan could never reshape the narrative on his presumed responsibility during the massacres of Rwanda as peacekeeping chief or on the Oil-for-Food scandal in Iraq. He was also blamed partially for Somalia and the Srebrenica massacre in Bosnia, when in fact his role was more that of an amenable bystander. The most serious damage was done to the UN Secretary-General's office when, in an unprecedented move, he retained a criminal lawyer who happened to be the same one that represented President Clinton in the notorious case involving Monica Lewinsky. The resulting negative impact was not only unfair to the UN but also to other valuable and formidable members of Annan's own family.

After the Assembly session that re-elected him to a second term, he thoughtfully mentioned that we could work together again. I then told him a story about Caesar during the Roman Empire. A person, usually a close friend, was regularly paid to stay by Caesar's side to remind him during overwhelming acclamations that he was human. Though the crowds were yelling "Hail Caesar," he should only get carried away for a brief fantasy, then return to running the empire. I would do so free of charge.

Working for the UN was not just a job for me; it was a commitment. One of the greatest advantages of being there was the opportunity to work with outstanding people who use their hearts and their brilliant minds to advance a cause in which I believe. While generally praising and supporting the Secretary-General, we also have to speak out clearly at times of disappointment. A credible, effective, inclusive U.N. is worth it.

Particularly as the UN's perceived role seems to be unduly eroding, it admittedly becomes challenging to defend a complex institution that I hold so dearly and that holds so much promise for our world. An effective UN is worth the effort.

CHAPTER VIII:

IT'S YOUR WORLD:
EXTENDED CONFLICTS

International peace and human development, the two main UN objectives, are facing serious challenges. Three glaring current worldwide challenges – terrorism, sectarian violence and migration hardly received even a semblance of a substantive international response. In an almost leaderless, increasingly fragmented world, the handling of peacemaking missions or peacekeeping operations eroded to the point of specific cases of embarrassment. As to human development, despite a formerly stiff upper lip, it is widely known that there are no funds left for basic requirements, and that all available funds are spent on emergency relief for migration of refugees. In fact, now that it is recognized at the highest level that displaced millions would require much more assistance, governments mainly reiterate earlier commitments, which they most likely are unable to meet, in fact.

The United Nations is not about merely hosting high level meetings and reproducing statements; its system is involved with every aspect of everyday life. When you post a letter, it moves across borders because there is the UN Universal Postal Union; radio signals are the International Telecommunications Union; airplanes fly within a system monitored by the International Civil Aviation Organization; the World

Bank regulates financial transactions; the World Health Organization looks out for global health. Although these organs are part of the UN system, they have fewer controversies in the media than the UN itself, for perhaps people would argue less on technical questions than on political ones. In other words, people are more willing to agree on their needs rather than their ambitions.

The UN's main objectives – peace and security, and social and economic development – may sound too general, but its operations have specific targets. Even conflicting governments collaborate on handling joint problems from contagious diseases to water rights to the flow of refugees. A Resident Coordinator oversees an agreed practical work program for priorities in each of the host countries

The human condition is not always attuned to instant solutions. Major issues take time before it is realized they are interrelated, and that their resolution could better be sorted out earlier in time together.

As one example, when the UN was established in 1945, the condition of women, who form at least half of the world population, was so lamentable that a special committee on their status was born to push for basic rights like their literacy and humane treatment. After thirty years, an international conference in Copenhagen showed some progress. It was mainly attended by female activists - with a large gap between delegates coming from the lands of plenty and others from oppressed areas seeking minimum rights like maternal and infant health and the right to drinkable water. Yet by the time a women's summit conference was held in Beijing in 1995, heads of State and/or their spouses showed up bearing the flags of a new era for women. By 2005, ten years after Beijing, a meeting at the UN General Assembly in New York was a women's power event.

When an ambassador of Sweden rushed a proposal in the early seventies to review environmental living conditions in cities and suburbs, even his own colleagues among other delegations wondered what was behind Stockholm's move. Still, after a UN Environment Programme was established in Nairobi headed by capable directors, questions persisted on its relevance, including its location in distant Gigiri, Kenya. Less than two decades ago, for example, talk of the "ozone layer" sounded more like an obscure scientific narrative. By 2006, however, it became so politically correct that it drew a Nobel Prize coupled with a Hollywood special award and topped by a tribute by hip hop artist Queen

Latifa. Support for freedom for peoples to decide their own destiny liberated from foreign domination took 30 years to show initial results. Since its creation, at least 135 countries were welcomed as new members of the United Nations, which is older than almost two-thirds of its members. Civil liberties were a serious issue even in the UN's host country, the United States, where the UN's Under Secretary-General Ralph Bunche used to join hands with Reverend Martin Luther King Jr., among others, chanting "We Shall Overcome". Despite lingering racial tensions everywhere, civil liberties are indivisible and legally established beyond any question around the world, crowned by the victory over apartheid in southern Africa where Nelson Mandela took over as the first president of a multiracial, unified state. Poverty, once viewed as a fated destiny for miserable masses, is now the main target of the Millennium Development Goals approved by a summit of heads of State.

The UN does not generate financial profit, nor does it charge for its work. A minimum token is paid for guided tours at UN Headquarters or postal services for letters mailed from there, yet it barely covers the cost of the staff involved. The Organization's budget comes from Member States and its special projects from extra-budgetary funds, including from particular Member States interested in specific programs. The UN is at its best when Member States agree on specific items and is handicapped when they disagree. At least the first seven secretaries-general tried to make an effort to promote consensus among the Member States, particularly permanent members of the Security Council with veto power. Whether navigating through the Cold War or mediating within the North-South divide, encouraging wider involvement of civil society, partnerships and grassroots, there was always an attempt to match what UN Member States want with what our ever-changing world politics demands. At a basic minimum, the UN provides a safety net when all diplomatic efforts fail to come to terms with a problem in a world of transition. It is where the international community, an all-inclusive community, agrees on basic principles that are then announced, recognized and pursued. When all diplomatic efforts fail elsewhere, the UN affords a wider framework for pursuing possible options for an agreement. It affirms international principles so that everyone will adhere to them and eventually implement them. Meanwhile, it offers a unique meeting place for officials, particularly those in conflict, and for international mediators to conveniently make contact, with or without asking for appointments.

Although the UN is not profit-making, it has to be cost-effective, making the best use of resources for each cause. The main debate about the UN is often focused on this: What do the Member States expect from the UN? Is it only an organization for conference services, arranging meetings simply to produce a calendar of events, or is it an instrument for the nations of the world to manage change and cope with emerging problems? No one questions the sovereignty of every member state duly guarded in the UN Charter. At the same time it is widely recognized that there are many issues and threats, such as terrorism, environmental erosion, natural disasters and drug trafficking, which can only be tackled through joint international action. The UN provides an unparalleled framework for addressing these and many other global challenges. If it is to be regarded merely as a meeting venue, countless hotels could provide the service instead.

The debate over the concept of the UN is not new. It comes up each time there is substantive change in the world, such as at the end of the Cold War, the North-South digital divide, Group of Seven, then Eight, then Twenty, changes of political systems, economic transitions, greater involvement of civil society and grassroots groups and technological advancement. The question of what kind of UN the world needs comes up almost every year during a General Debate.

Our world population has more than doubled in the last half century. It is estimated that by the year 2050, the population of the 50 poorest countries will more than double once again. Because resources like water, energy and fresh air are limited, the threat to human survival is increasingly apparent.

There is a widespread public misunderstanding about how the UN operates. Most people would probably be surprised to learn that the budget for the UN's core functions - the Secretariat operations in New York, Geneva, Nairobi, Vienna, the International Court of Justice and five Regional Commissions - is about four percent of New York City's annual budget and nearly a billion dollars less than the annual cost of Tokyo's fire department. The US, which provides the main share of the UN regular budget, contributes around $420 million a year, which is the equivalent of $1.42 per American. In comparison, Japan, the second largest contributor to the regular budget, pays $374 million a year, which is about $3.49 per citizen. UN peacekeeping has a special budget. The Organization spends less on peacekeeping worldwide than what the City of New York spends on the annual budget of its police department. Also the humanitarian and development programs under the UN banner have special budgets that rely on "voluntary funding" by member states.

The UN has no army of its own. Governments voluntarily supply troops and personnel to halt conflicts that threaten international peace and security and it is the Member States of the Security Council - not the Secretary-General - that decide where and when to deploy peacekeeping troops. Only about 20 per cent of the regular UN system's work is peacekeeping. The other 80 per cent is expected to help promote human development, prevent starvation, avert diseases, provide relief assistance, counter global crimes and assist countries devastated by war. About 60,000 people work in the entire UN system worldwide, which includes the Secretariat and 25 other organizations such as UNICEF and the World Bank. In comparison, McDonald's employs three times more people. And the UN has to respond not only to one need but to any relevant issue in the human condition.

The moment the Berlin Wall fell, I was at the Washington bureau of *The New York Times*. While washing my hands in the bathroom, its columnist Thomas Friedman, whom I was visiting, shouted across the door that history was being made, and he left for the office of Secretary of State James Baker. Back at UN Headquarters in New York, there was a feeling that some adaptation would have to be made. But no diplomat, head of state or senior official realized the extent.

When Germany was united, some officials dealt with it mainly as a deletion of one member, the Democratic Republic of Germany, and a change of the name of the Federal Republic to only one Germany. Even with the fall of the Soviet Union, a prevailing approach was to deal with issues as they arose. The first sign of adapting to change within the Secretariat was in dropping the policy of reserving specific posts for certain countries. A vaguely worded Assembly resolution had been interpreted to hand down specific posts, like Head of Library, Chief of Conference Services, and Director of External Relations, to succeeding Soviet citizens. While most of them made a serious effort, a minority took it so much for granted that in certain instances the occupants hardly bothered to make any pretense at work. One director was in the habit of drinking so carelessly that his bosses designated a loyal Czechoslovak to babysit him. Although the Czech's official task was to deal with non-governmental organizations, his main function was to keep the comrade company and carry him around when he was too drunk. Such embarrassing behavior did unfair damage to others sharing the same nationalities who truly did their best to represent their culture appropriately.

The new shift in internal postings encouraged regular staff to challenge the policy of predetermined national allocations. When a politically designated Soviet director at D-2 level (the highest regular staffing level) left, I insisted on applying for his post. When big power politics were invoked, I submitted my record for the judgment of Secretary-General Javier Perez de Cuellar, who firmly took my side. There was strong Soviet pressure on the then-Under Secretary-General for Administration, Martti Ahtisaari of Finland, who did not wish to unduly antagonize a veto-wielding neighbor when his name was being mentioned as a potential future Secretary-General. As head of the Public Information Department, Thérèse Paquet-Sévigny, a communications professional from Canada, proposed a formula placing me in the post of covering external relations while offering a Soviet a post as Director of Distribution. Then-head of personnel Kofi Annan swiftly implemented the promotion, calling me to pick up the documents right away to avert any further meddling. Ironically, while the Soviet diplomats were openly upset, the US mission was not pleased either; it had been seeking a promotion for someone else.

While the British. French, Soviets and Chinese seemed to have a planned approach to placing personnel in various appointments, the Americans did not have an active projection except when it came to certain "political" positions. They insisted on three senior posts - Under Secretary-General for Political Affairs; Administrator for UNDP, which they eventually gave away for someone they approved; and the Executive Director of UNICEF. During the Cold War, they also arranged to have a director in Political Affairs to watch the Soviet Under Secretary-General. It happened that every Secretary-General sought to have an American and a Soviet in his office until the fall of the Soviet Union to keep in direct touch and form a discrete back channel to Washington and Moscow. This system started with U Thant.

After the shock of Hammarskjold's death, the Organization was approaching turmoil. There was a war in Congo, the British and French had turned against the Secretary-General since he had blocked them in Suez, and the USSR was against him since he had opposed them in Hungary. While resisting the election of a new Secretary-General, the Soviets had proposed a Troika – a three-men team to run the place; they did not want one leading Secretary-General. U Thant's main preoccupation was to steady the waters and put the place in order. The newly elected Secretary-General in his wisdom recruited two assistants - one Russian and one American - who would keep in touch with their respective capitals. The Secretary-General was thus sheltered from *démarches* from their ambassadors' agitation. For a long time, there was a Soviet serving with U Thant, Peter Lessiovsky, an unassuming, clever man who seemed to have close contact with Moscow at all times. He was always around and responded to what Moscow wanted. The Americans likewise always had someone in the office of the Secretary-General who kept in touch with Washington. In some cases other Soviets and the Americans, besides those designated, tried to play that role and sometimes did. But they never replaced the two focal points, or channels of communication, which kept the Secretary-General well informed and the capitals aware of where the Secretary-General stood.

Particularly during the Cold War, there was the complication of having specific posts allotted to certain countries. In political affairs, a Soviet Under Secretary-General would be countered by an American heading a similar department. The irony was that the Soviet had an American director, and the American had a Soviet director, what in the eyes of cynical observers seemed like a jamboree of spies spying on spies. Amusingly, the same conflicting characters, after the fall of the Soviet Union, formed sort of an East-West partnership to exchange profitable business tips grounded in their past connections. Some of the most capable professional diplomats were allowed to survive. Those who knew the old system best, mostly "intelligence" people, stood to benefit most out of the eventual privatization, particularly in partnership with their former "capitalist" adversaries.

A visit to the former Soviet republics, which became known as Newly Independent States, revealed a lingering Soviet legacy, not only in the architecture and centralized control or the protocol of the diplomatic exchanges, but also in some communist leaders who refreshed themselves as reformed statesmen. For someone originating from the Middle East, their names as members of the Soviet Central Committee Politburo sounded too familiar. At least three former KGB chiefs took over as the "democratic" face of new countries. It may be because they had been the most informed about the outside world and knew their way through appearing to be attuned to updated demands. Since part of my job was to introduce heads of states when they came for a press conference, we normally needed a biographical note from their permanent mission to use in formulating some background words for their introduction to the press. In one case I received only one line, giving me the President's place of birth and the date on which he took office after "a free and fair election." Unsuspecting, I kept calling the permanent mission to ask for more information that was never forthcoming until it was whispered in my ear that their president had most of his life been a KGB chief. Even some of those who were once tough talking, never smiling "apparatchiks" who represented their countries in the Secretariat, returned all smiles and with a willingness to cooperate. The most militant leftists were reincarnated as pro-democratic free market advocates with all the politically correct rhetoric that impressed the right-wing conservatives in Europe and suddenly stood to the right of US Senator Jesse Helms. Media reports described a G-8 Ministers of Finance meeting in Germany at a lakeside luxury resort featuring American-style clapboard villas, rose-petal baths and tai-chi classes. Their unusual host: a long time agent of the former East Germany's feared secret police, the Stasi. Apparently, unlike generals, agents do not fade away - they just cross the street.

The allocation of posts to America and the Soviet Union during the Cold War was compounded by posts maintained by other permanent members of the Security Council. Although their high-level postings were visible, their allocated presence spread throughout all areas of interest. That meant that there would be no secret mission or confidential memo. Any meeting, comprised of three, would not be limited to the participants. Open information about closed meetings did not end with the conclusion of the Cold War but continued, though in a different formula often through press leaks. In one case an Under Secretary-General for Political Affairs after briefing the Council gently but firmly rebuked its members for leaking deliberations to their respective media. By the time he got to his office, he had a phone call from a correspondent of a press agency protesting his attitude. The problem was not that of spreading unwanted news, but in limiting the movement by any official performing a discreet function. That is why every Secretary-General had a few people whom he could trust with political tasks, regardless of who ran the political or peacekeeping department.

Increasingly, the numbers of senior officials appointed from various countries to be part of peacekeeping or political operations bore inevitable links with their governments, as many were diplomats on loan, hoping at least to return to their home base. Their attempts to influence decisions would be matched only by the flow of information they provided to their respective governments.

Initially, most Americans who joined the UN on their own steam were Democrats. Among the very few Americans I met in 33 years of service who were Republicans was Ambassador Joseph Verner Reed, an elegant aristocrat from Connecticut. He was assigned to the US permanent mission to the United Nations under President Ronald Reagan and then became Under Secretary-General for Assembly Affairs. Later he served in the White House as Protocol Chief under President George H.W. Bush but continued to support the UN in various capacities, pro bono. He was one of the most effective and capable pro-UN people in the US, volunteering his high-level services for so long that he became the Dean of the UN Special Envoys.

After decades of adhering to established rules and regulations, the UN's personnel department tended, in the late 1990s, to accommodate member states more readily, especially finding jobs for recommended diplomats at missions abroad.

The staff is the backbone of the UN with the Secretary-General as its personal leader. They need him, but also he needs them. For a revived UN, there is a need to adhere to the original rules of a highly credible international civil service; further, the Organization must, avoid excessively expedient appointments. Our young colleagues - males and females – should be prepared and encouraged to loyally grow within the system and evolve intellectually, while being constantly refreshed with selected new careers and creative new ideas. The more complicated issues may have simple answers. Good people usually produce good results. Good staff produce good leaders, good delegations would produce a good UN. And if the UN house is in order, it would be better equipped to help the world.

And the world indeed meets here, at the United Nations in Manhattan, New York. Yet it was not only Manhattan, not merely New York, but a whole wide world spinning before us. Some staff felt that the best period to concentrate on urgent business was between the closing hour of 6 pm and dinnertime. Holidays were merely opportunities to work without interruption. High season usually started around the third weekend of September with the opening of the general debate of a new General Assembly session. Particularly on special anniversaries, Heads of State took the opportunity to make policy statements and hold discreet meetings. For over a week, that international glass house on the East River turned into a vivid theatre of political operations. If each one of the visiting dignitaries extended at least one obligatory invitation to lunch or dinner, you could actually leave home without your credit card. A British delegate, Lord Caradon, was widely admired for going through an average of three dinners an evening with a stiff upper lip.

When Everyone Lost

War in the third millennium reflected a new world disorder where there was no definite victory or recognizable defeat. New businesses evolved, like security companies and military contractors on one side and subsidized militant zealots on the other. With fewer global wars yet more local conflicts, the lines between big power interests, regional power subcontractors and proxies became increasingly blurred. The widespread pain of so many innocent people exceeded any gain. In effect, everyone lost.

Since the UN establishment following World War II, the concept of a neutral mediator to help settle conflicts evolved in varied formats. A truly honest broker like former UN Secretary-General Dag Hammarskjold managed to mediate, for example, between the U.S. and China on the release of a captive pilot when both countries did not recognize each other. U Thant's unheralded role in defusing the U.S. crisis over Cuba with discreet, reciprocal steps helped avert a nuclear war. Javier Perez de Cuellar arranged for a ceasefire between Iraq and Iran and peace agreements for El Salvador and Nicaragua, in addition to helping to release Western hostages kidnapped during a tense conflict in Lebanon. Replacement of peacemakers and peacekeepers around the globe reflected credible confidence in a consensual UN role. The thrust of that effort was handled directly by the Secretary-General with a designated envoy as required. As need expanded, this was gradually extended through overuse and politically expedient appointments. However, the value of that role remains valid as dedicated staff do their best despite seeing that the credit for their own efforts was claimed elsewhere.

A weakened UN leadership with eroding credibility allowed for an emergence of some member states subcontracting conflict in their region in the hope of making political gain, advancing their national interests, or simply attracting attention to their new or renewed status.

Smaller countries acting on behalf of large ones was not new. Particularly during the Cold War, a number of proxies were promoted to play that role. In certain cases, some exchanged loyalties to balance their neighbors. When Ethiopia was traditionally pro-American, Somalia was pro-Soviet, but when General Mengistu turned Addis Ababa towards Moscow, President Syad Barre in Mogadishu turned to Washington. In time, both superpowers had to deal with growing egos of their protégés, especially those who they arranged or allowed to serve for prolonged years. Both shared the problem when a proxy would suddenly seek to become a partner. He would then be left to his own devices when facing popular outrage and international condemnation.

For example, the Shah of Iran, who was returned to power in a coup commanded – according to his wife's biography, by a police chief from New Jersey – and was hailed by US President Jimmy Carter as a bastion of democracy, did not face trouble merely because of a lavish imperial ceremony in Persepolis but when he presumed he could be the predominant authority in the oil-rich "Gulf", particularly if he strengthened his claim with an acquisition of atomic weapons. His wings needed some clipping, with unintended consequences. Philippines President Ferdinand Marcos was similarly promoted for years on the far Asian front. When he exceeded his red lines by personally killing his potential replacement Benigno Aquino, the most he was offered while facing overwhelming protests was an airlift to Hawaii. His loyal wife Imelda moved separately to New York and took three apartments in the building where I lived, one for her, one for lady friends and a third for security aides. She used to go to the nearby Holy Family Church, kneeling her way from entrance to altar and gave hospitable dinners where her favorite song was "*Because of You*" in Tagalog. When I heard it said one evening that her human rights had been denied I wondered in what way and was told, "the right to say goodbye to friends." On the French side, General Biddell Boukasa brutally ran the Central African Republic for decades until he decided to crown himself Emperor of the region and thought he could influence the outcome of the presidential elections in "Mother" France. Press reports started circulating that he kept human body parts in his refrigerator and widespread opposition to his exceedingly erratic behavior ensued. He must have been stunned to find out that it only took a telephone call to get rid of him. Another African leader, Joseph Mobutu, who as an army colonel led a decisive coup during the Congo crisis in the 1960s, promoted himself to Marshall, prolonged his name to Sese Seko, etc., and ran the country like a personal household for decades with external support; such was nurtured particularly as he hosted one of the most influential annual gatherings, a "safari club" of intelligence and security chiefs of most key countries.

When he too eventually crossed certain red lines, particularly relating to mineral resources, and was no more needed with the end of the Cold War, he was overthrown by public rebellion and allowed to take residence in the French Cote d'Azur where one early evening, in a clear signal, his chauffer received a speeding ticket while hurrying back with a pint of ice cream!

The USSR dealt with similar issues, whether in Southern Yemen or Eastern Europe, through "redeployment" of comrades who made public apologies and admissions of personal shortcomings as once-uncontested leaders disappeared into the sunset. In Afghanistan, with a change of positions in Moscow itself, Soviet-appointed President Najibullah could not find refuge, however futile, from advancing Northern Alliance troops, except at the office of the UN Representative, who by the way left for New York.

The use of good offices by certain governments to avert potential military confrontations in their regions was not new either, though increasingly rare. For example, the state of Oman, strategically yet vulnerably positioned around the Strait of Hormuz, the world's riskiest narrow passage on the inflammable oil-rich Gulf, acted for decades as an effective back channel between the US and Iran. Its quiet ruler, Sultan Qabous, and its experienced Foreign Minister Youssef bin Alawi, moved swiftly and discretely at the earliest hint of possible confrontation, often visiting key capitals during official holidays not to attract media attention.

Yet new subcontracting States in the third millennium seem to operate with a free hand almost uncontrollably subsidizing, recruiting and hosting a risky mix of characters blending UN official venues with unmandated action by a "coalition of the willing," without serious responsibility to protect innocent civilians. Colonel Muammar Gaddafi's initial role to sub-contract the conflict in Darfur was cut off by regime change. A wider and more sustained partnership developed between the Governments of Qatar and Turkey in diverting the so-called Arab Spring. However, they could not deliver on time in Syria, for example, let alone Libya. Some of its designated officials overplayed their management capacity by offering a free hand to known armed groups who once on the ground became involved in uncontrollable actions to terrorize innocent civilians. It was not only the resulting militant anarchy fractioning Libya, where, for example, a US Ambassador was assassinated. There was an overall regional atmosphere of open kidnappings, bloody murders and assaulting minorities who were an integral part of these countries' mosaic throughout history.

Small Actors' Influence

Civil conflicts are further complicated when not only government officials but local groups assume that big powers were closely interested in their every move. During an attempt in Beirut to open a crossing near the museum to allow people to move between the east and west sectors during the civil war, a head of an armed gang expressed readiness to consider it if he was contacted personally by US Presidents Reagan and USSR General Secretary Brezhnev. A senior member of the Lebanese government, who thought that his fame as pro-American had overwhelmed even the White House, asked to meet President Reagan while on a visit to the American capital. He took the encounter for granted. The impression he spread among local politicians was that "Washington was in the palm of his hands." If the US Secretary of State was not at the airport to welcome him to his "second home" he presumed it was mainly because of pressing diplomatic meetings at Foggy Bottom. After the frustrating delay to his quite persistent demand, he was given a brief appointment, known in protocol as a handshake or photo op. President Reagan initially pretended to listen attentively as his visitor elaborated on his strategic display of international relations with hints about his own primary role. When the President started reaching for his favorite jelly beans, the visitor sensed that time was closing in and paused for impact. President Reagan then looked at him with a congenial smile and said, "You know, while you were talking, I was wondering who you looked like. Actually you remind me of my old friend and fellow actor who came from Lebanon, Danny Thomas." Small actors may typically have little actual influence, but that often depends on the actual interest and leadership conveyed by larger actors.

Fragmentation of the Middle East

Fragmentation of the Middle East into religious and ethnic entities along the lines of the "Millet" system of the Ottoman Empire has been under discussion in certain academic circles for decades, at least since the early 1970s. A substantive seminar at Princeton University under Professor Bernard Lewis devoted special focus on that approach. Its political interpretation may have been initially experimented with in

Lebanon, which had been highlighted at the time by France's President Charles de Gaulle as a hopeful example for a harmonious mosaic, with varied religious and ethnic groups living together in productive peace. The divisive "Balkanization" trend then manifested in the breakdown of Yugoslavia, a prelude to the de facto-split between Iraq, Syria and Lybia. Sharpening of religious and ethnic tensions was facilitated by the failure of many secular governments to maintain the human dignity of their citizens. Successive coups exploiting Arab nationalist slogans imposed emergency measures on freedom in the pretext of mobilizing all energies to "liberate the Palestinians." The disappointing outcome was losing both human values and more Palestinian land. The Ottomanization angle was strengthened with the rise in leadership of Turkey's Prime Minister Recep Tayyip Erdogan, whose rhetoric invoked the role of famous Sultans referring to the victory over Byzantium almost 1,000 years old, yet with apparently still some particular meaning in that particularly sensitive area. Hosting, training and accommodating subsidized foreign fighters involved in the beginning of the Syria/Iraq conflicts financed by a number of officials and oil-rich countries provoked historic sensitivities.

Erdogan's selection of the area around Antikya (Antioch) was indicative. Less than 90 years ago, it was part of Syria until it was handed over to Turkey after the end of the First World War in a deal by the mediating powers, Britain and France, under the secret Sykes-Picot agreement. Antioch is a symbol revered by all Eastern Christians as a site of the first mass of Saints Peter and Paul. Every Patriarch of all denominations carries its name until today in their official titles. Sheltering and parading foreign Islamic gunmen with militaristic agendas with open acts of kidnappings and beheadings raised not only serious political but also social, cultural and ethnic issues. While it may have strengthened then-Prime Minister Erdogan's Islamic credentials, it sent an alarming signal against the Eastern Christians that they were a target. Regrettably, it unduly raised fragmentation among people who lived together in a mosaic society for centuries. Meddling by certain Gulf officials was perceived by some to reflect a schism between geography and geology. Urban societies in Mesopotamia, the Fertile Crescent, the Nile Delta and even the Yemen plateau have always been by necessity and nature inclusive, as they had to accommodate one another in approaching daily life. The oil-enriched mostly desert Gulf area has mainly been of singular composition despite the influx of foreign workers. The perception of internal survival would naturally be quite different. It was a sensitive yet unspoken difference between those who survived in institutional fertile societies since the dawn of history and these emerging younger, smaller, geologically empowered forces seeking to make their own version of history as they embarked on reshaping the region.

For about two years, from 2012 to 2014, a growing role of the Islamic State was reported without any serious concern except for a query about its last letter in English, whether it was in the "Levant, Syria, Damascus or Sham." Its destructive efforts seemed to fit loosely within an informally desired pattern to decimate regular armed forces and fragment the nationalities of middle class societies.

An alliance of former officers of the unwisely disbanded veteran Iraqi army and Jihadis seemed to form part of a practical framework of dividing Iraq into three main federal entities: one prompted by former Prime Minister Maliki's obsession with his own Shiite power in Baghdad, thus antagonizing the Sunni population into yearning to restore their ruling power even in their own separate space; and the Kurdish-run Government in Erbil with business and strategic focal points for personnel from varied allies. A trilateral set-up in Iraq, however volatile, yet controllable in the long run, was described by some media in the region as not be too different in practice from a proposal in 2006 by certain interested individuals with influence in key capitals.

A basic loophole in distantly perceived Big Power political plans – or lack of plans – was in unintended consequences. Instead of leading to a planned federation, "creative ambiguity" on the ground would result in a fragmented country where armed bickering may flare not only amongst varied sects but within each group in addition to contested claims on others. A "known unknown" to quote the US Secretary of Defense who led the invasion of Iraq, was the impact of unleashed forces which have no regimented discipline on raising the extent of chaos to levels that threatened national, regional and international security. Would it then be too late, or too cautious, for the "community of nations" to intervene effectively? Echoes from Libya and Iraq, let alone other "Arab Spring" countries would raise a more basic question: who used whom and, more regrettably, at what human expense.

A perception within the regional media that the United States was not initially seriously concerned about a role by the Islamic State may have been created because the governments providing operational support for it were US allies like Turkey and Qatar who host US military bases. The argument was that those who initially financed, helped train, advised or ISIS and Da'ish in Arabic should be well-known to interested governments which are capable of tracing not only movements of funds but transfers of equipment across or even within borders. Individuals from certain oil-rich countries could be publically identified. Even those living in Europe working with internationally known banks could not evade a tight, monitoring process particularly after the governmental oversight the US established after the catastrophic tragedy of 9/11.

When members of the Saudi ruling family became more visible targets for the Islamic State, active in neighboring Iraq and Syria, alarm bells started ringing in Riyadh for an urgent response. Questions had been raised on who would benefit from the escalating rhetoric and who was sorry now for encouraging it earlier. In a culture dominated by coded messages that would require an insider decoding, including through Twitter, who was sending what to whom? And how?

Many enthusiastic recruits were driven by wide media coverage of individuals involved in gruesome murderous acts giving them worldwide name recognition. A photo of ISIS "Emir" Abu Bakr al-Baghdadi presiding at a mosque signalled a leadership address to potential recruits as far away as Australia. It is no secret by now that a number of governments – or secret services – outside the Middle East had at least facilitated the travel of troubled armed security risks to fields of conflict in the hope of keeping them preoccupied elsewhere, only to have to deal with their return to their capitals with more troubling field experience.

While it is recognized that to everything there is a season, a time for war and a time for peace, it is also entailed that there would be someone to sort them out somewhere; a place to wage war and hopefully a place to arrange for peace.

As existential threats engulfed an already volatile region, there was very little effort to clarify coherently or consistently explain precise U.S. positions, at least to people in the area directly targeted. These glaring vacuums raised local interpretations with many drawing on conspiracy theories mostly unfavorable even among traditionally pro-U.S. groups.

The ability of the United States to effectively obtain active human feedback on the region suffered not only from problems with its agencies in Washington, D.C. that were confronted with political investigations, but also from three main events in the region itself: one was the bombing of the American Embassy in West Beirut in 1983, where a number of top experienced and well-informed field operatives were meeting, Another was the evacuation from Lebanon of the PLO's leadership, which made a special effort to open communications and valuable information channels to US authorities as well as other big power military and security officials to gain backchannel contact. The third was the bombing of the Pan Am Flight 103 over Scotland, where again a number of senior US officials were reportedly travelling. The point is that those who prepared these attacks must have known their targets precisely.

For some civilian victims in the troubled region, especially among minorities, the emergence of a growing military group like Da'ish solidly funded and efficiently organized, could not have expanded in a strategically valued area without the tacit approval of a closely monitoring big power and/or some regional allies who were reported to be subsidizing that group at least for a while. The Patriarch of Christian Chaldians, one of the most ancient sects in the world, Patriarch Rafael Sacco, openly accused "Western countries" of betraying Eastern Christians. A meeting of the Eastern Patriarchs, both Catholics and Orthodox, in Washington, DC. during September 2014 mainly aimed at drawing attention not only to the plight of Eastern Christians but also to what was maintained as lack of action or even attention. The references by the regional media to a possible US role prompted a former ambassador of Iraq to the UN and Washington to write a column in the London-based daily Al Hayat dismantling that claim yet in a way drawing more attention to it. It reached a point where the US embassy in Beirut issued a denial - a very unwise step as it led addicted conspiracy theorists to view it as a confirmation!

It was only when Da'ish over stretched its authority to the strategic Kurdish area, threatening vital interests that a clear and present danger became obvious. When an uncontrollable, confused policy started to backfire in echoes reminiscent of Benghazi, certain officials started pondering vaguely worded calls for corrective action.

A serious handicap for the US is the almost-dysfunctional foreign policy Establishment which started paying more attention to fund-raising than offering credible, experienced, informed advice. Traditionally, whoever was president, a natural combination of experienced former officials, academic intellectuals, informed communicators, members of "think tanks" interested congressmen and other civil society volunteers maintained an enlightened impact through intra-partisan dialogue on foreign policy issues. President George H.W. Bush, who presided during the fall of the Berlin Wall and the breakdown of the Soviet Union, was perhaps the last President to benefit from such valuable national assets. During the following Administration, particularly in the period between the catastrophic massacres of Srebrenica and Rwanda of 1994 and the unilateral invasion of Iraq in 2003, the role of that Establishment was overtaken by a mushrooming of presumed experts presenting partial views with misleading lack of practical knowledge. Regrettably the main preoccupation of several councils and foundations which were once-prestigious and, when necessary, outspoken, turned into mainly seeking funds even when a conflict of interest was clearly evident. An enterprising breed of experts emerged who measured their success not by the accuracy of their predictions but by the money they arranged or made. One such expert who was introduced at a seminar in the American University of Beirut as having influence on decision-makers in Washington at the time, puzzled his audience by boasting that he had bought his first luxury car from giving opinion on Iran and the second one on Iraq.

CHAPTER IX:

"IN CAMERA" OR FOR CAMERA

Any meeting of world leaders would not be complete without an exasperated remark about the increasing role of the media. Any diplomat will readily comment about the "CNN factor" in world affairs, while some United Nations officials diligently refer to a quip by a former Secretary-General that television has become the 16th member of the Security Council. Yet, while inspiring awe, admiration or disdain, journalists are left to their own devices. They have to find their own way as they rush in where diplomats fear to tread.

A common impression that professional writing is easy could easily be dispelled by anyone attempting it. The French author and philosopher, Voltaire, once apologized to a friend: "I regret the length of this letter. I did not have time to write a shorter one." Seen after completion only, media work is a creative outcome of professional talent and very, very hard work. Those in particular handling foreign affairs know that it can be risky indeed. In addition to physical danger, it draws passionate responses from any of the obsessively determined parties in any of the average 70 conflicts around the globe - let alone politicians at home and government officials abroad. Almost every prominent media star or pundit has had to pay his or her dues at every step on the way to the top. Once there, in a swiftly changing and competitive business, an Alice in Wonderland rule will apply: you have to run as far as you can to stay where you are.

Journalism, if that is still its name, is the most open profession. Anyone can participate; everyone can judge. Visible and vulnerable, an error is seen by millions; effective daily reporting is expected with a nod and a switch. A field assignment is the firing line through which a reporter is professionally tested. Most of those who passed it successfully earned their places as television anchors or press columnists. When a speaker introduced Thomas Friedman in a briefing about his second bestseller "The Lexus, and the Olive Branch", she described him as having the happiest job - he wrote what he thought, had it published twice a week in a most influential paper and got paid for it. While the leading foreign affairs columnist of *The New York Times* pleasantly went along, I recalled an afternoon in Beirut, when the impact of an explosion threw me to the floor, interrupting a call from New York. It occurred at Mr. Friedman's *Times* office nearby, one of the many risks he confronted with courage and a sense of humor as an active reporter in strange territory and an entirely different culture during a cut-throat period.

Similarly, I observed Dan Rather take an obvious risk while reporting to CBS on series of wars from Bosnia to Somalia, Peter Jennings negotiate in Tehran the unpredictable cross-currents of Iranian politics during the hostage crisis, Robert Fisk of London's *Independent* boldly checking his facts in the midst of heavy bombardment, Lauren Jenkins of the Washington *Post* and National Public Radio defying armed cordons among the 1982 siege of Beirut, and the BBC's John Simpson move in wherever angels feared to tread. There were always those who preferred the safety of their hotel bar, awaiting the informative return of their colleagues. But they remain on the waiting list of journalistic achievement.

During conflicts, there are media divas who drop in for a couple of days and there are those who regularly cover the terrain – they make a lasting difference. At times of war – during rocket exchanges, booby-trapped cars, air raids, kidnappings, sheer ruthless violence and armed confusion – you discover the difference between a real reporter, a mere informer and an amateur scout. In Beirut, Thomas Friedman never hid his faith and never lost his professional integrity. He moved amongst key players and simple folks alike with the same enlightened courage and basic confidence. Most importantly, he explored the forces behind the events and interpreted the most complex issues with the simplest everyday terms. Obviously, he has strong, firm views. One would agree or disagree. But he is always open for a tough argument, most likely with a cheerful outcome.

Robert Fisk was another ace reporter. His book "Pity the Nation", like Friedman's "From Beirut to Jerusalem", is a landmark reference on the conflict. Other outstanding reporters included Doyle McMeanus of the *Los Angeles Times*, Lauren Jenkins of the *Washington Post*, Tim Llewelyn of the BBC, and Julien Nundy of *Newsweek*. News agencies like Reuters, *Agence France Presse*, the Associated Press maintained their excellence during a most difficult period.

Perception of news value is comparative, often a precarious balance between tragedy and entertainment. News is also in the eye of the beholder; the problem is that what is published or broadcast passes through many beholders. It is not only what is fit to print but who actually thinks so. During the 1982 Israeli invasion of Lebanon, one journalist, Lally Weymouth of the *Washington Post*, visited the encircled area of west Beirut. With no water, electricity or food, most civilians were scrounging for whatever they could get between raids, artillery exchanges and naval shelling. She seemed deeply moved and, like all of us, passed through successive scary moments worth writing home about. As she prepared to leave after the third day, she mused over whether her story would ever get printed. When I thought it odd that such a story could not get through despite her excellent family media connections, she responded that it was mainly because her copy would arrive on the same day as the National Football League's Super Bowl. That same day, incidentally, bombs were falling so close that even the journalists had to rush to the Commodore Hotel's makeshift shelter, a former discotheque. ABC's Peter Jennings hesitated, preferring to work from his room on the Hotel's seventh floor. Minutes after we persuaded him to join the group, his room received a direct hit. Not only did Thomas Friedman cover the daily events effectively, but he also managed to file a complaint to his editor about lifting the word "indiscriminate" from his report on the shelling.

Aspiring journalists love taking notes; cautious diplomats avoid them. As the job title indicates, a reporter reports, clarifies or sheds light on a question. As the title diplomat implies, he or she wavers, covers his or her flanks or advances a favorite position. A journalist risks life and limb to cover a conflict; a diplomat takes the same risk to cover it up.

Journalists overestimate a diplomat's authority in making

decisions, while diplomats overestimate a journalist's determination to make trouble. Their work is so interlinked that although sometimes it is impossible to live with each other they have to work together. As a modus operandi is reached beyond a level of tolerance, some become the best of friends.

It took years to convince reluctant civil servants - the national and international elite - that surfing the web was quicker, cheaper and possibly less public than floating papers between offices and departments. Journalists were neither expected to go beyond the fourth floor of the 38th floor Secretariat building nor to cross into the General Assembly hall or Delegates' Lounge, although many of them did. Cameras were not allowed beyond a certain point within the Secretariat building. There were also security considerations. Eventually in 1997, negotiations with the UN Correspondents Association, headed by Raghida Dergham and Ian Williams, gave journalists and cameras more freedom of movement. That was the first year Kofi Annan took over, and we worked closely to persuade our colleagues that the media was not an enemy but a potential ally. By that time, CNN had designated a resident correspondent who was given the most favorable courtesy, by which he and eventually his boss valuably reciprocated.

Military officers are clearly more cautious, even suspicious, of journalists. Peacekeeping operations in particular were a challenge even to their professional spokesperson. Again, a natural inclination of the commanding officer is not to provide any information, lest it be used by the enemy. UN operations are different, at least in the sense that there should be no enemy. That was a serious conceptual question, especially for new peacekeeping officers. Once, while UNIFIL was being established in South Lebanon, a colonel commanding his country's troops referred in an internal briefing to *notre adversaire*. Brian Urquhart, then the chief political peacekeeper who was present, interrupted to indicate that, while we do have challenges and challengers, we do not have adversaries. While the politically minded functionaries were inclined to give more information, the military professional strove to prevent any information from being advanced, citing the safety of troops. In our situation, commanders refused to announce even the number of soldiers that arrived at Beirut airport en route southward. That would have made good sense if the airstrip had not been open, like the palm of a hand, to anyone on any hill overlooking Beirut. The assembling group could have been easily counted by any number of curious binocular-holders. Fortunately, UNIFIL Commanding Officers

"In Camera" Or For Camera?

General Erskine of Ghana and General Callaghan of Ireland, were skillfully open to press needs, each in their own way. Despite the inevitable frustrations of a rough neighborhood, they paid special attention to building a credible press office, eventually headed by Timor Goksel, who came from an information office in Ankara to become an integral part of the terrain for two decades.

One helpful supporter at that time in opening up to the media was General Siilasvuo, Coordinator of Operations in the Middle East. Based in Jerusalem, the cool Finnish officer was aware of the various political undercurrents. Having heard conflicting arguments during one of his early visits to Beirut, he told me to go ahead and deal with the press in any open way possible. His reasoning was different than mine. Resolution 425, which had just been adopted by the Security Council in March 1978, was not likely to be implemented immediately. He thought it might take some time, indeed a very long time;and that our best option was to be visible. The more we showed through the press that we were trying to help, the less blameworthy we would be, and a more peaceful atmosphere would prevail in our area of operations. If we made their jobs easier, they would make our task less difficult.

The problem was rarely at the top echelons, but in the entrenched clusters of bureaucratic officialdom. All Secretaries-General recognized the value of a friendly press and courted particular journalists, although some were more sensitive to negative reporting than others. Kofi Annan, who practically grew up in the building, personally knew most of the key media residents and was keen to open wider doors for them. His natural inclination to be open, patient and attentive gained him additional points as the role of the media widened and its outlets multiplied. A private public relations firm may claim some credit, but the inherent key to good press during Kofi Annan's first term was his personal attitude. He understood that, as the UN was at risk of creeping into obscure irrelevance, the only option was to open the gates - open to the media, open to key personalities, open the world organization to the world public. Yet that exposure would have to be institutional, not individual – otherwise, the Secretary-General would become inflated while the United Nations became deflated. Action by other senior officials should mesh with the same open rhythm.

Nowhere is the closed approach to the media more visible than in the way the Security Council operates. Current resident journalists are by now used to it, but the manner in which they are kept at bay - with their own consent – is striking to a now distant yet sympathetic observer. If political expediency dictates close "in your face" consultations, rare recent experience shows that open meetings could be more helpful to Council members and more useful to journalists.

For decades, yet in vain, the composition of the Security Council has been under review. That is a matter linked to the Charter. But nowhere does it indicate that the Council's business should be conducted *"in camera"* - that is, excluding the cameras. As the Council pronounces itself on various aspects of reform, it might look into its own proceedings, including the need to consider more open meetings.

Closed meetings are an obsolete relic of the 1970-1980s. During the last stages of the Cold War, the Soviet Union and the United States initially agreed that open controversies might not help a warming detente and agreed to have "adequate consultations" before arriving at a resolution. Within the secretariat at the time, a senior Soviet diplomat headed the Department in charge of the Security Council, while an American headed Political and General Assembly Affairs. When the exclusive "club of two" agreed, the rest went along; when they clashed, the others paid the price. When the other 13 Council members protested, they were occasionally brought into the consultations. Obviously, this club of two kept in direct touch through other channels. Mainly to keep their proxies in line with fewer open meetings and more "closed" consultations, a separate conference room was built adjacent to the Council with phones, lounge chairs and side entrances. As is usual in such cases, a conceptual theory was advanced. It was more productive to have a consensus resolution that everyone agreed should be implemented than a controversial one with a majority vote when those opposed may not cooperate. That concept may have helped in specific cases at the time. But an indiscriminate search for consensus would normally result in a substantively watered down resolution, holding the majority hostage to the interests of a minority. Furthermore, while it is preferable to obtain a consensus, a Security Council resolution, whatever the majority, is binding on all its members. That's what the Charter states. It also indicates that the "peoples of the United Nations" should be mobilized to support its objectives. How could that be done if they had no idea what was going on in the crucial area of their own peace and security?

In the UN's early days, most meetings were open. All meeting rooms had press seats with a special arm for a note pad. Outstanding journalists covered accomplished diplomats. And the world paid attention. New Yorkers, too, were able to identify faces and attitudes, giving them a feeling of relevance to those characters discussing world problems on the East River. The open debate of the Cuban missile crisis when Adlai Stevenson was waiting "until hell freezes over" for a response was widely followed; the icy silence by the Soviet delegate and witty understatements of the British were noted. Some American journalists even got a chance to meet closely with US Ambassador Henry Cabot Lodge, although it was famously said at the time that the Cabots spoke only to the Lodges, and the Lodges spoke only to God.

After all, the UN is a convenient place for unscheduled meetings, quiet diplomacy and international networking. At any given moment, a perceptive observer can judge the position of any country or any issue through an analysis of its action at the UN. A simple boycott by the Soviet delegation of an open Security Council meeting gave journalists the chance to report a historical decision to send UN, mainly US, troops to Korea. The sight of Soviet leader Khrushchev banging his shoe on his delegation's table, and even the utter silence of the be-daggered royal Yemeni delegate dressed in national costume, provided colorful coverage.

In the early 1960s ABC television was actively represented by John Scali, who later returned briefly to the UN as US Permanent Representative. It was while following the deliberation over the Cuban crisis that he coincidentally played a discreet role of mediation between the US and the Soviet Union. It is a tribute to his modesty that, while even those who hardly played any role claimed credit, Scali did not blow his own horn. Abe Rosenthal represented *The New York Times*, later becoming its managing editor. The *Daily News* and *New York Post* had permanent, UN-based correspondents. When Council meetings were open, consultations were quietly held at the Delegates' Lounge, the dining room; or in private residences; or at an agreed number of nearby restaurants that became almost an annex to the UN. The three western permanent delegates --US, France and UK -- usually held their own private meeting; sometimes, they invited the Soviet or the Chinese envoys, or both, depending on the stage of agreement. That interplay was detectable to a trained eye. A luncheon every month hosted by the president of the Security Council became a tradition. At first, it was for members only; later on, other guests and supporting secretariat staff were added. Diplomats were energized by the presence of journalists covering their meetings. Journalists were stimulated by the quality performance of the diplomats.

When meetings became mainly closed, and there was very little else to report, most American media organizations pulled out their regular correspondents.

A Security Council meeting at the level of heads of state in January 1992, which marked the end of the Cold War, stimulated renewed interest. Correspondents of mainstream media who were given wider access gave wider coverage. However, the Security Council maintained its practice of holding most of its real meetings *in camera*, leading mostly to coverage by rumor, spin or squawk box. With a new world, open societies and the communications revolution, Security Council members may find a new refreshing life in an open, transparent process. The sight of some of them leaking a story or beating one another to the exit microphone is as ungracious as the sight of hurried journalists straining to hear the last sentence of a self-serving "response to a question."

No secrets can be kept for too long in a multinational glass house. Anyone with real interest in the decisions of the Security Council need only hang around long enough on the second floor to meet a delegate out for a leak – even literally, as the men's room is located around the corner. That is how I found out one evening in December 1991 that we just elected a new Secretary-General. Without even asking, I was approached in the bathroom by an enterprising delegate while the Council was still in session, who thereby "leaked" to me the following: "We have just voted. It's Boutros."

There was a British saying that inside every diplomat there is a journalist trying to get out, and inside every journalist there is a diplomat trying to get in. The more the diplomat and the journalist operate in a gray area, the more the temptation to cross from one profession to another. Therein lies the difference between those who have a command of their profession and thus do it well and others who do not seem to know whether they are getting in or going out. A clearer partnership would help. Today there is a remarkable number of delegates and an equally professional number of journalists. All that is needed, for the UN's sake, is to plug in the public switch.[2]

---

[2] The UN staff, too, can help check the press. The sight of UN correspondents sitting in formal attire at annual dinners, celebrating and awarding each other in the most expensive New York venues, is sharply contrasted by UN figures indicating that more than 60 million displaced refugees are in dire need of urgent help.

"In Camera" Or For Camera?

Secretary-General U Thant used to say: "When a big power enters into conflict with a small power, the small power is likely to disappear; when a small power fights with another small power, the conflict eventually disappears; when a big power fights with another big power, the Security Council disappears." Increasingly, the media in its wider convergence is growing into a world superpower - maybe worthy of a permanent seat in the Security Council. It may be about time to send an invitation.

Going Hollywood

Involving artists, athletes, movie stars and public faces is a valuable initiative which has always been part of the thinking in the UN system, provided it does not overwhelm the basic cause or undercut the real work involved. It should focus on the issues, not individuals.

Anyone dealing with the public realizes that movie stars, football players, actors, artists and singers are more popular and have a more popular following than politicians. People trust them. The concept has not been overlooked in the past, but it had always been very carefully handled in a much more selective manner. For example, UN Day was normally an occasion for linking the arts with the UN. Dag Hammarskjold was the first to initiate that, as he invited an philharmonic orchestra and elaborated about Beethoven's Ninth symphony, which was played. We vividly re-launched the concept when Mr. Annan became Secretary-General, as he was very open to these popular pursuits. I initiated "Voices for Survival", where a limited number of creative artists like Luciano Pavarotti and others participated in different UN events. The idea was to have it very selective and focused, with limited invitees who were role models in their fields and embraced specific UN causes. Eventually, though, it became an open arena.

Originally, the purpose was to enlist those with a proven record and popular following to highlight a specific issue, while occasionally raising funds for it. The criteria were clear; the selection was limited to eight individuals. Then it got out of hand. Some UN officials were thrilled by the prospects of star-gazing, and movie stars designated as envoys needed to get down to Earth. One day an aide to Secretary-

General Annan sent me someone "highly recommended" to focus on Hollywood. I was expected to provide a senior officer post (P-5 in official jargon) for that "reform oriented" task. I explained that we have always had a good link with the motion picture industry, but that a framework had to be drawn on what sort of image the UN sought to project through Los Angeles and beyond. There were also specific limitations on the extent to which the international organization should be used to launder the reputation of certain actors specializing in projecting on film sexual violence, marital conflicts and drug traffic.

Within five years, the number of "envoys" rose from eight to hundreds. Anyone with some influence not only within the Secretariat but in any of the UN programs, funds and agencies would pick a favorite and issue a press release. The Secretary-General was kept from protesting by advice given to the newly honored stars to shower him with effusive praise. Particularly, divas who habitually focused mainly on themselves were reminded just in case – and in good time – to put in an appropriate word about the one who nominated them. The group grew to a point when an annual meeting was ceremoniously called. They were briefed on the vision of the "leader" and his unprecedented reform. Those who really mattered among them were given "talking points" to guide their facilitated media encounters. At an annual dinner by UN-based correspondents, my neighbor, Egyptian star Adel Imam, was puzzled about the briefings. Apparently those who had contacted him did not realize he was fond of his own compatriot, Boutros-Ghali. He did not mind listening to rave reviews of the current Secretary-General, which he thought was quite reasonable, given that they offered to invite him in the first place. But why, he asked me, did "they" make a point of criticizing all previous Secretaries-General?

Whitewash, Bluewash

The regular UN budget is closely watched by auditors and advisory committees. Less closely watched expenditures were in the area of extra-budgetary funds or in peacekeeping procurement and transportation contracts. The sums remained within cautious limits as influential powers competitively shared in having a number of their companies benefit from these arrangements. Drawing lines of what was appropriate were generally, if not always, clear. From the mid-1990s, however, lines between public service and private enterprise became increasingly blurred. A growing number of less controllable, almost secretive extra-budgetary funds landed with newly proposed UN projects, presumably aimed at introducing the private sector to play a public role, but eventually leading to occasional rehabilitations of certain politically risky firms or dubiously perceived individuals – a sort of reputation-laundering; a whitewash – or, under the UN flag – a bluewash.

A glaring example related to the business corporations that had been officially placed on a blacklist for supporting the apartheid regime in South Africa. They were its financial backbone and its political lobby worldwide. After the fall of that system, they were under a serious political cloud and sought urgent rehabilitation. Some new "strategic thinkers," who had recently joined the Secretariat and were prodded by private public relations firms, obligingly offered politically correct umbrellas. New ventures sponsored mostly by an official UN office or fund proclaimed impressive titles linked to "global contract" or "partnership with business" or "social commitment" with very little information regarding actual modalities of operation. Names of participants were not disclosed until officials were pressed for details.

By coincidence or design, a staff member known to some as "Puff the Magic Dragon," who transformed the original blacklist into whitewash or bluewash, was somehow brought into the inner circle and then swiftly promoted from an average P-5 post to a more senior post ending up as a Special Representative of the Secretary-General with the rank of Assistant Secretary-General – then, more recently, to Under-Secretary-General level in a key geopolitical posting.

In the UN context, any "envoy" can be effective only when presumed by the parties to the conflict to be serious and credible. A conflict of interest – no matter how distinguished an envoy – would undermine the performance of the mission. If an envoy is perceived to be interested in seeking to help an oil firm get a contract to explore in the host country, the government would be only happy to oblige with an expectation of an appreciative reciprocal signal through the UN's work. Similarly, if an envoy is also seeking consultancy deals or fundraising for a non-UN institute, governments will be only too happy to oblige, again in return for similar appreciation. There were at least three recent cases where an envoy with openly conflicted interests had to discreetly leave.

Additionally a number of former prime ministers or foreign ministers would need to display international credentials not only for tax purposes, but to seem relevant. Making money on the side would be a welcome bonus.

Entertainment and sports figures also sought bluewash when they felt public condemnation. The soccer star Diego Maradona, when caught in a controversy of drug abuse, donated his autographed football at the UN lobby to help children. Near the start of the millennium, a close advisor to a Director General of a UN agency almost specialized in locating prominently wealthy individuals with image anxieties, anxious to reward a sign of international recognition.

It got to the point where a number of normally cautious diplomats started wondering whether the time had become ripe to refresh themselves with abundant UN "holy water."

An unprecedented offer of $1 billion was an overwhelming red, white and blue wash to the reputation of CNN creator Ted Turner. However there were questions about how it was handled, or whether it was accurate or even legal to call it "UN Foundation" when decisions on its use were remotely controlled elsewhere; whether projects implemented, including some personalized ones, were within the framework of UN operations, and whether the extent of money and salaries paid were in line with UN policies, rules and regulations.

In a confusing way compounded by the communications revolution, use of the trademarked name of the Secretary-General in particular, and the UN name generally, tended to venture into uncharted territory, blending millennium-era calls with private Internet corporations, human rights causes and educational campaigns with rap albums.

Natural disasters were also accounting nightmares, particularly when accountability was weakened to allow for political considerations. One example was the Asian tsunami of 2006 and, to a lesser degree, the tragic earthquake in Haiti. More than $10 billion was raised but very little was indicated about the way it was actually spent. It was handled under the general supervision of the UN Office for the Coordination of Humanitarian Affairs.

The government of one of the struck countries, Indonesia, which became a member of the Security Council, could not be seriously pressed for details. Former President Clinton, appointed as a special envoy to raise funds, did so with effective enthusiasm and bountiful results, but again it would be awkward to monitor the man who practically appointed the Secretary-General. In her own understated sense of humor, Hillary Clinton pointedly thanked Secretary-General Annan for "giving my husband a volunteer job" when it was her husband who helped Mr. Annan get his job. After the 2010 earthquake in Haiti, where our UN colleagues led by Hedi Annabi gave the ultimate sacrifice, an assortment of mushrooming aid groups made it extremely difficult to keep accurate tabs. For example, one self-appointed supporter, a singer, helped himself first with $60,000 as a performance fee in a fundraising concert. Again, the former U.S. President was also there to raise funds. It may be added that President Clinton did extend a helping hand to Secretary-General Ban Ki-moon, who had been elected during a Republican administration, to be appropriately received in a President Obama's new Democratic Administration. The grapevine had it that candidate Obama in his early campaign, when he was still a weak candidate, had felt somewhat snubbed during a shuttle to New York by the then-newly elected Secretary-General and later, as President, responded in kind by delaying a joint photo or official meeting. A visit to Washington was arranged through Haiti, first to Secretary of State Clinton at the State Department, then to the President at the White House.

The UN took its most serious hit with Oil-for-Food, which some observers would claim was just the tip of an iceberg. A senior UN budget official indicated after his retirement that upon closure, more than $10 billion was handed over. Where did that money go?

While a bluewash by the UN has become more readily available to an interested power, whitewashing an awkward UN position had become less frequent. At least one hand did not wash the other.

CHAPTER X:

ELECTING A SECRETARY-GENERAL

Evolution of the Election Process

A sitting Secretary-General did not usually need to lobby too hard for a second term; his senior aides had a vested interest in taking this initiative on his behalf. Key delegates who had established close links with him were more than receptive, particularly those diplomats about to conclude their governmental appointment in New York who maybe hope to be positioned on a shortlist for upcoming Secretariat jobs.

In one case when a delegate happened to vote - with all other Security Council members – for Kofi Annan, his country's new government then rotated him out. He sought jobs discretely in various UN programs until someone advised him to approach the Secretary-General directly. When he did, he was offered an appointment as Special Representative residing in Cyprus - a country he had never known and an issue he had hardly handled. A decent and intelligent man, he kept away from controversial actions and concentrated on offering his home in hospitality to all parties. His loving mother specialized in making delicious "cookies for peace" - at least a positive step in that contentious atmosphere.

While it was politically correct for the incumbent to state that he had no interest in additional time, it was in practice advisable to pursue corridor contacts on the assumption that he in fact was. A certain

Secretary-General publicly warned his staff against lobbying for his second term. Loyalists nodded politely and carried on with their whispering promotional campaign. One senior officer, however, took him at his word. He may also have hoped, however slightly, that he would have a shot at the top post. After the renewal of the Secretary-General by acclamation, that staffer - referred to his colleagues as "Al Hadj" - coincidentally, yet graciously, left when his contract expired.

Early Elections

Originally, candidates did not publicly lobby for the Secretary-General's job. For the first time, the Security Council did not even bother to search for potentially more qualified candidates. Trygve Lie was brought in because they needed someone acceptable to the Soviets and the Americans. It was said that Stalin knew the Norwegian former trade unionist personally. Hammarskjold did not lobby for his job; in fact, he thought it was a pleasant surprise when it was offered to him. U Thant, who happened to be a delegate chairing the group trying to find a new Secretary-General after the sudden death of Dag Hammarskjold, eventually ended up being nominated himself. The French opposed him. Their official claim was that he did not speak their language. Perhaps the real reason was that he chaired a Non-Aligned group working effectively for the independence of Algeria, then considered an integral part of France. When it was mentioned in the corridors that President de Gaulle described him as "that short man," the Burmese educator called Ambassador Bertrand of France to say that he was at least taller than Napoleon Bonaparte. He did not really run for the office and refused another term as "a glorified clerk," as he described it. When it was agreed to designate him initially as Acting Secretary-General, he quipped with a straight face: "I am not a good actor." Waldheim did in fact run a discrete campaign, but he was not openly lobbying. The most dominant candidate at the time to become Secretary-General was a Finnish diplomat, Max Jacobson, but in that era the inside joke was that the weakest person was the strongest candidate. Habitually, all the big powers did not want a strong Secretary-General. Although they were occasionally or eventually surprised, they never missed an opportunity to hit their targets in time.

The Role of the Security Council

In a swiftly changing world, handling the selection of a Secretary-General by the five permanent members of the Security Council has generally deteriorated over recent years. A normal advance outreach to locate acceptable, qualified individuals with proven experience to handle pressing UN issues has been gradually replaced by internal political and sometimes personal expediency. The US, host country and still the most powerful member, continues to exercise overwhelming influence. Its position, however, has weakened when its traditionally consensus national bipartisan approach was eroded by internal national politics. Yet when it comes to the selection of a Secretary-General, it still maintains a decisive edge to this day. Russia, which took over the previous seat of the disintegrated Soviet Union, initially took a very low-key approach almost in line with the US position for about a decade. It gradually gained its own assertiveness, possibly due to incompetence by some of its competitors and maybe helped by a Minister of Foreign Affairs, Sergey Lavrov, who had more experience in UN matters than any of his contemporary counterparts. Nevertheless, for Russia, the selection of a new Secretary-General – Ban Ki-moon – boiled down to administrative and national gains; a post of Under-Secretary-General heading the European office in Vienna after the Geneva post was given to Kazakhstan's former minister Tokayev; and creating a new Assistant Secretary-General post in the Department of Peacekeeping to accommodate a recommended candidate to head a section on the Rule of Law (a duplicated area also handled by the Deputy Secretary-General and the Office of Legal Affairs). If nothing else, a vote by Moscow for a Secretary-General from South Korea on which is once boycotted the Council was a significant indication of a drastically changing world.

The United Kingdom had always exercised substantive influence in the Security Council, including the selection of Secretary-General, sometimes openly, often under a US guise. The first Acting Secretary-General, Sir Gladwyn Jebb, was British. Several critical resolutions, including 242 on the Middle East, reflected the handiwork of British diplomats like Lord Caradon. Sir David Hannay gave the admirable impression that he singlehandedly ran the Security Council. While most observers understood that Kofi Annan was brought in by the US Administration of President Bill Clinton, he was most welcome to London, which had nurtured him, his father and family since Ghana's Gold Coast days. However, since Tony Blair's transformation into a highly prized guest, job-seeker and lucrative consultant, the main interest by several UK officials in selecting a new Secretary-General was to locate senior-level posts. Blair himself lobbied to become Middle East Quartet coordinator, which he secured and maintained at least in theory despite his ineffective performance. Farcically, his successor in London, James Gordon Brown, was also given recently a 'for the camera' assignment as UN Special Envoy for Global Education. France, which for decades under Presidents de Gaulle, Pompidou, Mitterrand and early Chirac held the Council in suspense by maneuvering for its preferred candidates, drastically narrowed its demands. Since 1996, when a French veto on Mr. Annan was lifted in return for his position as head of the peacekeeping department, four sets of its diplomats have occupied it. During a reception at the Indonesian Lounge after Ban Ki-moon's Oath of office ceremony at the General Assembly, there was a somewhat comic moment when the newly elected Secretary-General told the chief peacekeeper in heavily accented French *"on va travailler ensemble."* There were of course additional demands for more of the same. The Foreign Minister who voted to elect Mr. Ban, Philippe Douste-Blazy, landed an assignment as Special Advisor on UN finances. For years, little was heard from him except occasional non-starters like imposing a UN tax on airline travelers worldwide (while his own income would remain tax-free). An outgoing permanent representative in New York was also given a nominal advisory task when recalled to Paris. Aspiring eligible Francophones from other countries started complaining that they have been overlooked in favor of a Quai d'Orsay clique, leaving some to transform the term "Francophonie" into "Francophoney".

The Chinese Seat

When China took over from Taiwan as a Permanent Member of the Security Council in October 1971, the process for selecting a new UN Secretary-General drastically changed.

Since 1945, China's seat was occupied by what was known as Nationalist China. Even after the establishment of the People's Republic of China by Chairman Mao Zedong in Beijing, back then Peking, an exiled Government in Taiwan maintained representation in New York. Practically, the Chinese role in the Council was taken for granted. Even the delegates themselves did not make many pretenses or demands other than in the area of national representation. Its highly educated and sophisticated diplomats made their statements mostly in English to the point where Secretary-General U Thant, and perhaps others, switched to the Chinese language interpretation channel for moments of relaxed silence. Its diplomats were satisfied with acquiring a number of jobs within the UN Secretariat for their nationals whom, incidentally, the People's Republic kept in place when taking over after sending them on a political "refresher" home leave visit.

The General Assembly's 1971 session reflected a changed balance of international powers. While US President Richard Nixon was seeking to exit from an exhausting, unwinnable, extremely unpopular war in Vietnam, Trudeaumania in neighboring Canada was instilling unprecedented confidence in that nation to pursue a distinctive national track. Gaullist France, which had its own Vietnamese moment and had already withdrawn from NATO command, was eager to display its "exclusive" role. Japan, the most influential US ally at the time, was edging for good-neighborly, though always cautious, relations. A changing China led by the astute political strategy of Prime Minister Zhou Enlai was setting forth a new vision of its international role. More to the point was the fact that the US President's National Security Advisor, Dr. Henry Kissinger, had already made two private visits to Beijing via Pakistan's back channel. Stalwart allies started wondering why they should be left out when the US administration seemed to be crafting the deal of the decade. In what some observers perceived as a reflection of internal politics, the US representative to the UN, Ambassador George H.W. Bush, a very popular delegate, was kept embarrassingly in the dark. He knew that Washington was instructing him to fight a losing battle in New York but carried on with professional dignity, gaining wide sympathy even from his adversaries.

U Thant, the first Asian Secretary-General, did not hide his support for the "restoration of the lawful rights of the People's Republic of China" as the official item was labeled, but he kept a sometimes-amused distance from active lobbying by all sides. The most senior Chinese staffer within the Secretariat, Victor Hoo, was expediently kept on for years pending a clear determination of the representation issue. An elegant intellectual with a discreet sense of humor, Hoo would quip that he would reach the official retirement age of 60 when the People's Republic took over. Draft resolutions calling for the "restoration" of the Chinese seat had been presented during several previous years, but mainly these were cosponsored by Albania and a limited number of States. That year, however, the co-sponsorship movement gained momentum, including endorsements from some countries in Europe,

Latin America and Asia, supported by regional groups like the League of Arab States and the Organization of African Unity.

The Chinese leadership had already dispatched its most capable negotiator, Huang Hua, as ambassador to Canada, enabling him to keep in touch and assess their chances from the proximity of Ottawa. The battlefront in the Assembly centered on whether the issue was substantially important to require a challenging two-thirds vote, or a "procedural," which needed an attainable simple majority – it was decided that a procedural vote would suffice. As a junior aide at the Secretary-General's office, I stood by the right side facing the podium as the votes were counted. When the numbers showed that the "procedural" won, a somber Chinese Ambassador Liu walked out with a steady step right in front of me as most delegates burst into sustained applause. An enthusiastic Tanzania delegation nearby, headed by Ambassador Salim, stood on their chairs rejoicing rhythmically in national style, prompting some reports that they were actually dancing in the aisles. Except for a festive General Assembly meeting to admit the "restored" member with the new representative from Ottawa sent in to take over, the new Chinese team moved very cautiously, taking time to assess pending issues and study UN machinery. Keeping most of the Chinese staff, they had to nominate a new Under-Secretary-General who would also reflect the general position of the Government leadership directly with the Secretary-General. The day he was presumably expected at the airport, he arrived by taxi from Chinatown.

When the People's Republic of China joined the UN, French satirical weekly *Le Canard Enchaîné* carried a double-barreled headline that played on the words of a popular proverb by claiming "ONU *soit qui Mao pense.*" It was an exaggeration to presume such a major key role within the UN when the Chinese Government was cautiously focused on areas of specific interest, including staff appointments, conference services and social development with a new and very tentative involvement in some peacekeeping ventures that would much later be fully developed. Over the years, a number of senior Chinese were sent to New York generally as heads of departments who stuck to their area of interest while fully participating in the Secretary-General's decision-making process. They cautiously kept a distance from getting involved beyond their officially designated areas. Obviously China always had particular political interests as a member of the Security Council, although in earlier days it sometimes "dissociated" itself from topics it sought to evade to the point that the use of the term "dissociate" in the

Council was mainly linked in observers' minds to the Chinese position.

A selection of a new Secretary-General was one of the first issues taken up when China joined as a permanent Member of the Security Council in the fall of 1971 with the right to exercise its veto. It did not seem to deal with this as a matter of immediate urgency as the outgoing incumbent, U Thant, was from Asia and a likely successor would be from elsewhere, most likely Europe or perhaps Africa. Yet automatically some names mentioned as potential front-runners faded away because they seemed unacceptable under the new circumstances. At the same time, a consensus by the "exclusive club of two" – the US and USSR – on Max Jacobson of Finland became less viable. An outstanding African, Under-Secretary-General and former Nigerian delegate Chief A.S. Adebo, who was waiting discreetly in the wings, was inauspiciously handicapped by the lack of diplomatic relations between his country and the incoming new Permanent Member.

Although it went along with the election and one-time renewal of Mr. Waldheim, China thought he already had "enough honor" and blocked a third term, which had been informally agreed between US Secretary of State Alexander Haig and Soviet Foreign Minister Andrei Gromyko. It also went along with the Latin American and two African candidates in return for specific understandings. But when it came to its election of an Asian, China punched its full weight. Even Ban Ki-moon would agree that he could not have become Secretary-General without China's full accord.

Like any devoted African, Nigerian Ambassador Ibrahim Gambari recounted later how he tried to get an African elected as Secretary-General at the time. He was coordinating the UN African Group and had cautioned his colleagues to avoid the 1981 experience when they stuck to one candidate and lost. This time, any of the listed six Africans would be acceptable; that is, the two countries representing the continent in the Security Council, Cote d'Ivoire and the Congo (Kinshasa) would vote "yes" when their names were polled. As a good Nigerian, he made his own discreet contacts to explore the chances of his compatriot, former General Obasanjo. He approached the Permanent Five, whose veto power could make or break anyone's prospects. Here, he explained, you had a proven, democratically minded man with a commitment to human development from one of the most populous countries in Africa, a most representative figure with recognized international standing. He later recounted that British ambassador Sir

David Hannay, a powerful diplomat who was once mentioned as the model for BBC farcical series "Yes, Minister." was fairly brief. "We need more a Secretary than a General," he quipped. French ambassador Jean Bernard Merimée responded bluntly: "Listen: he doesn't speak our language. Even when he speaks English, we don't understand him."

While it is the governments, not the "people of the UN," who select a Secretary-General, an emerging number of active individuals with adequate disposable means increasingly seek to influence the decision. They do this by floating an amenable candidate, not necessarily from their region, and thereby hope to acquire crucial support from certain key members of the Security Council – including, not least of which, some Permanent ones.

Security Council Muscle

China, of course, is not the only Permanent Member of the Security Council to throw its weight around. By the second term of Boutros-Ghali's tenure, as the Clinton Administration's campaign against him peaked in 1996, the highly connected Canadian international businessman Maurice Strong contacted a senior member of the Secretary-General's entourage. Mr. Strong had started his UN connection briefly as a young security officer, and returned decades later after a string of successful enterprises to head the UN Environment Programme. He then left and returned again as a key player at the environmental summit in Rio de Janeiro 1992. Of course, he knew the Secretary-General but not well enough to make a direct call. He was said to have offered to stop the negative political campaign. One version from a senior Secretariat official had him saying he would arrange "to call off the dogs" in return for a senior appointment such as the soon-to-be-created post of Deputy Secretary-General. It was mid-summer. Boutros-Ghali was spending time at a rented house in Long Island. Recognizing the close relationship between Mr. Strong and Vice President Gore, the official made a confidential call, then arranged for a UN car. At the time, the US administration was offering the Secretary-General a one-year extension. What happened during the meeting is best subject to speculation. A closely related source indicated that a compromise would provide a half-term extension, that is two and a half years, in return for a desired appointment. Perhaps the skeptical Egyptian professor sought some practical results before making a commitment. Or maybe he thought Mr. Strong, or even Mr. Gore, could not deliver. Although the full details may never be known, it is a fact that one month after Kofi Annan replaced Boutros-Ghali, Maurice Strong was appointed as the key leader of "the quiet revolution," the main "reform" process covering the whole Secretariat. That process created the post of Deputy Secretary-General and he became its founding de facto holder before another Canadian was eventually designated.

Differences between a new Clinton Administration and new Secretary-General Boutros-Ghali occurred much earlier than reported. While it is generally perceived that the Americans blocked the renewal of Dr. Boutros-Ghali, his undoing may have begun with his first open clash with the British envoy, Sir David Hannay, an effective diplomat and lethal adversary. Although Prime Minister John Major appeased the Secretary-General during a visit to London, their support was mainly surface deep, leaving the eventual action to Mrs. Albright.

Actually, disagreement with President Clinton's U.S. Ambassador started much earlier than an open controversy over a report detailing a tragic attack in a UNIFIL guarded south Lebanese town. A very limited circle knew that the tension started when, during a meeting at the White House, the U.S. president requested an appointment of a particular male political operative as a new head of UNICEF, to succeed the legendary James Grant. The Secretary-General indicated that he would rather need to nominate a woman with substantive experience. When U.S. Ambassador Albright pursued the request months later in New York she received the same response, only more pointedly, adding that if the U.S. had no female candidates there were already two Europeans available. Carol Bellamy, who was eventually appointed, proved to be one of the most caring, effective and popular heads of a UN fund. Clearly the Secretary-General paid a price later for standing on professional ground. The children of the world, however, received crucially needed attention. Incidentally, perhaps as a historic footnote, U.S. President Obama's Administration, with Mrs. Clinton as Secretary of State, proposed President Clinton's former National Security Advisor Anthony Lake as a new UNICEF Executive Director. Compared to his male and female predecessors his performance is at least open to question, particularly during a current catastrophic migration crisis.

When it became clear that Boutros-Boutros-Ghali was definitely out of the running, a number of delegates hurriedly searched for an alternative. Africa's most senior statesman, Nelson Mandela, who was the newly elected South African President, prepared a letter to the

Security Council presenting the continent's claim for the post and starting urgent consultations on possible candidates. Some Africans proposed Salim Salim, then Secretary-General of the Organization of African States, as an African candidate. Salim, who years before had stood on his General Assembly chair celebrating China's admission to the Security Council, had been vetoed 17 times by a previous US administration in December 1981. The purpose of those again floating Salim's candidacy may have been to test the claim by US Secretary of State Warren Christopher that any African candidate, other than the incumbent, would be acceptable. A deadlock was broken by Italian Ambassador Paolo Fulci, the rotating President of the Security Council. He obtained a consensus that only an African would be selected. He then asked African governments to officially submit names, using Horace's words: *carpe diem* - seize the day - before the opportunity was lost. He compared their reticence to the troops in Verdi's *Aida* who kept singing "Partiam, Partiam" ("Let's go, Let's go") without actually moving anywhere. When four African names were put forward, Fulci went to the 38th floor to ask the incumbent Secretary-General whether he wanted his name to be added to the others in a new vote. The response was no, he did not. "But then, what is your position?" the Council's President wanted to know. Boutros-Ghali responded in French: "*Je me mets en réserve,*" which Fulci interpreted as "I am suspending my candidacy for the time being". Announcing his motto as "speed to deliver in time," he proceeded to arrange straw polls among the fifteen Council members.

When Boutros Boutros-Ghali was fairly certain that his renewal was no longer on the cards, the name of Lakhdar Brahimi of Algeria started circulating. There were other names explored of mainly African potential candidates, whether in New York or at home capitals.

Annan's name was mentioned, but he had not yet officially run for the post of Secretary-General. Though Madeleine Albright and the Clinton administration were pushing for him, he was very careful not to speak publicly on the matter. Kofi Annan only made a deal with the French about heading the peacekeeping department when the French exercised their veto. When he was approached by the Chef de Cabinet, who told him he had to resign his office if he wanted to run, he explained that he was not officially running. Only during the final week in the process did Ambassador Gbeho of Ghana swiftly present Mr. Annan to the Council. Yet when some African and European delegates produced the names of several Africans, there was a leaning toward Lakhdar Brahimi. Gbeho then "threatened" Brahimi, a former Algerian Foreign

Minister. Brahimi, the Special Representative to oversee the peaceful transfer of democratic power in South Africa, who was surprised and visibly upset, had not initiated any political campaign and so the Ghanaian diplomat was sent packing. Our colleague Ismat Kittani arranged for lunch between Brahimi and Annan at the Delegates Dining Room. Eventually Annan came to utilize the valuable experience of Brahimi in two main activities: a comprehensive review of peacekeeping, and discrete handling of the UN's activities in Afghanistan and Iraq.

If relations between Brahimi and Annan were worked out, the relations between the African Secretary-General and Nelson Mandela – the most inspiring African of the 20th century – were not always at their best. Publicly it was all correct and polite, but perhaps certain opportunists around the Secretary-General trumpeting him as a "diplomatic rock star" sought to make him feel that he was more important than the legendary South African president.

I recall a gathering shortly after Annan took over, a weekly meeting with heads of departments before he was going to attend an African summit hosted by South Africa. A visit to Johannesburg with African leaders could highlight two major UN accomplishments: the fight against Apartheid and the granting of independence to colonial countries and peoples. I was therefore stunned when some senior officials suggested that he go to Johannesburg and "show leadership" by lecturing African leaders on good governance. To me it sounded a bit unhelpful and unwise. We had been raised at the UN to particularly respect leaders like Nelson Mandela, who had spent his life in prison defending human dignity. How could any one of us, particularly Mr. Annan, UN civil servants in the safety of New York when the legendary "Madiba" was in prison, now go and lecture him about the pursuit of freedom? Mr. Annan seemed to take that point after the meeting but it did not change his statement when he arrived in Johannesburg. I presume our colleagues were mainly thinking of building his image with the Western media. They all knew that Mr. Mandela would always be gracious. That point was carried too far when, as the world mourned the passing away of the historic leader, in an article by Annan in a leading paper it was lightly noted that Mr. Mandela called him "boss"!

A couple of months before Annan's election, the Department of Public Information had arranged for a TV summit at the United Nations featuring various figures from the industry, including heads and owners of TV stations. One item for discussion was coverage of conflict by the media and settlement of conflict by mediators. Since Mr. Annan was head of peacekeeping at the time, I had asked him to come in and speak on the settlement of conflict. It was in September, about a month before the actual voting process would begin. Annan was not yet officially a candidate but because he had been asked to join the summit, some within the Secretariat thought I was pushing for him to the post by introducing him to so many influential media representatives. Even some among Boutros-Ghali's close aides suspected that I was backing Annan. This was not the case, as Annan himself would confirm; I was simply putting together the best possible panel for what I viewed as an important event. We were having a discussion on peacekeeping, and it was only natural to invite the head of peacekeeping to participate.

The first session was held in the morning, to be followed by lunch with CNN's Ted Turner as the keynote speaker.

We were still in the meeting with the journalist Christiane Amanpour, speaking from London, when I was told there were some problems with the line connection with the UK. Then I was told that Ted Turner was out in the nearby Delegates' Lounge and wanted to come in to speak. My response was that we were in the middle of a scheduled discussion, and he would be speaking at length during lunch. Suddenly, Ted Turner swept in with his wife, Jane Fonda, who drew everyone's attention, together with Mrs. Boutros-Ghali. Kofi Annan, who had been interrupted, was obviously not happy. I was similarly unhappy at the disruption of a useful meeting and deduced that there was a political maneuver behind the scenes. Ironically, the same person who, I understood later, helped orchestrate that maneuver against Annan turned around the following year to claim ardent admiration for the new Secretary-General, bringing once again Ted Turner and his wife to the UN for a special dinner party.

Mr. Turner said he was upset that the US had not paid its dues. He noted that he earned a lot of money through shares of CNN and, if it were up to him, would like to pay a billion dollars to the UN but they would not let him. When he finished, I raised the question of donating money, pointing out that there was nothing preventing any person from paying a sum to the United Nations. If he wanted to pay a billion dollars, a fund could be set up for that purpose as long as they were without conditions under the UN rules and regulations.

The Re-election of Kofi Annan; a 'third term' for Africa

Kofi Annan could have had an unprecedented third term had it not been for his second one. There were no real problems during his first term, and the second was viewed as a done deal. There was some work to do because of an initial view that Mr. Annan was completing the second term of another African Secretary-General. The initial thrust to ensure a second term was to mount a concerted effort for a summit in the year 2000, an occasion for heads of state from around the world to attend and make speeches that usually start by the habitual praise for the Secretary-General. The second was to address peacekeeping issues on which Annan was very vulnerable in Somalia, Rwanda and Bosnia and Herzegovina. Brahimi came to the rescue, preparing reports and proposals about peacekeeping to address these failures. The third initiative was building up Kofi himself, "going Hollywood," and giving him the image of a diplomatic rock star. Meanwhile, those around the Secretary-General were making sure that any potential candidates would be nipped in the bud.

Kofi Annan typically allowed his team to maneuver for a second term as he stayed elegantly above the fray. According to the traditional rotation, the next term was designated for Asia. But one of the most active and capable diplomats lobbying his Asian group to agree on a shortlist, Ambassador Anwarul Karim Chowdhury of Bangladesh, suddenly slowed down. His party had just lost its respective national elections, and he was about to be replaced within four weeks. To his luck, the rotating presidency of the Security Council was turned to him for that month of June 2001. He managed to recommend another term on behalf of the Council for Mr. Annan to the General Assembly only days before his own term ended as the Permanent Representative of Bangladesh. Possibly a coincidence, immediately afterwards Ambassador Chowdhury was designated as Special Representative of the Secretary-General for the least developed of developing countries. Anybody who knows the UN well would know that if ever there were a non-job, this would be it. It only took two decades of debate to define the meaning of the terms "least developed" and "developing countries."

Annan barely survived this second term. It may be the curse of a second term, or it may be that with more time we all make mistakes eventually. It is a matter of conjuncture: what would have happened if Annan left after his first term? My personal guess is that he would have been one of the best Secretaries-General. Annan glided through the first term when there were very few serious challenges, and the main task was to present the Organization in a positive light. His human dimension, a ready smile and his considerable courtesy projected a welcome image in the homes of people - until later on when questions were raised as to whether he was just a beautiful figure or a true statesman. Maybe it would be unfair to expect him to handle so many issues that even big powers were unable to settle. He looked like a world leader, he walked like a world leader and in many cases he acted like a world leader. But given the players on the global scene at the time, he may have been excused for not exercising more leadership on behalf of the UN. He may have thought that to get along he had to go along and that he was saving the UN by not placing it in harm's way. Perhaps he was a very good navigator who avoided hitting icebergs and averted rocky territory. Whether he could have done more was a question interrupted by the Iraq war and the Oil-for-Food scandal. To put it in New York terms: Kofi's mojo was punctured by Kojo – his own son.

"Oil-for-Food" in Iraq was a lethal setback to the reputation of the United Nations and the credibility of its Secretary-General. What was officially intended as a noble humanitarian venture was transformed into an unmitigated disaster. While very few Secretariat staff members were involved, everyone's reputation was tarnished.

A most serious dimension was that the United Nations Secretary-General, with an entire Legal Counsel department, was compelled to employ an outside criminal lawyer, Gregory Craig. Clearly Mr. Craig did his job effectively. So did several other big players like former banker Paul Volcker and Deputy Secretary-General Malloch Brown, with the discreet help of the former World Bank Executive Director James Wolfensohn.

The Oil-for-Food program, initially discussed under Secretary-General Boutros-Ghali and later implemented and expanded under Kofi Annan, gave the UN unprecedented leeway in deciding substantive business deals. The main idea was to funnel all revenue from Iraqi oil and use it for importing food, medicine and other humanitarian goods for needy Iraqis. Because of the sanctions imposed by the Security Council, it was necessary to ascertain at specific border crossings that the imports were actually relief, neither contraband nor military or other "dual use" goods.

Initially a British firm, Lloyd's, was entrusted with the task.

However a Swiss-based company, Cotecna, was granted the lucrative contract. It was discovered, as is well known by now, that Kofi Annan's son, Kojo, was on Cotecna's payroll prior to, and after, the contract was awarded. When the issue was first raised, the UN Secretariat took several months to respond and even then clumsily denied that Mr. Annan's son was an employee of the company when it assumed the contract. It would have been better to swiftly and immediately clarify that Kojo was not Kofi; even in their local Ghanaian language Kojo means Thursday while Kofi means Friday. This was not done, however, and over time it became clear that Kojo, a non-staff member, had placed the UN in an unprecedented vulnerable position.

There were other aspects of the scandal, including those relating to the use of oil coupons for political influence that have taken up volumes of analysis. For example, diplomats and politicians from around the world who were friendly to Saddam Hussein would get special coupons to buy oil on the international market. They may have had no clue how to sell that oil but they could easily hand over coupons to an expert trader who would buy it at a discount and give them cash after taking a commission. A list of these individuals was eventually published after US troops occupied Baghdad and went straight to the Ministry of Oil. The list embarrassed a multitude of leaders and various cabinet ministers around the world.

More to the point was the impact on the UN itself, which ran the program without adequate oversight. The list named, among others, the head of the Oil-for-Food program, Benon Sevan, who had been personally appointed by Kofi Annan. He was an experienced and capable international civil servant, but even with the best intentions handling an unprecedented amount of billions put him in a vulnerable position. The accusation that Sevan may have diverted about $186,000,000 to his personal account would sound trivial compared to the total amount. He denied any wrongdoing and many of his colleagues believed him. Unfortunately, he did not explain himself clearly, convincingly and immediately to the media in time, while the UN Secretariat looked defenseless, encircled as it was with increasing accusations of corruption.

A committee headed by Paul Volcker, in an attempt to avert a disastrous exit for the Secretary-General amid calls for his resignation, determined to blame the UN system rather than specific individuals. A high-level team known as "FOK," or Friends of Kofi, helped in working out a gracious outcome with the help of Tony Blair, who talked personally with President Bush. Deputy Secretary-General Malloch Brown, later granted a lordship, took actual charge while Mr. Annan had to merely hang on for the rest of his second term. There was a great contrast between Mr. Annan's stature during his first term when he was applauded for enlivening the role of Secretary-General and his final years. Perhaps he was misled by an atmosphere of impunity that prevailed at the time in the international community, including in the Host Country. An attitude of entitlement fostered by those indicating how powerful and almost invincible was the Secretary-General may have tempted him to feel that accountability was a distant option. When told that the mainstream dailies of the world are behind you, that you are more popular in France than Chirac and more popular in England than Prime Minister Blair, and more liked in Scandinavia than any other person in the world (not to mention Africa, Asia and Latin America), you're inclined to feel that the small matter of a Mercedes imported from a Geneva auto show for your son would hardly draw a blip on the international screen. As seen in the movie "Wall Street", the motto of the time was "greed is good."

Another issue concerning Oil-for-Food was the bank where the money was deposited. Certain Swiss banks were initially considered but some delegates, including the United States, objected to the likelihood that secrecy of bank accounts there would erode transparency. Thereafter a French bank, BNP Paribas, was designated.

When the propriety of that decision was called into question, a Cypriot Security Council official, George Stephanides, was marched out of the UN building and his contract terminated. The indignant staffer brought a case to the UN Tribunal, providing documentation that the banking decision was done in full compliance with transparent instructions from senior officials and key members of the Security Council. He also may have threatened to spill the beans if squeezed further. Eventually, Kofi Annan called him at home in Queens to discreetly offer a post outside Headquarters.

It is regrettable that someone as media savvy as Kofi Annan allowed the case to overwhelm his reputation. It is also a pity Annan became a victim of a corruption scandal and had to abide by certain arrangements to survive politically. Moreover, it's a great loss for the United Nations that non-staff members like Kojo Annan and other diplomats and businessmen were able to bring down the reputation of the United Nations, which should have been defended more swiftly and effectively. A UN culture based on dedication, sacrifice, and enlightened hard work was mistaken even by Annan's successor, Ban Ki-moon, to be one of bureaucratic mediocrity, even corruption.

Certainly the Iraq situation complicated not only the Oil-for-Food program but Kofi Annan's standing in general. One awkward move in the lead up to the war in Iraq was the disappearing Pablo Picasso painting.

A replica of the historically famous and culturally valuable Picasso artwork "Guernica", which had been prominently displayed near the approach to the Security Council for 60 years, seemed to bother some influential party the day US Secretary of State Colin Powell was scheduled to brief the Security Council. It would, too, be visible to cameras displaying delegates entering the chambers to discuss the threat of war over Iraq; it may also appear behind the shoulder of the Council president as he addressed the press after the meeting. So the painting was covered by a curtain and flags of Council members. Ironically, among the flags abused to cover the masterpiece of the Spaniard who resided in Antibes were those of Spain and France. Fortunately, the cover was undone after a scandalized response, but the harm was registered in the form of embarrassment to the UN and, frankly, to the Secretary-General. After all, Picasso is Picasso and none of those masquerading as decision-makers around Kofi Annan can touch the tip of his creative brush.

The UN was almost crippled by the Oil-for-Food scandal. However, it raised an equally relevant question about $8.1 billion that the UN gave to the new occupation authority when that Program was closed. While the UN was handling it, there was at least some sort of an account, but where did that money then go? There was supposed to be continued international follow-up on expenditures, and yet the group established to control the money found that there was a $2.6 billion payment with no recorded contract and no action indicated; 89 cases where over $270 million were expended had no records to reference. Lack of transparency about where the funds went created an impression in the region that much of the money was looted while the Iraqi people - whose main concern was to survive - got nothing out of it.

Oil-for-Food was an internal earthquake. Serious failure by the UN leadership to respond to the accusations from the outset raised indicative questions. Instead of immediately explaining what the program was about, what were the political constraints, how procurement worked; instead of highlighting what had been accomplished while pinpointing certain admitted failures, the Secretariat lapsed into ponderosity. Instead of going openly clean, it chose to remain suspiciously silent. Between January and May 2004 when top notch teams of investigative reporters were digging damning material, nothing was heard from the Secretariat, except a letter to an editor when the Secretary- General's son was mentioned. Unfortunately, even that letter proved embarrassing; it denied any involvement by Kojo Annan with a certain firm, only to be proven wrong. That reflected a serious defect in a communication strategy preoccupied with the person of Mr. Annan rather than the institution of the UN.

Oil-for-Food eroded the U.N.'s role and demoralized its supporters. The Volker report looked like a deal to save Annan while hitting the UN, which was compelled to support his team with a $34 million budget. That money was initially taken from funds devoted for Iraq. However, when the new Iraqi regime objected, it was discovered suddenly that nine different UN agencies owed Iraq money for overcharged administrative expenses. Baghdad was compensated with the same amount of money Mr. Volker was paid.

Reaction from around the world on the Secretary-General's involvement demonstrated one of the peculiarities of being the head of a world organization with people from different nationalities and varied cultures. While the press in general attacked Annan, in some cases hypocritically, a close observer noted that certain omnipotent rulers may have considered it very strange that the UN Secretary-General could not even offer mediocre gain to his own son.

Kofi Annan deserved everyone's support, particularly at that difficult time. He was not at all helped, however, by some clearly identified people who were openly promoting their personal agendas and exploiting his prestige, while violating basic rules and disregarding established standards of international civil service. The longer he allowed them to do so, the more vulnerable he became.

Election of Ban Ki-moon

Like a traditional marriage, the election of Ban Ki-moon after Kofi Annan seemed to be arranged. He was the first Secretary-General to come from outside the UN system and UN culture, except for a brief stint as Chef de Cabinet to the President of the General Assembly in 2001-2002 when South Korea held that post. For the first time too, he came from a country that was still in conflict, with an overwhelming presence of foreign troops. Boutros-Ghali came in after Egypt and Israel made peace, but North Korea announced a nuclear test the day Ban Ki-moon was under consideration for Secretary-General. Some worried about the implications of a new Secretary-General with no record of any commitment to the Organization and with a new membership – South Korea had only just joined in 1991. To start with, carrying no political baggage could be a clear advantage, but that should be accompanied by a capacity to absorb, learn, explore and find out how to deal with matters in a multilateral way. Some pointed out that during the swearing-in ceremony of the new Secretary-General in the Assembly, there were two ongoing interests at the same time. There was a VIP group, overwhelmingly comprised of Koreans, talking, saluting and exchanging photos with one another, while the official meeting was proceeding. It was as if they had nothing to do with the process, although they were in its midst. These two separate streams appeared to only converge when Ban Ki-Moon took his oath of office.

His election was also an indication of how the world had changed. It was the conflict between the US and China that brought the war in Korea to the UN. However, after a half-century passed, it was a deal between the Americans and the Chinese that brought a South Korean to the office of Secretary-General. The French and British mainly negotiated for jobs, as did the Russians, but the fact is that if the Chinese did not want him, he would not be there. The administration of President George W. Bush seemed to want him, and the Chinese agreed for a price: for the first time a Chinese was given the leadership of a UN agency. Normally the most China got was an Under Secretary-General heading the translation section and conference services. In an unprecedented move, however, Dr. Margaret Chan of China was voted as Director General of WHO just before the vote in the Security Council on the new Secretary-General. Veteran observers noticed that the first statement welcoming her election was issued by the US delegate to WHO. In addition, the Chinese took a bigger department within the UN, gained a senior Deputy post at the International Monetary Fund and made further inroads concerning the World Trade Organization and other arrangements closer to the Asian region.

There were of course other candidates for Secretary-General at that time. There was a Thai Foreign Minister who tied all other Asians when he received an earlier endorsement from the Asian Group. Although a coup took place in Thailand and he lost every possibility of succeeding, he still forged on. That hopeless campaign, however, damaged one of the most experienced candidates, who was from Sri Lanka. India, which normally does not submit candidates since it is persistently seeking a permanent Security Council seat, had a sudden candidate in Shashi Tharoor, who somehow received his Prime Minister's backing. Prince Zeid, the Permanent Representative of Jordan, a very capable man, came in too late at the end of the summer and could not count on the vote of the Arab member of the Security Council, Qatar. All in all, the South Korean was the one working the hardest with arrangements made well in advance.

Incidentally, many admirers of Japan were disappointed at its ineffective, mainly ceremonial diplomacy. It seemed to punch way below its actual weight. For almost three decades, its diplomats have been running around verbally promoting the need for acquiring a permanent seat in the Security Council to the point of openly paying governments to vote, yet they were unable to get anywhere mainly due to lack of evaluation of the powers at play but more to the point due to the lack of imagination by traditional Japanese diplomats who seem to belong to one school, one perception and, obviously, a singular approach. Japan had an outstanding opportunity to secure the post of Deputy Secretary-General when its capable citizen, Mrs. Sadako Ogata, was briefly considered for that post. But some of its representatives thought it would detract from their request for the Council seat. A real, unique opportunity was lost by Japanese uncreative diplomats when in 2006 they could have put up a candidate for the post of Secretary-General. With some leeway they could have indicated a willingness to temporarily put aside the claim for the Council seat, which they should know they were not getting anyway, and offer a viable, solid candidate like Yukio Takasu for the role of Secretary-General. In a list of unknowns someone like Takasu, who had worked both within the Secretariat, in his own mission, as well as in the Foreign Ministry in Tokyo, and who was well-recognized and highly regarded by everyone and not controversial in any way, could have swiftly overwhelmed the campaign. However, they were too shy or too timid and actually too unrealistic, thus depriving their own country, indeed their own culture, from a real opportunity of leading the UN, to which Japan contributes substantively.

In any event, between the time of his selection and taking over at the UN, Ban Ki-moon made two statements with a positive impact: one official and the other in jest. In his official October 2006 acceptance speech, he spoke earnestly about his youthful striving days in his homeland and a committed belief in defending human dignity and effective international collaboration to handle real issues. The second was at a correspondent's dinner in December, at which he sang "Ban Ki-moon is coming to town" with many participants dancing to his tune.

He seemed keen, dynamic and ready to play a refreshing role. However, immediately after taking over, he unfortunately made two disappointing statements.

Before giving himself adequate time to credibly assess his new environment, he indicated his dissatisfaction with a UN culture that he said he sought to change. Adding insult to injury, he did not make the statement himself but passed that task to his close aide and eventual shadow Kim Won-Soo (dubbed immediately "Kim Too Soon"). It would have been understandable if Mr. Ban indicated a need to change the UN image, particularly in the aftermath of the Oil-for-Food scandal, but in one sentence he gratuitously antagonized thousands who devoted their careers and sometimes risked their lives for the UN. That culture, inspired by the likes of Secretary-General Dag Hammarskjold, who made the ultimate sacrifice while performing his duties, is that of dedication to UN objectives, exclusive loyalty to the Secretary-General and high-caliber professional work by proven international civil servants chosen from the widest geographical and specialized sources. Confusing the staff further, no alternative culture was proposed. Besides getting up early in the morning to go to work, there was neither clear indication of a specific focus, nor to a concept. Only Mr. Ban and Mr. Kim would know. That certainly did not help mobilize, inspire or guide his anxious and puzzled international staff worldwide, both active and retired.

If you listen to the skeptics, you would think that a Korean was picked as Secretary-General to do what he was told, with no institutional memory and no previous attachment to the UN as Korea joined the United Nations only in 1991. Indeed, loyalty to the Organization may be superseded by a political need to survive.

When by coincidence Ban Ki-moon took over while the main Secretariat building was renovated and interim offices were spread out among buildings over the Manhattan East side, some frustrated displaced staff referred to their new locations as "Bantánamo": Secretariat staff were getting ready to move out of their current offices. While an interim structure for Assembly meeting gutted the centre of the U.N. gardens and doors which used to be open over the years are being closed (for "fire" protection!), several divisions had already left the building (with Elvis!) to prepare for the promised renovation. By July, most offices, ten floors each, found their way across First Avenue. Even the same departments dispersed in different directions. Some claimed a certain favoritism as luckier ones just crossed the street while others were exiled to Lexington or even Madison Avenues.

Unfortunately, as a new Secretary-General with very little acquaintance with the UN system, Mr. Ban selected an even less experienced Deputy, a Minister of Foreign Affairs of Tanzania who voted for his election. An impression of vague leadership eroded a potential halo around the Secretary-General's office, disoriented the main staff, and possibly gave leeway to certain opportunists to advance their agendas. An appointment during the second term of an experienced Deputy, like Jan Eliasson, who was not only an active President of the General Assembly, Foreign Minister of Sweden, and a former Under-Secretary-General with varied assignments, but who was fairly active in mobilizing wider support for the UN Secretariat, might have been a more informed decision.

In the search of a new Secretary-General, somebody told me sarcastically that big powers only pick someone on whom they have something. The more skeletons in the closet, the more selectable the person would be. They may not need anything at the time, but when the time comes they would use it to push for their interests. Secretary-General Ban can sometimes act as a Secretary-General when required. Normally, any Secretary-General would have one or two assistants from his own country to help handle inevitable demands from their home country or deal with the local angle of their position, their "home cooking" so to speak. But no Secretary-General has given them so much influence by appointing them deputy Chef de Cabinet, or even any specific post, as with Mr. Kim, through whom everything has to pass, mostly in a non-official UN language. He has a different, more influential role to play than any other predecessor.

Though many qualities are changing at the UN and many need to be changed, some elements should be preserved, such as the Organization's culture of dedication, integrity and widely representative diversity. There were a few rotten apples who really embarrassed the staff, but that does not mean the entire UN culture is at fault. Before attacking it, Mr. Kim should have pondered the backlash. For example, does Mr. Park, who was deeply involved in the Oil-for-Food scandal, represent the Korean culture? No, he does not. Did the South Korean student Cho Seung-Hu, who killed 32 people in the massacre at Virginia Tech, represent the Korean culture? No, not at all. Then, do the one or two people who violated the rules of the UN represent the UN culture? Definitely not, in the same way that neither Mr. Park nor the Virginia Tech student represent Korean culture. The UN has its own culture. It needs to be updated, modernized, and adapted to emerging circumstances, but there now seems to be an attempt to attack the Organization's working culture as if it were to blame for all problems in recent years.

Another of Secretary-General Ban's early unfortunate errors was telling an internal town hall meeting that he did not need institutional memory, saying he could get it by pushing a button on the Internet. He immediately squandered his main available asset: his Secretariat staff who had taken an oath of loyalty to serve only the SG. It made them feel that their experiences did not count, that history begins with the arrival of the new boss with his new aides and possibly new appointments, and that there was no need for making a mark other than ensuring a record on the Internet. Practically, it sounded as if he did not really need them, and they were free to go. More serious was a perception that erasing the institutional memory of every society is usually a prelude to phasing it out. It reflected a very narrow management approach. International organizations could not be run by the Internet alone. Even Silicon Valley's largest companies like Google, Apple and Microsoft have recognized the basic need for human judgment and personal involvement, while of course taking into full account revolutionary electronic communications and the role of the Internet.

Election of Secretary-General Antonio Guterres in 2016.

By summer 2016, interest revolved around whether a woman would replace Secretary-General Ban Ki-moon. Following two Africans and an Asian Secretary-General, it was said to be Eastern Europe's turn, with lesser claims by Western Europe and Latin America. There was certainly a wealth of well-qualified women worldwide, some of whose names were already mentioned, like Irina Bokova, Director General of UNESCO, a Bulgarian, or Alicia Barcena of Mexico, who worked in ECOSOC with Maurice Strong, and was widely respected in the key capitals. It was even thought that German Chancellor Angela Merkel, might come to the fore. She happens to be a woman born in Eastern Europe leading a major Western country. And the joke was that with the UN in its current state, perhaps the popular singer Shakira might qualify.

There were also two male candidates with proven international management experience like Antonio Guterres, former UN High Commissioner for Refugees, who also served as Portugal's Prime Minister, and Danilo Türk, former President of Slovenia who also served as UN Assistant Secretary-General for Political Affairs.

When heads of state gathered during the last week of September 2016 for a General Assembly "High Level Segment", discreet contacts and exploratory reviews were held to sharpen the focus on electing a new SG. Practical confidential exchanges were accompanied by informal balloting at the Security Council to "encourage" or "discourage" official candidates eventually clearing the deck by introducing a red ballot for Permanent Members with Veto power. By October 5th., a consensus was reached. With Migration seen as the most pressing and challenging global issue, Antonio Guterres, a former U.N. High Commissioner for Refugees with ten years of proven dedicated hands-on experience seemed the uncontested qualified candidate; his performance as Prime Minister of his own country, Portugal, added to his other human qualities. The Council President for the month, Russian Ambassador Vitaly Churkin and U.S. Ambassador Samantha Power made a display of joint declaration, despite political divergences elsewhere, reflecting an enlightened determination to grant the U.N. its rightful role in international affairs. It is hoped that member states, particularly the Permanent Five will extend crucially needed support for the new SG to perform Charter designated functions, especially in heading a qualified dedicated unique International Civil Service.

But these refreshing efforts to open the selection process by publicly interviewing willing candidates and the push for a wider role by all member states are unlikely to change the basic structural fact that, while amenable to rhetoric and cosmetic transparency, the Security Council's Five Permanent Members with veto right make the decisive choice.

As head of UNHCR, Antonio Guterres brought a new sense of integrity to that body. It is further to be hoped that his practical experience in the field-work of the United Nations, rather than as a desk-bound bureaucrat, will inspire a new generation of the world's youth and bring a new air of positivity to the UN Secretariat.

Chapter XI:

FIVE SECRETARIES-GENERAL IN CRISIS

Baghdad-Tehran – A Gulf?

It took a war in Iraq for the public to find out that country invented the wheel. What did it take for world leaders to agree on what to do next?

With the looming threat of war over Iraq in 2003, Secretary-General Annan was caught in an escalating conflict where the stakes were high, while his means were limited. Pondering the task ahead, he observed that "the Lord created the universe in seven days, but He had the wonderful advantage of working alone." Mr. Annan had to work with the Security Council, particularly its Permanent Members, the General Assembly and world media, as well as an internal working group proposing different viewpoints. As he contended with competing interests of pivotal member states, he could only draw on his moral authority. Although in theory a Secretary-General commands multinational military forces, he must recognize the practical fact that they belong to governments with national interests. For example, decisions to refrain from air strikes over Bosnia were influenced by the positions of the British commanding officer and the French General on the ground. The moral impact of international legitimacy should not be underestimated. At times, the UN Secretary-General could play the role of a civic pope. The real power to take immediate action, however, does not rest with the person who symbolizes the Organization. His ability to move is constrained by the interests of key players. Some permanent members of the Security Council would wish him to do precisely what he is told. Less powerful ones would encourage a bolder approach as long as it was not at their expense.

The style of each Secretary-General differed in handling that intricate relationship, which often seemed like an intricate puzzle with no instructions. Dag Hammarskjold allowed his friends in the Council to draw vague resolutions so he could feel free to interpret them. Our devoted colleague Jean Gazarian of France, who had worked since 1945 on sensitive translations and retired as Director of General Assembly Affairs, enjoyed telling how stunned he was to receive a phone call directly from Secretary-General Hammarskjold asking why he used a certain word in a French translation of an originally English text of a Security Council resolution. Summoning his wits, Gazarian explained that his intent was to make a somewhat vague wording specifically clear. Pleasantly, yet firmly, he was told to leave the drafting as vague as politically intended.

After Hammarskjold's tragic death, his successor's main concern, while at odds with four out of five permanent members, was to stay steady in stormy political seas. Thus, U Thant opted for precision. Kurt Waldheim, who sought a second and possibly third term, studiously avoided issues irritating those holding veto power. A diplomat's diplomat, Javier Perez de Cuellar usually prepared the groundwork through discreet contacts to ensure a tacit consensus before venturing into an initiative. Boutros Boutros-Ghali, a former professor of international law, considered his office an active and autonomous partner with the Council. Lifelong civil servant Kofi Annan grew up in a culture that properly accommodated member states while maintaining an oath of office - not to take instructions from any government including his own.

While style mattered, each Secretary-General had to deal with the reality of an entirely different world. Conflict is a negative form of contact. In handling the contentious issues over Iraq, Annan naturally had to accentuate the positive; an initial consensus by all to work through the United Nations. It was a welcome opportunity for an Organization to provide an accommodating umbrella. Its Charter offers numerous ways out of emerging threats. Good offices, mediation, disengagement, observation, verification and enforcement are among a numerous range of workable options. Yet because he officially used the inclusive international forum, Kofi Annan tried to inch his way, stampeded by a restless and angry Administration of the host country in Washington, D.C., and frustrated by an irresponsive, almost playful attitude by its adversary in Baghdad.

For the first five years after he took over in 1997, Kofi Annan tried to show understanding to Iraq, a founding member, expecting a reciprocal response - or at least a better reading of what the international circuit can bear. Instead, its adamant leadership responded only in times of extreme pressure.

With a war looming in 2003, while Secretary of State Colin Powell kept in close touch with "Kofi, my man," others in the same administration perceived Annan's solution to the inspection process as part of the problem. Singling him out was unfair. A 1998 Memorandum of Understanding on searching residential compounds did have certain loopholes like allowing for advanced notice and entrusting accommodating diplomats with an intricate scientific task. That arrangement, however, was not concocted by Annan. It was drawn with all the parties and fully cleared by the American administration. He rushed to intervene when a crisis first arose in the winter of that year. When Security Council members like France and Russia floated the prospect of a visit to Baghdad, U.S. delegate Bill Richardson flatly opposed it in a meeting on the 38th floor, but after a weekend's private chat with Secretary of State Albright, Annan decided to proceed. A first draft Memorandum of Understanding on the search of presidential palaces, which was the main bone of contention, was prepared in New York and amended in Paris during talks with the French President, who was in touch with Iraq. With typical navigational caution, Annan sent an advance team, which included two personally trusted officers, an Indian and an Italian Swede. They were taken for a ride around unfamiliar complexes and went through the motions of holding measuring tapes across vast walls and opulent furniture. The main points sorted out in Paris were finalized during his visit to Baghdad. When Annan telephoned Dr. Albright to convey the final draft, Iraqi officials who were obviously monitoring the conversation felt certain that all was clear and Washington was back on track. Five years later, with a change of US Administration and an apparent change in Iraq government's attitudes, a war threat was more serious, particularly in light of the tragic events of 9/11 in New York.

The dealings of the Iraqi leadership with different UN Secretaries-General reflected its shifting fortunes and confirmed the inevitable need for a UN role. When Kurt Waldheim visited Baghdad in the seventies, Saddam Hussein was the rising Vice President to General Ahmed Hassan Al-Bakr; he was officially referred to as "Mr. Deputy" or "As-Sayyed An-Na'ib" in Arabic, which implied that he was the master deputy ruling in reality, while Al-Bakr was the figurehead. Except for discussing the general situation in the Middle East, there was no major issue on the agenda. In an attempt at diplomatic bonding by Mr. Waldheim, he made a point of demonstrating that the director of his office, Ismat Kittani was a former Iraqi diplomat. We were lodged in what used to be called the Palace of Flowers. Our Austrian colleagues admired the old architectural charm. For someone from the region, the blossoming roses could not dispel the eerie feeling that accompanied its new name - The Residence of the End. It was from there that King Faisal II and his family were seized, roped and dragged to death through the streets of Baghdad. As a special tribute to the guest, the hosts assembled in full regalia for the opening meeting. Facing Foreign Minister Saadoun Hamadi, who was a colleague at the American University of Beirut, I realized that his official revolutionary posture would not allow for a friendly smile; only a gracious nod. It was, however, our Iraqi colleague who committed an unforgivable error by behaving like a true international civil servant and taking his seat next to the Secretary-General.

The following day, Mr. Waldheim was advised during a car journey that Mr. Kittani was urgently required back in Baghdad. In response to a query, he was told that no specific post was contemplated yet, but an Iraqi citizen should come back at once all the same. That was a clear error of judgment by the Iraqi leadership - it was more of a loss for Iraq than to the United Nations. A qualified Chef de Cabinet was duly found but Iraq lost the opportunity of having a highly regarded internationalist to give it a positive image and exercise considerable influence in a key UN position. Years later, Kittani, a proud Kurd fluent in Arabic oratory, returned to New York as his country's ambassador, but it was a national assignment and not with the same impact.

Five years later, a brief meeting took place between Mr. Waldheim and, by then, President Hussein, during the conference of Islamic Heads of State in Taif, Saudi Arabia. The war with Iran had been launched, and the Secretary-General sought to explore a potential role in ending it during the last year of his second term in office - or hopefully as a qualifier for a possible third term. In a sitting room of an Alpine style lodge in a sprawl of villas built for that summit, Mr. Hussein opened by repeating twice through an interpreter that "some people love the sight of blood", possibly referring to the Iranians. Startled and clearly puzzled, Waldheim turned to me for a Byzantine explanation before I was politely yet firmly led to wait in the foyer. Getting no tangible results, the Secretary-General moved on to meet other participants with a new focus on the question of Afghanistan, which had just been invaded. It was a particularly popular cause with the Saudi hosts, and after initial consultations he advised us of a decision to appoint a member of the accompanying team, Javier Perez de Cuellar, as his special representative to handle that issue. Months later Don Javier succeeded Mr. Waldheim.

The new Secretary-General had to deal with the Iraqi president on two major events - the Iran-Iraq war and the invasion of Kuwait. Despite their military preoccupations, both Iraq and Iran extended their traditional hospitality while keeping a watchful eye on their shuttling visitors. Guards outside the guesthouse in Baghdad must have been caught off guard when our colleagues Alvaro de Soto and Giandomenico Picco took their early morning jog in the neighborhood's very tightly guarded yet deserted streets. A UN security officer who had joined from Geneva was spotted taking photographs, thus raising obvious suspicions; he claimed tourist curiosity, although, particularly in his line of work, he should have known better. Standard practice in these visits was for Foreign Minister Tariq Aziz to prepare grounds in detailed discussions leading to an undisclosed meeting with the President. A professional interpreter in military uniform would convey the leader's views with rhetorical, almost theatrical precision. He was a brother of a diplomat who was a member of the negotiating team and would make a point of finding out after each meeting how exquisite was his performance. Indeed he did consistently well. Good progress had been achieved in negotiations but the Iraqis may had been misinformed on the position of the Secretary-General and exaggerated the influence of some of his aides, who they suspected to be pro-Iranian.

Human nature being what it is, the UN team did have some internal differences, which may mislead an outside observer. Whatever the personal background, however, the Secretary-General, who listened attentively to all viewpoints, made all the final decisions. Everyone else was expected to follow. When traveling with the Secretary-General nobody counts but him. No individual grandstands or maneuvers at his expense. The group usually worked together as one team exclusively.

Our biggest asset was our international credibility. From time to time, though, a rotten apple crept through.

Once during a peace shuttle between Tehran and Baghdad, it transpired that someone had portrayed other members on the team negatively to the Iranians. We were seated next to one another in the ruling Majlis government chambers facing our hosts. While Foreign Minister Ali Akbar Velayati studiously peeled an ice-cool cucumber, President Hashemi Rafsanjani opened the meeting by asking about our backgrounds. In order to honor us appropriately as his guests, he said, he wanted to know precisely who we were. The Secretary-General immediately responded by briefly mentioning our names and deliberately explaining that his trusted team reflected the dedication of international civil service regardless of individual nationalities. Mr. Rafsanjani graciously nodded and sent each of us a package of special pistachios from his family farm.

Despite noisy rhetoric, both Iran and Iraq officials were inclined to peaceful negotiations. Both felt they knew one another better than any third party and were testing their way to what the other side would consider a fair settlement. Both were suspicious of outside "conspiracies" and "red lines," convinced that "world parties" will not allow any of them a decisive win. Yet each sought some sort of international accomplishment to show their people. In Baghdad, for example, a series of media-oriented conferences were held to review the significance of a battle around al-Fao. While Iraq television repeatedly showed the President explaining to a flow of visiting dignitaries the implications of his victory, Iranian officials dwelled on their military superiority giving as proof a higher number of prisoners they held. The Iraqis seemed to angle for a binding deal directly with the Iranians after a decent introduction by the UN The Iranians preferred to hang on to UN embroidered formulas and avoid signing anything before definitively ascertaining what their adversaries were up to. The two sides confirmed that they were poised to seize the right opportunity "when and if it occurred". That meant when the time was ripe for a final accord the composition of their negotiating teams will be changed accordingly.

One reason for prolonging the Iran-Iraq conflict may have been a misconception on both sides that the other regime was on the verge of collapse pending only one more push. The Secretary-General sought to dispel such miscalculations. In addition to maintaining close touch with potentially helpful personalities in the Iraqi-Iranian power structure, he encouraged permanent members of the Security Council to pursue their designated responsibilities more actively. New leaders of the two superpowers, George H.W. Bush and Mikhail Gorbachev, had embarked on shaping an orderly historical change. A prolonged bloody conflict in an area so close to the Soviet border, yet so crucial to U.S. interests, could trigger unwelcome confusion, let alone more tragic loss in human lives. Both were willing and able to intervene. Vulnerable oil-rich countries also helped in exerting their underestimated influence. By then they were exasperated with subsidizing an increasingly costly venture and seriously concerned about its side effects on their internal politics.

Iran and Iraq had unpronounced territorial claims that would tempt a frustrated loser or an over-confident winner. Although the Shah had waived his claim to Bahrain as part of a U.N.-brokered understanding prior to its independence, the ruling Sunni Al-Khalifah family in Bahrain had to handle delicately the passions of its Shiite population. The United Arab Emirates had a dispute with Iran over the seizure of three islands, while Iraq considered Kuwait a temporarily separated annex to its Basra province. Most borders amongst thinly populated states were not definitively delineated; disputes were settled by handshakes in honorable tribal fashion. A war that would exhaust the two big neighbors was not unwelcome for a while; prolonging it unduly, however, was like blowing into an unpredictable, possibly destabilizing desert wind. Even as both parties agreed to a Security Council ceasefire, a face-saving formula allowed respective leaders to claim some sort of victory. Each side could tell their internal audience that it could have gone further towards the total defeat of its adversary were it not for insurmountable pressure from world powers.

Reviewing its strategy after the cessation of hostilities, the Iranian leadership opened practical channels with its Arab neighbors, like Saudi Arabia and Kuwait, starting with basic vital questions such as arranging pilgrimages to the holy city of Mecca and pricing oil by OPEC. On the other side, the Iraqi leader accelerated his posture of uniquely acquired glory. Sensing a re-emerging world, Mr. Hussein felt entitled to claim the leading role in reshaping his strategic neighborhood. In practical terms that meant the super powers should reward him for services personally rendered over ten years and that the Arabs - particularly rich ones - ought to show more gratitude for his fighting on their behalf. A disastrous symptom was his invasion of Kuwait in August 1990.

Secretary-General Javier Perez de Cuellar swiftly attempted to avert the almost certain war. He made a special last ditch effort. During a tense meeting with Mr. Hussein in Amman, Jordan, he drew a practical picture of the bleak prospects and offered his good offices in accommodating a gracious way out, but was flatly, almost rudely, turned down. A side effect of a negative Iraqi attitude was a calculated approach by the Iranians to offer their help in the release of Western hostages held in Lebanon. An experienced Foreign Ministry official, Javad Zarif, a former member of Iran's diplomatic mission to the UN, was designated to discreetly guide and, if necessary, travel with a member of the Secretary-General's office in order to finalize specific details for each freed captive. In addition to demonstrating its key role in the region, Tehran may have sought to obtain a clear international indication as to who started the eight-year war in 1980. After the release of all the hostages, as agreed, it was noted that a report by the Secretary-General during the last month of his tenure put the onus for hostilities on Iraq.

The subsequent Secretary-General Boutros Boutros-Ghali was familiar to the Iraqi leadership from his days as Egypt's Foreign Minister during the crucial Camp David Middle East talks. Although they were at opposing sides of the inter-Arab cross-currents, a cordial working relationship was eventually established. Its architects were his Special Advisor, the retired Iraqi diplomat Ismat Kittani, and newly appointed Iraqi Ambassador Nizar Hamdoun, a senior member of the Baath Party and a former ambassador to Washington. Iraq had refused to deal with a successive number of resolutions by the Security Council after Desert Storm, delaying the launch of the Oil-for-Food program. It took two years to persuade Baghdad to go along. That signaled the opening of a new cordial relationship, for which Boutros-Ghali may have paid a price.

For his part, Kofi Annan's involvement with Iraq started in August 1990 when he was the head of the Office of Personnel. Immediately after the invasion of Kuwait, Perez de Cuellar sent him together with his own Chef de Cabinet to ensure the safety of the staff in the region and boost their morale. Annan's receptive approach to media interest gained coverage for his assignment when the press was looking for every angle on which to report about the crisis. That ruffled some feathers at Headquarters. As Perez de Cuellar flew to Jordan in an urgent effort to avert the war, an assistant advised Annan that "it would not be prudent" to talk to the press at such a delicate time. A reporter, Charlayne Hunter-Gault, an African American who had quoted him frequently, happened to join me in New York for lunch years later, in

December 1996. At the entrance to the delegate's dining room, we bumped into Paolo Fulci, the Italian Ambassador who was presiding over the Security Council's deliberations to elect a new Secretary-General. When he mentioned that it was almost certain that Annan would be recommended the following day, she wondered about the prospects of the fellow who had once rebuked him on Perez de Cuellar's behalf.

While still adjusting to his new job, Annan faced the Iraqi test sooner than expected. He instinctively felt his way around, discreetly making the mandatory contacts and seeking a way out. His 1998 visit to Baghdad, derided some five years later, was hailed as historic at the time. It provided conflicting parties with a ladder to climb down from and a fig leaf to cover concessions. More to the point, it averted a perceived war. Suddenly Kofi Annan received instant international recognition. CNN covered live his return to New York Headquarters. After being perceived as pro-Israeli, his popularity in the Arab world shot up. In Damascus, then known as the throbbing heart of Arab nationalism, he was mobbed by cheering crowds to the point that some of us were cut off from the official motorcade and had to find our way by local taxi to the next appointment with the Prime Minister. It was after such euphoria that Kofi's friends, propelled by a private public relations firm, initiated a quest for the Nobel Prize for Peace. An appointment of a Norwegian diplomat Terje Roed Larsen as special envoy in the Arab-Israel Peace Process was perceived as a step for that prospect to fly. His connections within the Oslo network could provide the wind beneath its wings. And any progress that could be achieved in the Middle East would be a welcomed bonus.

The Iraqi situation was generally contained for about five years. Benign yet profitable neglect was tolerated and tacitly approved by all the key players. A list of beneficiaries from Oil-for-Food contracts covered a range of permanent and non-permanent members of the Security Council, amenable politicians worldwide, plus a number of key individuals from a surprising number of nationalities.

Incidentally, during all the preparations and the discussions, there was one mechanism in the Security Council which no one ever talked about - the Military Committee. Its five generals from the five permanent members should be the most powerful part of the Council. They are supposed to meet bi-weekly to review the world situation and decide on issues, but indeed they did not. For a certain period during the Cold War they hardly did anything. They opened their files, made sure the agenda was empty, approved the agenda item and indicated the date for the next meeting. If the military committee had any role in encouraging or preventing the war in Iraq, no one could tell.

When talk of renewed conflict became serious, the Secretary-General, together with the United States, France, Russia, China, U.K. and non-permanent Security Council members like Mexico, Ireland, Norway and notably Syria managed to reach a workable peaceful option. It took eight weeks for the Security Council to reach Resolution 1441, adopted in November 2002. Every one of its fifteen members would claim an element of achievement. A delegate who managed to exchange a past tense for the present, replace an "and" by an "or" or drop a whole paragraph would immediately write home about it.

To be clear, the Security Council resolution did not authorize an invasion of Iraq. The consensus took into account all viewpoints but pointedly averted a reference to the military option. After all the UN is an Organization of peace. Yet a cleverly drafted part by one of the best American diplomats, Ambassador John Negroponte, could be vaguely interpreted by a keen permanent member to accommodate other options. That may be why, a decade later, particularly in light of the eventual Libya experience, other permanent members like Russia and China repeatedly blocked even a vaguely political resolution on Syria. After all, Russia's seasoned Foreign Minister, Sergey Lavrov, was in 2002 his country's Permanent Representative in New York.

Yet the UN is not in the business of beating its own drum. The day after the vote on Iraq, it was handling other pressing issues too. The Secretary-General was making proposals on Cyprus and Atomic Energy Chief El-Baradei was rolling his suitcase down First Avenue to take a bus for a weekend retreat with other heads of UN agencies on future programs. Credit is habitually left for member states. Failure is conveniently placed at the UN. More than one Secretary-General abbreviated his initials to mean "Scape Goat."

A War Already Won

Collective dealings with Iraq were naturally influenced by its bilateral relations, which in turn were shaped by a pivotal geographic location and abundant resources. A geopolitical perception divided the strategic Arab region into two main groups of countries: those in the near eastern fertile crescent with enviable geography yet deprived of oil, and those in the desert Gulf region with profitable geology yet deprived of water. Iraq enjoyed both: since its days as Mesopotamia, it boasted a blend of human diversity and natural resources that led to both cultural enlightenment and brutal conflict. Unlike any other Arab country except, perhaps, Syria, it had oil and water together with human power and social structure dating back to the dawn of history. Those not aware of the legal code of Hammurabi or the splendor of the early Abbasid Empire will recall folkloric tales of Scheherazade of the 1,001 Nights. That of course was long ago. What did not change was the strategic relevance of that land, by whatever name. If anything, Iraq grew more crucial, particularly during the Cold War when it was courted by East and West. Not only does it straddle Saudi Arabia, Kuwait and other Gulf states, which provide eighty percent of the world's energy needs, it also has long borders with similarly strategic countries: Iran, facing the Soviet Union (Russia); Turkey, guarding the southernmost flank of NATO; and Syria, at the heart of the Arab world.

Over three decades, as Saddam Hussein consolidated his muscle behind the local branch of the Baath Arab Socialist Party leadership, key capitals gave him priority attention, exchanging special envoys on urgent missions.

The United States in particular sought a special link. No foreigner knew the ruler in Baghdad better than authorities in Washington. Paying attention to Iraq was part of a consistent bi-partisan policy in that region. Under whatever concept and at whatever cost, it aimed to guarantee unfettered and unchallenged access to energy resources and safeguard its navigational routes without threats from any other power. President Eisenhower proposed a Baghdad Pact - a regional alliance involving Turkey and Pakistan. President Gerald Ford's Secretary of State, Henry Kissinger, arranged a deal between Iraq and Iran dividing the shared waterway; he also reportedly engineered the counter-productive expulsion of Shiite cleric Ayatollah Khomeini from the closely watched Iranian city of Najaf to the more media-oriented French capital, from which he successfully campaigned for a victorious return to Tehran.

President Carter particularly encouraged the Iraqi leader after the seizure of American hostages in Tehran. And when Iran seemed to be gaining an upper hand during the war, President Reagan restored balance by providing Baghdad with vital high-altitude surveillance reports.

Donald Rumsfeld was designated as a Special Envoy to the Iraqi leadership, and Iraq's Foreign Minister Tariq Aziz kept in regular touch with powerful individuals in Washington; a diplomat based in New York was on permanent standby in case of an emergency contact. President George H.W. Bush, preoccupied with historic changes like the fall of the Berlin Wall and the crumbling of the Soviet Union, still kept a wary eye on the increasingly restless Iraqi leader until the invasion of Kuwait.

But in the lead up to his Kuwait invasion, a line was drawn in the sand that Saddam Hussein could not fathom. He underestimated Washington's reaction, overestimated Moscow's support, and misjudged the French balancing act. Similarly, he inflated his fighting capacity, overlooked his diplomatic options and inflicted lasting injury on Arab interests he claimed to defend. More to the point, he confused the nature of the conflict. Arab governments repeatedly singling out Israeli occupation across their borders were shocked by a brotherly leader plundering one of their valuable capitals. A series of Security Council resolutions allowing enforcement action were indeed propelled by the United States but approved by the full membership condemning a flagrant violation of the UN Charter by the government of one of its founding members.

By 2003 Iraq, for all practical purposes, had been broken down under the no-fly zones into three parts. The north was already controlled by an autonomous Kurdish government, and the south was open territory for lucrative contraband and semi-legal business with neighboring countries. Only the central region was controlled by the national government in Baghdad - an effective war had already been won if the purpose was to break down the country. Ten years after the Kuwait invasion, and a new government, demarcation lines were getting sharper - and deadlier.

Opposition to the war that year sought not to protect Saddam Hussein but to prevent the spread of instability and a potential Sunni-Shiite conflict. Iraq's closest neighbor, Saudi Arabia, always favored the status quo to avert potential risks. More substantively, an armed conflict in Iraq could be a prelude to *fitna* - the instigation of ethnic conflict within the state. An Arab observer in Paris pointed out that the real risk in the region was not merely between Sunnis and Shiites but in the competition between Sunni oil and Shiite oil. The oil-rich eastern province of Saudi Arabia hosts a predominance of Shiites who are only a bridge across to Bahrain, where the majority are Shiites while the ruling family is Sunni. It was noted that most of the oil in the region is where the Shiites are located, except, in part, where the Kurds control nearby Kirkuk (a point of potential conflict with Turkey). With tribes knowing their way around borders, no country, as we have now clearly seen, is immune to potential trouble once the floodgates open.

Perceptions in Conflict

While American culture is the most imitated worldwide, U.S. policy is the least understood. America as a country is generally admired, while certain American politicians are disliked. A television reporter observed that during an invasion the American public sees the outgoing missile, while the Arab public sees the incoming one. These are two radically different perspectives that would not only be bridged through better media relations, but through a more mutually understanding approach. It is not a matter of good or bad positions but of conflicting cultural perceptions. An American matter of fact could be a British understatement, a French dilemma, a Russian option, a Chinese deal, an Arab suspicion, or a Byzantine conspiracy. And the Byzantines will insist that history proved their theories right.

An interestingly new element was that the first big war in the 21st century was also the first to be privatized. It was not just a war between national armies but of security companies and individuals. Private firms like Halliburton and Blackwater became household names under business contracts. The Iraqi and Afghanistan conflicts, among others, engaged not only companies run by former military officers but also adventurous, opportunistic individuals from various nationalities without accountability, eager to take personal risks for profit. International terror groups, military contractors and individual mercenaries seemed to have a sort of tacit alliance, as their respective conflicts benefited each other financially.

Privatized fighters or mercenaries, of course, are not a new invention. The Angolan war was mainly fought by them: those who sought the diamonds and those who wanted the oil. The infamous "Le Colonel" undertook the dirty work in Africa that the French and the Belgian colonial powers did not wish to be caught committing, under an assumed name of Bob Denard. The man born in Bordeaux as Gilbert Bourgeard and his clique of "Les Affreux" started during the Congo Crisis in the 60's - paid by companies - to search for minerals in

Katanga. He ruthlessly undercut the United Nations and its Secretary-General. One conspiracy theory about Dag Hammarskjold's death pointed to a missile that shot down the Secretary-General's plane (I had visited the site of his plane crash myself to pay respects and see for myself what might have transpired). Mercenary actions in Nigeria's Biafra war was popularized through a best-selling novel (and movie) entitled "Dogs of War". Although the phenomenon was always there, it is taking a more organized shape and gaining more acceptance. One reason may lie in the media-savvy participation of highly regarded former officers with stature in their powerful countries and in the failure of the international community. A fragmented international community paralyzed in leadership and ponderous in membership has given more ascendance to daring officers that are willing to do the job, although they are unaccountable and costs billions more than the UN. They may be part of the coalition of the willing, but - as someone suggested - they certainly form a "coalition of the billing."

More politically relevant, neighboring countries have grassroots links with Iraq. Saudi Arabia is historically close to Sunni tribes across virtually unmarked borders. Tehran has been long engaged with religious groups like the Aldawa party and the Bader brigade militias; and Damascus had long maintained its Baathist and Kurdish connections. The two successive Iraqi prime ministers, Ibrahim Jafari and Nuri al-Maliki, had taken long refuge in Iran, and President Jalal Talbani was particularly favored by Syria where he had lived in exile for years. For all practical purposes, the U.S. invasion ended by leaving predominant influence to Iran; some would claim it was in return for Iran's practical help in the U.S. taking over Afghanistan.

There was great hope that positive change would strengthen the diminishing middle class in Iraq. The real irony about the many years of sanctions was that they destroyed the middle class, the only power that could change Saddam Hussein. Doctors, teachers, lawyers, architects and engineers had to take other jobs in order to survive. Security hazards continued the erosion of that middle class, to the financial gain of politicians and foreign contractors. The same mistake that happened during the sanctions against Saddam was repeated post-Saddam, as the backbone of Iraqi society, including its professional army, medical doctors and academics became unemployed, paralyzed or exiled. Iraq used to be one of the most advanced countries in education, introducing gender equality in schools. Now women are afraid to walk on the streets. One of the most active and culturally enriched societies in the Middle

East fell apart for the entire world to see.

Iraq became even more confusing after Baghdad fell. When Saddam Hussein was on the run, a black joke was that President Bush was searching for him merely to re-install him in charge. Even Saddam may have believed that he would be spared, perhaps until the last minute. He may have thought that his old acquaintance with Mr. Rumsfeld in the 1980s would somehow serve to deliver a last-minute reprieve, and indeed, as it accidentally happened, when Secretary Rumsfeld left, Saddam Hussein was hanged.

It is generally agreed upon by now that the disbanding of the Iraqi army was a great blunder and one of the major reasons for the current situation in Iraq. Although the army had a Baathist slogan, it was a professional army and the bulk of the officers and soldiers were non-political. To the contrary, Saddam Hussein never trusted professional officers, imposed restrictions on them, and forced party members on them as commissars. After finishing off his own party members, he plunged the army into a prolonged war partially to exhaust it to ensure that it would not have the stamina to challenge him. The Iraqi army was the longest serving professional one in the Middle East. Disbanding it was used by conspiracy theorists in the Arab world to say that the purpose of the war was to destroy that army and turn Iraq into a weak divisible country. Americans running post-war Iraq immediately after the fall of Baghdad were at first puzzled by the embarrassed smiles of their local listeners when they expressed their determination to have a New Iraqi Corps, replacing the disbanded Iraqi army. They eventually discovered that the Arabic acronym for it, NIC, which they proudly repeated in public gatherings, was a popular Iraqi equivalent to an English four letter word for having sex. There was a blend of speculation within and outside the UN about the purpose of military operations, some trivial and some pragmatic and even some religious versions. Some groups were mentioning quotations in the Bible to claim the war was prophesied. They referred to Jeremiah's prophesy of how an assembly of great nations from afar would come and hit Babylon and the land of the Chaldeans, one of the oldest people in the world, an ethnic part of Iraq. A petition from a religious group speculated that the evil in Iraq was a continuance of the evil in Babylon and part of God's final day judgment, or would go on to predict that the war would be launched when Prophet Jeremiah took over. (It happened by alphabetic rotation that British ambassador Sir Jeremy Greenstock headed the Security Council during December 2002, in the run-up to the war.) As they say, you can always build an argument if some people believe its basic premise.

Time between meetings in the Security Council is normally designated to allow for bargains, arm twisting or waiting for one side or the other to blink first. With such high stakes, particularly between Colin Powell and his French counterpart Dominique de Villepin, there were some attempts at comic relief or amusing gossip. At the UN Delegates' Lounge, steps away from where Security Council members huddled to weigh-in on prospects of war, a veteran internationalist mentioned the Viagra Angle. It was claimed Iraq responded to American predominance by secretly manufacturing its home-grown product, proudly named Samagra. Unlike the "imperialistic" U.S. version, it claimed to have no side effects. Due to its role in boosting leadership morale, it could only be authorized by the President from limited quantities carefully stashed inside presidential compounds. Even Deputy Prime Minister Tariq Aziz would not have regular access; he was left to keep grinding his Cuban cigar until he puffed out a suggestion about how to outmaneuver former friend Donald Rumsfeld. One idea, according to the Baghdadi grapevine, was to offer the vigorous looking U.S. Defense Secretary the best quality samples of Samagra during a secret date sought on Valentine's Day. The proposal was discarded, however, as Chief Inspector Hans Blix demanded immediate unfettered access. The farsighted Swede hinted diplomatically that he would distribute material to overworked members of the Security Council. As to his colleague and successor in the Atomic Energy Agency, Mohammed El Baradei, he should be able to negotiate his own way in plain Arabic. Failing that, he will have to simply settle for Korean Ginseng which has the awkward side effect of raising blood pressure. The American-Iraqi duel between omnipotence versus impotence tempted other players. Germany and France hinted about a new response spearheaded by Bayer. That may explain a glimpse of a smile spotted in recent photos of the former German Chancellor, Herr Schroeder, who seemed to be sleeping better knowing that his compatriots were feeling happier. In Paris an analyst took a subtle dig at the world's "hyper-power" by indicating that while Viagra provided only a window of three hours in the boudoir the "old Europe" version would last the full twenty-four. In the midst of that transatlantic divide, a surprising initiative came from Syria. Its "Prescribed Feelings" was said to be drawn from a purely organic herb first discovered by mountain shepherds when they noted unusual commotion among their goats. Neighboring Turkey was not far behind, with its "Achievement of Age", a play on local slang clearly lost in the English translation. However, the Greeks were said to be considering a truly Byzantine response. "It is all in the mind," Greek Prime Minister George Papandreaou pointed out. Pulling cultural rank, the rotating President of the European Union felt entitled to intervene effectively between the Potomac and Mesopotamia. More to the point, he would evoke Aristophanes. In Lysistrata, the Greek tragic-comedian urged women to withhold sex from the warring men of Sparta and Athens until they bade farewell to their arms of mutual destruction. Could it be about time for women to take over again?

The UN Rôle

On March 24, 2003, I met Secretary-General Annan upon his request at 4 p.m., three hours after he had received U.S. Advisor on National Security, Condoleezza Rice. Unusually, there were some black helicopters circling around the Secretariat building and despite his usually calm demeanor, this seemed to irritate him. About halfway through our conversation, he wondered what those helicopters were doing. Alluding to the claim by certain ultra right-wingers, some of whom were having influence in Washington, D.C, that the UN would be invading the U.S. with helicopters, I responded: "I thought they were yours." Mr. Annan laughed and hit my wrist so that my loose watch fell on the leather sofa.

Handling the crisis in Iraq raised questions about the relevance of the UN, Bashing the Organization and its Secretary-General was not limited to only one side. While the Americans thought he was unhelpful and some American headlines called him "Kofi Annoying". world media generally portrayed the Secretary-General as an American puppet. Some Arab newspapers accused him of firing the first shot in the war by swiftly withdrawing UN observers from the Iraq-Kuwait borders. Prominent international figures like Nelson Mandela hinted that Annan did not have the guts to stand up for the principles of the Charter. After the fall of Baghdad, Kofi Annan himself felt despondent enough to curtail his appointments for two months and cancel scheduled trips. Those who met him noticed that he looked thinner, and acted somewhat ponderous, speaking with a hoarse voice, a sign for those who know him that he was getting tired and irritated. By July he seemed to recover and regain his public image of strength. Why then did the UN suddenly seem so vulnerable?

Since its establishment, the UN has been in the firing line for disgruntled leaders from all sides, the same ones who eventually resorted to it for a gracious exit. Soviet leader Nikita Khrushchev, who placed his shoe on a General Assembly seat and banged it repeatedly in protest, was only too happy to have a UN-sponsored arrangement out of the Cuban missile crisis. French president Charles de Gaulle referred to the UN once as "that thing," yet readily used the permanent seat in the Security Council to deal with Middle Eastern and other issues. France, like Britain, its ally in the Suez war that almost caused the Secretary-General to resign, are now exemplary members paying their dues on time and without conditions. While support for the UN in its host country, the United States, is consistently bipartisan, there was always some discreet and sometimes open political tension in that unique relationship of mutually high expectations. Democratic President Lyndon B. Johnson, piqued by the first Asian Secretary-General who did not agree with his policy on Vietnam, broke with tradition by boycotting the General Debate of the General Assembly. Similarly, under a Republican administration, an American ambassador wished the UN away from the U.S., promising to wave goodbye as its diplomats faded into the sunset. When alternative sites in Geneva, Bonn and Paris were offered, the same administration scuttled to block any move, however partial, at the behest of New York City, which receives through UN presence more money than the U.S. assigned contribution to the Organization. The smoothest period, under President George H.W. Bush, may have been mainly due to his previous international experience, including his time as UN ambassador in New York.

Governmental proclamations were not limited to big powers but extended to smaller ones, though with lesser negative impact. The most extreme case was that of Indonesian leader Sukarno, who announced his nation's withdrawal from the UN to form a bizarre organization of one. His successor Suharto arranged a gradual return. Another display was by Pakistan Prime Minister Ali Bhutto when the separation of Bangladesh appeared to be certain. After presenting his country's position he suddenly stood up in the middle of the Security Council chamber, took the paper containing the resolution in both hands and tore it apart, shouting, "This is what I think of your resolution."

The outcome over Iraq created an unprecedented risk for different reasons - suspicion, disappointment, or mere scapegoating - conflicting powers joined in a public derision of "people at the U.N.," although the UN reflected collective action or inaction of its Member States. A slight difference lies in a traditional discipline whereby the Secretariat is not as free, as individual governments are, to declare its own version of events — it would then risk offending at least one member state, let alone a permanent member of the Security Council. That was true in many controversial instances. Although Boutros Boutros-Ghali begged for 5,000 troops to avert a likely massacre in Rwanda, the Secretariat was generally blamed as countries that had turned him down were among those pointing the finger. Ceasefires were arranged between Arabs and Israelis by unheralded field officers, only to have the outcome claimed by some national governmental envoy. Hostages were released through quiet diplomacy, but publicly it was credited elsewhere.

The most tragic event to impact the UN role in Iraq was the attack on its headquarters in Baghdad. The UN lost valuable, dedicated, competent people in a very visible central stage as if someone wanted to send a sharp, brutal signal. It was an indication that the UN was losing its credibility in the third world. This was not the first attack on UN staff. Security of civilians in field has always been an issue, but in recent years there has been a pattern of growing attacks. There was a gruesome murder in September 2000 of three UNHCR workers who were hacked to death and their bodies burned in East Timor. A second incident was a coldblooded killing in Guinea with the abduction of a female colleague. The Baghdad bombing created problems, not only in undercutting any potential role there, but it also had repercussions within the UN itself. An initial official consensus was that if the purpose of the terrorists was to intimidate, the response should be swift and clear: we would not be intimidated, the mission would continue, the greater the challenge, the stronger the determination. However, just a week later, someone from the Secretary-General's office informed the press that we would be "lowering the flame."

Inside the United Nations

Presenting Luciano Pavarotti with his title as the first United Nations Messenger for Peace.

A signed photograph with "fratello" Maestro Pavarotti.

With Secretary-General Boutros Boutros-Ghali, showing Nelson Mandela, the first president of a free South Africa, a book by the Public Information Department on the fight against Apartheid.

Welcoming the King of Morocco, His Majesty Hassan II, to the United Nations; the only one to sign a photograph in gold ink.

The staff at my office, during a visit by Mother Theresa. Why are they smiling? Because she suggested getting them all married!

Presenting gifts to Mother Theresa during her visit to my office.

A moment of conversation with Mother Theresa.

Giving a photo of Mrs. Roosevelt holding the Universal Declaration of Human Rights to Hillary Clinton on its fiftieth anniversary.

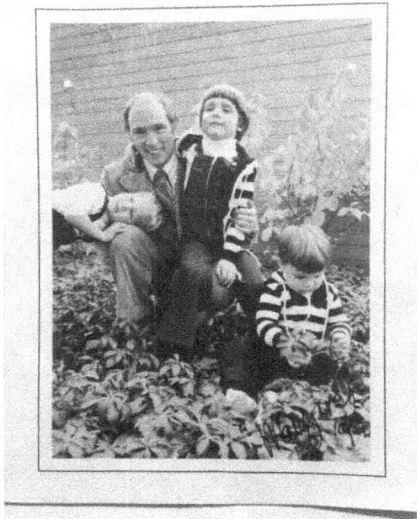

A personal Christmas card sent from then-Canadian Prime Minister Pierre Trudeau, with his three sons. The eldest, seated on his lap, is current Prime Minister of Canada, Justin Trudeau.

Delivering the results as the Special Representative to head the UN Observer Mission to Verify the Referendum in Eritrea – paving the way for a new UN Member State.

Surrounded by Eritrean women during the referendum.

With the President of the newly independent Eritrea, Isaias Afewerki.

A poster from the Eritrean referendum.

The front of a t-shirt, from the referendum, a remembrance of UNOVER.

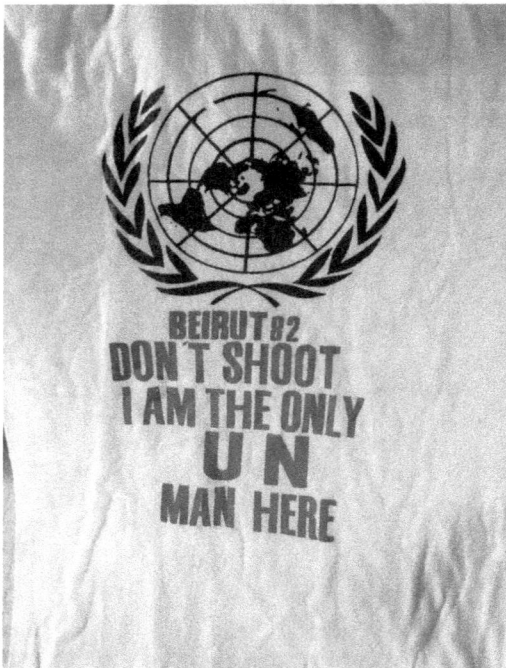

A t-shirt gifted to me by journalists in Beirut, after I was the only "UN man" who stayed behind during the Lebanese civil war.

With Kofi and Nane Annan, briefed by director Nadia Younes, who was later killed in the Baghdad bombing.

When I joined the UN: During a visit by George H.W. Bush, U.S. Delegate to the

UN.

Attending a panel discussion at the United Nations with Angela King and Dame Margaret Joan Anstee.

Crowds in Tehran surrounding UN visitors' car during the hostage crisis.

UN delegation of jurists visiting Iran's Ministry of Foreign Affairs, to visit the U.S. Chargé d'Affaires detained there.

A briefing in Tehran on the status of the hostages.

With Kofi Annan, at the United Nations.

Cyprus President Glafcos Clerides pleasantly advocating Food for Peace.

During a visit with a delegation from Beijing to prepare for the Summit on Women.

A signed photograph with Secretary-General U Thant.

A signed photograph with Secrtary-General Boutros Boutros-Ghali.

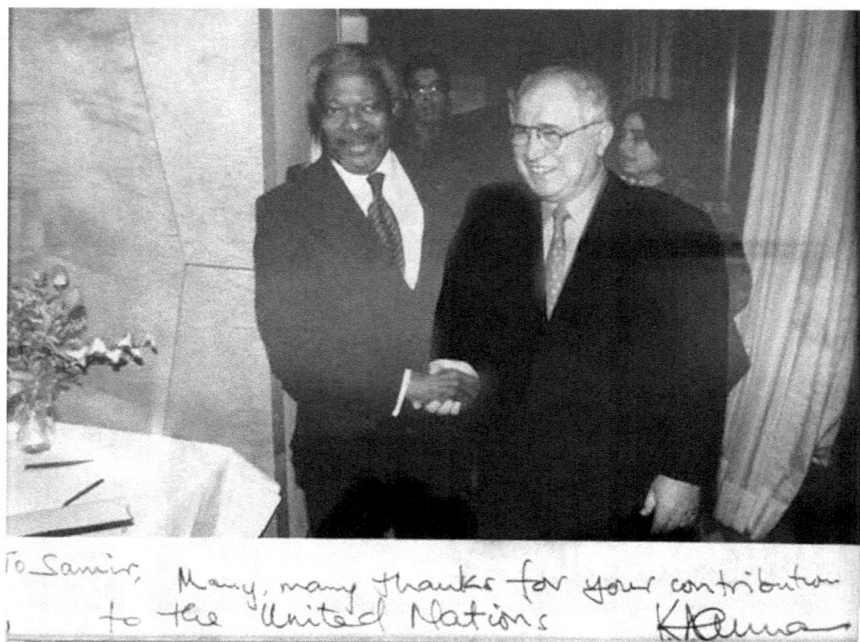

A signed photograph with Secretary-General Kofi Annan.

A resolution to raise the number of women to 50% in a number of departments was exceeded by raising it to 62%. Why were they all smiling? Because they were promoted!

A photo with the Information Assistants of the guided tours, one of New York's ten best public attractions.

A photograph of world leaders at the fiftieth anniversary of the United Nations; the opportunity to photograph world leaders together, without security guards, and witnessing this moment of vulnerability was worth all these years of work.

A shared hug with Secretary-General Kofi Annan at my goodbye party; director Nadia Younes was present as well (on the right), who regretfully died years later in the bombing of the UN office in Baghdad.

Chapter XII:

VITAL, CENTRAL, PIVOTAL, NO ROLE?

After the fall of Baghdad, an Anglo-American summit in Belfast envisaged a "vital" role for the United Nations. "Old Europe" immediately demanded the UN carry "the central role," then compromised with a diplomatic vowel movement to "a" central role. Egypt helpfully suggested "pivotal," while the Prime Minister of Sweden - not necessarily influenced by Hans Blix - felt that the UN should be "in the driver's seat." Even Kofi Annan, the UN Secretary-General at the time, seemed to waver between "important" and "effective". His designation of a "Special Advisor" on Iraq was immediately followed - lest anyone expect any substantive move – by an announcement that he will be based in New York and "would not be traveling, neither would he be putting forward ideas to the Security Council for considerations," but would be available to the Council "should they ask questions." An insider interpretation meant that this designation was interim; time out to search for future prospects while allowing permanent members to sort out their other relationships and agree on a broad direction.

By then, everyone needed the U.N., though for different purposes. The U.S., at least, had to obtain international legitimacy for its continued presence and future action in Iraq. That included lifting sanctions, phasing-out the Oil-for-Food program, overseeing the flow of oil and reconstruction projects, dealing with civilian Iraqis, and replacing the former government with a new one, which would become legally empowered to make commitments on behalf of the country. France sought to bring decision-making back to where it could wield more influence and perhaps exercise some diplomatic bargaining, hoping to regain some of its valuable ground lost. Russia hoped to negotiate through a valued veto its financial claims, together with its strategic interests; its "vision" of a new world order was described by its transient Foreign Minister as "a pyramid topped by the United Nations and its Security Council." Germany, a non-permanent member with notable influence, never abandoned its long pending quest for a permanent seat. The speed with which Saddam Hussein's regime fell and the chaotic breakdown of the Iraqi state must have caught most everyone off-guard. A strategic earthquake shook the region. In dealing with its aftershocks for some time to come, world capitals did not realize the value of working closer together. A politically safe demand for regaining the unity of the Security Council was a worthy target, easier proclaimed than done. The U.S. needed a more persuasive approach than merely displaying its military victory while other key members - presumed allies yet avid competitors - needed a wider vision than secretly hoping for the U.S. to get a black eye. Traditionally, the Secretary-General would try to help by exploring areas of joint interest and sensing the right timing for a step-by-step consensus. Through planned, often discreet initiatives, he or his representative would synchronize a re-entry into the collaborative diplomatic orbit of the all interested members, including the country directly involved, Iraq - a founding member of the United Nations.

Italian Nobel Prize winner Luigi Pirandello wrote a play about six characters in search of an author. Was it impossible for a UN Secretary-General to come out with a blueprint for a "five plus one" scenario? Admittedly, there were obvious constraints: some political, like the overpowering stance of the United States Administration; some structural, like the Eurocentric composition of the Security Council; and some managerial, like the absence of any senior official around Kofi Annan with credible standing in the region or practical grasp of its shifting crosscurrents. Still, the stakes were worth the effort, however painstaking.

In approaching a UN role for post-war Iraq, one option for the Secretary-General was to prepare and propose his own considered vision. A European summit in Athens, preceded by the Anglo American summit in Belfast, and followed by a G-8 summit of industrialized countries in

Evian, would have presented unique opportunities to propose it; unfortunately he was neither inclined nor in a state to do so. A second option was to wait for emerging developments, tacitly holding competing countries accountable for likely failure; that would require unusual spinning skills. The third was to designate someone to explore what could be done and how to do it. Initially, his team sought informal approval of only one name. A former Foreign Affairs Minister of Thailand, hardly familiar with the complex issues or the explosive region, was presented as a presumably politically correct choice. When the name of Sergio Vieira de Mello was mentioned, some around Annan were not enthusiastic. The charismatic Brazilian who started his peacemaking career with the UN force in South Lebanon and headed missions in Kosovo and East Timor would not be amenable to remote control. He could develop strong support among key governments, including from that of permanent members of the Security Council where he was highly regarded. His savvy handling of the media in several languages could draw eventual attention to his potential as a candidate to succeed the Secretary-General.

The prospect of his appointment to such a key role was particularly opposed by an internally influential team aspiring to push their own candidate to groom for the next top world diplomat should come from the Asian continent. They would leave no bureaucratic stone unturned to make Sergio's assignment more difficult in New York than in Baghdad.

Confronting the requirements of post-war Iraq was an unprecedented challenge. The UN was not the major player; its own Security Council entrusted that task to the "Occupying Power." It needed to set forth a carefully planned strategy with an incremental approach, while offering to the public a perception of determination and clarity. With its inclusive framework, it could draw on the best and brightest talents worldwide. If it sharpened the focus on feasible fields of operations, its leadership would move gradually, building on whatever limited agreement and consolidating every step with a growing consensus. Making peace is not just overseeing an absence of military conflict, it is sustaining a process of human development, consolidating the quality of human life and protection of human values. That is at the heart of UN work, and similarly at the center of the real issue in Iraq.

Usually, the UN operates more effectively not as a hammer, but like a comb or ploughshare, tilling a landscape to mix fruitful ingredients and create an atmosphere of peace. If basic conditions or a lack of minimal security did not allow for certain activities, others could be explored. If no role on the ground was deemed practical, then that would be appropriately, yet clearly, indicated; otherwise the UN will be held accountable for what it was not in charge of.

The UN could not be in Iraq merely as a diplomatic assignment or complementary operation, an annex. Instead, its team would need to show an active interest in the daily life of Iraqi citizens and stand out as a champion for human development and human dignity. That, in my mind, was the role that Sergio Vieira de Mello intended for the UN in Iraq. Strategically, the UN could be essential to strengthen the unity and sovereignty of Iraq, while working with neighboring countries whose own stability depends on what happens in Baghdad. To gain acceptance by its neighbors, however, any Iraqi authority will have to first win the acceptance of its own people. Any presence of the UN should represent the consensual will of the international community speaking with one voice to an Iraqi public facing fragmentation as ethnic flames threatened to tear the country apart.

To play a constructive role in Iraq, there was also a need to look outside the country's borders. Apart from the Palestinian-Israeli conflict, with obvious impact in the region, the U.S-Iran relationship had implications on the Iraq war. Unlocking the secrets of that relationship would in fact provide a clue to the future of the Middle East and beyond. The United States-Iran relations has since the fall of the Shah been more of shadowboxing than engaged conflict. Despite angry political rhetoric, the two countries have had many parallel strategic interests along the same lines, not only in the fall of the Taliban in Afghanistan and Saddam Hussein in Iraq, but in installing the political authority that took over. The United States and Iran also have common strategic interest in fragmenting a unified "Arab nationalist" vision, as both of them prefer a splintering of the Arab world into weaker compliant entities. While the U.S. clearly intended to have an uncontested presence, Iran's geopolitical position near the Strait of Hormuz straddling the Gulf and the Caspian oil rich basins would strengthen its claim to be recognized as a regional player and a nuclear power. Given the stakes involved, there was no doubt that at any given day, intermediaries in contact points like Dubai, Geneva, Beirut or elsewhere were trying to perfect a mutual arrangement.

With the massive presence of American troops in Iraq, one of the world's newest cultures came in direct dynamic and often explosive contact with one of the oldest. Through daily experience, they blended or clashed, fused and confused, in what could have been for both either a unique opportunity - or a potential tragedy. But while the repercussions of the Iraq war on an outstretched U.S. appear gradually over a decade, the impact on the UN was almost immediate. These included the fallout over Oil-for-Food; the bombing of the UN headquarters in Baghdad; growing skepticism about its work culture; and the shifting positions of member states in the Security Council. All of this presented an unprecedented challenge which has not yet been substantially faced.

In time, occupying forces found an exit, and the Iraqi people, survivors of seven thousand years, will continue to look after their own. For the UN however, its handling of the Iraq crisis was a serious blow to its stature, if not its relevance in these changing times.

The UN Headquarters Bombing

Just after 4:30pm on August 19, 2003, a cement-mixer truck bomb destroyed the UN headquarters in Baghdad, which had been set up in the early 1990s in the Canal Hotel and was now used by the UNAMI mission. At least 22 people were killed, including the UN Special Representative in Iraq, Sergio Vieira de Mello. Over 100 people were injured. Abu Musab al-Zarqawi, leader of the terrorist organization Jama'at al-Tawhid wal-Jihad, claimed responsibility.

This murderous terrorist attack on UN headquarters in Baghdad was unprecedented — the first assault on the UN flag in history. Before, there were individual deaths of envoys or threats against certain offices. This time, the immunity of the international organization -- its main trademark -- was violated, brutally. People whose only aim was to help were killed. An organization whose main objective is peace and development received a severe blow. Yet if the purpose was to intimidate, the first response was swift and clear: We will not be intimidated. The mission should continue. If one purpose was to try and divide members of the Security Council who differed about the war, a unified council met immediately and condemned the assault in the strongest terms. UN staff felt the strength of their bond as they hugged and exchanged consolation: the greater the challenge, the stronger the determination.

The bombing of the UN office in Baghdad was our 9/11, where we lost some of our best people. Staff exchanged stories about each of our colleagues and everyone had a human experience to recount. Sergio was a close friend of mine, and Nadia Younes, his Deputy had been my dear friend for 25 years. She was one of my closest colleagues as she made her way up the staff ladder from P2 to D2. In a gathering in New York after the attack, one of her best friends described her by counting the best things about Nadia: "She never talked down or pulled rank, never a hint of 'as the president of Pakistan said to me....' She never talked from her position, her age, her class. Her talk was never competitive, never pedantic. It was like her physical presence: unmannered, unaffected, no nonsense, straight-up stuff. No wonder the press liked her. She knew always knew and cared that she lived in a world of poverty, violence, injustice, sexual and racial prejudice – she worked in it, that world of pleading representatives of starving countries, phrase-parsing diplomats, grand standing politicians and wild-eyed religious fanatics of all stripes. All the oh-so-right-and-righteous-manly men. The manly men who killed her, in a war fought by manly men fighting manly men."

The dynamic Brazilian Sergio and the irreverent Egyptian Nadia – both unique international civil servants – made a perfect team with hope, energy and sense of humor. They shared a work ethic, an unflinching commitment to the objectives of the UN They were workers, not mere networkers, but somehow their performances networked for them. They were among the best that the UN system could produce. What happened to them and their colleagues in Baghdad was a shock to the whole UN system, and the staff held the UN leadership accountable for their failure to deal with the aftermath. There was a feeling that senior officials were being protected while junior ones were scapegoated. Mr. Annan's decision to discipline a handful of UN officials for failing to provide adequate security at Baghdad headquarters was not enough and many thought the Organization's top leadership should accept greater responsibility for the tragedy. The staff expected more accountability. First an investigation team was formed, an "independent panel" led by Mr. Ahtisaari, which was followed by another committee that produced another report. It was felt that both the report and the Secretary-General's response to it placed excessive emphasis on low-level individuals in the area of security. The only real action taken was to hit the politically helpless Security Coordinator, Myat Tun. As an isolated citizen of poor Myanmar, neither his government nor its Permanent Representative in New York would do much to defend him. Colleagues of Mr. Tun and of

Ramiro Lopes da Silva, the other person held responsible, found the actions to be unfair and biased. The investigation was not considered serious since it picked on staffers unable to defend themselves, while the "big shots" who took the decision in the Iraq Crisis Group regular meetings were not touched.

There was also a feeling that some of those around the Secretary-General had not been fair to Sergio when he was first sent as an envoy. He had recently been appointed as High Commissioner of Human Rights in Geneva, a favorite town, and wanted to consolidate his new role. He agreed to go only for an interim six months. Within the diplomatic community there was a general impression that he had the stuff to become the next Secretary-General. Some of those around Kofi who had their own agenda saw Sergio as the main competition. They blocked him from taking regularly visible positions for which he would have been easily qualified, like the Director General for Europe, or Under Secretary-General for Public Information. When his designation for Baghdad was imminent, they tried to undercut him by spreading the word that he was an American choice. In fact, he was very highly regarded by the French, with whom he had a deeply close link, admired by the Russians who dealt with him well over Yugoslavia, and the Chinese who knew him from Cambodia. Most member governments knew and liked him, as did the Americans after his brief visit to Washington. The loss of Sergio Vieira de Mello was not only personal in losing a close friend but a loss for the whole UN.

The Baghdad attack left the United Nations family in an emotional state of sorrow with a profound sense of loss. Those emotions could have flown into a channel of action in the right direction and for the right course. Our colleague and friend Sergio Vieira de Mello was also the High Commissioner for Human Rights, inscribed in a Universal Declaration. They include the right to live free from intimidation, freedom of expression, and freedom of cultural diversity. He died trying to fulfill his mission.

It's a Vigil, Not a Photo Opportunity

The passing away of loved ones is a particularly unique lifetime void. The untimely loss of my father at age 52 when I was 18, still in college, was compounded ten years later with the sudden death of my closest brother, Sami, on his 30th, birthday while working as a medical doctor in Kuwait's main hospital.

We had grown up together as roommates for 25 years and travelling to retrieve his body was uniquely agonizing, particularly when I was firmly though politely blocked from obtaining related details. Only his personal clothes were handed to me. His personal notes, insurance policy, bank account and further details on the cause of untimely death disappeared. Upon enquiring, I was told, incredibly, that he had not renewed his insurance (very strange for a struggling medical expatriate) and closed his account, oddly, because my understanding was that he was preparing to get married. Although one sheet of paper handed to me mentioned a "coronary thrombosis," a Lebanese doctor colleague mentioned that Sami was injected erroneously with a drug to which he was known to be seriously allergic. Curiously, although he was officially an employee of the oil rich state of Kuwait, no compensation, indemnity, or pension funds were paid. My main focus, however, was on bringing my brother back home. He had already suffered enough in his life, particularly as he struggled to continue his studies at Bonn University, having to swiftly learn a new language, after being forced out of his concluding fourth year at Beirut Medical School. An arbitrary decision by a politically appointed President sought to punish him as Chairman of the Student Literary Club after its assembly decided to hold a one-day demonstration.

Students at the American University of Beirut who were determined to speak their minds freely in the 1950s and 1960s did not realize at the time that the heightened tension of the Cold War would put pressure on their American supervisors to avert public demonstrations that may be used by political adversaries. On the other hand, a politically appointed president of the University perceived by students to have a security background placed all outspoken individuals together, even those belonging or openly belonging to different, contradictory groups. Socially, civil activists were dumped with Arab nationalists, socialists, liberals, together with a very limited minority of communist individuals; all were put together, thus bonding them totally against him. His threatening measures aimed to "kick ass" and instill fear, but became glaringly counterproductive, not only for the transient president but also for the credibility of the university, which had taken careful decades to build. Similarly, it took years later, particularly because of the civil war, to partially recover. By then even caring presidents had to face not only the usual sensitivities and differences on campus, but also a growing influence of antagonists outside its gates.

This antagonism ended up having violent consequences in some cases. Malcom Kerr, a pro-Arab scholar was killed at the university. He was born and raised, and died, in Beirut. An Arab scholar and father of Golden State Warriors basketball head coach Stephen Kerr, he was an Arabic-speaking American citizen who specialized in the Middle East. Once more, this was a tragic case of a good man who was violently silenced.

Although I was cornered into getting only one Kuwaiti narrative, however unconvincing, almost ruthless, my family needed to offer our loved one a gracious, affectionate farewell. As anyone with such an experience would know, the passing away of a close family member leaves a uniquely irreplaceable void. Decades pass; yet their living memory remains.

Even now I feel Sami's absence in my everyday life and devote two weeks in February to his affectionate memory

Within an hour of hearing about the Baghdad attack, distraught internationalists started arriving at the Dag Hammarksjold Plaza across UN Headquarters on First Avenue and Forty-Seventh Street. They embraced and hugged, some openly sobbing, some holding their tears. Volunteers offered candles. At about 7 pm, men and women mingling regardless of rank or prominence started lighting the candles from one another in dignified silence. Clerical secretaries mixed with Under-Secretary-Generals in the true spirit of dedicated civil servants. Every face seemed somehow familiar. Everyone looked like a friend. UNDP Administrator Mark Malloch Brown intently listening, confident as always; then-newly appointed Ombudsman former Jamaican Ambassador Patricia Durrant, casually attired as she joined in singing "Amazing Grace". Under-Secretary-General Nitin Desai, short-sleeved, silently grieving by friends. Retired colleagues like Leona Forman, a Brazilian compatriot of Sergio Vieira de Mello, and her husband, Professor Shephard, standing with members of the International Peace Academy. New Under-Secretary-General for Administration and Management Catherine Bertini compassionately exchanged consolations. Deputy Secretary-General Louise Fréchette arrived and delivered brief, sincere and effectively emotional remarks, then graciously stood aside in respectful silence. Sirens announced the approaching motorcade of the Secretary-General, though that was not necessary in such an atmosphere;

the vigil was just across the street, and he sometimes walked all the way home. Someone mentioned wistfully that it was an adviser's ploy to alert the cameras.

Kofi Annan was usually a master of handling emotional occasions, but it must have been a stressful day, plus the jet lag -- having arrived that shocking morning from Sweden. He seemed perplexed as one determined aide placed a lit candle in his hand while he hesitated as another gently edged him towards the microphone. He looked around as if seeking fresh oxygen among friendly faces, but then those determined handlers wanted him -- his head first then theirs -- facing the cameras. He made off the cuff remarks almost matter-of-factly, which was atypical, except for the last sentence when he seemed to regain his original self. But then again he was led to the corner of entry for a quick exit. Obviously seeking to linger on, self-appointed handlers kept him in place. Instead of consoling with affectionate colleagues and friends at such a sorrowful occasion, he was brought three nervous young girls to shake his hand, for the benefit of the cameras -- which, incidentally, turned elsewhere.

As UN speechwriter Ed Mortimer aptly pointed out in the *Financial Times*: "We are all in shock and may not be thinking straight." That is more reason for those in senior leadership position to reflect a dignified sense of shared sorrow. Most of them did. But obviously there were some who perceived a spontaneous heartfelt vigil merely as a photo opportunity.

Sergio was drafted to go to Baghdad. He reluctantly agreed and only for four months. It was known, and reported, that certain influential characters around Kofi Annan had other candidates in mind. He was too independent-minded, too charismatic, attracting too much media interest and presented too much competition. With his success in Kosovo and East Timor, and then Iraq, he became more visible and more "Secretary Generable." They sharpened their tools of ambush, if possible, without leaving a trace. They spread the word, not only in New York but unscrupulously through an appointed proxy in the mission itself, including someone who was sent on the mission to Baghdad. They whispered his name accompanied with a grimace, a grin, or a head-turn that he was "working for the Americans." Never mind that any member of that gang, with a reputation for licking any powerful hand, would have loved to be asked for a favor by Washington. Their irresponsible purpose was to get at Sergio's reputation and credibility, fingering him as if he was doing the bidding of the occupation forces. Who are they? The least we could do is make the point.

Investigation Report on Baghdad Bombing Raised Serious Questions

The adverse internal impact of the Baghdad explosion grew within the UN system as more facts were unearthed and more questions were asked. An "Independent Panel" led by former Finnish President and Senior UN official Martti Ahtisaari made specific observations on October 20, 2003, that the Secretary-General announced he would study carefully. Ten days later, on the eve of a gathering of heads of UN offices, programs and agencies, the Secretary-General sent a letter to the staff promising improved security. That, however, was not enough to contain the anger, frustration and sense of unapplied justice. The more the delay in providing a clear and tangible response, the stronger the pushback. Already staff throughout the system were insisting that those responsible, no matter how senior, be held accountable.

The panel concluded that "the UN security management system failed in its mission to provide adequate security to UN staff in Iraq," leaving the UN "open and vulnerable to the type of attack that was perpetrated on 19 August 2003."

The main conclusion of the Panel was that "the current security management system is dysfunctional. It provides little guarantee of security to UN staff in Iraq or other high-risk environments and needs to be reformed." The panel identified a lack of accountability for the decisions and positions taken by UN managers with regard to the security of UN staff. It said, "The United Nations needs a new culture of accountability in security management."

The report was released to the staff with a letter from the Secretary-General, who said he was "gravely concerned" with its findings. "We owe it to all those affected by the attack on our Baghdad headquarters -- the dead, the injured, the survivors, and their families -- to do our utmost to ensure that such failures are not repeated, either in Iraq or elsewhere. Indeed, we also owe that to ourselves and to each other," he wrote. He also announced a series of steps to implement the Panel's recommendations.

The issue goes to the heart of leadership, responsibility, and accountability, as well as to the performance and delivery of international civil service. In allowing adequate, but not prolonged, time for a responsible response and an indication of action, it would have been useful to produce the executive summary of the investigation, mentioned in the first letter by the Secretary-General, in ten days amid the general reaction of the staff. It was owed to the UN and to those who died to continue pursuing the matter.

Accountability For Baghdad: Forming Committees Was Not Action, Nor was Scapegoating a Helpless Myat Tun

Four months later, the stonewalling continued. The scapegoating of lower level staff seemed to be the order of the day. Higher level officials who competed in taking credit for decisions started competing in disclaimers. They may have attended meetings, but they did not really follow all the points raised. They received reports only to pass them on to officers with more time on their hands. They knew, of course, that there were risks and threats. They even heard the fallen Special Representative declare in the Security Council that he and his staff were "vulnerable." But you know how things happen, went the weak argument: a very senior person hardly had time to focus on any particular issue more than a few minutes -- half an hour at most.

Vague utterances should not be allowed to cover for the biggest tragedy that had ever hit the United Nations. People wanted accountability. A first investigation team was formed by Mr. Ahtisaari, but after a "thorough study" of this half-and-half report, another committee was formed from distinguished individuals who were expected to produce another report requiring further study and continued thought. The only action taken thus far was to hit the politically helpless Security Coordinator, a citizen of isolated Myanmar named Myat Tun. Certainly his permanent representative would not be knocking doors down to defend him. Even the preliminary Ahtisaari report pointed, however slightly, to specific officials in the higher chain of command. But then they were either too connected or too well informed to be provoked by tough action, however deserved. The attempt from "those above" seemed to focus the issue and the blame on "security." That should not work. There was so much emotion, credibility and conviction at stake to disregard time-consuming committees. The teflon was wearing thin.

Vital, Central, Pivotal, No Role?

Staff Continue to Raise Questions on Baghdad: No Due Process for Publicly Condemned Coordinator While Senior Officials Merely "Share" Reprimand Letter

While publicly dismissing two Security officials, the Secretary-General felt that he had taken "firm" action by sending a letter to the Deputy Secretary-General, who chaired the decision-making Senior Group on Iraq, and requested her to "share" it with its members. In fact, those members still appeared to be surrounding Mr. Annan at all meetings related to Iraq. They must have had a jolly interesting nudge-nudge when dutifully served with a neatly typed copy of the collective reprimand. One could not contain oneself when faced with such a "Yes Minister"-type situation mimicking the British satirical comedy show.

Meanwhile, *The Washington Post* reported that a group of mid-level UN staffers had formally protested Annan's decision to discipline a handful of UN officials for failing to provide adequate security at the Baghdad headquarters of the UN before the August terrorist attack. The staffers said the Organization's top leaders should accept greater responsibility for the tragedy.

In addition to the strong views expressed by the Staff Committee, two letters to the Secretary-General received wide circulation. They reflect feelings among staff throughout the UN system that senior officials were being protected while junior ones scapegoated. The two official reports produced thus far were described as full of inaccuracies and tailored to suit a selective attitude in dealing with accountability.

The first letter was written by Robert Turner, a survivor of the Baghdad blast. He stated in part: "As a UN staff member who was intimately involved in this affair and who will feel the impact of your decisions in this matter, I am very concerned at the lack of due process provided to Mr. Myat and Mr. Lopes da Silva. Your request that they resign from the UN Secretariat, while convenient for the organization, does not offer either of these staff members the protection provided them by staff rules."

He went on to say that Mr. Myat and Mr. Lopes da Silva "have been tried in secret by the Panel, arbitrarily sentenced by you, and forced to become the very personal manifestations of a failed security system, a system which you head."

He went on to express "serious concerns" about other actions, saying the Secretary-General "clearly demonstrated that politics are more important than staff security when it suits as there was no requirement in Iraq -- bar political -- that justified a continued presence under UN security regulations, after either bombing."

The letter cited other incidents that "sent the very clear signal that your office had no interest in supporting security decisions in the field that may be politically sensitive at headquarters."

Staff of the World Food Programme wrote a second letter expressing similar distress regarding disciplinary measures against Mr. Tun Myat and Mr. Ramiro Lopes da Silva. "It is our view that neither of our colleagues can be held personally or professionally responsible for the tragic events of 19 August 2003 in Baghdad." Expressing praise for those individuals, the letter states that "both the report and your reaction to it place excessive emphasis on individual responsibility over and above the United Nations system's shared responsibility for security."

Ignoring Lessons

All UN staff, friends and families of loved ones lost on August 19th were commemorating the event a year later. But a number of those who evaded any responsibility for decisions taken at that time were at it again, meeting that same day to select their own favorites to assign for Iraq -- not to send to the risky area of course, but to assign tasks and "co-ordinate" turf. But then no one could accuse that team of being sensitive. Kofi Annan was in Geneva when Sergio Vieira de Mello was buried. It must have been a very difficult moment for him. Presentable and solemn, he looked emotionally spent, befitting the occasion. Atypically, he misread several words. Drawing on his ancestral Ashanti tradition, he seemed to talk to the dead -- like carrying on a side conservation.

Those joining the New York commemoration, dutifully and punctually took their seats at 8:30 a.m. in the Trusteeship Council Chambers. Security officers politely and efficiently oversaw an orderly arrangement, and guides pleasantly welcomed and directed everyone to their general location.

Then it was like hurry up and wait. A piano player created a solemn mood as diplomats and staff awaited some signal. Nothing much happened except some whispers and rushed movements by volunteer helpers on the sidelines. As it became clear that proceedings will start with a Geneva connection, many started to shuffle. Someone could have taken the stage to fill in the time with some sensitive talk of welcome and a few suitable words to maintain the momentum. Or, at least the impressive video which had to be cut off abruptly could have been played earlier. Deputy Secretary-General Louise Fréchette entered, surrounded by fully uniformed guards, followed by a number of representatives of bereaved families and accompanied by a greater number of staff who volunteered -- or were asked -- to join them. The procession was advanced by the gracious and elegant Aminata Djermakoye, Protocol Chief, who rose, as expected, to the occasion. Lakhdar Brahimi displayed genuine grief with a dignified demeanor. Many eyes were on Ms. Fréchette, who had chaired the Crisis Group on Iraq, which staff representatives strongly felt got off lightly while junior staff were summarily dismissed without due process. The negative focus on her alone was neither accurate nor fair. Other senior officials were in fact making the real decisions. But somehow, she seemed intent on wearing that role. She must have changed from when she was the engaging and considerate Representative of Canada. We all change. But at least she is straightforward. What you see is what you get. She expressed understanding for everyone's grief. No doubt she was emotionally shaken and very much withdrawn.

In a clearly insensitive move, a circular sent out to all UN offices just before the occasion instructed staff not to devote any special conference room, office, statue, etc., to any of the victims. No Sergio prize. No Nadia Younes Press briefing room. The claim was to honor the group collectively, rather than individually. But the fact was that Sergio's charisma and Nadia's irreverent laugh still haunted those who lack enough self-confidence to accept other "diplomatic rock stars" or work with a wider team rather than through a closed clique.

After another year had passed, except for Deputy Secretary-General Louise Fréchette, no one from the UN leadership was present as staff assembled for the second anniversary to remember their fallen colleagues. Particularly those who were in the forefront of photo opportunities when the catastrophe first hit seemed to have found excuses and disappeared elsewhere. The Secretary-General was on holiday in Ghana, where he was reported to have received an accomplishment award. Yet he did find an occasion to make a thoughtful reference. The Chef de Cabinet, who actually had handled Iraq issues substantively was off that day. To her credit, Ms. Fréchette appeared and milled around. At least during some occasions, like at an important gathering in Canada, she defended the staff in their absence without seeking credit. And, unlike the rest, she did offer to resign.

We still remember those victims of ruthless terror. We recall their names, every one of them, with pride and sorrow. Each of us lost a friend and colleague: Sergio, Nadia, and all the others who gave the ultimate sacrifice. They died in order to make a difference in our world. They died for A CREDIBLE UNITED NATIONS.

"We believe in the UN flag that flew in Baghdad that day," said Michele Montas, a radio officer, on behalf of her colleagues. "WE DEMAND JUSTICE." Further, she stressed: "Without that clear message, others among us will be killed; others among us will be kidnapped." While senior officials generally ignored the event, staff around the world were smarting under what they feel was lack of accountability among those officials who were in charge of making the decisions. Two reports raised more questions than answers. Action taken, or lack thereof, smacked of expediency and spin, mainly hitting at mid-level officers and staffers with no political backing while big honchos who had supposedly met regularly on Iraq hardly got a slap on the wrist.

The most peculiarly accurate comment came, surprisingly, from Kofi Annan. An official statement reported him as saying: "The question of justice lingers, as no one was held to account for this crime."

It seemed that one of those around Secretary-General Annan believed in the eroding impact of diminishing memory. They lowered the flame gradually every passing year, in the delusion that accountability -- and people's profound agony – would fade away. Every passing year they focused attention elsewhere, possibly expecting that such a horrific crime would be somehow minimized. And every year the staff proved them wrong and remembered right. And if the Secretary-General, the UN Chief Administration officer, did not yet know whom to hold accountable, everyone else did.

As more attention and funds are allocated to security at Headquarters and certain areas in the field, the basic protection of staff depends on having a credible image stressing clearly their unique roles as truly independent representatives of the entire UN community, rather than seeming to project policies of particular parties. This was the main safety net for UN personnel over the first 50 years of the Organization's history, without any major accident. That continues to be the key for the personal safety, and indeed the success, not only the mere survival, of the United Nations.

CHAPTER XIII:

WHAT PRICE PEACEKEEPING?

The role of UN Peacekeeping reflects the impact of drastically changing times. A highly regarded asset over the first 50 years turned into a scandalous embarrassment. What had been a major source of accomplishment for Dag Hammarskjold following the Suez War, and of pride for Javier Perez de Cuellar, ended up being accused of allowing massacres in Srebrenica and Rwanda and awkward inaction in Darfur. It eventually drove Ban Ki-moon to declare that he was shocked "to the core" for repeated indications of sexual abuse. Those who were hailed in 1956 as Guardians of Peace, perceived worldwide as a uniquely creative UN initiative, were replaced by some in 2016 who were branded even by a UN senior official as having turned from protectors to predators. A main difference in time is that while the Secretary-General's mission was then complimented by helpful influential statesmen like Canada's Lester Pearson, the special envoy of the Secretary-General in the currently beleaguered mission is an obscure "fonctionnaire" from the same country as certain accused troops.

Peacekeeping principles remain the same. The difference in stature, performance and image is in the credibility of team leadership, extent of collective political support and dedicated determination at all levels to implement a designated mission.

How does a peacekeeping mission start? Why is it that some

conflicts have UN peacekeepers and others are outside its auspices? A non-permanent Council member once compared the Security Council's attitude to conflicts to that of the New York City Fire Department. There's a difference perceived in handling a fire that breaks out on Park Avenue and that in the Bronx. That may explain part of it. Delays to take action in a growing crisis are usually caused by member states calculating their own interest, pressuring one another or simply hoping the issue would somehow go away. The Secretary-General is normally on the receiving end, reflecting the nature of a prevailing consensus. He could, of course, try to have them move along or shame them into action, but usually the Secretary-General seeks to maintain useful and effective relations with key member states and would rather do so softly. Although a peacekeeping is always a process, any mission would go through a ladder of the following steps.

1. A conflict is brought to the attention of the Security Council by one or more member states. In certain cases the Secretary-General has the right to draw attention to a situation that may threaten world peace and security.

2. The Council would then give initial consideration.

3. If there is a general agreement, the Council will ask the Secretary-General to propose a plan of action, indicating for example the number of troops required and the amount of money needed, after surveying the options and feasibility, including the degree of participation and the ability to operate in the area directly involved.

4. To gain practical insight, the Secretary-General or other senior officials will contact key countries to insure the political will to proceed, the potential contribution of trained soldiers and the logistical support.

5. Theoretically, at least a careful selection process should follow, like ensuring a geographical balance, proven level of competence, and ability to work within the context of wider intra-national operation.

6. An additional requirement injected by U.S. ambassador to the U.N., Richard Holbrooke, was a medical test for HIV/AIDS. Whether that politically correct approach was rigidly applied or not is uncertain.

In practice, an emergency situation would give priority to putting boots on the ground, drawing from an already existing drill of "the usual suspects." In the first generation of peacekeeping mainly Scandinavian countries like Sweden, Denmark, Norway and Finland were the quickest to offer troops and cover their expenses, while Canada and sometimes the US provided logistics and communications. More recently, there was more contribution from developing countries, such as Bangladesh, India, Fiji, Jordan, Nepal and Pakistan. While soldiers from these countries are paid by their own governments on the basis of their national salary scale, the same governments are paid by the UN on the basis of standards approved by the General Assembly, where these governments have major influence. A large margin of difference is not coincidental. For example, a national salary for a soldier in Fiji or Bangladesh is much lower than the $1,027 the UN pays per peacekeeper, with $303 more for "a specialist" and $100 supplement for clothing and equipment. The main financial contributions for missions since the 1990s came from the U.S., Japan, Germany, U.K., France, Italy, Canada, Spain, China and the Netherlands. Some 120,000 uniformed personnel are currently in the field with the first all-female police unit introduced in Liberia in 2007.

The decision on missions would depend on the position of Security Council member states: 15 members, (five permanent and 10 serving two-year terms). A three-decade discussion on the composition of the membership reached nowhere. For example, an alliance of four influential members, Brazil, Germany, Japan and India, proposed adding ten more seats: six permanent without a veto power and four non-permanent. Another group, mostly led by Pakistan and Italy, wanted to add 10 non-permanent members who could be re-elected. The African Union, which is the most numerous consisting of 53 countries, proposed 11 additional seats, six of which would have veto power, two of them going to Africa. There was no outcome, since the matter was for practical purposes in the hands of the existing permanent members who, whatever their rhetorical positions, have a vested interest in keeping the structural balance of power. The Council, which first met in 1946 in London, still consists of its permanent members — China, France, Russia, United Kingdom of Great Britain and Northern Ireland, United States of America — and the non-permanent members that rotate every two years.

There was great optimism in 1992 when the UN was assigned to play a role in evolving a new international world order after a Security Council summit attended by its members head of state. Particularly President George H.W. Bush, a former Ambassador to the UN known for his experience; Russian General Secretary Gorbachev; French President Mitterrand; a new flexible Chinese leadership; and the U.K. government, always a UN supporter, all geared towards giving UN peacekeeping and peacemaking a chance. Ten years later, the situation totally shifted. Leadership changed, enthusiasm evaporated and opportunity ineffectively mishandled.

An added complication is that there are so many UN offices and agencies, most not shown to the outside world, also operating in the field. Taken together, there are scores of UN agencies, offices, funds and programs. The most prominent are the Specialized Agencies, such as the World Health Organization, International Labour Organization, International Telecommunications Union and the Universal Postal Union. These agencies are semi-autonomous. They have their own respective governing bodies and their own assemblies that elect their respective directors general, although they operate under the UN umbrella. Some of them have been operating since before the UN was established. They would meet once or twice a year for personal coordination but do not take instructions from UN Headquarters. For example, when the General Assembly years ago decided to boycott South Africa, some agencies like UNESCO joined enthusiastically but others did not. The World Bank explained that they were not in a position to stop dealing with any banks; ICAO, the International Civil Aviation Organization, explained that it was unable to interrupt any airline communications. There are additionally more than a dozen funds and programs, such as UNICEF, the UN Population Fund and UN Development Programme, whose budgets are based on voluntary contributions. Then there are also special ventures, where the Secretary-General may have more command but needs to accommodate balance of power. In a sense, the UN Secretary-General who supposedly runs peacekeeping is possibly first among equals, but he is not on full operational command. Sometimes even on his own turf, he needs to tread softly.

A mission normally will have a Political head, and a Military Force Commander, most likely selected from a participating country. Its timeframe is mandated by the Security Council, initially for a short period like six months but often renewable, sometimes for decades. The Cyprus mission has been there since 1964, for 50 years, surpassed possibly by the ones in Kashmir (UNMOGIP) and Jerusalem (UNTSO) which started in 1948. Even a relative newcomer like UNIFIL has been in Lebanon since 1978 - although "Interim" is still part of its name. In Haiti, intermittent missions have stopped and started since 1993. Successfully concluded missions include those in Cambodia, during three years starting in 1981, and in Mozambique, during two years starting in 1992. Eritrea in 1993 took five months from referendum to nationhood. Four missions broke down tragically in 1993-1994: Rwanda ended with a massacre of some 800,000 people, Bosnia with a massacre in Srebrenica of 8,000 men and teenagers, and Somalia with the famous Black Hawk down helicopter incident. Those responsible, whether the countries concerned or at the U.N., were never really held accountable, a serious drawback for credible peacekeeping. Some missions, like that in Western Sahara, have become such grazing ground to former diplomats and cronies to Secretariat leadership that some of those sent on a mission were the least interested in seeing it accomplished.

The French government at the time may have initially sought the peacekeeping post for the same reason the Clinton administration wanted Kofi Annan for Secretary-General: Rwanda. If President Clinton, like Mr. Annan, felt vulnerable about whether to interfere to avert the massacres, the French government would have felt vulnerable for protecting the Hutu regime. French military units had intervened earlier to abort a military assault by Uganda-based Rwandan rebels, headed by Paul Kagame, who five years later succeeded to take over as President. Since then, Rwanda tacitly blamed specific personalities within the French establishment, while French sources accused Mr. Kagame of shooting down the plane that carried the two Presidents of Burundi and Rwanda, signaling the outbreak of widespread massacres. While subsequent massacres against fleeting Hutus have yet to be adequately exposed, placing a French diplomat in charge of UN peacekeeping operations, including those in former colonies, gave that Permanent Member of the Security Council a protective and far-sighted advantage. Since then, it insisted on maintaining that post as an added condition for electing a new Secretary-General. The original one was the ability to speak French.

The whereabouts of the black box from that ill-fated 1994 flight is still an unsolved mystery. Why didn't the international prosecutor who investigated the case, Canadian judge Louise Arbour, ask for it right away? (By the way, Ms. Arbour was later appointed as UN High Commissioner for Human Rights.) Why was it briefly "discovered" years later at a UN depot in New York after French daily *Le Monde* raised questions, and why was the issue then conveniently and quickly forgotten? Another mystery concerned an urgent message sent from Canadian General Romeo Dallaire, Commander of UN forces in Kigali, to Peacekeeping officials at Headquarters to a serious massacre in preparation. It is by now known that he was told "not to exceed his mandate" nor take any preventive action. Books have been written about this failure to respond and whether some individuals in particular could be held accountable as culprits in international law. What is rarely known is that Dallaire's cautionary message had been sent dated 11 January but was only "discovered" three months later in April.

There is a growing need to seriously review the process of field operation appointments. There were constant promises of flexibility to attract new blood and fresh faces. Instead, particularly in the mid-1990s, many of the appointments were to accommodate well-connected staffers reaching retirement age, or diplomats not keen on going back home. Confusion is sometimes compounded by reviewed decisions to change not just the task but the name, too. In one country alone, the UN mission carried the following names in 1999: UNAMET, UNTAET, UNMISET, UNOTIL and UNMIT. Not only did the name of the mission change, but also the name of the country itself from East Timor to Timor-Leste.

There are also missions that could be under UN auspices but not under UN command. Even the controversial U.S. invasion of Iraq in March 2003 was given a vague but conveniently interpretable umbrella by the Security Council. There are negotiations on Darfur dealing with a hybrid force of the African Union and the U.N., with the Sudanese insisting on the command being African while the logistics could be offered internationally. There were also forces of specific nations that had a UN link but not a mandate; for example, the U.S. force in Sinai which replaced the UN Emergency Force (UNEF) there; or a European force in Bosnia; a Russian force in Tajikistan, and an almost forgotten Russian force in an area almost unknown called Transdniestria, located between Ukraine and Moldova; there were Australian troops in East Timor; and Russians in Georgia leading troops from the Commonwealth of Independent States. The same is true for the AMISOM mission in Somalia.

Despite recent negative reporting, recognized presence of certain rotten apples and the need for more dynamic performance, UN peacekeeping has had positive impact on maintaining world peace. The real value of peacekeeping can only be recognized when it is not available. UNEF went almost unnoticed and was sometimes ridiculed for ten years - but when it was withdrawn in 1967 a full war broke out. The total budget of peacekeeping worldwide for 2013-2014 was nearly $8 billion. The UN has repeatedly pointed out that such expenditure is less than half a percent of global governmental military spending. It is far cheaper than war. That justification, which some of us admittedly helped to evolve, could only stand, however, if accompanied by effective accomplishment.

The chief peacekeeper is officially the Secretary-General; he is the one entrusted by the Security Council to undertake missions and deal with member states from negotiations to consultations to reaching agreements. He is the one who matters. Staff draw their authority and their influence from him. Normally, most of those around the Secretary-General behave appropriately, but there have been occasional characters who assumed that it is they who run the Secretary-General, not the other way around. There are very exceptional cases when an occasional opportunist who would try to "deliver" the Secretary-General to some key member state in return for self-advancement.

There has always been a need for internal UN peacekeeping, either between departments, member states or different UN bodies. Tension has always been brewing between the Security Council and the General Assembly on the question of who takes the final decision. The U.S. in the early 1960s, when it enjoyed majority support in the Assembly, introduced Unifying for Peace, an amendment that provided that two-thirds vote of the Assembly could overturn a Council decision. It was introduced partly to avert a Soviet veto. However, after the U.S. lost that majority in the 1970s, it reverted back to the Council. That reflected the change of times. At first, the U.S. used the Assembly to overcome the Council, then it counted on the Council to overcome the Assembly. Before it was the Soviets who used the Council more, except for one issue in Korea where Soviet diplomacy learned a lesson after a strategic mistake. To show their displeasure, they boycotted the Council meeting where the decision was to be taken on Korea. They could not use the veto, and thus could not block the vote that sent troops that remain there until today.

Nine Degrees of Peacekeeping

Peace, like beauty, is in the eye of the beholder. For some countries, peace is equivalent to the absence of war, at least as long as the conflict is not in their backyard. For others, it means enhancing human development to avert the causes of war.

When the UN was established, it was felt that the absence of war was a passive achievement. A positive one would be to create a situation where war can be avoided; that is, as to take away the ingredients of conflict. That is why it was eventually announced that the other names for peace are human development, freedom, justice and human dignity. Peacekeeping was therefore not just about a ceasefire arrangement but taking into account conditions that create an atmosphere of peace. Admittedly, there is no ideal solution to any problem. There is a realistic image of what peacekeeping can actually do. As Dag Hammarskjold once said, "The UN was not created to take us to heaven, but to save us from hell." The idea of peacekeeping is to achieve a situation where more attention could be paid to human development, human dignity and freedom of choice.

A close look at conflicts where the UN was called upon to play a role will display differing aspects of involvement. There were situations like an outbreak of conflict after a 1969 soccer match between Honduras and El Salvador that resulted in *la guerra de fútbol*, the Football War. That fight was resolved fairly quickly, although it took a few victims, including the referee who misjudged the penalty kick that apparently started it. The ceasefire took effect only after six days. By contrast, El Salvador itself became involved later in an internal conflict, which required a higher degree of UN mediation. The "good offices" of the Secretary-General are usually available to contact parties to avert a conflict. To be able to do so effectively, observers are needed to ensure that the agreement reached was being implemented, which is a third degree of involvement.

Another aspect of peacekeeping is the art of opening confidential back channels, like passing discreet messages when two countries, such as Iran and the United States, are not officially in touch. The UN is a fairly convenient venue for adversaries to meet and talk without necessarily asking for an appointment. An inclusive meeting on an international issue would offer a place for testing the waters. An initiative under Perez de Cuellar on Afghanistan was a telling example. Initially it was a meeting called Friends of Afghanistan, where both Americans and Iranians joined, among others. With eight countries in the group, there was no way the two adversaries could not be in touch. United States-Iran relations has since the fall of the Shah been more of shadowboxing match than an engaged conflict.

The relationship between the two countries also highlights yet another form of peacekeeping: that of handling cases of hostage-takings or kidnappings. American hostages in Tehran in 1980 and Western hostages in Lebanon were both resolved through discreet negotiations in concert with a touch of public diplomacy. The UN was involved in the Iranian hostage crisis not just for the release of the hostages but to avert an explosive conflict. The Secretary-General visited Iran with such a mandate from the Security Council; accordingly, he had to create an atmosphere where the Iranians would feel that they were listened to. While the interest of the U.S. was to get the hostages out, the Iranian interest was that the Americans recognize their suffering under the previous regime, and that their regime change was therefore right and appropriate. Iran wanted to tell the world that their takeover was in response to oppression and to evoke international legitimacy through the UN. While the U.S. tried to influence Iranian politics, Iranian officials felt they could make a point in the other direction. It was no coincidence that the American hostages were released the day President Carter left and President Reagan swore the oath of office. Nothing is new under the sun. History, as someone once said, just repeats itself, only at a higher price.

Another type of peacekeeping involves the endorsement of separately negotiated arrangements, such as the Disengagement Agreement between Israel and Syria. The two countries were sworn enemies. But over time, since the agreement was signed, barely a single shot has crossed the border. They would fight through proxies elsewhere, but the two countries would not face each other directly.

The next degree of involvement, "soldiering for peace," is actual peacekeeping itself with the presence of troops, contingents from various countries, with the likelihood of some paramilitary action to respond to provocation, prevent an attack or suppress an outbreak of hostilities. Such operations require not only a decision by the Security Council but physical boots on the ground to observe while diplomats negotiate. As expressed by Socrates, "There is no order without soldiers, no soldiers without money, no money without an authority, no authority without citizens, no citizens without justice." Sending troops is a growth industry: there's been a six-fold increase in deployment since 1998 of the number of soldiers and military observers around the world. These are complemented, however modestly, with attempts at peace-building, like ensuring a peaceful transition of authority with free and fair elections. The United Nations Electoral Assistance Division played a positive role in hundreds of elections in scores of countries. It was not just an exercise in transparency or transfer of power. It also has a more lasting impact in countries where people never voted before; the UN helps to build "democratic muscles" that enable ordinary people to practice their rights and to speak out.

Of course, there are more levels of conflict than there are degrees of peacekeeping. There are conflicts by proxy, where two powers fight each other through another country. There are conflicts over resources, such as diamonds, gold and oil. And if the conflict over a football match was the most easy to handle, the most difficult ones are those that seem to be scripted in heaven, where people evoke God Almighty as their real estate agent. Other conflicts are not just limited to the living but also the dead, as for instance the Balkan wars that were an example of the legacy of the Ottoman empire. The names of villages reflect battles in the 1500s.

The Arab-Israeli conflict is another example. From an earthly perspective, the Arabs and Israelis are supposedly cousins. After a visit to the Middle East I returned through Newark airport. Joining a long line of people waiting for a taxi. I happened to be standing behind two people arriving obviously from the same region. One was a Palestinian Arab and the other one Israeli. Since there were a limited number of taxis, they very reluctantly agreed to share one, and by a rare coincidence it was written on the door of the cab that happened to pick them up: "Property of Isaac and Jacob, sons of Abraham." They disappeared into the sunset.

Yemen

My first UN assignment was as a press officer for the mission observing a Disengagement Agreement over Yemen. While there were military observers, mainly officers, I was the only one working on the civilian side under my boss, Pier Pasquale Spinelli, who was also director of the UN European Office in Geneva and mediator in the Middle East. Mr. Spinelli was an experienced Italian diplomat who blended a down to earth perception of a complex situation with a warm approach to his colleagues. While being clear and direct in getting to the point, he also managed to stutter and splinter vague words incoherently if he needed to gain time. Because of his other preoccupations I was left to move freely, which helped me grow into my own role. I discovered that my concern about communicating with my hosts in their local language was unfounded: the Yemenis spoke the most classical Arabic. At the outset I thought I was only meeting their intellectuals but when I met farmers in the mountains they would converse in the same way. It is generally agreed among Arabs that their origins came from that part of the Arabian peninsula. Yemen is known to have an old civilization, particularly with innovative approaches to farming and cultivation; terraces could be spotted even in some of the poorest regions. Yemenis insisted on keeping their traditional architecture even as they entered the 21st century. Laws prohibit buildings above a certain level, all with castle-like designs.

An added attraction to some of our northern European colleagues was the sunny weather. The capital, Sanaa, was placed on a mountainous plateau above sea level, so it was neither too hot, nor too cold. For some mysterious meteorological habit it started to drizzle every day at about three o'clock during the five months we were there. Our Scandinavian officers would rush during lunch time to take advantage of the sun in shorts and often without t-shirts, not realizing that the detained women of the former royal family were placed in a nearby palace peering and giggling, amused and amazed from behind their veils. We were accommodated in one of the former palaces of the Imam, who ruled by divine decree, that had been turned into a hotel. We also had the opportunity to visit other palaces, including one where the Imam kept the eldest sons of all tribal chiefs to ensure loyalty. There was a famous story at the time about when God was taken around the world to see how it would be in the 20th. century. An angel described each country, and the Lord Almighty expressed astonishment about all the changes made. He would not recognize any of them until they reached Sanaa, the capital, at which time He exclaimed: "This is Yemen." Before the Angel could inquire how quickly he recognized it, the Lord continued, "It looks exactly as I left it."

It was my first experience in working together with a group from different nationalities towards the same goal. On one occasion when our Canadian logistical team had a free day, we visited the sight of the first dam in history at Marib, which was built by the first woman ruler in history, the Queen of Sheba. As we approached the area by helicopter, with its high houses built on solid rock, the silhouette from a distance strangely looked like Manhattan. Our Canadian pilot seemed to be flying on visual and a general map, landing us in a location distant from the desired site. As we stepped out of the aircraft, we were surrounded by tribesmen coming out of nowhere. These men would normally take hostages and release them only upon receipt of ransom. Their leader was stunned when I addressed him in Arabic, informing him that we were under his protection. He assumed that with such uniforms, we could only be actors for a movie, presumably an Egyptian one. The chief expressed his undying love for actress Faten Hamama, suggesting he was available to marry her at any time of her choice. Assuming that his message was well received, he personally led us to the sight and back to the helicopter.

In Yemen I also started picking up UN terminology, learning for example that when an officer referred to a "sitrep" he was referring to a "situation report" sent to headquarters summarizing observations of the day. We felt it was about the end of the mission when I overheard on my radio one of the officers telling his commander that he had heard a number of shots from a mountaintop and asked: "should I record it for the sitrep or not?" An "obs" is an observation post and a "crypt," which in Greek refers to "a hidden body," meant a cable from headquarters conveying special information.

One communications problem was the inability to obtain any response from any local mission at certain times of the day. We learned that it was time for almost everyone to have *qat*, a plant with a drug-like effect. There were group sessions where friends would gather to chew it and exchange pleasantries — the busy ones chewed alone. The local term *takhzin* was derived from the word "to deposit" as the plant is "deposited" in the mouth, which gives it a bubbly look and with regular use stains the teeth. Fresh arrivals were treated mostly on Thursdays or at latest Friday morning. An invitation to join in a "deposit" is the highest form of flattery. The habit is spread wherever Yemenis, Somalis or Ethiopians are located around the world. At a certain time whole neighborhoods in Brooklyn would make it to New York's JFK airport to welcome the arrival of an Ethiopian Airlines flight carrying fresh products from home.

A development expert had explained to us that the widespread use of *qat* deprived the country of one of its most famous exports. It seems that a specially perfumed coffee used to be produced in Yemen and shipped out of the port of Mocha. The process of export and payment seemed to consume too much time for some of the farmers, who were persuaded that planting the high-inducing drug was not only quicker, as they cashed their sales in the local market, but also it would give them more that one season. Still, this habit did not diminish the ability of Yemenis to fight fiercely whenever their loyalty to the tribe was needed.

The tribal chief would traditionally decide which political

position to take. Once, days after arriving in Sanaa, we heard celebratory shooting in the air and noticed movements of armed tribesmen into the center of town, while the government radio announced that a certain tribe was coming to declare its loyalty to the Republic. About a week later in the mountainous territory of the loyalist side a similar commotion indicated a similar purpose. It turned out to be the same tribal leaders who apparently kept moving from one side to the other. We were informed that in return they only accepted gold coins. Until the 1960s Yemen's currency was mainly Austrian Maria-Theresa Thaler in silver or gold. An Italian doctor who managed to survive the transition of governments told me that he used to take his salary home in bags carried by porters. The chiefs of the two, sometimes three, main tribes knew precisely their favorite currency; they expected the real thing.

A successful oversight of a Disengagement Agreement depended on the cooperation of the powerbrokers in the region and their internal proxies. As the situation grew more stable, and both Egypt and Saudi Arabia arrived at an understanding to maintain a status quo, the need for a UN mission had expired.

South Lebanon - UNIFIL

Golden Beirut once offered a cosmopolitan world in a nutshell. Impeccable weather, glorious sunrises over the mountains and sunsets in the Mediterranean and starry nights added to the attraction. Young casanovas seeking to impress visiting young women would boast that they could snow ski and water ski the same day. Its laissez-faire attitude made it the main listening post in the Middle East – the most strategically located oil-rich region at the time. Beirut offered a colorful opportunity for instant fame to international journalists and diplomats. Some raised it higher. Many rewarded their host city with due acknowledgement, while some went astray or simply disappeared. During the 1950s and 1960s, the terrace of the St. George's Hotel bar was the main hangout for expatriate reporters. It offered a breathtaking view of the city, the bay and the mountains beyond. A practical advantage was that it afforded easy access to very important visitors staying at that unique hotel and served as a posh alternative to an otherwise expensive office. Everyone knew where to find them at any time. Besides, a few steps down was the most elegant beach in town where the most popular young women from prominent families would hardly exchange a conversation without displaying a charmingly accented comment of three languages at once: French, English and Arabic, in that order: "Ça va? OK? Yallah."

But by the late 1970s, things had changed.

UNIFIL was an operation that included both observers and participation of troops. Resolution 425, adopted on March 25, 1978, which established it, aimed at ensuring a withdrawal up to the Litani River of Israeli forces that had entered Lebanon; helping to establish the authority of the Lebanese government within the international recognized border; and maintenance of an atmosphere of peace in this area of operation. A resolution taken the following day, resolution 426, indicated how that could be done.

My involvement with UNIFIL started after I was asked to return to Beirut on an interim measure to take over the UNIC office there, particularly because the Secretary-General was involved in arranging for a peace process in the Middle East and started visiting key capitals to maintain momentum. Until March 1978, my work was mainly to travel with him in the region, to keep the press abreast of developments and maintain contacts with the media. I also maintained our library for visitors and ran the usual work at an information center. This changed when the newly arriving commanding officer of UNIFIL, General Immanuel Erskine of Ghana, arrived to take over. I had received indications from the Secretary-General's office and from the Under Secretary-General of Political Affairs, Brian Urquhart, suggesting that I should help the General in whatever way possible. Incidentally, when Brian Urquhart was about to visit Lebanon to deal with UNIFIL, he was urged by UN security to delay his trip because of a potential flare-up of local tensions. He tentatively and reluctantly agreed and waited a while in New York. During that time, he decided to take a walk in Central Park. He was mugged there. When the General arrived, he brought with him the French Colonel Salvin, who was commanding troops near the Litani area close to Tyre. Colonel Salvin had a reputation as a fighter; having lost one eye in Vietnam, he presented a fierce look. Although he was a very kind man, he was obviously also a tough soldier. It was interesting for me to watch the General showing him how to operate, explaining that we were not fighting anyone; rather, we were soldiers for peace. It turned out that General Erskine's first request of me was to pass a message to PLO Chairman Yasser Arafat to allow troops uncontested passage from Beirut International Airport to the South, where PLO armed units had full control of the city of Tyre. One of the problems of giving him the message was that the PLO leader had several offices and that even his closest aides referred to them by numbers or codes. I found him at the "University." That was the first operational contact between the UN and the PLO, and Arafat saw an opportunity for political advantage. He asked if the message I had was from the Secretary-General and then noted it as an official message, which he said he would discuss with his colleagues in the "command," including the chief of operations, General Abu Walid. While there, another leader, Abu Jihad, who was later killed in Tunis, came in. We had met before, and he said a few helpful words. Though Arafat obviously wanted to gain time to reassess, he suggested coming back within an hour. When I did, Arafat had already exited, but he symbolically left his fur hat on his desk while Abu Walid indicated an acceptance of the UNIFIL troops' passage.

Word reached the press that there were some contacts, but I was not free to talk about it. However, I felt that those correspondents staying in the Commodore Hotel were mostly friends, and if someone asked me that evening while I was having dinner, I would provide them a careful briefing on deep background. But none of my usual friends happened to be there. A reporter from the *Washington Post*, Thomas Lippman, stopped me to check the story. When I said that I was indeed the contact he looked at me doubtfully and left. When the news came up the following day, he told me he thought I had been joking. We understood from subsequent meetings that part of the delay was the attempt to reconcile the concept of a "revolutionary resistance" with reaching a negotiating accommodation.

Instructions were sent down from the PLO leadership to the field to cooperate with UNIFIL, although there was the inevitable daily friction with all armed sides. One of the main purposes of UNIFIL was to restore the government authority – then, as now. A weak Lebanese authority was further weakened by internal arguments, but somehow, miraculously, they managed to present a semblance of a government, and the foreign ministry kept its diplomats operating despite not receiving their salaries for months. The President, Elias Sarkis, despite a chronically tragic look of his sad eyes, maintained a steadfast, presidential air.

UNIFIL faced a number of handicaps. One was topography. It is in an area of mountains, valleys and streams where it is very difficult to detect people. When Israel discovered a hole in the fence they went after people for three days but could not find the infiltrators. It was the same thing for UNIFIL, which sometimes was accused of intentionally not finding people. This has become an even bigger problem for UNIFIL II, which is dealing with people from the area who by now know it very well. Peacekeeping cannot operate without the support of the local population. In a densely populated, topographically difficult area, UNIFIL, more than any other force, has to win the people over. There is a need for communication and the capacity to deal with people, to explain to them in simple, understandable terms that they are there to help. That becomes even more essential in a densely populated area.

The main effort was to get the Lebanese army, as a symbol of official Lebanese presence, to secure the south. While officially every side offered a welcome, all of them were against it since it would erode their own presence. Lebanese army officers were ready to move, their task was to assert the sovereignty of their land even if they had to die for it, but the decision was political, and the politicians felt they could not send the army before striking a deal. At one point there was an argument whether UNIFIL could help in transporting the army officers to the south. The response was that UNIFIL could not operate outside its area of operation. Outside that area, it was up to the Lebanese government to ensure transportation and arrival. An interim arrangement was to have the local police fill in for the government but that was not enough. Arrangements were made in what was thought of as a negotiated agreement by all sides, but the army force was shelled on its way by the pro-Israeli forces of Colonel Hadad, and it was decided at the mountainous town of Kawkaba not to continue.

As it became obvious that a "interim" assignment was turning into a longer-lasting task, a wider range of staff were brought in, and a larger headquarters was constructed, including residences for command officers who had lived for a while in Nahariya, across the Israeli border. A newly appointed Political Officer, James Holger of Chile, started visiting Beirut regularly: he was a friend from an earlier posting in New York. His successor, the perceptive and engaging young Sergio Vieira de Mello, though new to the region and the task, swiftly gained support from all parties.

UNIFIL was supposed to oversee the withdrawal of Israeli troops. It was assumed that they would do this in three stages. They performed the first two. The last and most substantive stage was scheduled for June 13, 1978. It was so definite that even international correspondents were invited to attend. However, the day almost passed without any visible movement. We were all standing at a posting called Abbasiyah. While the UN Commanding Officer and all of us were waiting there under a hot summer sun, we were first told that a leader from northern Lebanon, Toni Frangieh, the son of the former president, and his family had been assassinated. Whether it had anything to do with the scheduled event of the day was open to speculation. The other more direct development was when some correspondents dropped by to tell us that the Israeli army had withdrawn from the area of Marjeyoun in the southeast, handing it over to Colonel Saad Hadad, who they claimed was the representative of the Lebanese authority. That drove General Erskine back to Naqoura to receive instructions on what to do next. In turn, this caused confusion among some of the UN officers regarding whether they should confirm the Israeli withdrawal or not. If they did, that would mean that the resolution was implemented. There was also a decision to ask the Lebanese authority what it thought of all of this. That again became a problem since this was at a point where there were almost three factions of the Lebanese government: one against Hadad, one for Hadad and one in between. Apparently the Colonel continued to receive his salary from the Defense Ministry until the prime minister asked for him to be considered as a renegade. A note was received on June 13th from the Lebanese government stating that in order to facilitate the withdrawal of Israeli forces we could consider Colonel Hadad as a de facto force. That is why in the subsequent reports, the UN referred to the Israeli proxy forces as "de facto forces" and to those of the PLO as "armed elements."

I recall a reporter, who officially represented a major US television network, spent her time in the hotel lobby collecting information from her colleagues and regular streams of visitors. Her caution in a rough neighborhood was understandable, and so I was pleasantly surprised when she came to my office for a briefing in the spring of 1982 on a potential Israeli invasion, which I indicated would most likely happen through three main bridges in the North, South and Central routes. My disappointment was not that she passed on different versions raising difficulties for me with varied parties but that she had introduced a man accompanying her as her network's correspondent in a European capital, which turned out to be false: I spotted him after the Israeli invasion around the neighborhood in a different capacity.

While General Erskine was the commanding officer of the mission, the Jerusalem-based General Siilasvuo, from Finland, was the coordinator for the region. General Callahan, also based in Jerusalem, and who later became head of UNIFIL, was chief of operations. This provoked sometimes a need for internal peacekeeping as well. Fortunately, I had good relations with all of them. They needed my work, and I did not belong to any one of them from a management point of view. I did not work for the political department, and the head of public information in New York gave me adequate leeway to work with the Secretary-General's office, so I was almost on my own. In the first report of the Security Council my name was mentioned as helping the mission, which made me feel even more accountable. When General Siilasvuo visited to size up the situation, he was concerned we were not going to be able to implement on time. He told me that though there were many difficulties in implementing the resolution quickly, we could not look as if we were failing. Whatever I could do in the realm of the media, I was counted upon doing. I was told to consider myself "another contingent" and to feel responsible in that way. Further, I was asked to keep the Lebanese officials very much in the picture, and at the same time let them realize that we were not going to do their national tasks for them. They had to show that they were as determined to implement as we were.

While UNIFIL's first commander, General Erskine of Ghana, took press attention in stride with a ready smile, and worked with all of us in a smooth manner, his successor, General Callahan of Ireland, who was highly regarded as a professional and experienced UN observer, for some reason made a special effort to control the political and media narrative through the English-language weekly, "Monday Morning". An attempt to cut off the role of Beirut was impractical, not only because of the central interest of Lebanese authorities noted in the Security Council resolution establishing UNIFIL to confirm Lebanese sovereignty, but also because most of the world press were operating actively from there. While UN peacekeeping officials in New York worked closely and appropriately with him, they kept Beirut in the picture. In particular the Secretary-General's office sought to offer regular guidance and receive feedback from the Beirut office.

Despite a politically complicated situation, one crucial task was to encourage the 500,000 Lebanese that had fled to return to their villages and reestablish the Lebanese presence in the South. The hospital in Naqoura to start treating the locals, not just the army officers. Particularly those treated and their families felt like the UN was helpful to them. We encouraged opening schools and starting social work so that those who fled to Beirut, or elsewhere, would discover that going back home was not only a gesture of self-respect but also a way of returning to a semi-normal life that was even more secure than Beirut. We publicly urged them to come back, and they did come back. UNIFIL's main achievement was neither political nor military but human. Half a million southerners who had been forced to leave their homes returned and resumed their everyday life. Many Lebanese immigrants were encouraged by the fact that UN troops were there. And, for example, some of those who went to Africa and made money happened to be from south of Lebanon. They felt at ease coming back from Nigeria, Ghana and Senegal to where contingents from those countries were posted in their own homeland. A member of parliament who had been an expatriate in Africa offered lunches and parties for the returning immigrants to make them feel at home. Also UNIFIL soldiers did their best to encourage the local population to believe that they were not foreigners but part of the tapestry.

An Israeli invasion in the summer of 1982 bypassed UNIFIL and reached Beirut. Although it had been partially expected months earlier, very few believed it would reach the Lebanese capital. Most observers had thought it would blanket south Lebanon to force the PLO presence out, leading to negotiations with the government.

During that invasion, one of the remaining open restaurants in Beirut was at the Commodore Hotel, managed by the hospitable and protective Nazzal family, where international journalists continued to enjoy relatively normal meals. It was curious to see how some Israeli officers and certain Palestinians and Lebanese joined tables at the buffet.

When Israeli troops moved into West Beirut from the area near the Saint George Hotel known as Ein el Muraissah and took positions in the unfinished Sheraton Hotel compound by the Corniche, close to where I stayed in a shuttered apartment, I could spot from my kitchen window a number of soldiers changing into civilian dress, coming up the shortcut steps to the main Bliss Street and from there into town. I often wondered: whom did they infiltrate?

Despite receiving instructions to leave like the rest of UN staff, I decided to stay at my own risk out of the conviction that the UN should not give up on the capital of one of its founding members - which also happened to be the town where I was raised. Making an effort to be seen by the reporters as a symbolic UN presence, some reporters gave me a t-shirt that stated: "Do not shoot. I am the only UN man here." Like most people in a surrounded city, we were expecting action by the international community or "brotherly" support from Arab League States. Except for contact between the king of Saudi Arabia and President Reagan, who had replaced Secretary of State Haig with George Schultz, there was little noticed elsewhere. Instead, the only popular demonstration opposing the war was in Tel-Aviv.

UNIFIL was the first peacekeeping operation on which no agreement was signed. One of the biggest problems for the mission was that the two real forces at play, the PLO and Israel, did not recognize one another, which was partly the reason why no agreement could be signed. The Palestinian leadership at the time spoke about resistance and revolution, which was part of their worldview and self-identity, while the Israeli government focused on hitting its adversaries hard. It was obvious that Israel was waiting for a chance to attack and destroy the PLO, which the PLO realized. UN officials tried to convince Palestinian operatives, who were certain the Israelis would attack, to avoid giving them an excuse. Eventually, a de facto arrangement was reached. A ceasefire was arranged between the two parties through indirect efforts by my colleague in Jerusalem, Jean-Claude Aimé, and myself in Beirut, with full support of UN headquarters in New York – but there were other elements at play, and events slipped out of everyone's hands. And, as usual, credit was taken elsewhere.

The original purposes of establishing UNIFIL were certainly familiar to those in the Security Council and the UN Secretariat who met to vote on resolution 1701 in the summer of 2006, after another war erupted in Lebanon. There was a call to establish an international force that would have duplicated or eliminated UNIFIL. Even the UN Secretary-General, a former peacekeeping chief, when asked by astonished observers explained that based on his observations from his contacts it seemed certain countries wanted it under the U.N., while others wished it to be operating independently, "the coalition of the willing." But French President Jacques Chirac, who had in mind that the head of UN peacekeeping was a French diplomatic position, prevailed: UNIFIL was maintained with an expanded mandate.

Another operational shift was that from the French to the Italians. With a Frenchman as head of peacekeeping, a new Italian commander took over in the field; the head of the strategic unit in New York was also an Italian. Italy played an active role in UNIFIL II – the first conference to call for a ceasefire was conferred in Rome by Prime Minister Romano Prodi. The choice of location and eventual command may be due to Italy's Mediterranean location, lack of problems in the region and the overall popularity of Italians who in previous missions managed to gain the goodwill of the local population. In UNIFIL I, the Italian role, which came somewhat late, focused mainly on the helicopter unit. They created a jovial atmosphere, arranging for the best espresso south of the Litani, and holding UN Day celebrations with the participation of famous Italian artists. In one case it was felt that the transportation of a piano on the helicopter to raise the moral of the troops was worth it. While the new Commanding Officer was a general with a seemingly serious demeanor, the contact man for the first Italian venture seemed more at ease. Captain Cantatore, who insisted on being addressed by his full name, had also attained a promotion of which he was proud. Coupled with a university degree he felt needed recognition, he was known as Comandatori Dottore Comandatore Salvatore Cantatore. Pronouncing them all in one breath was a prerequisite to getting a free helicopter ride to Naqoura. Besides having many female admirers among foreign and local correspondents, our brilliant Comandatore was also an alert political observer with an accurate perception of serious events.

UNIFIL II, particularly from the start of 2007, updated UNIFIL I of 1978 in a number of political, logistical and strategic issues. The new level of troops was only slightly higher than those that had been originally deployed. Whether 2,000 more would do better was an open question. There was also the establishment of a "strategic command cell" in New York, which presumably would strengthen the hand of the commanding officer in Naqoura, while keeping in mind the political requirements of key countries. In effect, it meant containing the authority of the Commander on the ground. The mandate of UNIFIL was always under the Security Council's authority, which could therefore reconsider it, revive it and refresh it. The difference between the new and the old missions was mainly on the ground. While resolution 425 and 426 took into account Palestinian forces, UNIFIL II had to deal mostly with a homegrown population. There was a fleeting consideration to include Arab forces in the new formation, but those with institutional memory recalled that a number of Arab troops had earlier joined in a peacekeeping force within Lebanon under what was called the Arab Deterrent Force, which fizzled away leaving only Syrian troops in charge. The new force, a blend of UNIFIL strengthened by new logistics from countries like Germany and others, gave the international community a breathing spell.

Seven years in Beirut witnessing an internal war, two Israeli invasions, an Iranian Islamic revolution and the establishment of UNIFIL, inspired my affection for ordinary, hardworking people who are innocent victims of someone else's arrogant folly. It also gave me an insight into the workings of the media, and admiration and respect for most of the reporters who shared my experience and went on to gain higher ground. There were some, however, very few, who to say the least did not do honor to their profession.

Regrettably, for a long period, southern Lebanon became an international post office where every party, regional or international, would convey messages through UNIFIL or through action in or around the south. This was not limited to diplomatic exchanges but extended to explosions. A cynical military officer explained it to me by comparing it to the writing profession. Just like writers had a signature, so did certain mercenary troublemakers. Groups are known by carrying out specific acts almost as if they were signing it. Whether a kidnapping, an explosion, a missile, or hijacking an airplane, these various groups had their unique and diabolical ways of announcing their works. A consistent, experienced observer could tell which groups were sending what message through the south of Lebanon. One of Lebanon's most experienced statesmen, Philip Takla, commented on the numerous regional conflicts that find their proxies in Lebanon by saying that "other adversaries usually got pregnant elsewhere and delivered in Lebanon."

Eritrea

When the Security Council decided on a mission to arrange for a peaceful, sovereign, national government in Eritrea in December 1992, this region around the Horn of Africa was in bloody turmoil. In nearby Somalia, the emotions of downing U.S. helicopters and dragging soldiers in the streets of Mogadishu were still brewing. There was an armed upheaval within Ethiopia; tribal conflicts in Djibouti, which extended to the Afars in the port of Asab; and brewing tensions in Sudan. With tribal, cultural and historic links, events in all these countries were interrelated. There were also other nearby countries which had a direct interest, like Yemen, that was so close across the strait of Mandab that the inhabitants of an Eritrean island like Dhalaak wore Yemeni skirt-like cloths and headdress. Saudi Arabia was a refuge to a number of Eritrean political groups, immigrants and businessmen. Most advocates of the thirty-year Eritrean revolution were spread throughout several Arab capitals with a concentration in media centers like Beirut.

What Price Peacekeeping?

The keyword for the mission, UNOVER, was "peaceful," while the rest of the region was not. When asked to supervise the operation, my main thinking was of a communication, grassroots mission, rather than a classical peacekeeping operation. That means t-shirts instead of blue helmets. Instead of a contingent of troops, it was more effective to stress that we were not coming there to impose anything. The main effort was to get all of the population involved, not just politicians in large cities, which is why I went to every town, met every group and visited many schools, churches and mosques in the region.

Eritreans are a mosaic combination of Christians mainly, who speak the oldest Coptic language in the world called Gyz, and Arabic-speaking Muslims. When I went to Eritrea my relations with Secretary-General Boutros Boutros-Ghali were not at their best. Since I was by then running the UN information centres around the world, my job entailed the appointment of people in about 80 countries. Although the Secretary-General's approval was a regular requirement, Boutros-Ghali may have wanted to assert his authority in every detail. When designated Special Representative of the Secretary-General for Eritrea, some of my colleagues felt I was exiled. One of the Executive Office Officers even refused to pay my salary in New York since he thought I was finished there. However, in time I realized otherwise; Eritrea was very important to Boutros Boutros-Ghali, not only because he was a Copt, like many of the Eritreans, but also because it is the backyard of Egypt and part of its national security. That is why when the mission was accomplished I had his Agenda for Peace translated into Gyz and brought it to him as a present.

Asmara, Eritrea's capital, was sometimes described as a forgotten Tuscany. It used to be Italy's colonial paradise in Africa. Many of the Italians left beautiful, though deserted, villas behind. I stayed in an old one with lovely wildflowers surrounding it. Every house there had a caretaker that came with it; someone who looked after the tenant and did the cooking and the cleaning. I lived by myself and had a very thoughtful, helpful woman. A slight problem was she cooked spaghetti for me every day. At first I thought it was the only food available, but I noticed the markets were full of fresh fruits and vegetables. Since I have always liked lentils, I brought some home with me and put it in the kitchen. Yet, in the evening, there was spaghetti again. I asked my driver to explain in their own language, Tigrinya, what I wanted. But the answer was no, she could not serve me lentils. It turned out that during the war, people were deprived of everything and the only thing available was lentils. It was therefore identified with the poor, while rich, presumably important people would have Italian spaghetti. So I was deprived of my lentils because of her impression that I should be treated as someone important.

The image of the UN in Eritrea was very negative for years. There was an emotional antagonism because of the impression that the UN abandoned the Eritreans in the 1950s when their fate hung in the balance and a power-brokered deal was made to link it to Ethiopia rather than grant it independence. From the start, even for the safety of the mission, a crucial need was to turn around this perception.

It so happened that the first week of arrival coincided with the International Day for Women, March 8th. Not requiring instructions, the women of our mission took to the streets of Asmara to join, and in fact lead, marches celebrating the day. It also happened that women generally had a very crucial role in that society. Almost all of them fought in the war and therefore had a real impact on public leadership. Women were already part of the Provisional Government of Eritrea. When we arrived, there was a reception by the Italians. As I was talking to a UNDP representative, a hard working Englishman with the self-perception of being God's gift to the country, an Eritrean woman approached to say hello. The man looked at her asking: "Do I know you?" She answered kindly that she just wanted to say hello and reminded him that they had met once at an earlier reception. Still inspecting the woman, he asked if she worked in the hotel. Suddenly she stood up facing him, saying, "I am the Minister of Justice, I am part of the Eritrean Peoples' Liberation Front who fought in the mountains, I am a Colonel in the Army of Liberation. I would like to talk to the Special Representative. Please leave." This was a welcome and instructive beginning.

Intentionally, no one in our mission stayed at a hotel so the people would not see us as strangers. We lived amongst the population and walked around talking to those of our neighborhood. I did not even go to New York to report to avoid confusion with instructions. Once we were there, we were there. Our assignment was clear: to ensure a peaceful transfer and have a fair and free referendum with full participation of the population. We reached out to every corner of a country ravaged by 30 years of war. The infrastructure was totally destroyed. A trip that would normally take an hour took four or five since you had to go on byroads. The biggest challenge of the mission was that the people had never voted in their lives.

We had to work through the National Referendum Committee, although we also worked directly with people in the government. One of the challenges was to explain what voting was about and how people ought to come out and vote. Mobilizing them to do so was another problem. We also reached out to Eritreans who were abroad either as refugees or expatriates, to join in and vote. Every one of these countries had a special case, and we had to handle them separately without any one-for-all formula.

Sudan was a big challenge since there were about half a million Eritreans there. In Ethiopia, the country which had controlled Eritrea, we had to find a way for the Eritreans to express themselves democratically without provoking militant Ethiopians. People who had gone to Yemen were mainly from the south and were easily identified. Egypt had an embassy, which was very helpful. There were Eritreans in Italy, Scandinavia, the United States and the U.K. who wanted to vote, and we had to arrange for that. We made a point that all Eritreans in any country had a chance to vote. That necessitated a major information campaign to reach out to Eritreans everywhere, through word of mouth, newspapers and radio channels. We discovered to our delight that these communities abroad were helpfully interconnected. Problems arose in Saudi Arabia that were not resolved until the last minute. One complication was rooted in internal politics. The Saudi authorities had welcomed and hosted a particular group of Eritreans who were not amongst the current leadership, the Eritrean Peoples' Liberation Front, which took over Asmara. Of more concern: How could the Saudis allow the Eritreans to vote in Saudi Arabia when the Saudis themselves did not vote? I had to meet several officials outside Eritrea, while asking the Secretary-General to approach officials in Riyadh. The Saudis themselves wanted to reach an agreement in order to prepare good relations with a newly emerging neighboring country. The solution came through the discreet use of soccer fields. On the day of the referendum, the Eritreans in Saudi Arabia went to vote on huge soccer fields, rather than in government buildings.

About 120 United Nations electoral observers from 38 countries were trained in two separate sessions guided by the experienced chief observer, our Vietnamese colleague Dong Nguyen. In addition, an estimated 500 international observers and media representatives were present. Following their deployment, polling stations were visited to ensure that the observers had gained the confidence of the public and that they conducted themselves in a neutral and impartial manner. After three months of preparations there was an overwhelming majority of popular participation on the day of the Referendum, April 23, 1993. More than 90 percent of those who registered voted and 99 per cent of them said "yes" to the creation of an independent state. Exercising their free and fair choice, Eritreans went from oppressive occupation to statehood, from being anti-UN to pro-UN. When we went to one of the previously anti-UN strongholds, 50,000 people were waiting to greet us.

At every location where there were Eritreans to vote, there were UN observers. We had to use all the UN people we could find. In Saudi Arabia we had UNDP and UNICEF to help out, in Sudan UNHCR, in Italy the UN information center, and so forth. We also had observers from the African Union, the Arab League, from the Carter Center and all member states willing to observe. After three months of preparations to mobilize the people and raise public awareness, the people responded in a resounding way. In a signal of accomplishment, President Isaias Afwerki joined me in a UN car to a polling station where he was the first one to vote.

As we announced the referendum to have been generally free and fair, some academics were questioning, why "generally"? It was the need to be accurate. This was the first time these people ever voted. Old men were coming in who could barely walk and were so eager to vote that they left the curtain open and did not countersign properly. Neither could we tell joyous women dancing proudly that their vote didn't count. Since we had done the Referendum exactly on schedule, UN headquarters suggested we could take a week of vacation instead of rushing back to New York. However, after consulting with my colleagues I decided against it. We finished on our original April 27, 1993 date, packed up and left. Anybody who wanted to come back afterwards was free to do so, but we signed off on a mission accomplished. UNOVER was over.

The public announcement of the outcome of the Referendum was especially important for neighboring States. The key country was Ethiopia, the former governing power. I therefore made a point of getting out of Asmara to New York via Addis Ababa. And to avoid misunderstanding, I informed President Afwerki that I intended to meet with Ethiopian officials for that purpose. He agreed and wanted to help by arranging the appointments. When I arrived in Addis Ababa, I met with the Ethiopian Foreign Minister, and then with Ethiopian President

Zenawi, who graciously took note of the outcome and recognized the new country.

The Eritreans needed to follow up on the Referendum by requesting to become a member state of the United Nations. There were some who felt they needed breathing space, suggesting they wait a couple of months to join in September with a big celebration during the General Assembly. My advice was to get on with the arrangements at once while the world was on their side. In quickly changing times, and in an unpredictably volatile region, weeks may make a difference. The Security Council was about to consider the membership of Monaco, so an immediate Eritrean application would be received with equal attention and support, particularly by members who sought to show a North-South balance. I already had an application note signed by the President handed to me in Asmara by the Director of his office, Yemane Ghebremeskel. Time was too short for a senior official to come for the presentation. A young diplomat posted in Washington flew in and impressively - emotionally - read the required statement. Within days the two flags of Monaco and Eritrea were ceremoniously raised. Their membership was timely indeed. By September, a controversy flared between the Eritrean President, the UN Secretary-General and - to a certain degree - the U.S. Secretary of State. Had the application been delayed, the membership would have not been as smooth.

The Eritrean experience confirmed the view that the success of any field mission requires competent, effective communications with an enlightened sense of public opinion. I would add that women I have worked with were born communicators, had a warm understanding of other peoples' feelings and were therefore duly patient and effective when handling a problem. A number of women graciously working with everyday citizens could be more persuasive than a bunch of fully armed soldiers approaching with machine guns.

I would also mention a more personal aspect. When Boutros Boutros-Ghali became Secretary-General in December 1992, he had been staying at the UN Plaza Hotel, and I was informed that I was one of those considered to head the Department of Public Information (DPI). I therefore had to stay around during Christmas and wait for an interview with him. Meanwhile, my mother was sick in London. Being a workaholic, the only time I could see her was during the Holiday season. She was getting older and weaker, but I was told to wait in New York in the hope of being nominated as Under Secretary-General and head of

DPI. As it got closer to Christmas Day I wanted to phone my mother to tell her I might be delayed, but at second thought I hung up and went to the airport. Going to London to see my mother that Christmas was the best thing I have ever done - a few months later she passed away. If I had not gone, I would have never forgiven myself. Because I was not there for the interview, Boutros Boutros-Ghali may have assumed that I did not care for the position, or he may not have thought of me anyway. But I did not want to use my mother's illness as an excuse for not being there. Whatever the reason, one person, and then another, was appointed as head of DPI. Meanwhile I headed for Eritrea.

When I was sent on the mission to Asmara and presented my papers to the President, the letter I had received from the UN to hand over was dated March 1st, my mother's birthday. I also noticed that unusually my name on the letter included my father's name, Habib Sanbar. Normally just my first and family name were listed. This gave me the strong sense that my parents were with me and that therefore the mission was going to be a success - which it was. It also happened that when my mother was very ill in London, she had been looked after for three years by Eritrean women. My mother wanted to live by herself and therefore had maids to help her. The Eritrean women were away from their country to raise money while their husbands were fighting. Whenever I went to see her she would tell them: My son works at the U.N., he will help you. I repeatedly explained that I did not work in a relevant area; I was rather in the press section, working with public information. But my mother kept telling them that her son would help them - and eventually I did. So when I came back to New York I thought whatever happens, happens. Two people were appointed to head the Department of Public Information while I was kept away from it, but for some reason it did not work out for either one of them. By November 1993, I was asked to take over. I am not superstitious, but I have the feeling that the blessings of my parents guided my fate.

Hostage Taking - The Alec Collett Case

A coded message from our information center in Athens in early April 1985 said that a telephone caller, claiming to represent the kidnappers of British hostage Alec Collett wanted to speak to someone in New York representing the Secretary-General. A follow-up noted that the hostage's kidneys were failing, and they did not want him to die on their hands; they would release him outside the Meridian Hotel in

What Price Peacekeeping?

Damascus on April 26[th]provided a representative of the Secretary-General was present. Secretary-General Perez de Cuellar had known Mr. Collett, who was a freelance reporter. At the time of his kidnapping in Lebanon, he was on a short-term assignment with UNRWA. Thus, he was a United Nations employee under the responsibility of the UN Secretary-General. Legally he carried a UN laissez-passer, covered by the Vienna convention, giving him immunity and protection. When discussing the message with Don Javier, it was agreed that we needed to explore this option even if it might be a hoax. I would go to Athens to await a phone call as indicated before the 24th to be available, just in case, and then possibly proceed to Damascus.

It was supposed to be a secret assignment, which in an intergovernmental mechanism meant facing political and logistical obstacles. Secrecy carried a personal risk. I had no papers or written instructions to show in case of a challenge. The head of Political Affairs was unhappy over the fact that someone from outside his department was being sent. Brian Urquhart, a British citizen like Mr. Collett, felt that his staff had been working on the case for months, but when it seemed close to a successful outcome, someone else came in to close the deal. I therefore hesitated to go if, in addition to personal risk, I would have difficulty with a fairly influential colleague for whom I had the greatest respect. After further discussions with the Secretary-General and his Special Assistant, Alvaro de Soto, it was decided that I would proceed anyway, to Athens as a first step; then I'd play it by ear.

I carefully considered whether I should notify the Syrians. Although my Lebanese passport would allow me to enter Syria without a visa, it would be sheer folly to assume that I would be able to hang around the Meridian Hotel in central Damascus and take over the hostage while the watchful Syrian authorities merely stood idly by. I thus approached the Syrian ambassador, who happened to be an old friend. He showed me around his official residence on Manhattan's E. 65th Street, which once belonged to former President Nixon (the story went that he was paid one million dollars more than he had asked). To avert any misunderstanding, I mentioned that I would arrive in Athens and possibly go via Cyprus with Syrian Airlines to Damascus. I explained it had something to do with Alec Collett - which he would have known anyway - but avoided giving him further details. The Ambassador had gently cautioned me that, as we were on Syrian property, he would have to notify his government of anything I said. I knew before I went to Athens that I could not do it single-handedly; I would need support while there. I therefore handpicked a capable and trustworthy officer from UNIFIL - a French Captain who knew the region very well. I proposed that he would meet me with his car in Damascus. In Athens, no phone call was received during the two designated days. I consulted my colleague Alvaro in New York. He thought that, since the kidnappers did not give a positive signal, there was no need to take an unnecessary risk.

I learned later upon return to New York that on the 26th, the day I was supposed to retrieve the hostage, UNDOF Headquarters in Damascus, which was under the Political Department, and which opposed my visit, had sent armed personnel, carriers and jeeps to surround the Meridian Hotel on the chance that Collett would be released in their hands. If anything, that action was counter-productive, as it may have frightened the kidnappers and aroused their doubts about the U.N.'s intentions. It certainly alerted the already nervous Syrians that something extraordinary was going on. I also found out that the Syrian Airline's plane from Cyprus on which I had tentative reservations was delayed from 8 p.m. to midnight for "technical reasons".

A few weeks later there was a newspaper appeal, again from the kidnappers, that Mr. Collett needed dialysis for his kidneys. They designated a leader in Saida, south Lebanon, Mustafa Saad, as a contact point to negotiate a release in return for some demands that they did not announce. The Secretary-General thought that I should go again and contact Mr. Saad, whom I knew. By this time, Mr. Urquhart was replaced by Mr. Goulding, who felt similarly offended and insisted that if I went it should be a secret mission with no media coverage. I then took two trips. The first was unnoticed except by those directly involved. From Damascus, I was driven by a Syrian colleague who headed the Beirut Information Office. We were delayed about two hours for the appointment. The friendly Mr. Saad, who had been blinded by a mail bomb, explained that he was merely trying to help in a humanitarian cause. He did not know his contacts representing the kidnappers but had been given a list of prisoners in British jails who they wanted released. I explained that this was beyond my capacity. For information purposes, I attached that list to my brief report to the Secretary-General upon return to New York.

Given the opposition of my two British colleagues within the Secretariat, I was surprised and puzzled several weeks later when approached by Virendra Dayal, the Chef de Cabinet of the Secretary-General, who told me that the British authorities would like me to go again and ascertain the fate of the hostage. They wanted me to go even if I did not get any result; just the effort would do. It seemed more like internal politics, though media was still off-limits.

Before that trip, I met with the experienced British Permanent Representative Sir David Gore-Booth in the Indonesian Lounge next to the General Assembly. He suggested that I should call on the British ambassador in Beirut and their Chargé d'Affaires in Damascus. Relations between Syria and the U.K. at the time were very tense. Such contacts, which would be obviously monitored, would put me under a shadowy light. The ambassador also mentioned the likelihood of taking along with me from London a daughter of Mr. Collett, asking me with a vague smile whether I knew what she looked like. I could not figure that one out but eventually assumed they would send with me someone else. In London, at the Foreign Office, the two men I met did not seem like traditional diplomats and were introduced under general names like Mr. Barrett and Mr. Jones. One of them had no clue about my background and the other inquired about the route I was going to take. When the question of the "daughter" was raised, I pointed out that it would be very risky for her to come along. Instead of saving a hostage, I feared the kidnappers would gain one more if I brought along a strange woman, even if she was Collett's genuine daughter.

In Damascus, I met Syrian Vice President Khaddam, with whom I was familiar since he had been Minister of Foreign Affairs. He was famous for being the first to know and the last to admit so. He said that the appeal in the press, like the previous alert, was made to embarrass Syria, and that the group of kidnappers picked a blind mediator who would not be able to identify them. Commenting on my loaned UNDOF car, he said he was receiving me in a personal capacity; if he knew it was official he would unfortunately have declined. He then shifted to Middle Eastern politics, pretending that the Collett case was totally irrelevant. Syrian Foreign Minister Al-Sharaa, who must have had an inkling about my purpose, passed a message through the chief of protocol that he would only see me on a courtesy call. He was also an old personal friend who was a regular visitor to New York. But again, he did not want to discuss the matter in his office.

When I proceeded to southern Lebanon to meet with the designated mediator, I purposely avoided Beirut since I was told to evade the media. My heart sank as I bypassed my beloved hometown, going straight to Saida. I arrived there in the midst of an Israeli air raid. I was touched later to find out to what extent the ever thoughtful Javier Perez de Cuellar, my Secretary-General, was personally concerned, inquiring through every channel about my safety. The mediator, Mustafa Saad, handed me the list of names that he was told should be released in return for the hostage. I again explained that I had no authority in that area and would not get involved in an issue other than that of releasing our colleague. After about two hours of discussions, it occurred to me that the matter could be handled elsewhere, possibly in a meeting held between representatives of the kidnappers and of the British government at a place where the British could feel at ease and the kidnappers would have some sort of leeway. Remembering the first coded cable, I suggested Athens but later understood that Cyprus, the divided former British colony, would be more convenient for both. On the way back from Saida, I stopped at the home of Princess Zeina Arslaan, who had once worked with me. She was pleasantly surprised and graciously offered assistance in any way from her prominent family house in Khalde, near Beirut International Airport. I used their phone to call the British ambassador, who was very pleasant but did not seem keen on a meeting. I got the impression that he already had his own line of contact. While there, I took the opportunity to go to the nearby spot where the kidnapping took place. It was important to explore the exact location to get a physical feeling about the likely group that had influence there; if they were not directly involved, at least someone on the ground would have an idea about who passed through. That area was almost a no man's land. No group was predominant in that thin stretch between the airport and the Mediterranean Sea, which made it more likely for a professional intergovernmental sort of team to operate. Talking to some connections, my understanding was that a group calling itself the Armenian Liberation Army could have been involved. That would either have been a cover, or if it really was them, they normally would have been a front in big power politics. Why would they be interested in a retired reporter on a part time job?

The kidnapping was most likely a tragic miscalculation. Those who knew Alec Collett recall that he enjoyed speaking with impressive rhetoric. Others mentioned that, in need of a survivor job, he just sought to impress. Anyone who would hear him for the first time would assume that he was a very influential man with impact, not only in London but in other world capitals. Of course, in a place where any foreigner was closely observed, everyone is suspect until proven otherwise. An informer watching a foreign newcomer from New York assigned to UNRWA for a special period and talking big words with a British accent would be certain that the man was a real catch. If it was done with an Armenian cover, which at the time was Soviet related, someone higher up would have discovered that they had the wrong catch. They would have passed him on to another group, which in turn tried to see how best they could trade him, possibly for friends in English prisons. When no result was achieved, they may have "sold him" to someone like Colonel Gaddafi, who may have thought he could use him to settle scores in his open conflictwith the government of Margaret Thatcher. Perhaps it was the British "stiff upper lip," or a negotiating tactic, but the British government did not seem too keen on the hostage as one of their own. They were more interested in operative information, such as finding out who the kidnappers were, how the Syrians operated, with whom I was in touch, and what by-roads was I taking, rather than getting the man released. That may be business as usual in intelligence circles, but to me it was unfamiliar ground.

The Secretary-General's interest was humanitarian. Each side, as usual, tried to use the UN for their own purpose: the kidnappers wanted to drag us into a dialogue in search for a deal, while the British authorities naturally sought more intelligence. In a way I felt, particularly during the second trip, like some British operatives were putting me in harm's way. It did not take much insight to realize that I was under surveillance while in the region. Yet the British Chargé d'Affaires in Damascus would call my hotel, asking me to arrange a meeting for him with Vice President Khaddam. Sometimes he sounded like he was giving me instructions. I made a point of staying at the Sham Hotel in downtown Damascus. I often sat on the roof by the pool listening to music on my headphones, just to be seen outside by all those in nearby offices so they would know where I was. Once when I came into my room I found my headphones broken; someone must have wanted to double check what I was using them for.

A colleague in the Secretary-General's office was puzzled by why certain British individuals were trying to erode my credibility with all sides, including with other British officials. They sought to make it appear to the Syrians and to the kidnappers as if I worked for the British, which was putting me at great risk. As I had always maintained excellent relations with the U.K. mission, I wondered what was going on. Taking over someone else's turf at the UN would not justify that sort of action, and I was sure that our British UN colleagues were not behind it. My first guess was that I was being used as bait, even if kidnapped, to track the kidnappers. A darker suspicion revolved around a frustrated field operative with a lethal approach and perceived grudge. Anyway, I had a feeling that something wrong was taking place that did not fit with the British diplomatic pattern of conducting business. My mission was becoming too closely involved with security services, which admittedly is not my area of competence.

When returning to New York, the so-called "secret mission," which we kept from the press had already spread around in the Secretariat. The Chef de Cabinet had told the head of my department, who in turn alerted the director with whom I officially worked, but with whom I already had a tense relationship, a Soviet functionary from Armenia. Particularly if the Armenian Liberation Army was involved, that meant more difficulties with him; not only was he perceived to be well-connected in Moscow, but he returned later to become the Foreign Minister of Soviet Armenia. He sent a note for the file, saying that my absence from Headquarters was not authorized. That would put me in a very vulnerable situation if anybody mishandled me. Having survived Beirut during a civil war, I felt I could manage my way. But a more worrying side was financial. The executive office would not pay me for travel or per diem. The Secretary-General's office managed to pay me during my first trip, but the second time I had to find another way within the system to retrieve the funds.

Clearly the UN itself was not yet ready for such an operation unless the one entrusted with it was given full flexibility and unreserved political support. It would mean working directly and solely for and with the Secretary-General. Only then one can get the funds to travel and authority to negotiate. Otherwise, you are unable to operate with almost everybody in the building knowing where you were and what you did. Iranian leader Hashemi Rafsanjani personally went to Damascus to oversee the release of some Western hostages, a UN administrative officer would not refund the staffer sent on a secret mission by the Secretary-General unless he received an approved itinerary together with a list of those contacted, including their addresses and telephone numbers. The flexibility of working directly at the Secretary-General's office empowered my colleague, Giandomenico Picco, when he discreetly helped in the release of other Western hostages. He would travel and move as required. Noting the Secretary-General's valuable interest, Iran placed one of its most able and sophisticated diplomats, Javad Zarif, to accompany and support Picco's involvement; he returned later as his country's permanent representative in New York and years after that became its Foreign Minister. You cannot operate a secret assignment effectively unless you have a free hand, and you cannot have a free hand unless the top man says so to everyone else. Perhaps the UN itself sometimes needed more internal harmony. After all, peacekeeping begins at home.

CHAPTER XIV:

CHANGING PATTERN OF WAR,
CHANGING NATURE OF PEACE

The UN's singular success in achieving peaceful statehood for Eritrea, with Ethiopia's agreement, was eroded a few years later through politically expedient multiple appointments with tragic impact on the ground.

At one point, at least seven Under Secretary-Generals and Assistant Secretary-Generals were presumably handling the Ethiopian-Eritrean boarder dispute: a Special Representative of the Secretary-General for Ethiopia and Eritrea, Legwaila Joseph Legwaila; two deputy Special Representatives of the Secretary-General for Ethiopia and Eritrea; a Special Representative for the Humanitarian Crisis in the "Horn of Africa", a post first held by former President of Finland Martti Ahtisaari, then replaced by a former Norwegian Prime Minister; a Commander of the UN troops between the two countries, Major General Rejender Singh; one Assistant Secretary-General in Asmara, and another Assistant Secretary-General in Addis Ababa. The outcome? Too many cooks, too much confusion, very low credibility, competition of moves, lack of focus on the brewing tension and threats of renewed war. On top of it all, the Secretary-General ended up receiving an unusual publicized rebuke by the President of Eritrea. Except for Ambassador Legwaila and General Singh, appointments were made not to settle the conflict but to accommodate a politically expedient needed elsewhere. The former Canadian Foreign Minister Lloyd Axworthy, appointed as a Special Envoy "over" Ethiopia and Eritrea was giving up by the summer 2005.

In Kosovo, where the UN had a unique role to play and to prove its worth in a time of deteriorating reputation, again appointments were made to accommodate a powerful government elsewhere rather than nurture a people in need. Five representatives were appointed in the first five years. Such action did little to assure a traumatized people that the UN was serious about their fate. Only the first, Bernard Kouchner, and the last, Sören Jensen-Pedersen, had any real expertise in the field. Dr. Kouchner knew how to handle Kosovars and win the media but was seen as anti-Serb. After him, Hans Hakkerup of Denmark behaved like he was still Prime Minister but with no back up resources. He was disliked openly by the Albanian majority without winning over the Serbs either. Michael Steiner was hated by everyone. His arrogance provoked even his own German compatriots. It was commonly known that his appointment was an accommodation to Chancellor Schroeder after an embarrassing scandal at Moscow airport. When the noise faded, he was recycled by his government as its UN Geneva envoy. When Harri Holkeri took over, the former General Assembly President from Finland boasted that his advantage over others was that he had never been to Kosovo. He then proceeded to demonstrate his ignorance. He gave the impression that he neither read his briefings, nor was he interested in anything to do with his daily duties. During his nine-month administration, civil services were at a standstill and worse: no water, no electricity, and no work. The economy was sliding and security non-existent. No one in New York wanted to know. The representative in Kosovo was THE representative: unquestioned even while in the host area - like the UN - reputation was going downhill.

Also in Kosovo, in addition to the "High Commissioner" there existed posts of Deputy Special Representative for Institution Building (OSCE) and Deputy Special Representative for Reconstruction (OECD), the first occupied by a German and the latter by a Briton. Another post, Special Envoy of the Secretary-General, was established to carry out a comprehensive review of Kosovo. This one had been occupied by Norwegian diplomat Kai Eide but was then assigned to the always-available Martti Ahtisaari, who indeed was well versed on the issue from his days of delicate negotiations with former Serbian President Milosovic. Mr. Ahtisaari, a former UN Under Secretary-General for Administration, had sterling credentials beginning with his role in the independence of Namibia. In addition, there was a Deputy Special Envoy of the Secretary-General for the Future Status Process for Kosovo and a Principal Deputy Special Representative.

In Cyprus, the kindest of diplomats, a former ambassador of Poland who had voted to elect Kofi Annan, was appointed as chief of mission. Zbigniew Wlosowiez had never set foot on the Isle of Venus before. He made up for it by outright hospitality to everyone, introducing kitchen peacekeeping: warm, hearty meals topped by his thoughtful mother's tasty cookies. Another non-residential Special Representative "for" Cyprus (Zbigniew resided "in" Cyprus), Alvaro de Soto, was based in New York, traveling only as required – which was not much. De Soto, who later served as a Middle East envoy, had proven experience in Nicaragua and Guatemala. A discreet, well-connected Peruvian with sharp wit and understated demeanor, he had little patience for Byzantine intricacies. His main effort was to co-ordinate with other interest parties what became known as "the Annan plan," which was unraveled by a popular vote. At the time, two Under Secretary-Generals, one Assistant Secretary-General, topped by no other than the Secretary-General, "lent their shoulders to the wheel," as the Secretary-General would say. The result was worse than when it started. Visitors to Cyprus a year later could still notice the negative impact. "Oxy Annan," using the Greek word for "no," it was said, when in fact the plan was not actually his. It was mainly the work of a very experienced British diplomat, agreed to by the European Union and by Washington. The Secretary-General tested it during a meeting at the Swiss resort of Birkenstock. He adopted it and insisted upon having a popular vote without a similar determination to mobilize for it. That double designation drew questions about possible conflict of interest when a Special Envoy "on" (as opposed to "in") a former Foreign Minister of Australia hired a "speakeasy" political consulting firm which was repeatedly conducting business with companies in a nearby capital directly involved. His successor, a Norwegian diplomat, wisely gave up the title early 2016 to focus on his work with the Davos World Forum, leaving the task to an experienced, competent, highly regarded insider, Lisa Buttenheim, who returned to New York as Assistant Secretary-General for Peacekeeping.

Sometimes a private invitation to dinner would promote reconciliation much more than protracted meetings. Once, after I had introduced Cyprus President Glafcos Clerides at a press conference, I went back to work. Then, as always for three decades, the Cyprus crisis revolved around the need to arrange a fruitful meeting of hearts and minds between the Greek and Turkish leaders. Leaving the office late that evening, I walked out with my colleague dealing with Cyprus, Alvaro de Soto, who elaborated on difficulties in arranging for such a meeting and possible approaches for achieving it. On the way home I stopped at a Chinese restaurant on 44th Street, off of First Avenue, to take out my dinner. Spotting President Clerides there, I recalled his jovial remark to me - that morning he had said that we seemed to enjoy the same kind of food. It also seemed to apply to his Turkish counterpart Mr. Rauf Denktash, who was also spotted in the same restaurant. Whether they walked back together to their separate hotels remains unclear.

Sometimes the drums of war can be overtaken by a good taste of peace. Alvaro de Soto is someone who knows this well. He had joined the UN as Special Assistant to his compatriot, Secretary-General Javier Perez de Cuellar, initially as "a bird of passage." Predicting a temporary stay, he remained for 25 years. Although he had nothing productive to show for his achievements in Western Sahara, he played a major, though unheralded, role in peaceful arrangements for El Salvador and Nicaragua, operating until midnight of the New Year in December 1991 to seal a conclusive deal for Central America. At the time, in the midst of delicate, often stormy, negotiations between warring parties, he called to find out about the possibility of arranging a good meal of Arabic food. It transpired that there were secret meetings in New York among the warring parties in El Salvador, and one of the leaders, Mr. Handel, was of Arab descent. A dinner break was in order; so why not some hummus and shish taouk?

Western Sahara was another arena for distinguished envoys with undistinguished results. The most famous was the legendary James Baker, former U.S. Secretary of State, who peacefully and promptly quit when his proposals were not implemented. He was replaced by another American, then by a Dutch diplomat who felt important enough to circulate his proposal to Security Council members before securing the approval of new Secretary-General Ban Ki-moon. He was replaced by a retired U.S. diplomat with expertise in Syria. There was a "Personal Envoy" of the Secretary-General and another "Special Representative" of the Secretary-General. Apparently, one travelled around the world, and the other around the region.

Africa had at least 30 "Specials". As a general umbrella, there was a Special Advisor for Special Assignments in Africa and a Special Advisor on Africa plus an Assistant Secretary-General for Africa at the

Department of Political Affairs. Then there was one in Burundi: an Executive Representative and Head of the UN Integrated Office. Central African Republic also had one, initially a General from Senegal, whose name was often confused with a dedicated close aide of Mr. Annan in New York. What he did there remained a mystery. Côte d'Ivoire had four. Again the same formula as in Kosovo was applied. Special, Principal Deputy Special, Deputy Special - with an addition of a "High Representative for Elections." Widespread violence there with an escalating number of victims did not seem to call for a serious review, even with respect to that just-referenced presumed election.

A more tragic designation was in the Congo, which went by the official acronym of DRC. Over 3.3 million died there between 2000 and 2005. A politically accommodated "Special Representative" there was an obscure Amos Nemenga Ngongi, who was replaced in 2003 by William Lacey Swing, an apparently well-connected American and former aide to Mr. Annan. When reports on sexual exploitation by peacekeeping troops were widely disseminated in mid-2005, Mr. Swing was called to the UN Headquarters. Reporters in the building were alerted by someone in the Secretary-General's office that he would be asked to resign that afternoon. Instead, a subsequent statement indicated that he still had "a lot of work on his plate," meaning someone in New York backed down. It transpired that Mr. Swing had the strong support of the company of friends he kept. Two years later he was still there with two equally Special Deputies: a former Ambassador and a development expert who most probably ran the whole operation. The farce continued, under changing names.

Brewing trouble in the Congo should have been of no surprise to the international community, which reacted only too late and mainly to media headlines. Observers doing their homework would have seen it coming. Special Representatives in the Congo were caught off guard. And what about the other 16 experienced diplomats hovering around the neighborhood? For several years, the Under Secretary-General for Peacekeeping Jean-Marie Guéhenno, himself an appointee of political expediency, had been visiting that Francophone African region almost regularly. Did he not notice anything? What was his take on the situation? Any proposals? He had noted "an unexpected opening" with the assassination of Congo President Lauren Kabila and the election of Kabila's son Joseph. At the time, the French diplomat stressed the need to "exploit that window of opportunity." What followed was more of the same atrocities, compounded with more reports of sexual exploitation by peacekeepers. When massacres got out of hand in gold-rich Bunia province, where some powerful countries had real vested interests, a new force was sent under "UN auspices" - an increasingly evolving formula meaning less control by the UN and more by the country offering troops. Six hundred poorly instructed and poorly motivated Uruguayans gave way to 1,400 Europeans, mainly French, to be followed by some from Bangladesh - with varying approaches but almost similar outcomes.

As usually happened in cases drawing media attention, a press release announced that "a multi-disciplinary assessment mission" was dispatched to the African sub-region "to determine measures to be taken for implementation of a comprehensive, integrated and resolute approach to the issues peace, security and development in the region." More terminology in the air meant more casualties on the ground. One more high level exploratory mission meant more special envoys - presumably pro bono - but travel expenses, plus per diem for days on duty, cost more than a regular salary. The list continued. The "Great Lakes" region had a "Special Representative". So did Guinea-Bissau, presumably for peace-building support.

Liberia had three headed by a true team leader, Alan Doss, an Englishman who served in varied delicate posts. There, at least, a UN success story was accomplished: a relatively free and participatory election after years of atrocities. Another relative success was in Sierra Leone, where after years of brutal turmoil a former UN staff member, President Ahmed Kabah, was elected in a popular, internationally supervised election.

In hopeless Somalia, one was more than enough; almost nothing was accomplished. Former Dutch Minister of Cooperation, Jan Pronk, assisted by two deputies, initially dealt with Sudan's Darfur tragedy with continuously frustrating results. Then there is an office of the Special Representative of the Secretary-General for West Africa headed by a former Mauritanian Ambassador in Washington and Paris. Also, the Rwanda 1994 memories obviously inflicted a deep scar. Although it happened under Kofi Annan's watch as peacekeeping chief, all powerful member states should share the blame for refusing to intervene on time. It is common knowledge by now that the UN representative on the ground, Canadian Lt. General Romeo Dallaire, sought to take preventive action but was handicapped by instructions from New York.

Latin America and the Caribbean had fewer Special Representatives than any other continent. A High Level Representative for "the Latin American Region," the highly regarded Under-Secretary-General Diego Cordovez, served until a change of government in his own country required him to become Ecuador's Ambassador in New York. A "Personal Representative on the border controversy between Guyana and Venezuela" has been in place since October 1999. The "Stabilization Mission" in Haiti has a "Special" plus a "Principal" Deputy and a regular one. A similar listing applied to Afghanistan. In Asia, Cambodia and Myanmar (former Burma) have only one each since the year 2000. Ban Ki-moon's outgoing Chef de Cabinet Vijay Nambiar was designated as Special Envoy to Myanmar, having drawn questions on his role during a civil war in nearby Sri Lanka. After initiating positive movement, he then vaguely disappeared from the diplomatic radar, first by having general statements issued on his behalf, rather than directly, then vague silence. In East Timor, officially named Timor-Leste, there were three. Tajikistan had one for "Peacebuilding" under the overly optimistic acronym "UNTOP".

A curious, almost amusing, appointment in Europe was that of an envoy for talks between Greece and the "Former Yugoslav Republic of Macedonia". With the breakdown of Yugoslavia, the Macedonian province claimed statehood, which was internationally approved except for a dispute over the name. Among their abundant claims to historic fame, the Greeks remain especially proud of Alexander the Great of Macedonia. Athens therefore blocked the name of the new republic until a compromise was reached. The envoy, Matthew Niemetz, who was appointed in December 1999, hinted - very discreetly of course - that he was likely to come out with a common understanding by 2006. In 2014, a statement on his behalf indicated the possibility of a meeting.

Another representative in Africa with a work description that raised a number of questions was the Special Envoy of the Secretary-General for the "Lord's Resistance Army-affected areas" operating in Uganda. There was neither an indication how its Special Representative would operate, whether through divine intervention, in prayer or by direct talks, nor whether he should turn to New York for guidance or work on more spiritual connections. Nothing tangible was heard from him for awhile. Equally obscure was the post of the Special Envoy of the Secretary-General for Humanitarian Needs in Southern Africa, who presented occasional reports with no apparent accomplishment.

In Haiti, the mission has been as confused as the situation in the country itself. At the initial period, when a coup occurred and the Clinton administration was pushing for a return to "democracy," former Foreign Minister of Argentina, Dante Caputo, took over as the Special Envoy of the Secretary-General. However, Mr. Caputo had difficulties with both President Jean Aristide, who accused him of working with the Americans, and, on the other side, the Americans, who thought he was playing a Latin-American game. The controversial death of Commanding Officer General da Matta Bacellar started a string of unstoppable rumors, particularly that he had an argument that evening with the Special Representative of the Secretary-General about the role of the mission. Despite a firm and clear announcement that the death was a suicide, it did not dispel a conspiracy theory, which further eroded the work of the team. The last thing it needed was the catastrophic earthquake with a 7.0 magnitude where more than 100 dedicated staff headed by a really special representative, Hedi Annabi, lost their lives.

All eyes were on U.N. Secretary-General Ban Ki-moon as he was in Haiti on 17 January giving a press conference amidst the ruins of Port-au-Prince. The whole country was in catastrophic shape. Millions displaced in the streets. U.N. Headquarters had fallen apart, about 200 U.N. staffers unaccounted for. The two most senior U.N. representatives, Hedi Annabi, and Luis da Costa were just declared missing. Mr. Ban, the symbolic figure of the international community, was highlighting the need to clear the bottlenecks and co-ordinate delivery of humanitarian assistance. In the midst of devastation and tragedy, TV photographers managed to zoom in on a man with distinctive Far Eastern features seated behind the Secretary-General using his own mobile phone camera to photograph himself!

Nepal has had several envoys. It was first handled from a distance in the hope that the King would make up his mind about what kind of Government he preferred. After experimenting for a while the job landed on Ian Martin, described as someone who knew the players in the region. That same description was applied to him when he was sent to East Timor on a Special Mission to handle the 2006 crisis when the Special Representative there, an expediently appointed Japanese, seemed hopeless.

Special Representatives in the Middle East were almost overlooked by former Secretaries-General Boutros-Ghali and Annan until an appointment of Mr. Terje Roed-Larsen as coordinator, first for

Gaza, and then for the Middle East. This was a hard-working, almost obsessed Norwegian diplomat who was reported to have had a yet-unclear role in the Oslo accords, which he seemed to later disavow. Mr. Larsen insisted on being the main representative in the region with little input from anyone else. He had good relations with both the heads of the Palestinian authority and Israeli Prime Minister Shimon Peres. Later, he had problems in Syria and Lebanon and eventually in Ramallah. He expanded his role to contacts with other Arab countries, such as Kuwait, Bahrain, and Saudi Arabia, gaining substantive financial support for a venture under his direction, an International Institute for Peace. He kept a UN title as Special Envoy on implementing resolution 1701 of 2006 over Lebanon which remained unimplemented by the time he left in the summer of 2016.

Although the UN's role in Iraq was still unclear in 2006, there were four "Specials" on it: a Special Representative, two Deputy Special Representatives and one Special Adviser. In addition, there was a high level Coordinator with the oversized name: "the Secretary-General's High-level Coordinator for compliance by Iraq with its obligations regarding the repatriation or return of all Kuwaiti and third country nationals or their remains, as well as the return of all Kuwaiti property, including archives seized by Iraq," a position held by Yuli Vorontsov from Russia for several years.

While the Secretary-General officially selects the Special Representatives, it was not always entirely in his own hands. Kofi Annan's wish to send Sir Kieran Prendergast as his Special Coordinator for Lebanon was blocked by an unintended consequence of a letter Mr. Annan had sent to President Bush indicating that the situation in Fallujah, Iraq, could have been resolved with less indiscriminate killing of ordinary civilians. This was received with an angry response from the President. Mr. Annan's defenders claimed that the letter was drafted by Mr. Prendergast, who subsequently fell on his sword. Instead, a Director in his office, Geir O. Pedersen, was sent as Special Representative for Southern Lebanon until his mandate expanded to other areas.

In brief, there were too many Special Representatives with too little impact. Originally, the designated Secretary-General's Special Representatives had an impressive standing. There were only few of them, and they had defined tasks. They were looked at almost with the same awe as the Secretary-General and directly represented him. They would not be taken lightly, and they carried themselves in a very dignified, impressive and credible way. The Special Representatives listed above are all distinguished people. The issue is that their appointment was politically accommodating to them – not necessarily for the citizens of the host country. The point of having a Special Representative was to prepare the groundwork. The Secretary-General would then come in only to crown an achievement, to sign an agreement and oversee the finishing touches. He should not have to end up looking for a refugee camp, which has disappeared on him somewhere in the desert of Darfur.

Darfur, one fifth of the Sudan, was caught in multiple conflicts: shepherds vs. farmers; Arabs vs. non-Arabs; African vs. non-African. It is an uneasy neighborhood with rough neighbors. Across the northern border lies Libya, where leader Colonel Gaddafi exploited it to settle scores with another neighbor, Chad, whose conflicting parties in turn settled their scores through Darfur. Most coups in Chad had been hatched in the seclusion of Darfur, while many Darfur rebels found in Chad their launching pads. There are complex tribal relations throughout the territory. Any serious attempt to deal with the Darfur situation should not only focus on the links between Khartoum and Darfur but take into account those neighboring countries and their tribal connections. The Sudanese government in Khartoum was not above using one group against the other to divide and rule, while appropriating the best of fertile land to offer it to a selected few. "Fur" was not the largest tribe, but it happened to give its name to Darfur (the "home of Fur"), now infamous for helpless famine and ruthless death under the eyes of an unhelpful world.

To outsiders, the perception of Darfur was mostly audio-visual. A complex evaluation of a destitute situation was abandoned for a colorful presentation: the helpless and the ruthless. While there was an abundance of victims, there were also an increasing number of culprits. Many of those supposedly protecting the farmers have indeed been raping women of their own tribe, committing atrocities in their area of control and looting aid convoys. "Rebel" groups were splintered into at least a dozen fighting for turf, recognition and funds. The role of big power politics only added fuel to the conflict and made a very bad situation even worse. A humanitarian red flag had been raised by civic society activists, with limited international notice, until an influential American envoy with religious interests returned to take over as the U.S. Ambassador to the UN. When the Darfur issue was raised at a Security Council informal consultation, the response was vague, taking into account the position of the Sudanese government. It was only when the campaign gained an emotional edge and the African group faced an awkward challenge that some diplomatic action became inevitable. That meant more media posturing than field action. The African Union was gradually prodded into assembling an overly prudent peacekeeping force with little impact. China, a discreet player which purchases about 80% of Sudanese oil, joined in the friendly persuasion of the Sudanese government to agree to a "heavy package" prepared by a hybrid Afro-UN monitoring venture. Since 2003, when Darfur was brought to the attention of the world, until the spring of 2007, no action had been taken. By then 200,000 people had been killed and 2.2 million displaced.

By the time the UN got involved, Secretary-General Annan was caught between the desire to consider growing public attention, particularly by civic groups in the U.S. and Europe, while avoiding to provoke the Government of Sudan. He was already in a vulnerable condition because of negative reporting on Oil-for-Food. In semblances of action, he timed his visit to Sudan with that of his only and possibly lonely friend in official Washington, Secretary of State Colin Powell. That may have helped him in Washington but eroded his credibility on the other side. Khartoum may have concluded that it was better to deal with the real power than with its proxy. Darfur became an increasingly complicated tragic situation as more countries got involved, either to demonstrate sympathy, offer practical help or exploit the situation for political pressure. Even an African expatriate like Mr. Annan was taken around in circles when he visited the area with a plane-load of journalists. The refugee camp selected by his aides the evening before had actually disappeared. A photo opportunity with a group of old ladies was arranged as a consolation prize.

The first special envoy sent was a Dutch development minister, Jan Pronk, recognized for his persistent efforts on Climate Change. His framework compact was known jovially as UNFUCCC. He had been looking for a UN post since applying years before for the job of Administrator of UNDP, which was given to an Englishman, and then a post as High Representative for Human Rights, which was offered to another Dutch politician, former Prime Minister Ruud Lubbers. Pronk was a clearly dynamic man with the best of intentions, but his main challenge over Darfur was to find out the real intentions of a mixed bag of conflicting parties and nail down practical arrangements. Unwisely, he also launched a website in which he pontificated about the situation, often reflecting personal views rather than the UN position. Unwittingly that provided a pretext for the Sudanese authorities in their delaying tactics. They considered him *persona non grata*, and the Secretary-General, wisely noting he had only a few months to go, let his contract expire at the end of 2006.

During this period, Sudan's President Omar al-Bashir was officially accused by the International Criminal Court, along with wide media coverage, of genocide, crimes against humanity and war crimes. Intriguingly, these charges seemed practically overlooked after he agreed to the split of South Sudan in 2011. In 2016, he indicated a readiness to leave by 2020.

There is a pressing need to regain the clarity and credibility of envoys' functions. When member states wonder what the Special Representatives were actually doing there, it is time for a courageous review. There is also the financial aspect. Representatives who claim they were not being paid a salary are deceptively wrong. It is not difficult for a Special Representative to find a reason to travel: it takes a phone call to the Chef de Cabinet. Their per diem alone is a costly burden of their mission. The Special Representatives of the Secretary-General were a crucial part of UN peacekeeping, and it is time to ask whether the proliferation of these appointments made any real difference in resolving the conflicts or actually added more confusion to already intricate problems.

Generation X of Peacekeeping

Could an officer from a national army turn into an international servant at the drop of a hat? When a general who was about to take a helicopter from Beirut to southern Lebanon some years ago to join UNIFIL realized he was still in his country's uniform, he opened his briefcase, placed a UN elastic band on his arm and replaced his paratrooper's cap with that of a UN peacekeeper. These days the opposite may be true - former UN peacekeepers may replace their international hats with their national ones. Whatever happened to UN peacekeeping? Why is it that the crown jewel of the UN eventually turned out to be a major embarrassment for the Organization? The U.N.'s peacekeeping operations were more impressive when it had fewer resources. So why is it that this, the pride of the United Nations with two Nobel Prizes, became its field of embarrassment?

There may have been a generation change. Earlier operations were clear, signed and sealed with agreements between parties. More recently operations were far less clear, with forays in varied, internal battles, sometimes unknown enemies and with an uncertainty of how to measure success. Initially the UN had no enemies, it was there to help, to play a constructive role and not to fight any party. Introducing soldiers as peacekeepers arose in 1956, 10 years after the UN was created, when troops were put on the ground. The first generation of peacekeeping was that of high-level negotiators who mediated, observed and endorsed and guaranteed mutual agreements. This generation was initiated by Folke Bernadotte, with the proximity talks, and continued by Dr. Ralph Bunche on the island of Rhodes in 1949, resulting in the first armistice agreement between Israel and the Arab armies. It created a group called UNTSO (troop supervision observers), which mainly was composed not of foot soldiers but officers as observers. Based in Jerusalem, it had several sub-offices in signatory countries, such as the Israel-Lebanese Mixed Armistice Commission (ILMAC).

Canadians would proudly claim that their former Prime Minister, Mr. Lester Pearson, was the father of peacekeeping since soon after the 1956 Suez war it was he who developed - in cooperation with Dag Hammarskjold - the first actual peacekeeping force, the UN Emergency Force. Mr. Pearson indeed worked with the Secretary-General so relentlessly that his family missed him. Surrendering to his wife's pleading he retired, but his absence from the UN was brief. Before long, after spending full time at home, perhaps his wife suggested he should find a new assignment.

When UNIFIL started, it drew on the ILMAC presence. It had new officers but kept the old structures. There was an argument on whether UNTSO and ILMAC existed or not. Each country had its own political interpretation. In the early days of UNIFIL there was a need to have Lebanese and Israeli officers meet to work out a few details on the border in Naqoura. The Lebanese officers claimed to meet under the General Armistice Agreement from 1949, while Israel claimed they were meeting to discuss current issues which had nothing to do with the old agreement. For the first time soldiers were dying under a flag that was not their own country's. While there were always those soldiering outside their national borders, it was mainly either to promote their own countries' interests or their that of their own. For the first time in history, the United Nations signaled that there are those who willingly dedicate their lifetime career - even their life – for human and international peace.

There were pioneering prominent examples like Folke Bernadotte, Dag Hammarskjold and Sergio Vieira de Mello, but there were also thousands of others that went unheralded and unknown.

The early 1990s witnessed a generation of miserable failures. A renewed world order was on the horizon, which was actually more accurately described by Paul Valéry's "new world disorder." Missions that witnessed massacres like in Rwanda, Somalia, and Bosnia were deep embarrassments for the UN and the beginning of the downfall of credible peacekeeping. Neither the Secretary-General at the time, nor officials directly involved, realized the extent of the damage. Some of those directly handling Srebrenica were on leave. Some were promoted up to the level of their incompetence and found their way up the ladder with keener instincts to cover their tracks.

In one of his disarming moments, Kofi Annan wondered whether SG stood for scapegoat rather than Secretary-General. The fact remained that while there were certain powerful countries that should have been held responsible, the UN Secretariat itself mishandled Srebrenica, Somalia and Rwanda. By the time it unsuccessfully tried to explain its way out of it, it was already too late.

A new field task for the UN was "running" a country or province by introducing administrators and police officers, as in Kosovo and East Timor. The new era of peacekeeping was not just observing and reporting or intervening in a conflict but also building peace and order. "Peace Building" was initially criticized when first proposed by some key countries in the Agenda for Peace by Boutros-Boutros-Ghali on the ground that the UN would be interfering in internal affairs of member states. A famous outcry was that of Republican presidential candidate Bob Dole, repeating the name of "Boot-ross Boot-ross" Ghali in his political campaigns, as if the UN Secretary-General was about to take over the United States, let alone the world.

Despite several peacekeeping reviews, the peacekeeping performance did not improve much. There was a discussion, for example, about whether it would be possible to operate selectively and only intervene where results seemed feasible. In a speech to the General Assembly, President Clinton stated that if the United States had to say "yes," the United Nations had to learn to say "no." Being selective is easier said than done. Trouble spots do not await official permission. The Secretary-General was caught between the two standpoints and was quoted saying both that we had to be more selective and not intervene everywhere and, at another time, that we had no choice but to intervene since crises were imposed. The Clinton administration also presented a policy of "thresholds." After a certain number of losses of its soldiers, the U.S. would get out. That policy played into the hands of their adversaries. In Somalia, for example, rebels made sure that the U.S. suffered enough victims to push them to withdraw - which they did. This approach also explains the confused attitude of the U.S. in Haiti and its reluctance to accept any preventive role in Rwanda. But this also affected UN peacekeeping.

UN soldiers were used as human shields in Bosnia, where three soldiers were tied to ammunition dumps after an air strike. Not a single member state demonstrated the political will to take on the Serbian army, except later on in Kosovo when the credibility of the U.N., together with the soldiers, were in retreat. In a somewhat public gesture, Special Representative Yasushi Akashi was singled out for blame and left to flap in the wind. They took away his authority to allow strikes, although everyone at headquarters knew that the amenable Japanese would hardly decide on his own. In fact, it was tantamount to delivering a victory to Serbian militant Karadzic, who had refused to see Mr. Akashi. The civilian Special Representative was caught between two UN generals, a British and a French; a ruthless Serbian general; thug and smuggler Karadzic; and an isolated Dutch general who had to make his own decisions with his troops in Srebrenica. Whatever the reason to have him there, he should have been supported more clearly and effectively. If not, he should have been withdrawn. The basic problem was that no homework was done about the region. After the failures of peacekeeping in the early 1990's, peacekeeping started to transform once again through a series of events that shaped another generation.

The Changing Nature of War, and the Changing Meaning of Peace

A new balance of power in the Third Millennium led to fewer wars but more conflict. It was not national armies clashing, but all sorts of ghost enemies fighting and operating through various means. A new feature was the use of mercenaries, an increasing trend around the world that finds its expression in "wars of the willing;" those involved in the conflicts were not merely national armies but also private groups. Whether it was in Afghanistan, Iraq or elsewhere, many governments started turning to subsidiary private players, representing a confused and confusing private extension of governments. Those involved were supposedly disciplined former officers who remained in touch with government officials. Because such mercenary security companies had experience in confidential operations, they were contracted to undertake tasks officially off limits to regular forces. Their adversaries soon responded in a similar pattern. Whole countries, even regions, turned into "no man's lands" with no accountability. Operations by mercenaries were profit-oriented, uncontrolled and even unobserved. No rules applied. They focused on delivering specific targets, regardless of the means or the implications of actions taken on relations amongst member states.

Some "think tanks" justified using them, particularly in situations where ruthless, tough measures were required. A number of influential highly respected former senior officials joined some of these well-known contractual firms, which by now are managed like established profit-making businesses. The fact remains, however, that their vested interests would be in continuing conflict; the U.N., in turn, would want them off the field of play. Security companies may perceive the UN as competition, because they seek lucrative contracts in areas where the UN would operate at a minimum cost on a publicly audited budget. That may be the influence behind the lack of support for any effort to rebuild an effectively strong U.N.

"Peace" today really means "managed conflict." The meaning of victory is even more slippery. With unknown adversaries and undrawn battle-fields, a new era emerged with less clarity and more violence. This raises the question of staff safety. Although often included in agreements between the parties and the U.N., a risk arises when there are no agreements, when it is not clear who welcomed you and who did not. That would require flexibility, mobility and above all strategic thinking with a preemptive approach if possible. But then officials prefer to react to a crisis than prevent it, even at a much higher cost.

X-Rated Peacekeeping

Tragically, the new millennium brought out reports of "X-rated" UN peacekeeping. Instead of selfless sacrifice, honest mediation and leading by example, the old faithful and newcomers alike were treated to unprecedented accounts of child molestation, sexual exploitation and illicit gold-for-guns trade offs. Astonishingly, no one was held accountable. The same Special Representatives, the same accused troops, carried on business as usual with an occasional proclamation from Headquarters about a zero tolerance policy. When the Secretary-General himself was under a cloud over Iraq, the last thing he needed was an argument with France over its main Under Secretary-General or with the U.S. over his Representative in the Congo. How could he seriously discipline accused Pakistani officers when his long time Chef de Cabinet was a Pakistani who had worked with him as deputy during the preceding catastrophic mission? One of the main peacekeeping directors in New York was himself a Pakistani General (who spent profitable time in Timor-Leste ensuring that his son was placed there before returning to Headquarters). Such questions when internally raised were countered with a legalistic answer: that the responsibility for the behavior of troops lay with their governments. In fact, it was in the interest of Pakistan to clarify that very few individuals were involved and that they received their due punishment. Unfortunately, no such transparent action was forthcoming. The same applies to other countries implicated for lack of immediate response. For example, certain troops accused of sexual misconduct in the Central African Republic included Gabon, the country of the Secretary-General's Special Envoy there. He was seen at his cleaner's on Manhattan and 2nd Avenue more often than he tried to explain – or maybe relinquish his position.

Changes of Structures and Personalities

Modern peacekeeping today was caught between the end of an old order and emergence of a new, not yet defined one. A chronology of events and changes among leading personalities drastically affected it. The first major blow in earlier days was the tragic death of Secretary-General Hammarskjold, who personally handled the most intricate assignments to the point of ultimate sacrifice. He died while on a peacekeeping mission.

His successor U Thant was increasingly challenged by the outcome of the 1967 "Six Day War" following the withdrawal of UN troops from the buffer zone of Sinai. A prolonged war in Vietnam, a country neighboring his own Burma, coincided with his term of office. As a Buddhist master, U Thant must have been particularly pained at the sight of monks burning themselves in protest while he was struggling almost daily to find a peaceful role. The loss of his son added to his sorrow, hidden from diplomats but visible to anyone looking into his mournful eyes as he started repeating in his baritone voice that he would not wish to be "a glorified clerk." Despite frustration, he maintained a firm grip on peacekeeping with solid backing by its pillar, the legendary Nobel Laureate Ralph Bunche. An African-American human rights activist, Dr. Bunche was ably assisted by a small team of experienced professionals. When U Thant left, his successor Kurt Waldheim depended entirely on the remaining team.

Waldheim gave Brian Urquhart an almost free hand as the potential for a growing UN role in the Middle East was - at least officially - supported by the two superpowers of the time. He did his job so well that, regardless of nationality, he became known as Mr. Peacekeeping, clearly overshadowing other high-ranking colleagues.

When another Under Secretary-General Javier Perez de Cuellar was elected to lead the Organization, Urquhart and his close associate since the 1960s in Congo, F.T. Liu, were about ready to retire. Don Javier capably foresaw a period of detente among the five Permanent Members and initiated timely interventions to settle pending conflicts like Nicaragua, San Salvador and the Iran-Iraq ceasefire, which helped the release of Western hostages. Peacekeeping was supported by a discreet, yet effective, role of the Secretary-General. By then, a new diplomat arrived from London to take over Political Affairs from his compatriot. As Sir Marrack Goulding started to assert his role and defend his turf, the second tier of command, which was holding the fort, found their upward mobility elsewhere. James Jonah, Virendra Dayal and Jean-Claude Aimé took more senior positions in other Secretariat posts, while another mainstay of peacekeeping institutional memory, George Sherry, retired. Naturally, the new crop did not acquire the same stature as the outgoing one.

For a long while, UN peacekeeping had a well-known address. People handling it and countries contributing to it were easily identifiable. An established mechanism worked to the general satisfaction of the international community. A set of countries and officers seemed ready to join in and operate at short notice. Those handling peacekeeping among countries and within the UN knew each other well. Perhaps because the conflicts were clearer, the parties were more openly collaborative. Agreements would be more quickly endorsed and generally followed. The Political Department submitted genuine progress reports. Field operations worked mainly because they were overseen by a unified team of experienced international civil servants with the UN oath of office foremost in their commitment. None of us thought of Brian Urquhart as British, or James Jonah as a Sierra Leonean, but as bona fide international officers. Like Jean-Claude Aimé, our colleague from Haiti, once wrote: we were all like one UN. The only person that mattered in making decisions was the Secretary-General. There was no personal credit for achievements. Even when the Secretary-General himself accomplished a task, there was always a careful evaluation of the need to claim it publicly. Would it be premature, would it preempt future tasks, would it irk a needed country in search of its own victory? There was no rush to announce. That gave special announcements a special value. It also made key countries more trusting of the UN. They felt confident that if they approached the UN on a delicate issue, it would be handled in confidence.

Media diplomacy is an essential ingredient of effective peacekeeping. There was a difference between grandstanding for the media and helping the media to cover a conflict; the first tends to exploit reporters, the second would treat them as partners. While it was essential to allow, indeed seek, the widest spread of public information, it may be equally worthwhile at times for communications to take place in a discreet, confidence-building atmosphere in order to obtain genuine results.

Secretary-General Perez de Cuellar was a master of discrete diplomacy and valued selective announcements. While he nudged the Permanent Five to have more regular gatherings, he would focus on a specific issue with a specific target in mind. He managed - very elegantly and softly - to push them to agree, again without claiming any credit. He would have them meet in his office for lunch to deal with one of the hotspots around the world. A staffer or two following the issue would brief assistant delegates. Spokespersons François Giuliani or Nadia Younes would make specific, informative announcements. Regular peacekeeping went on despite looking as if it took a backseat to diplomatic initiatives. The Secretary-General sent his own envoys, mostly drawn from inside, to handle a particular case within a certain timeframe. He personally followed their effort and evaluated the outcome.

There were very few, if any, open-ended, politically expedient envoy assignments. While working in Public Information I was, like others, asked by the Secretary-General to perform other functions as well. As head of the information centres around the world, I received interesting daily reports. It was natural for me to continue briefing the Secretary-General while working closely with my colleagues.

A new era happened to coincide with the election of Boutros Boutros-Ghali as Secretary-General, as if he was entrusted to reshape the world. He was encouraged by a summit during his first month in office, where heads of states asked him to prepare a global plan. Agenda for Peace was produced in more than 65 languages and adopted by the General Assembly. Sustained by his own legalistic view, he felt he could play an unprecedented role, which made several powerful countries feel uneasy. Some of them wanted a secretary, although they would tolerate an accommodating Secretary-General. On the other side, Boutros Boutros-Ghali felt that member states were asking too much without giving adequate practical support. Whenever member states complained, he would just grin and bear it. As he repeatedly told his often-enraged wife, he was paid to be blamed.

The relationship between Boutros Boutros-Ghali and the Security Council was delicate. He came after Perez de Cuellar, who had a smooth experience, and after the Kuwait war, where the Security Council had played an overwhelmingly decisive role following a wise approach by first President Bush and Secretary of State Baker aimed at building an alliance of countries to implement UN resolutions. The most predominant member of the Council was U.S. Ambassador Thomas Pickering, a very capable professional who managed to win the Council's support on every issue. Another prominent member of the Council, who because of the nature of that conflict had to take an essential role, was the British ambassador Sir David Hannay. Sir David was of the view that the Security Council decided in all peacekeeping matters and that it was the Council, not the Secretary-General, which should dictate the pace. That clashed with Dr. Boutros-Ghali's view. His natural approach conflicted with that of these ambassadors whom he suspected were trying to undercut him. He would rather call their prime ministers and deal with their presidents than argue with the ambassadors. In fact, some of his staff used to record which ambassador got the shortest meeting. The winner was a Jamaican ambassador who only received a one-minute handshake. There was also a clash with some Council members over Bosnia and former Yugoslavia. Those who disagreed with him worried that the Secretary-General, because he was an Orthodox Copt, may have had sentiments for Orthodox Serbs. The Secretary-General, for his part, felt that when Council members arrived at agreements, such as that in Dayton, concerning Yugoslavia, they settled the easy issues and stuck the UN with the difficult ones. In an unusual step, he designated a Special Representative to the Security Council, a former Indian delegate who would cover all meetings but carefully avoid making decisions without clearance. In a symbolic move to signal his autonomous role, the seat of the Secretary-General was left unoccupied when he did not personally attend. That, to say the least, irritated particularly powerful members.

Throughout this contentious atmosphere, and maybe for other political considerations, the authority of peacekeeping was diluted with a split into two different departments: the Department of Peacekeeping Operations and the Department of Political Affairs. In turn, Political Affairs was split into two different divisions, one headed by a Russian and one by a Briton. Peacekeeping was entrusted to Kofi Annan, a former (successful) Director of Personnel and Budget. It may have been a coincidence that all those disasters from Rwanda to Srebrenica to Somalia followed one after the other on his watch. On the other hand, Annan, as head of peacekeeping, may have been partially to blame, but it would not be fair to blame him alone for an inherited assignment. Maybe he did not have the tough, possibly aggressive personality to deal with that brief, or maybe it was mainly the structure he had inherited that did not allow for actual hands-on intervention. In any event, many Africans still blame Annan for Rwanda, in particular, and hold him accountable for it. When Oil-for-Food was becoming a problem, I happened to meet a Francophone African delegate at a grocery store who claimed that the embarrassment was God's revenge for the victims of Rwanda.

From Professional Work to Political Games

The loss of institutional memory, fragmentation of command at Headquarters, and a glaring failure by the peacekeeping leadership to cope with at least three catastrophic missions was compounded by a bickering atmosphere with and within the Security Council. In such conditions, an average performance by the missions in the field was almost miraculous. As the UN supposedly mirrored the world and depended on member states for budget and authority, it took some time to cope with unprecedented historic changes, including the fall of the

Soviet Union, the predominance of a "hyperpower" like the United States, globalization, electronic technology, the communications revolution, ruthless terrorism, fragmentation of states, growing ethnic strife, religious extremism and continued worldwide erosion of governmental authority. It became very tempting for several key member states - large, medium and small - to corner the UN into impotence unless it became their exclusive proxy. And the door to what turned into a political bazaar was opened when the post of Under Secretary-General for Peacekeeping became part of a deal to select a new Secretary-General.

While there were always "understandings" about a geographical and cultural balance, a blatant political bargain not only eroded the Secretary-General's stature but undercut the credibility of peacekeeping as the genuine representative of international legitimacy. Such a perception of bias would place their missions and the security of personnel at risk. When France placed a veto on Kofi Annan to become Secretary-General, he offered to give them his own job. He took with him to the 38th floor his deputy and two close directors who kept in frequent touch with their former colleagues. Fortunately, the first man nominated by the French government, Bernard Milllet, was a professional communicator and an experienced manager. There were no immediate challenges at the time to test him, but he stabilized the situation and gave the perception of running a coherent operation. His replacement, Jean-Marie Guéhenno, did not have the same standing, particularly within the Secretariat or among Francophones. Despite several years in the building, very few staff-members knew what he looked like. Besides Darfur, which had been brewing for years without preventive attention, millions died or were displaced in the Congo. Reports about sexual exploitation and arms for oil mushroomed, causing further damages to what was left of peacekeeping prestige.

Although politics had always been in the background, appointments have become blatantly expedient. There seemed to be more interest in finding jobs for "important" people, rather than solving the problems in conflict-tom countries. An added attraction "special" was that there was no age-limit; some stayed way beyond retirement, age up into their 70s. Not only retired diplomats or relatives of current ones, but also immediate family of senior Secretariat officials, found in this a helpful entry to evade staff rules. There were well-publicized cases, known sarcastically as "family-planning." Aiming to accommodate led to an abundant number of Special Representatives whose vague tasks were endless.

Internal complaints of "family-planning" were no secret. They were known within the Organization and in member states. The assumption that locals in the host countries did not notice it was totally wrong. They knew more than those at Headquarters. A prerequisite to the success of a mission was to impress the people of a host country with the feeling that we are there to help them. Appointing retired ambassadors to accommodate political interests did not send the right signal. There may be a classification of "developed" countries and "underdeveloped" countries, but there is no such thing as developed and underdeveloped individuals. In the developing world, sharp and brilliant people noticed mediocre appointments, and that eroded the role of the mission. While some in New York may not lose sleep, over in the host country it is a matter of survival. A failed appointment takes away the importance of a mission. Yet, it kept happening over and over again. It would be unfair, perhaps, to blame the Secretary-General, particularly when he was in a vulnerable position himself. One could blame not only those assistants using his name but member states for their persistent pressure.

The need to cover failures in previous peacekeeping operations like Rwanda and Srebrenica may have influenced recruitment of some who were in positions to know precisely what happened at the time. Simply look at the list of senior level appointments made after the then-chief of peacekeeping and his deputy became, respectively, Secretary-General and Chef de Cabinet.

Member states seeking jobs at the UN was nothing new, but it was never so widespread or so blatant. Now it has become an open quest. As a Secretary-General for the first time in UN history was hit by so much scandalous reporting, he would seek help that was thereafter duly rewarded. Even dedicated UN countries that used to provide unquestioned support to the Organization had to join in overtures for posts to accommodate their senior officials. To be sure, the majority of delegates were doing an admirable job. They clearly saw the link between their national interest and that of the UN. They know that there are things a country can do on its own but others that can only be achieved by working through the UN. Certain diplomats, unlike any time before, openly demand posts for themselves or some of their compatriots - or even relatives. In several cases when appointed, these interim officials would remain attached to their governments and planned to return to their national service. Some appointees would receive subsidies from their governments, while other regular staff of course do not. That is a violation of the code of international civil service. It created distinctions between staff and raised questions about the real purpose of appointing those who would feel compelled to accommodate their country's instructions rather than UN objectives.

Vulnerable on Procurement

A persistent loophole in peacekeeping missions was in the area of supply and procurement. Billions of dollars were involved with minimal oversight. In some missions, "administrative officers," however junior in rank, acted as if they owned the whole operation. One of my first experiences during the early days of UNIFIL was with an administration officer who withheld field cars at will from senior officers, while he had two readily available for his own use. He somehow managed to get three per diems in a roundabout way. Based in Vienna, he moved himself to Gaza, Golan and then to Lebanon. That had a demoralizing effect on soldiers: this fellow who was just moving around the office, not risking his life, had the best residence and was paid the highest salary. Generally, field procurement officers were dedicated regular staff who did a good job, especially compared to what happened in private contracting firms and in national countries. There were efforts to investigate UN procurement, as there were always a limited number of wheeler-dealers who had been left unidentified for years.

The Office of Internal Oversight Services (OIOS), established under Boutros Boutros-Ghali with independence to investigate potential violations, uncovered a number of serious flaws that were corrected. Still, a number of junior staff who were paraded out of buildings and publicly told not to return did not receive their due apologies when it was proved that the mishandling was in fact higher up. After an initial buildup of OIOS by a German diplomat, his successor was implicated in controversies that wiped away from his marked achievements. Accusations by staff representatives that a successor exploited his position, for example, to promote a female colleague from a very junior level to the most senior one over a weekend, remained uncleared even after he left. When Secretary-General Annan took no action, someone with institutional memory recalled an almost similar incident in the mid-eighties when Under Secretary-General for Administration Management Martti Ahtisaari sought to ramp up the promotion of a female colleague from a junior level to director but was courageously blocked by the then-decisive chief of personnel Kofi Annan. The perception that the OIOS investigator needed investigation raised credibility questions, although it did not entirely cripple the work of that office.

A major investigation of field procurement was conducted in 1994 upon the request of the Secretary-General. It implicated in particular two senior officials. During a visit to Geneva, Dr. Boutros-Ghali issued instructions to fire them. The Under Secretary-General for Administration and management advised otherwise, presumably to avoid a publicized scandal, and suggested handling the matter discreetly. One of those implicated, a European, found a niche elsewhere. The other was made to disappear out of sight at an equal level post in Vienna, only to return to UN Headquarters in a more influential position when the peacekeeping chief became Secretary-General. Loose money tempts the most pious, and there were widespread whispers of irregularities in procurement. As the most visible area with the largest expenditure, peacekeeping attracted the most attention. But its extra budgetary finances meant less supervision. Unfortunately, the price the UN had to pay was not only in loss of reputation and accusation of corruption, but it cost more dearly in the loss of human lives. In 2004, a UN chartered helicopter crashed in Sierra Leone killing 24 people. The incident, like several others before it, raised questions of who hired the transport company, and who ran them? The investigation, once more, was vague, but the conclusion was clear: Helicopters fly; it is corruption that kills.

Growing to an unprecedented level worldwide, "field operation procurement" turned into a multinational business. Influential or newly established companies from different member states took an active interest – with cover from their respective governments. A Procurement Task Force appointed to assess corruption found that a privately owned firm, which had been involved for many years in some of the U.N.'s most sensitive operations, claimed to have spent $100 million on fuel in Sudan alone. That was very questionable, since there was not yet even a fully fledged UN force in Sudan. During the same period, eight UN junior officials were placed on suspension on accusations of corruption, but six returned after proven innocent. Unfortunately, as the UN started to display zero tolerance with proven culprits, their identified partners in business companies remained generally untouched.

Attempts to counter widespread negative reporting by announcing some proposals did help a little. They covered "strategic management of procurement; UN acquisition management; and internal control measures." A procurement control implementation team, a bidding oversight committee and an inter-office group were set up to review supply and insure transparency - it remained to be seen whether these proposals would lead to actual progress. Initial observations indicated that business continued as usual, together with open interference by those who should be overseeing strict adherence to the rules. In a well-known case in the fall of 2007, the head of the Office of Oversight Services Inga-Britt Ahlenius requested in an email the appointment of a personal acquaintance- the head of a department her office had just investigated - as "Director of Procurement Services." She urged her colleague Alicia Barcena, Under Secretary-General for Management, to make sure to attend the meeting where the choice would be made. An obstacle was raised by the experienced controller, Warren Sach. The fact that the chief investigator pushed for a key appointment in a highly vulnerable and visible area of presumed "reform" reflected not only bad judgment but glaring indiscretion.

Damaged Credibility

Negative reporting on peacekeeping in recent years had an impact also on the most UN important asset: its credibility. Until recently it was perceived as an honest go-between that was not taking sides but was there to help. Once that perception changed, its capacity to deal with serious problems was gravely eroded. Apart from contributions from member states, of course, the UN has neither soldiers nor a budget of its own. The only way it can perform is when all parties believed its presence to be to their advantage. Clearly, developments in Iraq crippled the UN for at least five years. The apparent lack of a role for the U.N., or at least the vision of a role, or even some clue about the real situation on the ground, was compounded by the attack on the UN office in Baghdad. In part, Sergio Vieira de Mello may have agreed to go to Iraq for a temporary period to help lift its stature and confirm its usefulness. Perhaps the terrorist attack on him and his team, a professional, mercenary operation, was to undercut that role, to dismiss it immediately and totally.

Further negative impact was caused by a lack of effective, coordinated communications. A multitude of spokesmen for offices, missions and specialized agencies at the Headquarters and in the field did not bother to coordinate their versions of events. There were instances in

Rwanda where three UN contradictory accounts were quoted in the same press story. A fragmented approach resulted in a fragmented image. During a brief period when Kofi Annan was the head of Peacekeeping, there was a serious effort to develop a joint approach, but it eventually faltered when some of those around him consolidated their own turf. For a while, Annan held regular meetings with the Department of Public Information on every operation and closely consulted on appointments of press officers. Indeed, Annan and myself met together regularly with all of our colleagues. We encouraged them to have regular contacts and arrange meetings between various spokesmen of missions to get to know each other and exchange personal experience. Instead of competing, they started to positively assist one another. There was more attention to predicting potential problems and handling them with mainstream media. The better access that good reporters received to cover a problem, the more helpful their reports were in handling it. That meant regular informed and informative exchange, consistently and patently, not only when headlines or photo opportunities were sought. To cite one of Dag Hammarskjold lesser known remarks: "Easy successes with the public are possible for a juggler, but lasting results are only achieved by the patient builder."

The systematic targeting of Public Information operations had an unintended - or in some cases intended - consequence of depriving peacekeeping from a crucial ally. Particularly UN Information Centres in countries contributing troops or money had played an underestimated role in maintaining media support, alerting Headquarters in time to handle upcoming difficulties and collaborating with peacekeepers on how best to project their case. A rash political decision in 2003 to close the offices in key capitals of "Old Europe," like Athens, Lisbon, Copenhagen, London, Madrid and Paris, was later recognized, too late, - to have been catastrophic. Perhaps the one who regretted it most was the one who engineered it: Secretary-General Kofi Annan clearly missed the enlightened dedication of UNIC staff when fighting for his survival.

Worse than scapegoating the media was the tendency to blame the people of the country for the failures of peacekeepers. An attempt to put the blame elsewhere occurred in an astonishing communiqué, in March 23, 2007, that dealt with "developments unfolding in Kinshasa." As anyone with institutional memory would recall, the UN had dealt with the Congo since the 1960s, returning off and on, receiving deadly setbacks, accomplishing occasional successes and sometimes nurturing a tolerable atmosphere of peace. A recently revived mission was marked with accusations of inefficiency, incompetence and child prostitution, while every neighboring country was involved, either directly or through militant proxies, in grabbing what they could out of the country's resources. The solution according to one official at UN Headquarters was for the Congo to have "a new political culture." Whatever that meant remained a mystery. But it was counterproductive, because it did not only convey a condescending approach, but a tone reminiscent of "colonial days." Blaming the victims was not really the best way to defend a dysfunctional operation.

Strategic UN leadership and Peacekeeping cannot be separated. The political brain is needed to guide the driving and use the brakes. When I first joined the UN, U Thant had a vision of what the UN could do. Besides the regular daily work of departments, he wanted a group around the Secretary-General that looked at the bigger picture and reviewed the current developments to try to ascertain its thrust. If it would not be able to predict a potential problem, it would at least give an idea about the nature of what was brewing. What interested the Secretary-General were practical events with impact on the daily life of citizens around the world. While each country has its sovereignty, there were also problems he felt that needed to be faced together. He called for an international think-tank which would look at trends in order to avoid tomorrow's problems. At one participant said: If we cannot change today's headlines, we can make tomorrow's headlines better. The Secretary-General drew on a number of experienced intellectuals with practical experience - either generalists with specialized interests or specialists with a generalized approach. The Chairman of the Royal Institute for International Affairs Chatham House in England, Sir Kenneth Younger, was brought in. So was the general director of the most prestigious French establishment institution at the time, École Nationale d'Administration, Prof. François Gazier, and outstanding intellectuals from the third world. After U Thant left the Group faced problems both from within and from outside. Those within the UN handling daily matters did not want the oversight board. They claimed they were conducting business with member states which they did not want exposed to others. Governments, particularly mid-sized, feared that such a prominent group would take away some of their decision making since no one could challenge intellectually such a team. It was allowed to fade away. Now, as a British diplomat would say, where you stand depends on where you sit. That is, what you see is what you get.

Casual Advice for Peacekeepers:

- Try quiet diplomacy first.

- Double check your facts on the ground; don't dive into an empty pool.

- Involve as many active parties as possible; it is better to have them inside shouting out than outside shouting in.

- Pay close attention to the voting practice of the Security Council members and not only to their speeches. You may have their full sympathy, but not their vote.

- Be careful with hot air; do not start lecturing the population that you were there to promote world democracy, world peace, or that you are God-sent to save them all. Avoid rhetoric and stick to the practical and what you can deliver.

- Do not underestimate the locals; level with them. Do not try to outsmart them, it is their turf, they could easily outsmart you. Furthermore, they outnumber you.

- Do not step in the *hosinga*; be careful to learn what is sacred to them to avoid getting into unwarranted trouble.

- Interpret, do not translate. Try to perceive what they are trying to communicate to you rather then translate literally what is being said.

- Smile, but do not laugh; hum, but do not sing. Join your hosts, enjoy your time but do not overdo it as if it were your party.

- The moment you feel you are above everyone, and those around you tell you how important you are, immediately go back down to earth. Whoever you are, wherever you are, there is always someone above you.

- Lead from the front, not from the backseat. Consult with your colleagues, raise their morale, take courageous decisions, and hold yourself accountable to them. And always defend them.

- Do not forget to say thank you.

- Do not judge a soldier by his hat. He may have just borrowed it.

- Think locally, act globally. In peacekeeping you need to reverse the famous motto and first take into account what the global picture is, then think how you are going to implement it locally.

- Do not volunteer for a mission in Turkmenistan if you cannot readily remember the name of Gurnebguli Berdymekhamedov, which has to be respectfully pronounced as is. How could you efficiently negotiate with someone whose name you cannot pronounce? One problem in the field is that everyone else's name is difficult. Sometimes it may sound differently than spelled. From Latin America to Eastern Europe, a negotiator will have to master the precise way of referring to the senior official concerned. If you think that the name of Recep (pronounced Reshab), or Tyeb Erdogan of Turkey (pronounced Aerdogan) are difficult to enunciate, then try Poland's former foreign minister Wlodzimierz Cimoszewiz.

- Honor your word. Never give the impression of flip-flopping or of hiding your intentions. You are sunk the moment you're suspected of deception.

- Whatever is on your mind, keep your hands clean.

- Secret contacts do not mean secret agreements. They are preliminary feelers, fishing expeditions, or at best a prelude to a clear, recognizable deal.

  Avoid any announcement until an official agreement is reached.

CHAPTER XV:

THE INTERNATIONAL CIVIL SERVICE: AN OVERLOOKED ASSET

Member States form the mind and body of the UN. Its vibrant spirit is amongst operational staff. Any Secretary-General needs them in the same way they need him. They are his main asset, and he is their leader. Countries, including his own or other powerful nations, offer contributions or lend support to his (or hopefully soon her) efforts. It has been said that he needs the big powers to survive and the smaller powers to succeed. But the only full-time, continuous, unswerving loyalty comes from the talented, dedicated, widely representative, multi-disciplinary staff. When inspired and effectively motivated, the UN could accomplish breakthroughs on pressing issues. If fragmented and demoralized, the people who comprise the SG's staff would simply await signals of changing times.

An unprecedented international civil service started taking an experimental, evolving shape with the creation of the United Nations in 1945. While it has varied historical roots, its novel role was in drawing on an inclusive collaboration of world talents to credibly facilitate and implement decisions by member states. It is recognized that each country has a national sovereignty that would be further strengthened when wider challenges, particularly in an increasingly interconnected world, were handled jointly. The precise functions of this service, headed by the

Secretary-General, depended not only on its credible performance but also on the extent of support at any given time.

James O.C. Jonah, a former UN Under-Secretary-General, described the international civil service as "unique because you are not working in a national civil service. You are working in an environment where you have different nationalities, you have people with different values and you have to learn to work with all these people for a common goal. It is those who work in the Secretariat of the Organization, programmes and agencies of the UN family who are able to translate the hopes and aspirations of the peoples of the world on whose behalf the Charter was drafted and approved."

The United Nations Charter gave a clearly international character to the Secretariat, calling, in Chapter XV, for a Secretary-General and such staff as the Organization may require, with the Secretary-General serving as its chief administrative officer. Article 100 declared: "In the performance of their duties the Secretary-General and the staff shall not seek or receive instructions from any government or from any other authority external to the Organization. They shall refrain from any action which might reflect on their position as international officials responsible only to the Organization."

The Charter's Article 101 next called for appropriate staff to be "permanently assigned" to various United Nations organs, forming part of the Secretariat, and set forth as the paramount consideration in their employment and conditions of service to be "the necessity of securing the highest standards of efficiency, competence and integrity," with due regard to the importance of recruiting staff on as wide a geographical basis as possible.

It is the prerogative of the Member States to define what they want the United Nations to be able and to do – to outline their vision of the goals they want to attain and to set priorities. In recognition of this overarching authority, the Organization's founders sought to establish certain boundaries. Thus, in addition to instructions on the neutrality of international staff, Article 100 of the Charter called upon each Member of the Organization "to respect the exclusively international character of the responsibilities of the Secretary-General and the staff and not to seek to influence them in the discharge of their responsibilities."

The International Civil Service: An Overlooked Asset

Clearly, the framers of the Charter recognized that an international civil service of this kind could not be made up of persons indirectly responsible, however indirectly, to their national governments. There was also agreement on the need for immunity to protect officials from pressure by individual governments and to permit them to carry out their international responsibilities without interference. Throughout the Organization's history, however, Governments have attempted to influence the selection and international loyalty of UN staff.

International tensions, changes in governments, concern with national security – all had their repercussions on the still-fragile institution dedicated to the international community, Secretary-General Dag Hammarskjold recalled, and governments not only strove for the acceptance of their views in the various UN organs, they also concerned themselves, in varying degrees, with the attitude of their nationals in the Secretariat. Some governments even sought, in one way or another, to revive the substance of a proposal defeated at the 1945 Preparatory Commission in London for clearance of their nationals prior to Secretariat employment. Other governments on occasion demanded the dismissal of staff members who were said to be inappropriately representative of the country of their nationality for political, racial or even cultural reasons. That is why the Charter Articles underwent a continual process of interpretation and clarification in the face of pressures from Member States on the Secretariat.

It was a matter of fundamental principle, the Secretary-General insisted, that the selection of staff should be made by him on his own responsibility and not on that of national governments; therefore the interest of governments in placing certain nationals, and barring the employment of others, had to be subordinated to the independent determination of the Organization. At the same time, practical considerations required the Organization to utilize the services of governments to obtain applicants for positions as well as information as to their competence, integrity and general suitability for employment. And so, while the Organization had to accept assistance from governments in obtaining relevant information and records concerning possible applicants, the Secretary-General consistently reserved the right to make the final determination on the basis of all the facts and his own independent appreciation of those facts.

The Secretary-General also invoked the relevant Charter

principles to the assertions made by some Member States that the Organization should switch from the system of permanent appointments in career service to a predominant system of fixed-term appointments to be granted mainly to officials seconded by their governments. Such a concept, said Hammarskjold, ran squarely against the principles of Articles 100 and 101.

Hammarskjold believed that, in his day, the UN had increasingly succeeded in affirming the original idea of a dedicated professional service responsible only to the Organization in the performance of its duties and protected insofar as possible from the inevitable pressures of national governments; and that this had been achieved in spite of strong pressures based on historic tradition and national interests. He tempered that optimism by observing that the international Secretariat would not be what it was meant to be until the day when it could be recruited on a wide geographical basis without the risk that then some would be under – or consider themselves to be under – two masters in respect of their official functions. The independence and international character of the Secretariat required resistance to national pressures in matters of personnel, he declared.

For United Nations staff around the world, Dag Hammarskjold remains, some five decades after his untimely death, the UN's most distinguished Secretary-General, an inspiring leader of spotless conduct and unflinching courage – in short, the personification of the truly independent, international civil servant. For him, the United Nations represented the proud, credible and effective reflection of human dignity and maturity of mind, and he kept his Organization at the center of international life. He dedicated his life for a better world, and gave his life for peace. What has happened, since his death in 1961, to Hammarskjold's vision?

What does it say about the current state of the international civil service when UN staff-management relations are at their lowest ebb, with virtually no communication between the sides over reforms that greatly impact the staff? When staff is mainly concerned about job security and self-preservation following the elimination of the system of permanent contracts, which brought with it a sense of independence from special interests? When the Organization's reputation and credibility have been tainted because of charges of corruption and mismanagement, of sexual exploitation and harassment against senior-and low-level officials alike? When certain senior officials are perceived to ignore or violate staff rules and regulations with impunity? When staff see senior officials accused of misconduct let off lightly with a slap on the wrist? When the UN's credibility is so eroded that terrorists target and attack UN staff, including the bombing of the UN headquarters in Baghdad with the tragic loss of 22 lives? When Member States today seek to influence the filling of even entry-level posts? By all accounts, the international civil service today is in disarray – a very sorry state of affairs indeed.

Addressing United Nations staff on January 9, 1997, shortly after assuming office, Secretary-General Annan said the selection of a career staff member for the position of Secretary-General carried with it a recognition of all staff – the team – and he counted on the staff's continued support, commitment and dedication to the essential work of the Organization. "Service with the United Nations is more than just a job. It is a calling. No one joins the Secretariat to become rich and famous, to be appreciated and applauded, for a life of ease and comfort. We join the United Nations because we want to serve the world community; because we believe this planet can be a better and more secure place; and because, above all, we want to devote our time, our intellect and our energies to making it so. Wherever we are – in New York, Geneva, Vienna and Nairobi, in the regional commissions, the information centres and every mission, programme or operation – and whatever task we may have, political, technical, military or clerical, we are there because we want to ensure a brighter future for all the human race," he said.

He drew loud applause when he spoke of real reform: "For those serving the world in the last years of the twentieth century and preparing it for a new millennium, I will strive to ensure that Member States recognize your efforts and grant you the best conditions of service possible." He praised the staff as the Organization's "most precious asset" and said, "We are nothing if not a team. There is no alternative to the United Nations. It is still the last best hope of humanity." Regrettably, those words later did not translate into practical action.

In fact, by all indications, during Mr. Annan's tenure, the International Civil Service was subjected to consistent, corrosive pressure. While report after report reiterated Mr. Annan's lofty vision, each new set of reform proposals seemed to please mainly influential Member States, creating a widening schism between the Secretary-

General – the UN's Chief Administrative Officer – and many of his personnel, as represented by the Staff Union.

In 2002, staff representatives issued a statement expressing their longstanding view that the international civil service involved job security to ensure that every staff member was able to retain their independence from individual, influential governments. They noted that the original concept of a permanent appointment – the very cornerstone on which the United Nations had built its global Secretariat – had been diminished and was even threatened with extinction. They further pointed out that being an international civil servant required physical security to discharge their functions. While some degree of danger would always been involved, they expected reasonable levels of protection from the constant threats of kidnapping, torture and murder. Staff felt this minimum standard was eroding. Contracts were becoming less secure and the principles of dedication and loyalty that had guided the Organization for decades were now secondary to technical skills. Staff rightly felt that they were not producing commercial products on an assembly line, and that there should be a higher standard of treatment than that exported from the private sector. "There is no need to privatize the United Nations," one said. "We can excel and be relevant and still be the Organization that our founders intended with our principles and ethics completely intact."

For his part, Mr. Annan repeated his praise for staff as the "principal asset" of the United Nations but did not directly consult with them.

Paving the Road For Capable Women

The first female head of a large UN Department (public information), Thérèse Paquet-Sévigny of Québec, Canada, was a pioneer. Having worked closely with her, the struggle for gender equality was one I passionately supported and did my best to advance.

The first International Conference on Women was held in Mexico City in 1975, and International Women's Day was declared on March 8th of that year. The day had been commemorated since the beginning of the 20th century in various places on various dates, but this was the first universally declared commemoration. The Conference also adopted a Plan of Action. This was the first worldwide recognition of women's roles in peace, security and human development. Before that there were dispersed initiatives, for example on educating women or advancing equality, but March 1975 marked the first universal approach. It was also the first consensus to end discrimination against women and call for their full and equal participation. Conferences that followed in Copenhagen and Nairobi pushed for practical action at the UN and individual Member States. A landmark summit in Beijing in September 1995 on the occasion of the UN's 50th anniversary produced an historic declaration reaffirming commitments to equal rights and the "inherent human dignity of women and men."

Included among the Beijing recommendations was a call for the number of women in decision-making posts at the UN to be raised to 50 percent. By the year 2000, the appeal was not limited to governments and civic groups but widened to call upon individuals - men and women - to play an active role in influencing policy and mobilizing public opinion.

The momentum on women generated appointments throughout the wider field of UN operations.

When I headed the Department of Public Information in 1993, the number of women at the P-5 level and above in that Department was about 30 percent. After two years later, it rose to 65 percent. That was not done to favor women but to strengthen the UN. My belief in women as born communicators was proven by experience. The women with whom I worked over the years were impressively competent. My impression was that as society had cornered women throughout the centuries, they had to explain and defend themselves not only to society in general but to members of their own families. For women, communications meant survival. As described earlier, a stark reminder of the capabilities of women was demonstrated by the immediate impact our team of female staff members had upon the movement for democracy and independent statehood in Eritrea.

The designation of Ban Ki-moon's Chef de Cabinet, Susana Malcorra, in November 2015, as Argentina's Minister for Foreign Affairs, added to the list of genuine contenders for the top UN post as the campaign escalates in 2016. Her experience in the private sector as a prominent IBM executive in Buenos Aires, followed by international public service at the World Food Programme in Rome, and peacekeeping in New York, could offer persuasive credentials, particularly if Latin America agreed on one official candidate. In addition to the five permanent members of the Security Council, the voting members and other members would be Angola, Malaysia, New Zealand, Spain, Senegal, Venezuela, Egypt, Ukraine and Japan.

Talk about geographical turns for the post of Secretary-General is mainly for jockeying purposes, and repeated references to Eastern Europe overlooks not only factual background but political shifts in a changing world. The Eastern European Group was initially a political alliance supporting the former Soviet Union, balancing the Western European and "others" alliance supporting the US. While political lines were scrambled with the fall of the Berlin Wall, it seemed politically expedient to interpret it geographically mainly for balancing purposes. Some would push the boundaries around to interpret it in general European terms. Geographical rotation was not essential in electing two Scandinavians successively (Mr. Trygve Lie and Mr. Hammarskjold); a third European was in line, an Irish General Assembly president, when an Asian, U Thant, was surprised by a practical consensus. When he refused a second term, it was not extended to another Asian. Instead, Mr. Waldheim of Austria was elected. While African diplomats presented Selim Selim of Tanzania to succeed him on geographical grounds, a Latin American, Mr. Perez de Cuellar, was elected in a last-minute vote. However, as a long as geographical grouping remains, even nominally, Eastern European candidates would naturally stake an obvious claim. Especially qualified women from anywhere in Europe would have credibility.

Diplomatic talk now about a turn for Eastern Europe would gain more credibility in case of a regional agreement on one credible woman candidate, like the Director-General of UNESCO, Irina Bokova. Another effective political claim will most likely come from Western Europe. For example, Chancellor Merkel represents the most formidable female candidate for the post. She combines geographical and gender requirements together with proven experience, political stature and credible leadership abilities to revive an eroded UN. But then again, most Permanent Members of the Security Council would not welcome a powerful Secretary-General.

The all-female contingent introduced in Liberia in early 2007 first raised the question about the role of women as peacekeepers. Before that, they were limited to specific areas such as field hospitals. Some were boasting about how many women they had in their force, but it turned out they were mostly nurses. The first prominent woman in peacekeeping was Margaret Anstee, a very capable British intellectual who served as the Secretary-General's Special Representative in Angola.

The uncomfortable issue of sexual harassment was eventually confronted head-on by the United Nations, but the zero tolerance policy was first applied – unfairly, as it turned out – to a woman, Carina Perelli, who was the first publicly announced target.

Some insiders had the impression it was more a question of settling a score. Ms. Perelli had received attention for her successful training of a wide segment of Iraqi citizens to vote for the first time. Media photos of Iraqis displaying their ink-stained fingers gave credit to the UN unit under her leadership. When US President George W. Bush singled her out in a public statement, it most likely raised the ire of some aides around Mr. Annan who already had what some around him thought was a nervous breakdown after the fall of Saddam Hussein in Baghdad, together with the growing Oil-for-Food scandal. Here was the US President, who had overlooked repeated overtures from Mr. Annan, Condoleezza Rice's sympathy toward him notwithstanding, openly hailing one of the SG's staff.

Yet all of a sudden certain officials very close to the SG appeared to be reporting to him about Ms. Perelli's alleged abuse of her staff, including "unwelcome advances," "a constant stream of sexual references, jokes," and the use of "sexually explicit, coarse language." And so in 2005 she was summarily dismissed. However, in March 2013, the UN Administrative Tribunal ruled in favor of Ms. Perelli. It found that her dismissal was not sustainable from a factual and legal point of view and ordered either her reinstatement or two years of net pay as compensation. Meanwhile, Ms. Perelli seemed to have gotten on with her life, running her own consulting firm and handling other private contracts. Her junior accuser at time, Salman Sheikh, was recommended a couple of years later by Chef de Cabinet Iqbal Riza to a much-higher paid job in Qatar and then moved on afterwards.

Indeed, our "macho" world was sometimes reflected in the attitude of a very limited number of senior government officials who behaved as if they bestowed a favor on females – particularly junior ones – when making sexual advances. A former Prime Minister of a

European country who was appointed as head of a UN agency initially explained away a formal complaint of repeated harassment by telling the press that he was merely being friendly. In another case, when a Secretary-General called in a prominent diplomat, who happened to be from Asia, to caution him against bothering one of his secretaries, the man seemed more flattered than offended; he felt he had finally sealed his reputation as an international playboy. One Prime Minister repeatedly boasted that he needed only thirty minutes to dominate a woman. He certainly got what he deserved when he rashly approached Secretary of State Condolezza Rice during a meeting in New York. Vanity claims were not limited to one region. A European Foreign Secretary regularly boasted to his agreeable entourage about what he would accomplish with unsuspecting female interlocutors; mercifully, he was eased out by his Prime Minister at the first reshuffle.

Although consensus about "zero tolerance" is yet to evolve particularly in distant field offices, it is hoped that these very limited cases, however, are not typical and are unrepresentative. In fact, in a worldwide operation that involves individuals from multiple cultures, we need more courageous women in UN positions of responsibilities, not less.

CHAPTER XVI:

WHO IS WORKING FOR WHOM?

To ensure appropriate performance and guard against corruption, the establishment of an Office of Internal Oversight Services (OIOS) was a welcome, though politically motivated, initiative. Normally, the Office of Human Resources and Management or the Controller would perform such functions through specifically indicated units. Having an external, independent, senior official heading a small, dynamic, supervisory team made sense assuming that the one in charge was above suspicion. Confidence that the Office was neither taking sides internally nor making deals externally was crucial to its potential success. Its first chief, appointed in 1994, Karl-Theodor Paschke, was indeed a presentable, impressive diplomat from the Federal Republic of (West) Germany before its unification. Gaining a reputation for easy accessibility and common sense, as well as being a talented jazz musician, he was limited by a somewhat narrow perspective of his initial staff and, more to the point, by accepting "supplementary support payments" from his own government, to cover his residence accommodation; which was a violation of the same international civil service staff rules which implementation he was entrusted to ensure. Additionally, there was political pressure on him not only to offer suggestions but also to "deliver bodies," meaning drastic staff cuts. He maintained a respectable posture despite displays by some of his staff of occasional partisan sentiments.

On occasion, Mr. Paschke discreetly complained to me about an "(East) German" in the evaluations unit of our department, hinting that the man was a longtime Stasi agent. I had heard that same complaint from a number of the Federal (West) German mission staff over several years. There was little administrative action that could be taken in response. Besides, the "Eastern fellow" stuck carefully to work requirements, at least within the office compound. When his contract expired as he had reached retirement age, I would not, indeed could not, bend regular staff rules to arrange for an extension. He sent me an angry, threatening message, which I merely attributed to anxiety. I was therefore surprised when I heard that he was offered a short-term contract with OIOS – the same team that had been complaining about him. Mr. Paschke genuinely denied the arrangement when I checked with him, only to confirm it later on, somewhat philosophically. However he accommodated his short-term recruiters, now that he passed away, may he rest in peace.

Superpowers, small powers and proxies

Perhaps big powers need to compare their lists of agents: they would find substantial duplication. Considering a unified list would help save funds, which could be usefully redeployed in helping poor countries rather than arming deadly conflicts. When working in Geneva, a seasoned observer once recounted an event decades earlier when the superpowers, basically the United States and USSR, were trying to sort out Laos, where apparently three fighting factions were led by three princes from the Fung family. One was pro-American, one was pro-Soviet and a third was neutral. The main operational fight was for "the Valley of the Jars," in a strategic area reportedly taken one day by one side, regained by another, and acclaimed at other times by the third. During a conference in Geneva, the leaders from Washington DC and Moscow explored how to persuade the three leaders to arrive at a peaceful arrangement or, in today's language, "a political solution" for the conflict. It seemed like an almost impossible task until a connoisseur was told that the three brothers were having a great time together at a famous nightclub, Bataclan, in the old city.

"Who's conning who?" as New Yorkers might say, has been the eternal question in politics, as in daily life.

Who Is Working For Whom?

Hardly anyone would take note when adversary operators meet at quiet, secluded spots or at socially welcoming resorts like Gstaad, Verbier, or St. Moritz, away from the eagerly publicized ego trips to Davos. More senior key officials with more available funds and more time to spend would also opt for Cote d'Azur, from Cannes to Saint-Tropez. And what happens in Monte Carlo stays in Monte Carlo. Other more recent locations include the new palace-style hotels by the Gulf. A spot like Dubai gained stature and popularity with both business and political people where banking facilities are easily handled, where similar languages are spoken and where both Iran and its adversaries in the Gulf could also run their daily work uninterrupted. Afghanistani, Pakistani or Indian key negotiators would advise on the best Asian restaurants there.

An open policy initiated by the founder of Dubai, Sheikh Rashed Al-Maktoum, was dynamically advanced by his son, Sheikh Muhamad, who, perhaps to compensate for the lack of oil revenues, initiated very ambitious projects for Arab media and international business. When I visited the country in 1975 with the UN Secretary-General, it was mainly a limited town, though enterprising and more open than most of its neighbors at the time. The main show item for us was a highway under construction. Sheikh Rashed genially told us that he acknowledged some comments about his opening the country to various groups and said, with an engaging smile, "We told everyone the mosque is open, the school is open, and the hotel with a bar is open. Our people pray at the mosque, outside, wherever they wish to visit reflects their personal choice."

During the Cold War followed by a cold peace, an exclusive club of two had more quiet understandings than open differences. Spheres of influence were almost demarcated and with some occasional exchanges.

Syria acted as a subcontractor supported by the US when its troops entered Lebanon in 1976 upon demand of Maronite Christian leaders to avert a possible takeover of an alliance of leftist and Palestinian forces. Israeli Prime Minister Yitzhak Rabin in his biography indicated a preference for an army with a known address, however hostile, to a chaotic armed presence on its northern border. The Soviet Union, Syria's traditional military ally, withheld comment. When visiting New York from Beirut a few months later for a briefing at UN Headquarters, I gained valuable insight from two senior officials. One was the US Under-Secretary-General for Political Affairs, William Buffum, who once served as Ambassador to Beirut, and Mikhail

Sytenko, the UN Soviet Under-Secretary-General who had served as Head of the Middle East Department in his country's Foreign Ministry. Both were keen on finding out the situation on the ground and had a positive insight of what could be done to deal with it. A newly appointed Director in the Department of Public Information, who occupied a post which was traditionally reserved for staff from his country, told me he was the spokesman for Soviet leader Brezhnev when visiting Damascus a week before the move of Syrian troops into Lebanon and that they were not consulted nor alerted in advance. Initially, the Arab League formed an "intervening force" but Saudi, Yemeni, Sudanese and others left with the bulk of Syrian soldiers under an Arab international blanket. President Hafez Assad, a master of intricate balancing, who impressed even the unimpressible, angry Dr. Henry Kissinger, managed to have the US, like other powers, on his side, however discreetly or openly, as when he sent troops to join the US-led coalition to liberate Kuwait in 1991.

By the way, the first time I saw Dr. Kissinger he was still a distinguished professor of international law at Harvard. He was in the seat in front of me at a Broadway play by Woody Allen entitled *"You Know I Can't Hear You When the Water is Running"*. My first impression was why was he smiling in a somewhat conspiratorial way as if he knew more than we did? It took years for me to find out.

Lebanon has for decades been a target for fragmentation. It symbolized a unified popular will of its varied people from different religions and cultural backgrounds to live together in a creative, free, peaceful mosaic community. After the state of independence when leaders with joint nationalist appeal led the country on the international stage with a clear consensus on foreign policy, successive conflicts created a class of politicians who had local and personal interests but no special national appeal. Even with that, a vulnerable political class mainly seeking to please and despite varied attempts to fragment the unity, the Lebanese people remained determined to live together and stick to their way of life.

During Mr. Annan's first – and my last – official visit to the Middle East, we stopped in Beirut. The Lebanese President, Prime Minister and Parliament speaker had formed what they proudly termed a "troika," indicating how they shared authority. While everyone protected his direct interests, in fact each one of them was beholden to Syria, the predominant power at the time. In every meeting there were three Lebanese note takers. In a smaller circle at the Prime Minister Hariri's residence before an official dinner, our Secretary-General unexpectedly asked, "Did you meet Prime Minister Netanyahu?" Visibly uncomfortable, Mr. Hariri responded with a curt "No." It occurred to me that this was one of the new Secretary-General's main purposes. He was a close friend of the Israeli Prime Minister, to whom he successfully suggested upon taking over that it should try to enter the UN regional groupings so as to get a turn in memberships for various bodies. He was very friendly with Shimon Peres and other Israeli leaders who substantively helped in his election. Yet he was equally friendly with Arab heads of governments, who later took the first step in suggesting his re-election to a second term. With such affectionate standing with both sides, it was puzzling why Mr. Annan did not play a more effective UN role. It may have been that he sensed that to maintain such prized standing he should not push the envelope too hard. Anyway, little known to our visiting team, Mr. Hariri was having his own side battles, as I eventually learned. The following day in Damascus, President Hafez Assad seemed bored, yet politely patient while awaiting some special message or proposal from a reportedly US imposed new UN Secretary-General. He was used to strategic sessions with visitors like Henry Kissinger, Warren Christopher, and Yevgeny Primakov, where exchanges touched on the destiny of the region. Now he was contending with an introductory visit that was literally and truly just that.

The President had known me for decades from meetings with various Secretaries General, and, having learned from his thorough briefing that I would be leaving the UN, he initiated a friendly conversation, perhaps after concluding that nothing new was forthcoming from official talks. He invited me to see from the window the highway that lead to Beirut and chatted amiably. A keen observer must have spread the word across the border. While the UN delegation continued to Jordan and Israel, I returned via Paris, where I discovered that Mr. Hariri was looking for me. When we met alone at his home on Avenue Aena, he suggested that I ask to see the Syrian Ambassador in Paris to tell him that during our visit to Beirut, he – that is, Mr. Hariri – was the most outspoken in defending the Arab cause; that President Hrawi and Foreign Minister Boueiz seemed wavering, while the Prime Minister was clear and determined. As usual in such situations, he prodded and wondered what I would be doing after leaving UN service, and about the cost of a pro-Arab public relations campaign around the world.

Still in my New York state of mind, I had expected Mr. Hariri to raise UN-related issues but not to get into internal Lebanese matters, which he knew I carefully avoided, especially when complicated by Syrian predominance. When responding I happened to address him casually as "Brother (Akh) Rafik." He paused for a while staring inquisitively in my face, then almost muttered, "Akh Samir?" Both of us realized then without further exchange that we had connected decades earlier in Beirut. When he called to follow up from his private plane while in Saudi Arabia, I was having lunch at the Tour d'Argent restaurant with a UN colleague, who was very impressed, not knowing what the call was about. It only dawned on me as I returned to my hotel walking by the riverside, that perhaps there was a much deeper and more serious problem. Rafiq Hariri, one of the richest, most connected, best protected, widely popular, prominently positioned businessman-politicians, must have been very nervous to grasp on a straw in the wind, like my occasional chat in Damascus. It did not occur to me to wonder about what he would be so very much concerned.

Brutal incompetence in mishandling a limited student demonstration, al Dara'a, habitually loyal to the regime, led to wider popular rebellion which eventually became complicated by extensive outside interference and the involvement of many foreign and domestic fighters proudly displaying brutal operations. The U.S. cut its relations with the regime while Secretary of State John Kerry continued his rightful quest for a peaceful solution. Incidentally, a main reason President Bashar al-Assad remained in Damascus despite public predictions to the contrary years earlier was not merely due to Russian or eventual Iranian military support - crucial as it is - but because the Syrian middle class, a surviving mosaic throughout history, resented the boastingly brutal and destructive alternative. Regrettably, while politicians on all sides adjust their calculations, the oppressed, dispersed and migrating millions of Syrian people pay the tragic price. First, the oldest Arab capital city, Damascus, was shaken daily, then Aleppo was bombed to a pile of rubble and dust. Syria, a unifying symbol for the region for centuries, has been torn apart. It is not just a shortcoming of internal leadership but of a worldwide sense of fragmentation.

A firm regime based on complex alliances drawn by President Hafez Assad strategically and patiently over decades, inch by inch, was swiftly dispersed by his unexpected heir. An easy inheritance meant an uneasy rule. A new clique of arrogant, greedy, insensitive young relatives viewed authority as a family gift rather than a national governance duty. Their claims to reign, however, were not matched with a capacity to rule, particularly with an increasing number of complaints mainly about mistreatment. Even when trying excessive oppression, their main instrument, a group locally known as Shabbiha, had grown too old to scare even young school children. Despite occasional lapses, however, relations between Damascus and Washington DC remained mainly operational particularly with a new Minister of Foreign Affairs in Damascus who was his country's Ambassador to Washington, a Deputy Foreign Minister who served at the UN Security Council in New York and a new Ambassador to the U.S. focused mainly on building links with security departments through offering valuable information.

CHAPTER XVII:

E-DIPLOMACY: WHERE'S THAT BRIDGE?

Is all Foreign Policy Financial? Follow the Money

Recent dialogue concerning Iranian nuclear capacity entails major financial implications for all countries involved. Iran will retrieve from the U.S over $100 billion of formerly sanctioned or frozen funds. The US Secretary of the Treasury, Jack Lew, provided examples, in an Op-Ed Friday August 14, 2015, in the *New York Times*, of how "scuttling the nuclear agreement would mean economic disaster." Other sources mentioned that American airline business will initially receive one-fifth of it, about $20 billion, as Tehran buys new airplanes to renew its ailing airline. French, Dutch, Italian and British oil companies and German banks are not far behind. Russia, China and Japan – the corporation of which, Amano, helped certify the technical feasibility of the accord – were angling for the inside track. Even negative reaction to it generated a sizeable profit to certain powers when fearful oil-rich Gulf countries with readily available cash sought to pay even more for very reassuring arms deals. Rulers who started paying a decade ago to avert the shadow of a scarecrow will suddenly be shaken further when the crows actually land on their backdoors.

The visible loss of sovereignty by any state, particularly historically recognized ones like Iraq and Syria, raise questions concerning the vulnerability of all other states in the region. There are still lingering, though unspoken, sensitivities from the demarcation of borders based on the Sykes-Picot agreement. Jordan, Iraq, Saudi Arabia and Egypt, for example, may still have some borders to clarify; so do most states of the Gulf that gained independence from the British Crown in the 1970s. No ruler of Iraq, whatever the nature of the regions, had recognized officially the independence of Kuwait, formerly considered part of Basra province until oil was discovered. Lebanon and Syria have intermingled border points and have not even maintained diplomatic relations until very recently. The thrust of Nasser's "Arab revolution" was to build one borderless nation. The independence from British-French mandates in the late 1940s created vested interests within the agreed borders of each country. Rulers are keen not to push the envelope too far.

Scaring vulnerable oil countries despite differences is not limited to public rhetoric. When Saudi Arabia has $700 billion in cash reserves, money shakers are not limited to arms dealers seeking commissions. When the United Arab Emirates or Qatar had similarly unprecedented funds, "shaking the Sheikhs" turned from tactic to strategy. Ironically, most of their go-betweens running back channels between proclaimed adversaries seem to whisper the same sentence with a wry smile: "They lie to us; we lie to them."

Going back to the 1979-1980 issue of U.S. embassy hostages in Tehran, there was, even then, a view that they would have been freed quicker if some frozen funds of the Shah's regime in U.S. banks were partially released. Also, while Western hostages were held in certain parts of Lebanon, certain international mediators gave the impression that some kind of a mutual, open recognition, including even partial release of those funds, would facilitate Iranian help in intervening with some of the kidnappers. When they were freed, however, it was not "politically feasible" to complete the deal. Interestingly, the young Iranian diplomat at the time seconded to help UN mediators in that area, Mohamad Javad Zarif, became his country's Minister for Foreign Affairs decades later when negotiating the nuclear agreement.

The Islamic State in Iraq and Syria, under whatever name, which makes rhetorical claims about spiritual purity, has full-time operatives handling financial business, including all black-market deliveries sustained by varied climate companies authorized by governments, including European ones. Visibly loaded trucks pass through borders without being blocked or targeted by air or ground forces.

E-Diplomacy: Where's That Bridge?

Every side gets its cut. In closed areas of Iraq and Syria, former notorious contraband smugglers suddenly adopted names with religious factors, turning a Dakmaq into a revered Abu something. Praying Emirs visit sectors of the faithful, while business goes on as usual – particularly by Chechnyan, Turkmen, Tajik and other fighters who have settled down with their families to replace the fleeing original inhabitants. Control or destruction of cultural heritage, including antique religious turf, is another source of income. While claiming to obliterate historic statues under the pretext of preserving only God's almighty image, profits are made at a higher price in readily available private markets, sometimes through highly regarded commercial firms. Ransom for hostages is another source of ISIS' financial profit. Anyone in doubt would need to check with someone negotiating the release of detained soldiers, or those trying to save kidnapped bishops, or those who helped to release nuns from the ancient Christian town of Maaloula. A specific oil-rich Gulf country has played a role in substantive payments. The recent release of a French female volunteer in Yemen was no exception, though back-channeled by the effective Foreign Minister of another.

Who transformed notorious contraband smugglers into leaders of rebel groups under new presumed religious names? Did certain faraway countries that initially facilitated travel or passage of subsidized fighters to Syria and Iraq eventually end up being caught, unprepared, on the receiving end? How did multi-social towns like Raqqa in Syria and Mosul in Iraq fall relatively easily to the "Islamic State"? Where is the Iraqi governor that fled after surrendering Mosul? Why were Arab Christians specifically targeted for intimidation, evacuation, and migration? Why did certain international mainstream media overlook the destruction of historic towns like Maaloula (where Aramaic, Christ's language, is still spoken), the obliteration of other predominantly Melkite Catholic villages, and the kidnapping of Eastern Bishops, when they would usually headline the arrest of one person of their interest? Why did officials in interested key foreign capitals avoid raising the issue despite receiving factual, uncontested reports? Were there much earlier attempts to cajole Arab Christians from leaving the whole region? Why? The valuable richness of the region is its multicultural mosaic society, where varied religious sects and social groups lived productively for thousands of years. Was the aim of these sectarian attacks to undercut their historic cultural value?

Regardless of intergovernmental relations, there are those who believe that financial considerations were behind most political decisions – particularly when governments are short of cash. For example, the decision to go to Iraq may not have been limited to kick out Saddam Hussein, but because there was an ocean of cash. Dissolving the Iraqi professional army, which proved to be a catastrophic decision, was interpreted by some to mainly give certain security contracts to specific companies. According to published reports, one such company received a *billion* dollars to unsuccessfully build up security forces, in addition to $99 million to help the army. Another received $48 million, let alone billions in other contracts paid for from available cash or from the revenues of Iraqi oil.

Although the occupying army could not protect the National Museum of Iraq, with some of the most valuable artifacts and treasures in the region, it managed to protect the Ministry of Oil and find the place of Saddam Hussein's billions of hidden cash. In the confusion of the first two years amounts like $20 billion disappeared. Looting the museum was an indication of things to come: insider information led to organized crimes and individual adventures. It also showed disregard for the cultural heritage, giving ordinary people a feeling not only their land and their resources, but also their souls, were being plundered.

Even when Saddam Hussein was hiding, he was reported to have kept billions of dollars in cash. It is by now common knowledge that the military acumen of ISIS was drawn from former professional army officers who were disbanded by occupation envoy Paul Bremer and were readily available when paid handsomely – particularly as they had a real incentive for payback time.

A disappointing indication of the erosion of leadership in powerful world capitals is how surprised they seem by efforts that failed. Ironically, the prediction by the president of the most powerful country in the world that a ruler of distant Syria would step down within a few months may prove to be the reverse; that is President Obama might be leaving office before President Bashar al-Assad. The US in particular had a superior edge in its international decisions when drawn from a consideration of its overall national interest based on its humanitarian resources. Instead, in recent years, political and foreign policy decisions seemed to focus mainly on military clandestine actions with mostly counterproductive results. Perhaps President George H.W. Bush was the last to consider decisions by a highly recognized, experienced national security team. In a historic irony, President George H.W. Bush brought his country to the status of an unprecedented and uncontested world power, a mostly inexperienced yet boastful Foreign Policy team of President Clinton unduly eroded it, particularly when failing to stop massacres like Rwanda and Srebrenica, and then his son, George W. Bush, drained it to vulnerability.

Indeed, ours has become an uncivilized world, with brutal, ruthless atrocities unprecedented in history. Yet there seems to be no consensus on how to effectively respond.

All Politics is Financial

Additionally there is an often blurred financial business angle in most conflicting developments. The Ukrainian conflict, to mention another issue, began over accusations of corruption. The emerging Presidential leader was a chocolate billionaire. Russia had already seized a most valuable asset – Crimea.

In ancient relations, China's predominance was not due to its military strength but its financial reserves. Today it may have more US dollars than most countries, possibly including the US itself. Japan and Korea played their political roles through obvious financial dealings. Even with respect to the appointment of Secretary-General Ban Ki-moon, some openly mentioned that financial deals were made with at least ten countries holding seats at the Security Council. An opening in the military rule of Myanmar was first tested in a trade deal with Korea, facilitated by Mr. Ban's pilot visit, which was followed by others. By now, the once so-called "Asian tigers" softened their claws as more vulnerable regimes in Malaysia, Singapore and Thailand pursued new ventures to refresh their economic heyday. Influential power across the border areas were those drug handling in the "Golden Triangle." Afghanistan remains the largest heroin producer in the world. Who is making money from this?

In Africa, financial considerations revolve more on natural resources from oil to uranium to fertile land to updated interests like material used in making cellphones. Though the notorious conflict in Darfur was mainly about irrigated territory, a neighboring water conflict in South Sudan is really about cuts in oil commissions. About half of the 54 African member countries have had the same rulers for decades; it may not be due to force alone but rather because they managed to financially accommodate local groups while ensuring the interest of influential foreign powers – and most likely pocketing sums for themselves in cash or real estate abroad. Otherwise it's hard to explain why Teodoro Obiang Nguema Mbsango can rule oil-rich Equatorial Guinea for more than 37 years, since 1979, and can have someone suggest an international prize in his name while his son, a minister in the government, enjoys a residence with one of the best ocean views in California.

Foreign relations of course are much more complex than mere finance, yet after crossing – by which I mean buying or selling – that "Bridge to the 21st Century" in an almost bankrupt world economy, most intranational action seemed to be about compensating loss or accessing gain. After the voluntary surrender of Communism, the capitalist system is being criticized not by rhetorical leftists but by some of its prominent figures, including an Executive Director of the World Bank in Washington, DC, and the manager of the most influential business gathering in Davos, Switzerland.

New business enterprises, particularly attuned to digital communications, have shifted billions of funds in an unprecedented financial landscape. These have refreshed the global outlook, replenishing new areas and substantially influencing basic decisions within countries and across borders, including the structures of major media. That was reflected in the way the *Washington Post* was bought by Amazon, and the *Financial Times* by Japan's Nikkei – which was able to pay, as LEX put it, about 2.4 million for every journalist on that paper. It could also be easily pointed out that private companies like Apple and Google have more cash than most governments.

While the UN Charter mentions "the peoples of the UN," not just governments, its current status and structure is not yet stretched out enough to take a crucial, mainstream role in a swiftly changing world where financial business decisions are causing the effective impact. That may be why most influential decision- and opinion-makers these days travel to Davos during January's snow and attend the annual General Debate of the UN General Assembly during New York's sunny September.

E-Diplomacy: Where's That Bridge?

E-Diplomacy Recognized

The diplomatic community initially viewed the advent of the Internet as a suspicious intrusion on their exclusive realm of informed power. The attitude changed after discovering that, far from complicating their professional life, it would facilitate their daily chores. While a secretary would deal with technicalities, using the required applications, the diplomats would be even more informed without exerting greater efforts or making too many visits and calls. In a more relevant, individual way, the ambassador no longer had to act or feel like a glorified concierge during visits by heads of State seeking hotel arrangements, restaurant reservations and introductions to friends. Effective emails would do.

Diplomats normally believe that information is power. What some may fail to recognize, however, is that digital technology or e-diplomacy could and does enhance human relations but does not replace the human touch. Any ruler or leader who would rely only on push-button technology instead of similarly seeking human institutional memory and live communications and advice would end up like a pretentious, vain emperor without clothes.

E-diplomacy officially arrived at the UN when the Blue Directory listing delegates for the year 2000 also listed their e-mail addresses. It had made some headway a few years earlier as a UN website was approved, and when a limited number of ambassadors started carrying bulky cellular phones in their briefcase to be pulled out on occasion in a corner close to a window. Unfortunately, it was inevitable for "IT" to become politicized. When the Secretary-General rightly wanted to establish a group to review its international implications, the backstopping team was not composed of technology experts nor communication professionals but overworked routine staffers from the Economic and Social Development Secretariat.

The Philippines was the first country to witness a political revolution through Motorola and Nokia. Its parliament deliberated for weeks in vain, concerning clear cases of embezzled millions. Opposition organizers communicated to web-crazed Filipinos on their watchbands the precise time and place of intended demonstrations, with an overwhelming response. The president, a former actor and television buff, was caught totally unaware. Within three days of digital networking, there were enough crowds approved by the widely influential Catholic Church and tolerated by the Army - to force his humiliating departure. Egypt's Tahrir Square popular revolution that ousted President Moubarak was popularly facilitated through Google, Facebook, and other social media.

In an increasingly interconnected world, the objectives of diplomacy remain the same, but not the role of diplomats. It is still customary to list every ambassador to the United Nations as "Envoy Extraordinary and Plenipotentiary". While some are more extraordinary than others, the purpose was originally to bestow on an envoy far away from home credible authority to make major decisions. As communications shifted from the Morse code to telephone, telex, fax and internet, together with travel potential at twice the speed of sound, the Plenipotentiary became less potent and had "pleni" instructions from home about what to do.

A signboard on the road to London's Heathrow airport wondered whether a meeting abroad was really necessary. It hinted that you could conduct business with equal efficiency when using the advertised solutions. Surely teleconferencing offers a useful method of communications. But such dialogues also raised so many pending issues that even more incentives for travel are created.

A Day In the Life

A new burden for ambassadors in a shrinking world was the mushrooming of so many national issues with international implications bringing so many directives from home. In classic diplomacy only the foreign minister demanded prompt action. Now almost every senior member of the government requires added attention, let alone those stopping by on holiday visits. Foreign ministers are more inclined to take over tasks in New York, particularly if there is a visible issue and their country happens to chair the Security Council or the General Assembly.

In one case, an ambassador in New York, a former Secretariat staff member, obtained an agreement to be elected president of the forthcoming session of the General Assembly. It was Europe's turn in that mostly ceremonial yet visibly prestigious position, and its representatives were persuaded by their colleague that his small country could represent them. Other regional groups went along. About two months before the official election in mid-September, the British

Broadcasting Corporation, naming the ambassador, reported the news. An avid listener, his Minister of Foreign Affairs, was impressed. On reflection he considered that such a lofty assignment demanded his own presence, not merely those of his young ambassador. Swift phone calls were made and notes were faxed around to world capitals to get the right name straight. By opening day the minister was indeed elected Assembly President, an assignment that required prolonged stays in Manhattan while continuing to run the Foreign Ministry. His political stamina was further demonstrated when he was elected president of his own country. As to the aspiring ambassador, he found great empathy among his colleagues before quitting and finding another international job.

Even Foreign Ministers are superseded by their Heads of State. The first Security Council Summit in January 1992 was chaired by British Prime Minister John Major during the U.K.'s rotating presidency. By then, summit meetings for regional, cultural, linguistic, economic and financial groups of countries had become so habitual that the term "sherpa," which is Nepalese for Mount Everest climbers, has become an essential part of international slang. Countries consider hosting such meetings a matter of national prestige, plus a bonus of economic profit. At the millennium summit in New York more than 150 heads of state, 800 delegates and 5,000 journalists stayed in the city's most expensive hotels, dined in the best restaurants, and used the most advanced communications and most luxurious transport. A minimum of $300 million was spent. That amount is peanuts compared to the expenses of hosting the heads of the seven richest countries, known as the G-7, to which Russia was added. The record goes to Okinawa, Japan, where $8 billion was reportedly dispersed in three days. By the way, one item to discuss there was how to handle the pending debts of poor countries. As wild demonstrations accompanied summits in Sweden and Italy, some heads of state started questioning the need for so many gatherings. If something went wrong some sherpas could be held accountable. Moreover, it all could be conveniently pinned on the over-intrusive media. If victory has many parents, while defeat is an orphan, the blame game never stops – only the players change. A bungling politician would conveniently blame a loyal diplomat. An erratic government could easily blame the United Nations.

In earlier high-level meetings, an indiscriminate appetite for photo opportunities overtook valuable time needed to set forth effective international strategies. Governments seemed to count on the UN Secretariat for basic proposals, while the Secretariat avoided the impression that it was nudging delegates sensitive about their sovereignty. A conference is successful only where a balance is reached between what the Secretariat could propose and what governments would dispose. Yet attention to historic photo opportunities is not new. In 1936, the Italian army had to enact its entry into Addis Ababa three times until the newly trained photographer got it right. As privileged authority of an ambassador decreased with frequent appearances by their chiefs, demand on their time increased. Not only did they have to ensure the highest level of bilateral meetings but also arrange the most convenient hotel rooms and secure reservations in elite restaurants. They still had to carry on with their regular work, which may not necessarily be crucial but always takes time.

After a succession of late nights and early mornings at the airport awaiting visitors from home, a European ambassador expressed a wish to retire as a plumber in New York's Park Avenue. He said other options like a concierge in a posh hotel or a manager of an elite restaurant were considered and discarded, because they demanded too much foot- and legwork. A plumber in a wealthy neighborhood, on the other hand may not require manual labor. He would simply charge for consultation visits to bored ladies who would love to boast about having an ambassador in their service. The technical work can be left to a subcontracting assistant. Instead of having to wait at airports or reserve hotel rooms and restaurant tables, others will have to wait for him to decide when and where to plug the pipes. Although the suggestion was made as an entertainment over dinner, some other diplomats present started entertaining it.

"A Day in the Life of a UN Ambassador" was aptly described by Samuel Insenally, former president of the General Assembly and permanent representative of Guyana, in a January 2000 issue of *www.unforum.com*:

> "It is 6:30 a.m. in the morning when I awake to the persistent ringing of the telephone. On the other end of the line is my Foreign Minister, reminding me of the brief he needs for an upcoming CARICOM meeting. By now fully alert, I remember that I have a Working Breakfast with a group of colleagues to discuss the Reform of the Security Council. As I struggle to get dressed and off, I think to myself what a never-ending chore! Not only do we have working lunches and working dinners but we now also have working

breakfasts sometimes even on the week-ends. Is nothing sacred any more?

"The breakfast proves, not unexpectedly, to be an ordeal. After five years of considering all conceivable options for reforming the Security Council we do not seem to be anywhere near to reaching general agreement as called for by Resolution 48/26. One keeps on hearing the same views meeting after meeting, year after year; only the faces of the representatives on the carousel have changed. With this discouraging thought, I leave for our Mission and our regular staff meeting at 9:00 am. I have less than an hour to review the day's programme of activities and arrange for representation at the various meetings being held at UN Headquarters. Invariably with our small staff, we cannot hope to be everywhere since, unlike the atom, we cannot sufficiently split ourselves to be able to adequately attend to the multiplicity of issues which today engage the international community's attention at the turn of the century. Still we manage and often are called upon to play Leadership roles out of all proportion to our size. Sufficient unto the day, however, is the Agenda thereof and however difficult we must make the effort to cover it as much as possible.

"This morning the General Assembly is meeting to discuss a number of important issues of interest and concern to us. Some consultations on related resolutions have to be undertaken and a few statements finalized. Not without reason is the United Nations described as a "talk-shop" for the diplomats who dwell there are doubly condemned not only to making long statements but also listen to those delivered by their colleagues. In between, we must slip out for "bilaterals" in one of the adjoining lounges or the 'souk' as it is now called, since for the greater part the business which is conducted there involves lobbying or being lobbied for positions in the international system. It is simply amazing how much time we spend on this international horse-trading. Soon it is lunch-time and again, because of conflicting commitments, I am obliged to run around like a beheaded chicken. First, a presence must be put in at a seminar being held in one of the committee rooms by a group of NGO's and for which my attendance had been promised some weeks ago. My participation in the event is fleeting however, since I must soon be off for a lunch hosted by one of my close colleagues to promote one of his country's candidacies. As luck would have it, I find myself sitting opposite him at the table. I will simply have to find something to say in reply to his words of welcome. Since I dare not speak for the other guests, I content myself with praising the meal and the virtues of continuous campaigning. I then hurry back downstairs to catch the tail-end of the symposium only to find that it has just concluded.

"The afternoon session comes all too quickly with more of the morning's activities and some appointments with Secretariat officials and one outside of the building. At about five p.m., I hurry to another venue downtown where I have been asked to speak on the subject of the Role of the United Nations in the Twenty-First Century. Yet another speech but one that I do not mind giving since the organization needs all the support and understanding it can get from the outside world. No sooner is the address finished that it is time for me to dash off to several receptions being offered by sister missions. My attendance at these is perforce perfunctory since at 8:00 p.m. I must be ready for a dinner engagement - mercifully the last event of the day. Around eleven p.m. the sumptuous meal ends and I hasten to take leave of my hosts in order to do some reading and writing for the next day's programme. By then, of course, it is the next day and I am so tired I cannot sleep. Eventually, however, after counting several sheep, I doze off into the arms of Somnus to await the next day's travails."

An unpredictable world may confuse diplomats, but most of them take it in stride. A constantly puzzled look on the face of a European diplomat was explained by a flying experience: he was once proceeding to Rome when his plane was hijacked to Cairo, while on another occasion he was going to the Egyptian capital when he was forcibly diverted to Rome. Aspiring diplomats may look purposely busy and act combative mainly to make a point. Generally, however, diplomats handling international matters are more open to novel ideas than they would let show except through glimpses of dry humor. When the Soviet Union and its allies were crumbling, an Eastern European diplomat defined a "paranoid" as someone in full possession of the facts.

E-mail, fax and cellular contact have changed the style and structure of diplomatic occasions. Receptions on national days or lunches and dinners to honor someone are not normally meant to be fun parties, though many are enjoyable indeed. They are actually an extension of work through social means. Particularly senior Secretariat officials know their way around the building enough to enter visibly and leave discreetly. Except for the Secretary-General, who would salute the host and respond graciously to greetings for a measured period of time, others plan their way gradually to a side exit. Almost everyone has a reason for showing up. Being there, even by accident, is a step in the right diplomatic direction. Some information casually heard or purposely leaked, bumping into someone who may turn out to be helpful, or hearing a suggestion floated informally to break a deadlock are merely part of that two-hour window of human bonding.

In earlier times, at a United Nations with less than half the current membership, most officially invited guests were known by the hosting ambassador or the chief of protocol. Instant communications with a wider attendance created an awkward information gap filled initially by a veteran, heavily accented Austrian Maitre d'hôtel in full black tie uniform designated by the management of the dining hall to make discreet introductions. It was soon noted that the man's passion for ceremonial courtesy was not always matched by attention to detail, like the precise name or function of the approaching guest. He would stand by the entrance, approach the next in line with his ear and announce you as heard. During one of the first receptions given by the Chinese away from their official Mission, I was waiting behind my direct boss, Under-Secretary-General Chief S.O. Adebo, who, like his wife, was dressed in colorful Nigerian national costume. In a thoughtful gesture, our Chief brought along his personal assistant, who happened to be a compatriot of the hosts. The enthusiastic announcer first declared the arrival of "General" and Mrs. Adebo. Then, he clearly amused the ambassador by introducing a very Chinese-looking young woman as their Nigerian daughter, "Miss Adebo." Later, upon retirement, the Austrian was replaced by someone who took pains to court guests and hosts alike.

Everyone seemed to appreciate the precise discretion of that new maitre, Norman, except for one puzzle: no one knew *his* full name.

Wider invitation lists made it difficult to comply with an obligatory notice that attendance in a certain hall was limited to an indicated number of persons. With some flexibility it could always be explained that not all those invited will actually attend, and then who is counting anyway: except possibly the Japanese. On one occasion a delegate from that country was preparing for a reception to be given by his Tokyo boss on a forthcoming New York visit. He liked the place in a tower building nearby but observed a notice indicating that the number of those allowed was five persons less than those on the invitation list. When the manager said that at least five of the intended guests may not in fact show up, the young diplomat quickly responded: "When the Japanese minister of Foreign Affairs invites two hundred Japanese, the two hundred will attend."

Another aspect of international life that changed in means but not in substance is that relentless curiosity of host countries to know more about the life and times of their accredited diplomats. It has become wildly recognized to the point that a host country, even an adversary, is habitually informed of the name and title cover under which a foreign secret service representative is operating in their realm.

During a television interview in New York on new changes in a reshaped country, the host expressed admiration for his guest's flawless American English. He may not have known that the younger man was brought up in Washington, D.C., where his father reportedly headed his government's secret service station. Diplomats seem to accept such "cloak" matters in stride as long as no "daggers" were involved. Some even take it with a grain of salt, like talking to a flowerpot at their dinner table or addressing a plant in the Delegates' Lounge. An Australian female diplomat was sure her phone was bugged but unsure by whom; she spent many an evening whispering sexual fantasies hoping to excite and frustrate presumed listeners. Some others approached this reality with tongue firmly in cheek. Diplomats posted in Moscow at a certain period recall that their colleague from Zaire (now Congo) was advised that his Mercedes, like that of all other ambassadors, could no longer go to Finland for a check-up; Soviet technicians were quite capable to provide the required service. It was understood that sending their cars to Helsinki was a diplomatic way to avert a re-bugging in Moscow. But when nothing much could be done about it, the ambassador wrote home to suggest reciprocal service. Thus the authorities in Kinshasa approached the Soviet ambassador there insisting on servicing his car. After reluctant bargaining, countered by Zaire's insistence, he had to give in. When the car was returned, embassy technicians searched for the planted bugs without success. Suspecting a more advanced "imperialist" technology - and curious to get it - the car and the ambassador were eventually recalled to Moscow. The simple fact was that there were no bugs to plant but they had bluffed their way to make the point and humor their ambassador, Monsieur Fato.

As frequent summit gatherings diminished the role of diplomats, there arose a new emphasis on security and protocol. Dr. Boutros-Ghali was fond of recounting how as a former foreign minister of Egypt he had to wait with counterparts from other countries in New Delhi for their designated bus, until he decided to take the one immediately following his own President's car. While Indian hosts were holding foreign ministers at bay, they allowed him through under the impression that he was the head of internal security.

Other than the principals, the only two people visibly noted during the UN millennium summit were the chiefs of Protocol and Security. In making arrangements for a round table, security considerations come first. Convenient conference rooms like those of the Economic and Social Council, the Trusteeship Council or conference rooms 1, 2 and 3 were bypassed because they were partially exposed to the East River. Those with institutional memory recalled an attempt three decades ago by an angry Cuban to fire at the building across the river from Queens to protest a visit by Fidel Castro. Now, with advanced weaponry and more than one determined adversary to any or all of the multiple rulers, security aides successfully argued against taking risks, however calculated. While armed boats patrolled the river, visiting dignitaries surrounded by their bulky escorts with plugged ears and whispering shirtsleeves, accompanied by discreetly helpful UN officers, were rushed down as ceremoniously as feasible to the safety of the first basement. A wall separating smaller rooms 5 and 6 had to be hurriedly torn down and a special security checkpoint requiring a special pass was erected.

After a direct threat to the UN in the aftermath of September 11, 2001, attendance of a high-level general debate postponed to November 10 required at least three special passes: to cross from Second Avenue, to enter from First Avenue and to get to the Assembly hall. Considering the alternative, delegates and staff went along collaborating with the ever-polite, yet firm, security.

Even during regular sessions of the General Assembly the building is now closed to visitors for the first week when several senior government officials are expected to participate. It is difficult to argue against security questions, particularly when you are not exactly clear about what they are. Those directly handling them know more than you do, and you would not wish to be responsible if something went seriously wrong. One point of argument at a certain time was about the number of public visitors allowed to take a guided tour. The visitor service is one of the very few revenue-making operations. It provides an international flavor to the public - particularly students - and is a lively communications tool; the message is individually delivered and personally received. After a campaign including posters in key world airports to "visit the UN; it's your world," a notable increase in visitors was welcomed. But the security service felt that they could only be allowed to tour the building in a maximum of fifteen persons. That meant not only splitting large groups but devoting more guides to a greater number of tours.

About a year later an acceptable arrangement was reached. Little known then was the fact that the first bomb attempt at the World Trade Center in 1993 had also marked the UN as a target. Even when the Secretary-General announced in frustration that he did not care for his personal safety, he was very politely reminded: what about the others?

Always on alert to evade potential trouble, an experienced security team ensured respectful treatment of diplomats and staff alike. After all, the span of modern international relations extends beyond accredited ambassadors to include unheralded achievers and ordinary individuals everywhere to cope with the constant challenges of daily life. Working in their various fields they may not make today's headlines but help shape the consensus of an enlightened international will. It is not by chance that for the first time in history, the second millennium ushered in a world where freedom is an individual's undeniable right and not a ruler's benign favor.

Through a persistent campaign led for more than 50 years by the United Nations community, the racial apartheid system was dismantled and the principle of self-determination for countries and peoples became universal law. There are more checks and balances, more transparency than ever before. Advances in medicine, science and technology widened a hopeful perspective of life. Despite obvious inequalities, resources are shared more responsibly, and political predominance is expressed more in economic competition than with military domination. There may be more questions than answers but then, why not? As Khalil Gibran, the Lebanese-American "prophet" wrote to a friend: "There are no keys because there are no doors; here it is - life - not locked away from our sight but all around us." When I joined the United Nations over 30 years ago, the main concern was the financial crisis. That sounds familiar today. Suspending the voting rights of a Permanent member of the Security Council for not paying its dues was so close that the Assembly President had to gallop through the proceedings to avoid a contesting vote. At the time, the culprit was the Soviet Union. The position formulated then by U.S. Ambassador Adlai Stevenson remains one of the most eloquent statements on the need for all member states to pay their dues in time and in full.

Reform was another pressing issue, and Dr. Ralph Bunche, who won the Nobel Peace Prize for his Middle East work in 1949, was charged upon his return with overseeing it. Some thought of it as bookkeeping, but most considered reform a search for excellence and the best use of available resources. Since the most valuable and available resource is the staff, reform was practically implemented through three main sources: the leadership of the Secretary-General, the approval of member states and the implementation by the staff. If a UN financial crisis and reform were regular facts of life, should the UN just keep doing what it does and hope for the best? Not really.

Entering a new millennium, the UN has to succeed in order to survive. Our swiftly changing world, with revolutionary shifts in borders, social fabric and communications leaves no other option for the United Nations but to reflect the dynamics of its membership. That would mean, briefly, an open and participatory operation with sharpened focus on current issues and wider partnerships. A strengthened internal public information culture is needed to highlight the relevance of its programs to everyday people in everyday language. Its partnership with the media is crucial. Its focused opening to private groups is even more so. Experience has shown that some groups have more say in formulating public policy than official committees. Some cities may have as much importance as their country's capital. An Italian saying *"Roma la capitale, Milano il capital"* would apply to New York, Rio de Janeiro, São Paolo, Sydney, Lagos or Johannesburg. One need not recall names of individuals who acquired international influence across national borders and have more valuable impact than most government officials. That is where Kofi Annan made a special difference. He made it one of his priorities to widen partnerships with the private sector and selectively involve the business community.

During the height of the UN financial crisis, when the U.S. Government publicly declared it had no intention of paying its dues, an attempt was made to seek the advice of the American business community. A representative group of "old" money like David Rockefeller and new market hedge funders were assembled on the 38th floor. An analytical presentation by Dr. Boutros-Ghali stressed the urgent need for money to help development of poor countries. Development, after all, was essential for stability, which is a prerequisite for sound investment. An educated population was more inclined to have a voice in shaping its destiny, hence its impact in promoting democracy. Enhancing the quality of life would cement human dignity, which, given its confident spirit, would oppose tyranny and oppression. It was also pointed out that some large firms which had been obliged to support apartheid or dictatorship may welcome an opportunity to offer "conscience money" and signal their enlightened role in a new era. As the group started to discuss an appropriate mechanism, a "reality check" was injected by a participant who reportedly made billions on currency fluctuations. Development was "a dirty word," he said, which should be scrupulously avoided when approaching his field because it was market forces, not human needs, that made the difference.

The initiative was picked up again by Kofi Annan when a small powerful group was formed, including former US Treasury Secretary Robert Rubin, who may not have realized that he was the one behind the idea of gaining support for the UN through the business community. While in office, he had mentioned it to a prominent columnist who casually passed it on in a conversation with an international visitor.

Business people know that the first lesson in finance is that money is a coward; it runs away at the first sniff of risk. And it is commonly understood that financial credibility depends on public perception. Countries and organizations, like banks, gain and lose accordingly. Recurring reports about non-payment of dues to the UN, coupled with lack of practical, political support, not only eroded the standing of that organization at headquarters but its operations everywhere. In the midst of the Western Sahara conflict in North Africa, the Secretary-General's special representative, Johannes Manz, landed in Nouakchott, capital of Mauritania. Airport. Authorities refused to refuel the plane, requesting immediate payment. At the time, UN credit was not acceptable, but the personal Swiss credit card of Ambassador Manz was more than adequate to allow for takeoff.

E-diplomacy stimulated a wider involvement by members of civic societies, creating new para-diplomatic groups who work like diplomats and look like diplomats but are not diplomats. The bottom line is that they don't cast a vote. Lunches, dinners and self-briefings may help change a diplomat's mind but not his country's vote. Opening words like "upon instructions from my government" mean not having to say sorry to last night's hostess. Given policy guidelines through closer communications, a diplomat has the freedom to use his inventive talents to make an argument but not to change approved policy.

A good diplomat may turn a messy situation into a civilized disagreement. A hurried politician could turn a fair disagreement into a messy misunderstanding. United Nations officials are often caught between diplomats trying to play politics and politicians taking over as diplomats. No complaints are made though; it is just another day in an imperfect world. But what is a U.N. spokesman to do when cornered to respond instantly and repeatedly to good questions by capable reporters? A U.N. Secretary-General was once in the midst of delegate negotiations between Arab and Israeli parties on controlling and maintaining a ceasefire agreement. As the situation drew out for weeks with little to tell without provoking potential opponents on either side, the spokesman kept using terms like the situation was "fluid" or that the Secretary-General, who was pursuing his contacts with all parties, was "flexible," "open to all sides" or "keeping the momentum." When the discreet good offices succeeded – for whatever short period – an appreciative Secretary-General sent his press assistant a token gift with a handwritten note; "to Mr. Fluid from Mr. Flexible".

For a while, a Peace and Security Section within the Secretariat was called pst... PSSST!

"Corridor diplomacy" got a new meaning as many restrictions have been imposed on internal movement within the U.N. Security Council meetings are mostly "closed," "for members only," or "consultations in progress." Even representatives of key countries like Germany, Italy, Senegal, or Chile would not venture to explore what was going on inside. Accredited reporters are kept behind iron hedges from approaching delegates except when invited to ask questions or listen to statements. Reaching upper floors, particularly those of the Secretary-General, would be a rare reward. A new practice urging staff to find their own space on particular floors within widespread cubicles continues to be for most a daily challenge. Staff without adequate credentials are not allowed into the Delegates' Lounge which in its current format now resembles an internet café except on Friday evenings when it turns into a disco bar. Retired staff are not allowed during the General Debate of the Assembly; they cannot bring a visitor, or even a spouse, anytime. The inevitable outcome is having so many people hanging around side corridors biding their time exchanging views on where they stand.

It is not easy being an international diplomat in a world changing with the speed of light and a profession torn between yesterday's tradition and today's technology. Similarly, it is not easy being the United Nations when some of its members are dismembered, and others are, like itself, financially strapped. While its main concern with human condition remains unchanged, its two main objectives of peace and development are no more what they used to be.

For its first 45 years, for example, UN peacekeeping was concerned with settling conflicts between two or more countries with an endorsed agreement. The UN intervened, mediated, supervised, offered good offices, observed or performed any of the 18 functions maintained in the Charter, mainly through dealing with governments. For that it received two Nobel Prizes. But suddenly peace had to be kept within, not across, borders. Limited wars were replaced by mushrooming conflicts, while faltering governments were superseded by warlords. Religious or ethnic backgrounds were exploited as a cover when the clear objective was raw power or sheer looting.

Somalia, possibly the first of the catastrophes, was an obvious case. All members of its population are of the same religious sect. A former Italian colony, it was first a Soviet naval base, then an American ally under the same ruler. With the Cold War over, it was left to its own devices. When photos of starving children appeared on television screens worldwide, each of its regions had its own warlord. Its capital Mogadishu was split among an alliance of factions, which mainly exploited teenagers, shorter and lighter than their machine guns, that they waved precariously on wildly driven jeeps. Most people suffered, as opportunist chieftains scrambled for turf control - and shared in the popular *qat* drug trade. Assistance agencies had to pay local gunmen to be allowed to help the victims. And even a decade later no one could adequately explain the disappearance of six million dollars in cash from the UN administrative office there. Pakistani troops, who shared the same religious faith as Somalians, bore the brunt of casualties. Unlike UN troops in earlier missions, they were not observing borders but operating in unfamiliar urban jungles. Americans were duly shocked at the sight of their young marines dragged through the streets of a poor foreign country they thought they were helping.

In Afghanistan, people who were united to fight the Soviet invasion clashed over power, which included control of opium fields, some gems and minerals, like Lapis Lazuli, and a prospect of a proposed oil pipeline in the South. By now it is common knowledge that Afghanistan was the world's largest producer of opium. The Taliban, which literally means students of religion, had no qualms about growing fields that stretched from their "spiritual" capital of Kandahar to the northern town of Iruggar and east to Jalalabad near the Pakistan border. Their adversaries in the Northern Alliance indulged in the same trade when they were within the tiny area they controlled off the Panshir Valley around the town of Feyyabad, close to the border with Tajikistan. Its main route flowed through the central Asian Republics to Europe. Whenever international pressure mounted to stop the trade, corrupt officials resorted to the cynical old ploy of seizing some minor smugglers to demonstrate their energetic adherence to the rule of law and deviate attention from the big deals.

Before the return of general order to Lebanon, a record heist was performed in downtown Beirut during the infamous fifteen-year-old war. With only one exception, all armed factions who were claiming to fight each other under varied pretexts joined in a coded understanding to empty the vaults of the British Bank of the Middle East. It contained the largest amounts of cash, plus the richest deposit boxes of Beirut's world-renowned gold market traders. When the looters first failed to open them, international specialists were invited. More time was needed; thus a ceasefire was suddenly declared by all sides "in the interest of the suffering public." When heavy drilling seemed to be required to break down the unexpectedly thick vaults, a battle was staged. Gunmen fired away in every direction but inward in order to drown the noise. The job took three days and netted an inappropriately shared minimum of $500 million.

Again, during the war, with an electricity breakdown and night curfews, some Beirut residents obtained radios, not necessarily to listen to international stations but mainly to tune into the frequencies of the fighting parties. The most interesting part was after midnight. Protagonists traded the usual insults about each other's families for hours until interrupted by an authoritative voice that advised all to shut up and listen carefully. Using agreed code words, he would indicate that some valuables, such as for example "eleven marbles," were passing through specific check-points at a certain time. All sides should ensure safe passage and will be rewarded accordingly. Later, during the Bosnian war, I met on the plane from Vienna some journalists who had covered Beirut. As we waited for my missing luggage in Zagreb, they ticked off a number of projects of joint financial and political interest between politically disputing parties. It seemed that while UN troops patrolled mapped streets, local thugs used shortcuts. And while under-armed and politically under-supported international soldiers were blind-folded and tied to lamp-posts, some of the regional adversaries ridiculing them were actually partners in contraband markets, particularly petroleum, liquor and cigarettes. Under the banner of nationalism, notorious thugs who plundered the region had silent partners in various ethnic camps. The public assassination of Serbian militant Arkan in the main lobby of Belgrade's biggest hotel was a double-edged signal: it was a threat to those contemplating to provide inside information to prosecutors in The Hague Tribunal and a nervous indication that Mr. Milosovic's regime was starting to crumble.

Then there is always, of course, the world's oldest profession. With so many stressed, tense, frustrated, angry, scared, greedy, gullible, destitute, hot-blooded, short-tempered people in so limited space, young women and men are the most vulnerable victims. Networks operated through lucrative Balkan transit spots arranged border crossings for illicit human cargo from countries of the former Eastern European block to those in the Western democracies. When clashes broke out in the summer of 2001 between the predominantly Serb Macedonian government and an Albanian militia, NATO and European Union senior officials attempted to intercede for an end to hostilities. Skeptics from the region predicted that the fighting may indeed stop, not due to the persuading skills of international dignitaries visiting the capital Skopje, but because of the interrupted prostitution business in Velesta. That obscure village on the border with Albania had become a vital link in the illicit trade. Ironically, peace negotiations eventually took place in the neighboring resort town of Okhrid. In nearby Bosnia, turf sharing blended with financial violation was rampant enough to cause an investigation by a US government agency. Cigarette smuggling through Montenegro was so widespread that its former foreign minister was sued by an Italian prosecutor in Naples.

When the U.S.-sponsored Dayton accord on Bosnia-Herzegovina was mentioned at the UN Security Council, an exhausted interpreter amused participating delegates by inadvertently referring to it as Daytona Beach, a resort in Florida. Indeed, Bosnia's capital Sarajevo, used to be an international resort before the break-up of Yugoslavia. A typical battleground for other people's wars and political intrigue, it prompted the spark to World War One when Archduke Ferdinand was assassinated in its main street. A history professor at the American University of Beirut, Dr. Zaine Zeine, was fond of recounting his visit to the museum there. As he thoroughly inspected the chariot that had carried the Archduke, he noted the traces of only two bullets, when historical evidence indicated the assassin had shot three. Before raising the matter with the curator, the professor realized that the third bullet must have hit the victim.

For years, the war in Angola had several ideological covers and political pretexts. Like those given for most other conflicts around the world, nothing could be further from the truth. Almost all those closely involved knew that the fighting was between those who controlled the oil and those who controlled the diamonds. It was simply diamonds or oil, except that far too many innocent people were victims. A report by the UN Secretary-General mentioned that over ten years approaching the new millennium, about five million people had lost their lives or livelihoods to such conflicts around the world.

Angola was just one example brought to the attention of the international community through a panel report to the Security Council. It noted that large quantities of arms and military equipment were imported mainly as a result of four key factors: the willingness of certain countries to provide certificates to facilitate the passage of arms and militia equipment through their territory; the interest by supplying countries to sell weapons with little or no regard for where those arms would actually end up; and the eagerness of international arms brokers and air transport carriers to act as intermediaries. A fourth factor had been the capacity of the Angolan groups to continue to pay for what it wanted through mining and selling diamonds illegally on major markets. The Panel confirmed that the critical fuel supplies for military operations had been facilitated by a number of former or current heads of state to circumvent Security Council sanctions. Briefly, embargoed diamonds worth over one million dollars were smuggled out of Angola each day, constituting an estimated five percent of the year 2000 supply of rough gems. With all the money made from mineral gems, 90% of Africans have not even seen a diamond.

Another case was the Congo. In a welcome display of straight talk, a report by a "Panel on the Illegal Exploitation of Natural Resources and Other Forms of Wealth" in the Congo, briefly known as the "Plunder Report," was transmitted by Secretary-General Kofi Annan to the Security Council in early 2001. It demonstrated the cobweb of greed that drained the natural wealth of several African countries. Those who invested in tension and conflict were basically exploiting their paramilitary prowess to make profit at the expense of millions of displaced innocent people. Key players in the Congo, Rwanda, Uganda and Angola, as well as accommodating or hidden partners, formed an administrative organization, a financial network and private companies to support the endeavor. Individual actors, assisted by three private airline companies, busily used planes provided by a non-African mercenary. There were six such companies on the Rwandan side, while Belgian Sabena cargo reportedly air transported material from Kigali, Rwanda, to European destinations. The management of Sabena in Kampala and Brussels refused to make anyone available to speak to the Panel. Several small banks also played a key role. These included Union des Banques Congolaises, whose ongoing operations were in areas controlled by Rwanda; Banque Commerciale du Congo, which was linked to Belgian consortium Belgolaise; Banque Commerciale du Rwanda operating in Kisingani, Bukavu and Goma; Banque de la Confiance d'Or, a family-owned business; and Banque de Commerce, de Développement et d'Industrie (BCDI), an active newcomer in Kigali whose shareholders, the Panel was told, included a combination of nationalities.

From diamonds to coffee to forest wood, timber and gold, let alone the dumping of counterfeit money, an assortment of deadly enemies united to plunder the region. In one example, the Panel chose to focus on three key actors. First and second Ugandan Major-General (retired) Salim Sateh, alias Khaleb Akandwanaho, and his wife, Jovia Akandwanaho. According to the report: "He is very popular in the army and pulls the strings of illegal activities in areas controlled by his forces. James Kegini is his right-hand man." His wife seemed particularly interested in diamonds, the report stated, adding that she was "at the root of the Kisangani wars." She wanted control of the diamond market there "after having confirmation from Mr. Khalil of the Victoria Group that it was a good and feasible idea." General Kegini is former commander of military operations in the Congo and was "the master in the field; the orchestrator, organizer and manager of the most illegal activities related to Ugandan troop preserves in north and northeastern Congo."

Local actors in that field could not be separated from the structure they served; some names kept coming up on several occasions. They included Ali Hussein, who played a major role in gold and diamond deals, always having a Rwandan citizen in attendance. Another was a Colonel Kabarebe, described as a "facilitator." A third was Tibere Rujigiro, one of the main financiers during the 1990-1994 war. A unique case seemed to be that of Aziza Kulsum Gulamali, whose vague status was compounded by her access to various passports. She lived in Nairobi; Bukavu or Brussels, "depending on her schedule." Her occasional alliance with Rwanda seemed to be at odds with her previous involvement in arms trafficking in support of its deadly adversaries, the Burundian Hutu. In an attempt to explain her partnership role, local officials in the Congolese Goma province said, "She was so useful that she would bring in $1 million monthly."

The Fight For Resources

Basic natural surroundings like air, earth and water are now open to conflict or concord among nations. Competition for valuable natural resources is not limited to profit-making firms or powerful individuals but extends to countries whatever their type of government. Mostly small wars are fought over oil and minerals. A future focus may be the Caspian Sea, believed to have an estimated worth of $3 billion in gas and oil reserves; already projected foreign investments in exploring it is estimated at $60 billion. Any mediator in the Middle East who overlooks the critical value of water will be making a basic miscalculation. River Jordan, Lake Tiberias, the Euphrates between Iraq, Syria and Turkey are now familiar names in political mediation. Attempts to divert waters have almost always led to armed conflict under other pretexts. The flow of the Nile could explain the delicate balance of relations between countries depending on it, from Egypt, Ethiopia and Sudan to Tanzania. Arranging for a peaceful transfer of authority in Eritrea, one had to take into serious account the unhindered availability of its ports of Massawa and Assab to its neighbors. Water is more basic and in many places less available than oil. It is a question of human survival and a clearly stated matter of national security. It will be misleading to assume that all military conflicts among groups or countries are motivated by profit or a search for resources. But they certainly take a more brutal turn and require a more complex handling when creed blends with greed, triggered by a fleeting sense of power and driven by a misconception of what each side can get away with.

New approaches to peacekeeping may invoke age-old remedies. Nelson Mandela had some advice for the women in Burundi. After relentlessly trying to shame Burundi leaders into an elusive reconciliation, one of the greatest human leaders of modern times resorted to one of the oldest approaches in history. He called on Burundi women to do what the Greek women of Lysistrata did to stop their men from going to war. No sex unless they refrained from fighting. The sex for peace formula succeeded in old Greece but apparently needed more inducements in Burundi. That further inducement came from the European Community, which promised about $550 million on reconstruction funds in case of reconciliation. Widespread conflict over natural resources changed the basic requirements of peacekeeping. Traditionally, diplomats and soldiers were needed. It is about time to bring in psychiatrists and cartographers. Wars, hot and cold, have ended,but they were replaced by conflicts - 34 to 78 at any particular time. A main difference is that ninety percent of the victims in conflicts are not soldiers, but civilians.

Announcing "the end of history" to intellectual applause meant reinventing geography. The Soviet Union scattered into 16 states from Armenia to Uzbekistan. Czechoslovakia was split between Czech and Slovakia. Yugoslavia became a former state limited to Serbia and Montenegro, while Croatia, Bosnia and Slovenia became UN members. Kosovo, still a "province" caused the first war by NATO, while the rest of the Balkans was truly balkanized. One of the most populous countries in Asia, Indonesia, gave way to the creation of East Timor. Breakups meant new members of the international community played a role both as partners in change and parties to disputes. The Caspian Sea is a simple example. Until the 1990's, the two states of Iran and the Soviet Union had to make sharing arrangements, despite their differing political systems. It was mainly about caviar and oil, let alone tacit security deals. Now, there are five, after the creation of Azerbaijan, Turkmenistan and Armenia. More competition meant more pollution and less caviar. But the big prize was oil. Powerful conglomerates from different countries sought drilling and marketing rights, raising the political stakes and siding with the accommodating country. Agreement about the extension of territorial waters was not merely a matter of national sovereignty but commercial enterprise. Azerbaijan, for example, insisted on its due mileage in the sea, while Iran held the position that the Caspian was a very large lake to be equally shared by all. A dispute over pipeline routes and who should benefit from controlling their safe passage may explain several armed, often ruthless, conflicts in that region from Chechnya to Georgia, Abkhazia to Nagorno-Karabakh. Visiting firemen could not solve these military disputes without businessmen and geologists finding a discreet settlement for claimed interests.

Some Pacific islands find themselves literally trying to stay above water. Having enjoyed a fleeting popularity at the dawn of the internet age, the government of Tuvalu is now preoccupied with relocating its 11,000 inhabitants before the sea level rises in about 50 years to engulf its territory. It has already approached its Pacific neighbors, Australia and New Zealand, for possible shelter. The Kingdom of Tonga had to protest publicly when $26 million disappeared with a former broker who had been designated as the King's court jester; he must have been laughing all the way to the bank. World membership by these countries is a welcome exercise in inclusiveness. It means that all the world is a stage. That requires more patient understanding while trying to orchestrate concerted action to meet successive crises. At the UN, seated as they are in alphabetical order, that may cause some awkward moments. During the height of the Iran-Iraq war in the 1980s, their respective delegations had to exercise discipline amongst those seated behind their main representative, avoiding eye contact but having to share neighboring seats. Their joint adversary, Israel was also within earshot.

Selling the Bridge

Although the concept is old, the practice of a concerted inclusive effort by all the world's countries to handle a particular problem is relatively new. Comprehensive multilateral diplomacy only started in the mid-20th century, initially through the abandoned League of Nations, then more firmly with the United Nations. Before that, treaties were signed and alliances formed on bilateral links between two countries or a balancing role between the predominant, the careful and the helpless.

Now, while each country maintains its full sovereignty it realizes that there are pressing problems that could only be faced through a concerted joint effort. These include terrorism, environmental waste, drug trafficking, money laundering, international crime and viral epidemics. Other obvious examples of inevitable collaboration in everyone's daily life include public safety, transport, technology, health, banking, refugees, immigration, exploiting children in zones of conflict, and emergency relief. In handling all these issues internationally, either everyone's on board or everyone is in trouble. The opening words of the UN Charter express the determination "to save future generations from the scourge of war." An inscription near its main entrance quotes Isaiah: "They shall turn their swords into plough shares." That was an instinctive response to the horrors of two world wars. Yet averting further destruction seems to be a passive objective unless accompanied by economic and social development. Human dignity and respect for the quality of life are perceived as basic necessities to ensure peace. The problem is not with the faith, as the clergy would say, but in the faithful.

New challenges to peacekeeping have eroded the other main UN objective: economic and social development. Since the beginning of the 1990s most available funds were diverted to emergency relief and humanitarian assistance. A long established motto that development was the other name for peace became too hollow to attract donors in days of moral fatigue and financial uncertainty. International development itself started scouting for a new name, possibly something related to good governance. It sought new sponsors: fewer governments, more civil society groups. As UN peacekeeping is no more what it used to be, development faces a similar challenge. Yet the two main basic human needs remain the same: food and security. Therefore the unprecedented global coalition against terrorism could be most effective when matched with an equally vigorous coalition against poverty. Graffiti in a Parisian metro station in the 1970s declared "God is dead," signed "Karl Marx." In the 1990s someone wrote under it "Marx is dead," signed "God." Diplomats were caught mostly unaware with the end of an ideological Cold War. While intellectuals lapsed into ponderosity, politicians swiftly adapted their calculations; older ones shifted between positions, new ones triangulated them.

Former members of the politburo of the Soviet Union were reincarnated as democratically elected heads of newly independent countries advocating free markets; some even designated special representation on Wall Street. Poland, capital of the military Warsaw

E-Diplomacy: Where's That Bridge?

Pact of eastern European countries became a favored member to join NATO. In the West, several former anti-war activists took over the reins of power; one became President of the United States of America. Others equally charismatic became prime ministers, chancellors and foreign ministers. One of their most competent socialists took over a term as Secretary-General of the NATO alliance, against which he had spent his youth demonstrating in the streets of Madrid. In some instances, diplomatic circles were amused by a crisis of cross attitudes. Formerly frowning delegates from former communist countries appeared at UN headquarters beaming with smiles and loaded with jokes, while the usually modest easy-going western diplomats had to put up with some of their self-important allies determined to "tell it like it is" to the media first, then to their colleagues. Most telling was an alliance of interests between extremists on both sides of the Cold War. An emerging grouping of "East-West" combined some former Soviet apparatchiks with their former adversaries in the U.S. It was further proof that old networks never die. They just cross the street.

Better national governance became a politically correct pressing international need. Drastic changes led to the erosion of moral authority, particularly as more of those in influential control were perceived as corrupt or immoral. While some news organizations overplayed an intrusive approach, it was mainly thanks to the press that corruption was exposed and oppression relieved. As Albert Camus once put it, the Press may be sometimes very bad but bad press is far better than no press at all. That was recognized in the International Declaration of Human Rights, when Article 19 underlined freedom of expression. The first worldwide conflict of the 21st century was neither between regular armies nor feuding groups. It was started by a limited group of individuals who exploited a noble religion as a tactic and depended on brutal terror as a strategy. It was a visibly shocking side of negative globalization and needs to be met with an equally global determination and resolve.The response requires prolonged focus and resolve by the concerted determination of the international community. It not only involves the hardware of military action or the maintenance of political momentum. More to the point, it ought to extend to the software of the human mind, heart and soul. What would be worthwhile, therefore, is to consolidate international resolve within a definite moral framework, inspired by the UN Charter, The Declaration of Human Rights made in 1947 after the turmoil and outrage of a world war needs no revision but rather a refreshed demonstration.

Many of those advocating globalization failed to highlight one of its most valuable achievements. While stressing technology, gadgets and market forces, they overlooked a major theme: civil rights have been globalized. Assaults on human rights could be more easily exposed and more widely opposed. A main adversary to globalization is ignorance, which begets fear. Active opposition may come from organized labor or mobilized anarchists. But globalization's main shortcoming is the inability to win the vulnerable middle classes, who are not clear what it actually means to them. Wide coverage of annual meetings in exclusive resorts only serves to confirm their suspicions that only a certain clique of businessmen and politicians are the main beneficiaries. Possibly the next meeting of the exclusive Davos group could place on its agenda the need to enlighten the rest of the world. Pope John Paul I, who was in office only one month, thought that the modern human spirit was like an exhausted car frequently interrupted from smooth driving by a diet of marmalade and wine rather than oil and gas. When the chips are down, there is a risk that financial insolvency could be compounded by moral bankruptcy. Only a creative balance within a unified society could ensure a dynamic response where every aspect matters and everyone counts. In that the private sector could play a far more crucial role than government. In a tragically leaderless world, Pope Francis has inspired more awareness of global issues than any senior national official.

As usual, unprecedented change came suddenly, swiftly shifting priorities across and within countries. As the old order changed it did not yield place immediately to a specific new one. Novel concepts were tried, applied, or discarded depending on better value, most impact or least relevance. The United Nations found itself in the most difficult position, reflecting a stunned world caught between political rhetoric and hard facts.

While approaching a new millennium, almost everyone invoked a vision of a new bridge. Particularly the President of the host country and heads of state who attended the 50th anniversary of the UN in 1995, like those who participated in the summit of 2000, announced their determination to build the "Bridge to the 21st Century." Building a bridge to the future is not novel in political rhetoric. Lenin invoked it to present the Revolution of 1917. Revival of the term 78 years later by some leaders of the Western world refreshes the claim that history could repeat itself once as tragedy and once as farce. A seasoned observer, who tried but failed to locate that bridge anywhere, could not escape the feeling that a new world order, or disorder, is yet to be framed. Until then, Planet Earth seems to run on automatic pilot. That need not be cause for urgent alarm. In trying times, many prefer mechanical precision to human frailty. As a matter of fact, life, like a heartbeat, never stops bouncing with opportunities while pounding with challenges. The prospect of a bridge may be politically impressive with a hint of a stable approach to a solid future. But it is far too static for our advancing human destiny: more open, participatory and inclusive now than ever before. It would clearly face formidable obstacles, particularly from within its own nature; we will stumble and fall, then pick ourselves up again and keep moving. Whether history "proceeds in disguise wearing the mask of the previous stage" or is shaped by the determined will of outstanding and ordinary individuals could be argued with so many other theories by so many willing intellectuals. A veteran internationalist will assume with Arnold Toynbee that history is not a final harbor but an ongoing voyage.

In any case, soon after the advent of the 21st Century, it was realized that the ceremoniously promised bridge was nowhere to be found. Anyone who would still claim to find it deserves to buy it.

The End of the UN As We Knew It

With the new Millennium, anyone entering the UN's New York Headquarters had to use an electronic card. In practical terms this means that at least the Security department will know at what time any individual entered the UN building, when they left and for how long they stayed. Until the end of the 20th century, the Security Section was handled by a few supervisors in the office of Building Management which was part of the Department of Management. The Security officers did their normal work with a chief who handled complaints and supervised the team. Several years later, by 2007, it had grown into a whole Department of Safety and Security (DSS), first headed by a former chief of Scotland Yard in London with the rank of Under Secretary-General.

The bombing of the UN headquarters in Baghdad and the loss of our colleagues prompted and raised questions of security within the UN. However, instead of taking more security measures in the field, this traumatic event was used as a pretext for expanding DSS in New York with a budget of about $90 million. Apart from raising sensibilities between New York and the field, extensively widened security measures introduced at Headquarters gave UN veterans the feeling that there has been a drastic change in the way the new UN management perceived the world and deals with its own people. There was a time when the UN was entirely open, all staff members knew each other and the Secretary-General walked around offices, double-checking on performances, without escort except for the chief of the section visited. When I joined the UN, its security officers were not even carrying arms. They were trained to judge people based on honed instincts. They were welcoming to visitors, and if you were a regular staff member they got used to seeing you and did not demand to check your pass every time you entered. That world, of course, is long gone.

Once after using my new electronic card to meet someone at the UN, I was taken to the Security Council Chamber. I was struck by the sight of an officer with a search dog next door to the Council's consultation room, where only delegates were allowed. The dog started barking, but its handler never bothered to calm it down.

Visitors are not the only ones affected by the changed approach; staff members are as well. There are now separate passes for people who can enter certain areas. While someone new, possibly on a temporary assignment, can get to the Security Council, the General Assembly, the Delegates' Lounge and even have access to the Secretary-General's office, a retired person, no matter what retired rank, has only limited access to certain areas. One can wonder if someone who just happened to join the UN would be more loyal than someone that spent – and possibly even risked – his or her professional life serving the Organization. Though the retirees are the UN's main support in the outside world, in such situations they are made to feel less than fully welcome.

Moving within the Secretariat itself has taken a totally different turn. Let alone the restrictions to the Secretariat office, cafeterias and lounges but access by staff and retirees to the offices of the Secretary-General on the 38th floor has become exceptionally challenging. While all six elevators went up there any time of day in addition to a service elevator, now, since 2014, with a new "master" plan, the masters of the universe have restricted any regular movement above the 37th. floor. Now even Ambassadors that have meetings with the Secretary-General would have to stop for elaborate check up before they are escorted by special security one floor up. The resulting atmosphere is neither cordial nor convenient – nor conducive to collaborative teamwork.

E-Diplomacy: Where's That Bridge?

Whether effective or otherwise, newly introduced restrictions created a feeling that a visitor is suspect until proven innocent. The perception of the Organization has changed. There is an Oath of Office that pledges to take no instructions from any party, not even one's own government, stressing full exclusive loyalty to the Secretary-General and the Organization. Personally, I mounted a copy of the oath and displayed it prominently on the wall of my office as a reminder to myself and all visitors whose interests I tried to serve.

Most staff abided by this compact. However, the spirit of international civil service, which has been the very basis of the UN, is under stress from within. The generations who joined the UN at its creation year when it was the main framework for international legitimacy, retired around the year 2000. No special effort was noted to install that spirit in newcomers and give them the needed training nor inspire dedication to the UN. Indeed, there were certain cases to the contrary among some transients who seemed over-educated about privileges or benefits and under-educated on principles and values.

More to the point, a spirit of teamwork has to be reformed. Meritocracy does not mean competitive focus on solitary performance. On the contrary, to encourage merit you have got to encourage teamwork and loyalty. To make this system work, it is crucial to have leadership by example that inspires from the front. If the staff see that the leaders and chiefs of section follow the right course of action, then they will go along. What is crucial is to refresh a culture of collaborative, dedicated work and loyalty to the international civil service with a commitment to deliver with excellence on behalf of all member states with due respect to all of them, especially the permanent members of the Security Council, with a determination to make them feel that the UN belongs to them. The UN can perform its best when member states realize that the Organization exists to carry out their collective will.

Member states should be made to feel that a top-quality civil service is in their best interest. Inevitably a number of individuals brought in around the turn of the millennium came with no checks or balances, and their appointments often evaded long-established rules or regulations. It disappointed regular staff members who looked forward not merely to stop at a transient station but to building a career deserving total dedication.

As it approached Seventy, the UN faced a serious issue of credibility, management and performance. It was not a legalistic question or financial issue or a matter of semantics. What was described a couple of decades ago as creeping irrelevance by an outgoing president of the General Assembly has taken hold as a number of newly designated senior officials, representatives and envoys were allowed to taint the UN's name through media reported scandals or glaring conflicts of interest. It may be worth repeating that working at the UN is not just a job, it is a commitment. That is the difference between a non-profit organization with an inclusive human objective and a for-profit, business promotional enterprise. It was always said that the Secretary-General needed big powers to survive and small ones to succeed. It could be added that he also needed the staff to deliver. A culture of dedication, credible service and a dynamic and relevant UN is crucial for effective international relations.

The UN was bound to change with everyday life, let alone a constantly changing world. Change, habitually described as reform, depended on the intentions of those proposing it. It could be either a strategy or a tactic depending on the time required to accomplish a particular target. It could be aimed at turning the UN around to accomplish its tasks completely, or to transform it from an advocacy forum for human causes with international legitimacy into a mere servicing theatre.

Experience proved that unified team work is not only ideal policy but practical politics. Member states big and small get better delivery. The Secretary-General needs the loyalty of dedicated staff as much as they need his inspirational mobilizing leadership. A dispersed Secretariat would confuse member states, diminish results and erode credibility. Its strongest links become its weakest. Cosmetic change particularly when imposed by politically expedient appointees could be counterproductive, seeking headlines at the expense of their own people would self-destruct like a shooting star. Those who led by enlightened commitment made a difference. Genuine updated change, always necessary to enable the UN system deal effectively with expanding and pressing issues, could best be accomplished through informed partnerships of secretariat staff entrusted with implementing it, wide membership of delegations, civil society groups and inclusive media support.

UN culture is about giving everything for the cause of peace; it can be found in the actions of Secretary-General Dag Hammarskjold who died for the cause, soldiers for peace who sacrificed their lives without fanfare, and our colleagues who were lost in Baghdad. All these people are examples of the real UN culture, the thousands of unheralded people who devoted their lifetime careers to the UN and risked their lives for peace. To start hitting at the UN culture is a deliberate effort to undercut the independence of the international civil service - a very risky endeavor indeed. A strong UN is therefore in everyone's interest. To try to undercut the UN culture is an attempt to end the UN as we know it. The alternative is chaos.

CHAPTER XVIII:

WHERE ARE THE LEADERS?
REVITALIZING AND REJUVENATING
THE UN

There was abundant good will but limited leadership during ten days of a General Debate at the UN Assembly that started September 25, 2014. A habitual contender, the President of the United States, did not pretend to try that year. President Obama sort of dropped by, made a statement geared mainly to an American audience, and left. He did not even stay for the traditional lunch where, on behalf of all heads of state and government, he would offer the key toast. Another option, under the rallying banner of "Francophonie"," would be France. But its newly elected president, François Hollande, who made being *"Monsieur Normal"* the theme of his image, acted accordingly. The South African President Jacob Zuma looked somewhat subdued after a tragic mining crisis in his country. Brazil's Dilma Rousseff, who demanded a Security Council permanent seat, was not yet widely recognized. The new heads of the so-called Arab Spring countries were actually old, exhausted men trying to cope with suspicious public opinion abroad and angry women and youth at home. Egypt's President Mohamed Morsi was ousted in a public uprising a few months later. Russia's Putin was not there. Absent also was Turkey's Recep Erdogan, who was instead in Istanbul preparing perhaps the revival of the Ottoman Sultanate. Hamid Karzai, once the darling of mainstream media to the point that his choice of Afghani robes would be analyzed, looked desolate and alone as he spoke to almost no one at 8:35 pm.

Clearly, there was no Nelson Mandela; no Pierre Trudeau or John F. Kennedy; looking way back, no Nehru or U Thant; certainly no Dag Hammarskjold.

After President Obama finished his speech at the Assembly, the meeting's chairman and the UN Secretary-General were expected to shake his hand and return to the assembly. Instead, they disappeared with him. The podium was left unattended for 18 minutes. Delegates from 193 countries first started exchanging whispers, then louder conversations across rows as a variety of cellphones were produced. Some, like Robert Mugabe of Zimbabwe, slumped in their chairs. Sheikh Hamad Bin Khalifah, Emir of Qatar, appeared glad to find his stunning wife, Sheikha Mozah, next to him. Nervous Libyans looked more nervous. Puzzled Albanians looked more puzzled. Kazakhstan and Turkmenistan did not seem to notice. As a heavy-set delegate with a thick briefcase ran around in circles desperately seeking to find his place, a veteran observer noted that the confused scene somehow symbolized our drifting, leaderless world.

At this crucial period, there is not one single national leader commanding a truly international appeal. It may be a sign of our anxious, uncertain times. Ironically, an electronic signal at the highways leading to Manhattan during the General Debate announced: "UN Meeting. Expect Delays."

Expect more of the same for a while – but hold on to your dreams.

A crucial key to an effective, refreshed UN role is to encourage youth to join its ranks and to place women in more executive positions, especially in communications: the UN image needs a real, renewed effort in this field and in a world where perception often is reality.

Despite discouraging signals and disappointing politically expedient appointments at various levels, UN objectives continued to have motivating appeal worldwide, particularly among young men and women ready and able to serve. The Organization's universal vision and inclusive framework is uniquely inspiring to a growing number of civic groups and individuals seeking to make a difference in facing the challenges of survival. Many of them are already inside the UN system. The majority of civil servants are by commitment eager to serve the greater global public good. Many others are aspiring to join in. What they need is to be directed by a credible, inspired and inspiring leadership.

There have always been discussions about opening the UN doors wider to rejuvenate it. I recall upon arrival at the UN, I helped draft the first resolution by the Assembly on the need to involve youth more effectively in its work. My expectations were slightly lowered after the first meeting of the inter-agency working group to implement the resolution. It was chaired by a retiring man who knew best how to draft a report acceptable to member states rather than how to open recruitment doors. Unemployed youth are awaiting in key countries, but much more has to be done than to declare August 12 as International Youth Day, or hold occasional meetings or Model UN's.

It was almost farcical during a certain period that calls to rejuvenate the UN with youth coincided with arrangements to "rejuvenate" retired former colleagues. There is no retirement age for the Secretary-General or Under- or Assistant Secretaries-General. All others had to leave either at 60 or 62. Some, however, found their way back, blocking posts for younger staff. Since movement is linked to open vacancies, the system gets partially clogged, not allowing fresh air or new blood to come in. There were questions about favorite retirees returning on special contracts. They all knew the rules very well; it was done in a manner that may not be illegal, but certainly improper and contrary to the claim of rejuvenation or reform.

A standing rule specifies that a retiree who returns on a special assignment would not be allowed more than a specific amount capped at a fraction of what they used to earn. Yet the number of favored retirees returning in the late 1990s was higher than at any previous time before. Awkwardly, some directors or senior officials – even an assistant-secretary-general and in one case a former under-secretary-general – who had received sizable sums upon retirement, returned at a much lower P4 or P5 level. Working under direct supervision of their former subordinates was embarrassing and demoralizing for the rest of their colleagues.

Understandably, experience is needed to guide newly appointed staff in specific areas: where the expense to the Organization is limited to a given timeframe, or a certain undertaking for a couple of weeks; or where someone can provide specific knowledge of a special case. Several UN resolutions underline rejuvenation of the Organization. But that does not merely mean new computers, walls or electronic entry passes. There is no alternative to the human factor; it is people who make the UN, not the key cards or the walls.

So many talented young people yearn to play a useful role. Kofi Annan reconfirmed this in one of his first pronouncements when taking office, indicating that he would seek to integrate young blood. What actually happened was to the contrary, as any observer would witness. His own Chef de Cabinet was the oldest ever to hold that position. There may have been a reason for this, but then there was no need to make repeated announcements about rejuvenation when some newly appointed individuals could hardly plod their way along the corridors of power.

In order to ensure commitment, loyalty and institutional memory, a corps of effective staff of all ages is crucial. The leadership should inspire staff while leading by example and remaining firm in not tolerating dead wood. That means having a mobile multi-functioning staff with emphasis on effective delivery as a path to career development; relevant training as a prelude to change assignments; accountability to enhance credibility; and recognition that everyone at all levels is a valuable member of the same team.

Where are the Leaders?

Three international summits held within one week of September 2014 hardly received any relevant public attention. The presence of over 120 heads of state and government did not seem to have an impact except on New York City traffic. A one-day conference devoted to climate change was not noted for substantive decisions, despite opening and closing appeals by Secretary-General Ban Ki-moon or supportive public marches the day before. The only statement gaining special note was by the president of a Pacific island who cautioned that it was literally going under water. A Security Council meeting about terrorism, particularly the threat of the Islamic State (ISIS), was dutifully recorded and reported; however; the only related noteworthy statement in Arab media was an admiring reference to a position expressed by the President of Argentina, Cristina Fernández de Kirchner, that those described as terrorist adversaries today had been presented as "supportive allies" of yesterday. At a third occasion, the General Debate, which normally was an opportunity for major policy declarations, the main competition seemed to be limited to jockeying for position on the list of speakers after traditional Brazil and the host country, the US. Otherwise, there was a shifting focus and ponderous search for priorities. Most speakers at these gatherings traditionally made important contributions on major current affairs. Lack of public interest may not be just a communications failure, though that should be seriously considered. Rather, it raises a number of questions not only about the value of high-level meetings these days but about wider prospects in our increasingly close yet surprising disconnected world.

Is the UN no longer inspiring? Has it lost its once-central role in the mainstream of international relations for good? Is it a weakness of leadership, the erosion of the international civil service, or a breakdown of its framework mechanism? Is our world falling apart because there are no cohesive leaders, or is it leaderless because its states are fragmenting?

Is it a worldwide crisis of leadership? A lack of confidence in governments? Or a growing trend of popular indifference?

Did national leaders with an international standing just disappear or have they turned into local politicians with divided and divisive strategies obsessed with mere survival rather than a historic vision? Did strategies turn into tactics and tactics into political theatre?

Have the majority of heads of state remained far too long in powerful authority, some for a minimum of 20 years, to any longer inspire a majority of their populations, including women and youth? Is the UN leadership vulnerable or is an outdated framework breaking down? Has a ponderous membership slid into futile confusion? Will a new UN leadership with an inspiring profile help?

Is the UN a mirror of an increasingly clashing world, or are mirrors no more as relevant as iPads are abundantly in hand?

Are "halos" out and "selfies" in? A symbolic question could not be avoided or averted: did the President of the US and Prime Minister of Denmark gamely share a selfie at the funeral of the hallowed Nelson Mandela?

Again on symbolic moves: is it "helmet" time rather than radiant charisma? Anyone with institutional memory could wonder when watching a self-proclaimed "ordinary" President of France scurrying on his scooter at dawn to the Élysée Palace once occupied by the legendary Charles de Gaulle?

Is it time to reevaluate charisma?

Is the new digital media to blame for privacy interference or habitual human frailty expressed and exposed? Is it speed pending accuracy? Consumer rather than public interest? Is it a swift predominance of the new news or failure of the old ones?

Is taboo taboo'd?

With the number of emerging players yearning for the past are we getting back to the future? If so how distant? Is it the Big Powers' understanding after the fall of the Berlin Wall? Yalta in 1945 after World War II? Versailles in 1919? Skyes-Picot around 1916? Westphalia in 1948? The battle of Kerbala in Iraq in 680? The Caliphate itself centuries earlier than the black-turbaned Al Baghdadi in 2014? Is it a yearning for an Ottoman empire in an era where Sultans ruled from the Balkans to the Red Sea, or is going further to the fall of Byzantium a thousand years ago when, as the quip goes, the Holy Roman Empire stopped being holy, or Roman, or an empire?

Are changes in names and structures within States causing confusion, or is confused politics leading to change? Did Yugoslavia split, for example, because of an externally devised plot, or was it plunged into a tragic search for status after Slovenia decided it had enough guarantees to declare a state with least damage? By the way, when the daughter of former Yugoslav President Tito's close Indonesian ally Sukarno took over as President of that country, his son was sent as an accredited ambassador to Jakarta; however, were there several changes in the name of all concerned? It was Ms. Megawati Sukarnoputri who received Aleksander Broz as the representative of Croatia.

Was Yugoslavia a separate case because of its Balkan position, or was it a prelude to a trend of fragmented states into smaller ones and smaller ones divided into entities? How come some states in periods of transition, like those that became independent after the fall of the Soviet

Union, maintain the same leaders with different status and a new rhetoric while others faced quite a different fate?

How are we to spot the difference between cosmetic and substantive name change, and who would bother to do so, except those directly involved?

In some cases, name changes are simply a logistical convenience or a practical expediency, for example when Cape Verde which carried that name since its independence from Portugal in 1975 decided to change it thirty years later to Cabo Verde; most other countries took it in stride with hardly any notice, except Canada and Cambodia plus some UN secretariat staff. Every year the Secretary-General picks, lottery style, the name of the country that gets front-row seat at the forthcoming General Assembly session. Others would follow in alphabetical order. As the change to Cabo was done in October 2003 during ongoing General Assembly meetings, it entailed a changing of chairs two delegations ahead.

In practical terms when making crucial decisions in an increasingly fragmented, leaderless world, are instincts overwhelming reason, mercenaries undercutting heroes, and computers replacing institutional memory? Or is it simply time changing, that is, to use the other UN working language, "*C'est la vie*"?

Has our planet entered the fragmentation zone? The absence of leadership habitually turns divisive. Why has the unity within even traditionally solid, unified countries come to face open challenges?

Who would practically benefit out of thriving on chaos?

Is the lack of effective action to confront visible common danger mere incompetence, ponderous musing or a conceived determination? By whom?

Has life become too fast through communications technology for formal institutions to cope, let alone average people? Or are institutions taking their habitual time to tame technological speed?

Have movie stars and pop artists collectively discovered the UN, or did their business agents unearth a discount in performance expenses when it is done for a humanitarian cause? For example, whether Ban Ki-moon won over Beyonce or Jay-Z made a better deal with Samsung was an open question.

Why are at least two "advisors" kept on the payroll of the Secretary-General's office for 18 years beyond any maximum limit? Are they a front, and for whom? A back channel? Or merely "bluewashed" freeloaders with convenient New York residences?

Would it be the end of the UN as we knew it? Do we have a refresh button on its leadership? Or, to put it in musical parlance, did Elvis leave the Building for good?

Would it be the "Big Bang" or the "Big Deal" between prominent allies and their proclaimed adversaries? What would that entail? Or would it be an extension of a managed understanding of parallel interests and perceived differences? If in doubt, try bargaining for a Persian carpet in the bazaar?

Has a long-serving UN envoy expanded his mission with his own leeway to arrange for a strategic understanding between certain Gulf States and Israel? Are there any specific indications of that key arrangement which seems to be intentionally overlooked?

Is Saudi Arabia the real target behind the extending, expanding armed confrontations in the Arab region, particularly Syria, Iraq and Yemen?

Besides the standard concept of a strategic alliance between the US and Saudi Arabia, what precisely is going on during those senior officials' visits, mainly to Riyadh,but also to Washington DC?

Saudi Arabia has both incomparable oil bounty and a unique religious significance, in addition to a particularly strategic location. While the port city of Jeddah was its main point of entry for business, pilgrimage and diplomacy, its capital Riyadh was transformed from a historic town into a major metropolis by its "Emir" (Governor). For decades, Prince Salman, who also operated as the "general manager" within the Royal family, was its main discreet conciliator and practical communicator. When he took over recently as King, pressures of a swiftly changing world and a tragically contentious area would naturally affect a new leadership strategy.

Where Are The Leaders?

Its traditional posture was to maintain a conciliatory role. Its leadership followed a balancing approach, extending its stature yet carefully keeping a distance from disruptive direct clashes. Its internal unity and external prominence could be unduly pressured by persistent distraction elsewhere. When gradually drawn into prolonged militant conflicts nearby, particularly involving uncontrollable subsidized foreign fighters, would inevitably make it vulnerable not only to foreign security infiltration but to internal tension. Its valuable resources, including its precious human assets, would be drained and its prominent role unduly tested by varied adversaries –and even by presumed allies with an eye on the biggest prize. Its main threat most likely is from within; it is for others to exploit internal issues and expand areas of dividing. It may therefore be best to focus on enhancing external solidarity and internal unity through conciliatory measures and a consensus-derived vision of the future.

How advanced are the prospects of a substantive connection between Saudi Arabia and Israel, and, in turn, with Gulf countries? The question was particularly raised in July 2016 after a former Saudi General who had served in Washington, D.C. openly visited Israeli officials in Jerusalem. How did these relations evolve? Who was involved? Was it earlier than the recent clash with Iran? How many backchannels were used? As the Saudi Interior Ministry officially forbids such contact, at what level were they authorized? How indicative were other public encounters at varied conferences like those by former Saudi Intelligence chief Prince Turki, whose father King Faisal was popularly known for taking an entirely opposite position? A factual, informed review would shed a perceptive light on the shaping of a shifting regional structure. Incidentally, the assassination of King Faisal signaled a new era of gradual divisiveness in the whole region. A generally tacit consensus amongst national leaders with regional appeal and international following was slowly but surely replaced by a variety of rulers using rhetorical slogans to incite tension within and across borders. An unintended consequence was an evolving militant fragmentation that more recently took a sharp emotional edge with a complicating sectarian cover.

There may be signals of reconciliation between Israel and Saudi Arabia, perhaps also prompted recently, even before the open clash with Iran. There have been approaches of back channels before the open clash with Iran, and there were several areas of connection; for anyone who is interested, they could follow.

Was a growing interest in the role of the Shia-populated areas due to theology or because they happen to live where key oil fields are located? In Yemen, is the fight between Houthis, al Qaida allies, government troops and a combination of forces about conserving the unique nature of the world's oldest capital, Sanaa, or about Bab El-Mandeb, the southern tip of the Red Sea to the Suez Canal, the basic navigational link between Asia and Europe? Was the need to stress the sensitivity of that strategic location a main reason behind a move by neighboring Oman to host a meeting on Iran nuclear capacity with US Secretary of State Kerry, Iranian Foreign Minister Zarif and European Commissioner Catherine Ashton then Mogherini? Oman has a highly experienced, though very discreet, Minister of Foreign Affairs, Yusuf Bin Alawi, who most likely wanted to illustrate that the potential to block the flow of Gulf oil through the Strait of Hormuz was a weapon almost comparable, but of course not at all similar, to having a nuclear deterrent?

Would the "new" Saudi leader begin exploring alternatives to resolve the crises in Syria, Iraqand Yemen? Would a number of Russian, Iranian and Turkish actors start placing their most flexible foot forward?

Is the concept of the Millet System in the Ottoman Empire, a title of a seminar led by Professor Bernard Lewis at Princeton in the 1970s, about internal sectarian (Millet) governance making loosely interpreted implications? Is that why Turkish President Erdogan is openly "Ottomanly"?

What is the most serious threat to the world's most dominant power, the United States of America? Is it an attack from another power, which would bring massive retaliation? Competition for influence around the globe? Or is it really internal instigation to split ethnic groups and fragment social entities in a federation of states superbly strengthened by its unity and freedom rather than separated by its differences? Shouldn't any US administration approach fragmentation of other countries abroad with utmost care as that contagious sentiment may spread universally? Isn't it a basic US interest to solidly stress in word and deed unity of social fabrics and sovereignty of federated states to signal the unique edge of its own example? Particularly in a free democracy, generally admired globally and closely observed by differing regimes? Shouldn't representative officials and their competing politicians taking public positions be welladvised to pay more attention to their international pronouncements and be more aware of their impact abroad?

Maybe by accident or design but why is it that whenever the declared masters of the universe face undeclared bankruptcy a conflict erupts that raises growing concern and leads to a rewarding intervention? That role is not limited to governments but extends to a growing number of stakeholders who could be in certain cases more influential than some perplexed governments, which would eventually wait to follow suit? As the main source of cash lies in oil-producing Gulf countries, is a strategically threatening situation the surest way to "shake the tree"?

Experience proves that irregular subsidies to foreign fighters, however their perceived interim usefulness, will come back to haunt their initial mentors. Shouldn't powerful Governments, particularly in open and free countries, be more carefully firm in dealing with their allies as well as adversaries on this risky issue? Is the hand that gives more corrupt than the hand that receives? Occasional mainstream media reports seem to expose one rather than the closer other. For example, why would a cash-rich Gulf country recently buy $90 billion worth of almost unused military equipment over four years unless its rulers were seeking survival guarantees in troubled times? Why would another one recently pay $11 billion in two years from a European country except to buy protection against a perceived aggressive neighbor? How many "devils" were there in the details?

Giving and taking is not restricted to the powerful and the rich; it varies in character from adventurous pirates in northern Somalia, to diggers for natural resources in the Congo, to those benefiting from the world's largest opium market in Afghanistan, to tobacco smugglers in the Balkans, to those stealing historical artifacts from Syria and Iraq, to others in the Asian Golden Triangle of Myanmar, Thailand and Cambodia, to a line of politicians trying to explore yet unexplored unproven prospective oil fields off the coast of Lebanon, Israel, Cyprus and Gaza.

Clearly the US Secretary of State and Iran's Foreign Minister are experimenting with rebuilding a relationship "one drop at a time," which may not work as new demands accumulate with more time and with interest. Yet there are several other parallel political, academic and business contacts by, through and in other countries on varied ventures with so many intermediaries who prefer to remain in the shadows. As an Asian diplomat would say: Does where they stand on an issue depend on where they are seated?

What precisely is the "Islamic State for Iraq and Sham"; "for Iraq and Syria"; "Iraq and Levant"; finally, "Islamic State"? Why was it astonishingly easy for it to recruit and mobilize before taking over resourceful territory? Who exactly is Sheikh Abubakr El Baghdadi? In the region, where everyone is known to the last distant cousin and the latest social activity, how come very little has been known or reported to be known about him earlier by a usually inquisitive media? Have we reached an era of selectively convenient amnesia? Who decides what to forget, and who is entitled to remember?

Anyone who has lived in areas of conflict knows that announced names could represent a convenient cover, or a colorful diversion. Why after five years is there almost no informed public reporting on who precisely wields operational power within that "State?"

Why did certain officials in the active Gulf country of Qatar financially subsidize for at least three years, foreign armed personnel from distant countries to inject them in the Arab region under the blasphemous claim that they were serving the hallowed, gracious Islamic faith? Was it to gain leverage in the region? Balance other active players? Deliver a promise to an external source? Participate in breaking down Arab society? And in whose interest? Will the official who had to fall on his golden sword after a tragic outcome try to come back with a little help from his friends?! A widely publicized declaration by al Qaida and its allies in 1996 pledged an international jihad against "Crusaders and Jews". Should ISIS issue a declaration of gratitude to certain prominent Western countries and influential individuals, who facilitated the takeover by their allies of most of Libya and other territories?

"To whom would I submit my resignation?" Yemeni President Ali Abdullah Saleh gave that answer when asked whether he considered leaving office after a quarter of a century in power. Did other colonels like the one in Mali and elsewhere maintain the same logic until they were finally awakened by the source to whom they should have responded without question: their own people? By the way, President Saleh was the only Arab official to attend the funeral of US President Ronald Reagan in June 2004. He was televised arriving at the official mass at the cathedral wearing his national robe and turban and placed in the forefront of official mourners. Even when the USS Cole was bombed in his territory no suspicions were raised. Ten years later in November

2014, ex-President Saleh was officially sanctioned by the US for helping Houthi rebels to undercut his successor in Sanaa. What happened in between?

With widespread reports of gruesome acts of terrorism of pronounced counter-measures, shouldn't more attention be paid to what officials in the region directly involved actually do, rather than what they proclaim?

When will self-serving, profit-seeking opportunist politicians be replaced by an inspiring, popularly credible national leadership that would not only abort catastrophic foreign deliveries at home but help spread positive reconciliation throughout the region?

A prevailing era of conflicting powers, confused countries, fragmented States, self-declared terrorist groups, erosion of authority, public apathy, degrading poverty, and the tragic displacement of millions of refugees is further complicated by an uncontrollable mix of the regular and irregular, orderly and disorderly, powerful and power-obsessed, rich and rich-seeking, poor people defending their community and ruthless adventurers seeking gains, perplexed State and frustrated stateless, a seemingly hopeless affairs of state.

Attempts to handle divisive conditions and catastrophic migration tragedy through "high-level" gatherings with varied names like "coalition of the willing," "Group of Eight," "Group of 20" over the last decades didn't deliver a convincing response. Should its main source of hope be in the upcoming generation of youth and women, plus the remaining faithful who aspire to a better and brighter world? Is that all that officialdom could do? Isn't it time to explore really seriously and practically how to strengthen, refresh and energize the only inclusive framework for all the world's member States with a universally agreed objective? Doesn't the UN, humanly imperfect and institutionally indispensable, offer a hopeful, perhaps only, available alternative? Isn't a new UN leadership, with active, credible participation of the "peoples of the United Nations" as indicated in the Charter, and a sharper practical focus on handling urgent issues, worth a determined quest for human survival?

CHAPTER IX:

LEADERS BEARING GIFTS: IT'S YOUR WORLD

Almost everything in the UN Headquarters, from the symbolic to the practical, comes from somewhere around the world and reflects a shared undertaking. The Security Council chamber was donated by Norway. On a wall outside the chamber's entrance a mural of Guernica depicts the scourge of war. The Trusteeship Council, which originally dealt with the granting of independence to colonized peoples, was donated by Denmark, and the Economic and Social Council chamber by Sweden. One of the most coveted conference rooms, the elegantly compact Room Number 8, with flowers carved into oak-paneled walls and wall-to-wall green carpeting, came from the United Kingdom, which also donated the limestone facade of the General Assembly and Conference building. Sixteen coffee tables and 70 chairs were donated by Austria to refurbish what was formerly known as the Viennese Café in the basement; it was subsequently renamed the Cafe Austria.

Even before entering the building, a visitor can spend some time admiring artwork thoughtfully spread out throughout the grounds. A 16-foot equestrian statue in the North Garden, given by Yugoslavia in 1954, symbolizes peace, represented by a woman on horseback carrying an olive branch in one hand and a globe in the other. A "children's fountain," named after a donation by American students, stands in front of the Secretariat Building and is sometimes illuminated in the evening. The architects who planned the fountain wanted a pattern of alternating black and white pebbles to decorate its surrounding floor. White pebbles were easy enough to find, but the problem was where to get the black ones. The Governor-General of the Greek Dodecanese Islands sent a sample of a traditional pebble mosaic used in Lindos, a small town on the island of Rhodes. When the offer was accepted, wives of local fishermen gathered 760 sacks of the black pebbles from the shallow waters off the coast of Rhodes. The fountain was paid for through contributions totaling $50,000 by American children. It was dedicated on June 26, 1952, the seventh anniversary of the signing of the Charter in San Francisco, and a plaque highlights it "as a gesture of friendship to the children of the world and a constant reminder of our hope for a peaceful world through the United Nations."

Although the water in the fountain circulates via the United Nations' air-conditioning system, some of the organization's managers insisted on turning it off during a period of fiscal crisis that coincided with a water shortage in New York. The purpose of this shut-off was to make an impact on public perception in the host city and to send a political message to the host country. They were overruled by more optimistic colleagues, and for a while insiders measured from the state of the outside fountain the status of shifting internal influence.

Next to the fountain are two unique works of art. Dag Hammarskjold had often privately expressed the wish that the circle in front of the Secretariat building would one day be adorned with an appropriate sculpture. He had also indicated his view that such an artwork might be most suitably executed by his friend, Barbara Hepworth of England, whose work he greatly admired. This wish was fulfilled in memory of the late Secretary-General through a grant from the Jacob and Hilda Blaustein Foundation. Mr. Blaustein was a United States delegate to the United Nations. The sculpture, 21 feet high on a granite plinth, is entitled "Single Form." It took 20 months of work by the artist, who inscribed in the abstraction near the top "To the Glory of God and the Memory of Dag Hammarskjold, Ndola 17-9-61." She indicated that it symbolized "his idealism and singleness of purpose." The late Secretary-General had also greatly admired the sculptor Henry Moore, with whom he had discussed having one of his works on the grounds. Nineteen years after Hammarskjold's death, on September 17, 1982, "Reclining Figure" was unveiled. It is a bronze casting, standing seven feet long and four feet high, and it graces the front lawn.

These gifts have been placed in the open outdoor public area, two of them visible and the third tucked away at the far northern corner of the garden. Visitors entering from E. 46th Street will find to their right a huge replica of a revolver twisted into a knot. This gift was offered by Luxembourg, although the work is by a Swedish artist. Objections were both conceptual and artistic. Civil society groups, staff members and several delegations found the sight of a gun, in whatever form, at the visitors entrance of an organization of peace somewhat disconcerting; others found the work grotesquely ugly. Everyone went along in the belief that artistic variety was a price to pay for political consensus. Another sculpture on the left side of the entrance, "sphere within a sphere," may sound better in Italian, particularly since it is the work of Arnaldo Pomodoro. Objections to its placement, mainly because it had already been sold or placed elsewhere in Manhattan, were overruled, because it was officially presented by the Foreign Minister of Italy in a very brief ceremony.

A third gift may be more amusing. For years persistent approaches were made by a group of individuals to install a bronze replica of a huge African elephant. It was claimed that the purpose was to provide a vivid image of wildlife and highlight the role of the natural environment. Two Secretaries-General turned down the relentless campaigners, who finally found willing sponsors and a receptive audience. New aides working under the banner of "A UN Open for All" agreed, particularly highlighting the African dimension of the offering. At the official ceremony, delegates were as surprised as the accommodating Mr. Annan to find out that the casting had been made while the elephant was in very obvious heat for a mate. Very soon, curious staff and resident correspondents hurriedly rushed to witness and exaggerate the unusual endowment, while officials found excuses to hotfoot it to other engagements. Taking charge, a Pakistani aide put his head to his hand and decided that the bronze-white elephant in custody could be located in the wilderness near E. 49th Street, surrounded by adequate shrubbery.

Outside the General Assembly Hall stands a mosaic panel created in the Andalucian style of the twelfth century. This gift was offered by King Hassan of Morocco, and inscribed upon it, next to the preamble of the Charter, "We, the peoples of the United Nations," reads a quotation from the Quran: "We created you male and female and made you into nations and tribes so that you may know each other. The closest of you to Allah is the most righteous."

Across from the mosaic is a unique Persian carpet that was presented by founding member Iran. Canada donated the steel doors to the Assembly building's entrance, where the Foucault Pendulum, a device that demonstrates visual proof of the Earth's rotation, was given by Queen Juliana on behalf of the Netherlands. The pendulum hangs next to a life-size stainless steel model of the Russian Sputnik, the first spacecraft, just yards away from an impressive seven-foot tall replica of a statue of the naked Poseidon of Artemision, God of the Sea, offered by Greece. Nearby, a free-standing composition donated by Marc Chagall hangs in memory of Dag Hammarskjold and those who perished with him in that fatal air crash near Ndola, Zambia. The cost was met by United Nations staff. As Mr. Chagall described it himself during the unveiling ceremony on September 17, 1964, "On the right side of the panel you will see mankind, with its yearning for peace, its prophets and its victims. In the center is the symbol of peace itself. On the left, above and below are depicted motherhood and the people who are struggling for peace: The main thing is not to just see it, but to feel it." It is appropriately located near the entrance to the Meditation Room, a sanctuary of silence bathed in soft fight. This room had been frequented by Secretary-General Hammarskjold and was open to staff until recently.

Another of Hammarskjold's favorites was a garden overlooking the East River, with an exquisite collection of flowers. The garden had been popular among those working in the neighborhood, particularly around lunchtime. On many a sunny spring day, it seemed like an open-air healthy alternative to a singles bar. That was before it closed to the public; first to expand the garage underneath, and then for security reasons. In the garden area stands a sculpture by Evgeniy Vuchetich, donated by the former Soviet Union in 1959 and entitled "Let us beat swords into plowshares." Another nearby gift was added to commemorate the 1987 signing of the Treaty on the Elimination of Immediate Range and Shorter Range Nuclear Missiles, known as the INF Treaty. Staff approaching the building from the northern entrance cannot miss a 39-foot, 40-ton strange depiction of Saint George driving a lance through the dragon's head.

The dragon itself is a hull from a decommissioned missile. It was explained at the time that in Soviet perception the dragon symbolized nuclear war - not the mythological beast of Christian tradition. Donated three years before the demise of the Soviet empire, it was entitled: "Good Defeats Evil."

Countries competing for a Security Council seat or a prominent position habitually produce a timely and visible signal. When Nigerian chief S.O. Adebo presented his country's sculpture, "Anyanwu" (the Sun), a woman clad in the regalia of an ancient kingdom and symbolizing the rise of a new nation, some delegations thought that placing it strategically along the way to the Security Council Chamber indicated that the Nigerian was a candidate for the post of Secretary-General. A Polish President of the General Assembly could not conclude his year's term in office without demonstrating his country's intellectual prowess by placing a bust of Copernicus at the entrance to the Library. A Liberian General Assembly President brought the UN an inlaid mahogany table that was rapidly placed in storage. Sometimes the mere placement of an object is challenged. A "Dialogues of Confucius" tablet was offered when China was represented by Taiwan. Calligraphy on a green marble plaque indicated the concept of *Ta Tung*, where mutual confidence and neighborly spirit prevail,"and all men are assured an abundant life." However, the plaque was removed after representation of the Peoples Republic of China was restored, and the Republic gave two gifts on the same day, October 7, 1974. A lush tapestry of the Great Wall now hangs on a wall in the North Delegates' Lounge; it weighs 280 kilos and was woven with more than 50,000 yards of wool, knotted 500,000 times. An ivory carving depicting the construction of a gigantic Chinese railway crossing over 600 miles stands on the third floor of the UN conference building. The carving shows a suspension bridge spanning the river over which Chairman Mao's army forced their way during the Long March. A third gift came from Beijing in 1995 "dedicated to the 21st century": a centenary treasure tripod representing "stability, tranquility and peace."

Even two close allies like the United States and Japan had a discreet, ongoing dispute that inevitably reminded them that they had once been at war. A Japanese Under-Secretary-General for Public Information initiated an elaborate display on Hiroshima and Nagasaki. It took another Japanese Under-Secretary-General to dismantle it years later. For over 20 years, that grim exhibit dominated the expansive first floor corridor connecting the General Assembly and Secretariat buildings. It contained statuettes and artifacts of remnants found in Japanese cities devastated by the first atomic bombs. A long glass wall, which normally looked outwards, was totally covered with black depictions of wailing women and sobbing children. At the time, an additional Japanese contribution was made "to improve the tour route" taken by visitors. A controversy then arose about whether a plaque should be placed in recognition of the contributor who had reportedly been accused of alleged war crimes. Mr. Sasakawa, the contributor, won.

Almost annually, the Mayors of Hiroshima and Nagasaki were ferried to UN Headquarters, with the typically appropriate receptions, conferences and roundtables, led by the senior Japanese official within the Secretariat and coordinated by the Japanese Mission. A pilgrimage became almost compulsory to all Japanese visitors to New York. Bus-loads were dropped off on E. 46th Street and First Avenue where they would immediately proceed to the exhibit, quickly observe the Japanese peace bell outside and hurriedly leave to explore the Big Apple. As they paid full rate for the tour, no one complained, least of all the exquisitely delicate Japanese guides whose one-hour tours were reduced to ten minutes. Everybody was happy.

The United States Mission, however, was not pleased. When the Deputy Permanent Representative made a *démarche*, the fearless leader of the Public Information Department diverted the blame to the staff of Public Services, who ran the guided tours. When the better-informed American came back, the accommodating leader supported some sort of a compromise gesture. A large portrait of President Reagan and USSR General-Secretary Gorbachev shaking hands was placed on a pillar, highlighting their agreement on a treaty on the non-proliferation of nuclear weapons.

Even when a non-Japanese was in charge, the arrangement was respected. Then suddenly, in the year 2000, the Japanese started expressing wider interest in the Japanese peace bell, which had been lying in the shadow of the tall Secretariat building. It was moved to a central position, then surrounded by some young trees, then expanded with an artistic zen-like stone arrangement. It became an increasingly tasteful display of landscaping that reached completion by taking over the whole area just in time for the Millennium Summit. A special reception was held with a ceremony at the Delegates' Lounge and attended by visiting Japanese dignitaries. Viewing the sight from the second floor, it looked like a masterful Japanese garden. The view became equally clear from the ground floor.

In the subsequent absence of visitors during the Assembly period, the opportunity was taken to dismantle the artifacts from Hiroshima and Nagasaki. With only one statue left in the corner, the darkened glass wall was fully restored to its original transparent view. From the inside, the garden and the peace bell appeared in full splendor, and the haunting exhibit was gone. Was this a symptom of the end of history, as Professor Fukuyama had predicted, or simply a deal whereby the atomic exhibit was given up in return for the garden? No one knows except for one simple fact: the Japanese senior staffer who had approved the move was soon recalled for another undisclosed assignment elsewhere.

Some gifts disappear through natural erosion. A plaster cast of an ancient royal sarcophagus presented ceremoniously by President Amin Gemayel of Lebanon on an official visit in 1982 was enjoyed outside the Delegates' Lounge until it started to disintegrate. A senior Lebanese staffer arranged to have it stored pending receipt of a more lasting one upon the occasion of a future presidential visit.

At the time the UN was created, the first gift was its very own compound. For a mere $8.5 million, in 1946 John D. Rockefeller helped to purchase the land, a former slaughterhouse on Manhattan's Turtle Bay; that amount of money may now buy merely one luxury penthouse apartment in the same neighborhood. The following year, in 1947, a group of architects from the United States, France, Brazil, Sweden and the Soviet Union started working on a unique design that creatively blended the concept of international peace with visionary modem architecture.

As the host country, the US combined official gifts with private donations, symbolic presentations with practical material. A memorial stairway from the North Terrace to the garden came from the Governor of New York State; an ornamental fence surrounding the UN grounds on First Avenue from 42nd to 49th Streets was given by the City of New York; Ralph Bunche Park across from the UN on 43rd Street was donated by the Mayor. A library of scientific literature and a four-ounce rock from the moon's surface with a plaque bearing messages from 73 Heads of State (the size of UN membership in 1970) presented by Apollo 11 astronauts are but a few examples. Some others include a Norman Rockwell mosaic entitled "The Golden Rule," which shows people of different nationalities banded together with the inscription "Do unto others as you would have them do unto you."

France donated three paintings, including a tapestry called "Le Ciel" (The Heavens) by Henri Matisse, which hangs in the Secretary-General's office on the 38th floor, and from the same artist is a collage entitled "Torch of Hope",used for a UNICEF greeting card. Made of yellow, blue and black paper, the original can be seen in the outer office on the same floor. Pablo Picasso's famous tapestry, "Guernica," named after a town destroyed by bombing in the Spanish Civil War, is on loan from Mrs. Nelson Rockefeller. A Salvador Dali painting (known as the "Painting"!!) bears a five-handed motif reflecting the five continents, while a rose symbolizes the "flower" of international cooperation.A mural by Jose Vela Zanetti depicting man's continued struggle for lasting peace was offered by the Guggenheim Memorial Foundation and blankets a wall on the third floor outside the General Assembly Hall. Its story begins with the destruction of a family and ends with its resurrection. First it shows the agonies of war, but then a hopeful emblem implants justice, human rights and reconstruction.

When it comes down to placement of this panoply of international offerings, the priority within the corridors of the compound is the same as that in the host city of New York: « location, location, location." Diplomatic maneuvers to obtain the most visible spot available are habitually handled at the highest level. A country's cultural reputation and political standing, let alone the extent of the ambassador's perception at home of his influence in the Secretariat, can come into play. Increasing interest by governments and sponsored artists has required the establishment of two groups, each headed by an Under-Secretary-General. A Gifts Committee decides on acceptance, giving priority to countries not yet represented. Guidelines indicate that the art "should as far as possible reflect the culture and history of a member State, which is responsible for installation, maintenance and insurance of the gift." Preference is given to original art and smaller works. An Exhibits Committee reviews requests for thematic displays at specific locations, such as the Visitors Lobby of the General Assembly, a basement neck leading to conference rooms, and a third floor corridor linking the two buildings. Consistently outstanding displays are those offered along the guided tour route. This also applies to a joint annual presentation by all programmes, highlighting a special message. Temporary exhibitions are held for short periods in the Secretariat building, between the entrance and the cafeteria; these require the approval of a Staff Recreation Council.

While almost every corridor or wall is now loaded with some sort of artistic touch, the only overlooked area had been the Library entrance. A long corridor leading staff from E. 42nd Street to their offices and language classes remained dimly lit and bare. Very few delegates ventured through it. It seemed as if the divide between a rich North and poor South applied also to artistic treasures with the confines of the same international building.

That situation was improved in 1997 when colorful, prize-winning posters and photos - and better furnishings - illuminated the walls; an active lounge for non-governmental organizations also added to the atmosphere. A comprehensive alphabetical list of gifts presented to the United Nations by governments, organizations and individuals was produced as a public document by the Public Inquiries Unit of the Department of Public Information. It provides a concise description of dates, locations and donors. Even for someone who might have spent a lifetime in the building, this list has become indispensable for jogging one's memory and quoting the precise context as part of one's personal narrative. I'm reminded, for example, that in September 1963 King Zaher of Afghanistan presented a lapis lazuli inlaid table with the UN emblem in white marble; it is displayed in the reception room of the Secretary-General, whose varied special envoys met the exiled monarch in Rome over the last two decades in the hope that his return would help restore peace to that tormented country. Armenia presented its holy "Khatchkar", a manuscript on stone dating back to the thirteenth century; it was an astonishing spiritual experience for me to meet their late Catholicos, the highest patriarch, who was born and brought up in Lebanon.

Several countries have donated miniatures, carpets, murals and leather crafts. Prince Sihanouk of Kampuchea presented his own work, "Khmere". An oil painting, "Corazon de los Andes", was provided by Chile, while Colombia donated its outstanding Alejandro Obregon's "Sun Rises in the Andes". And Cuba gave an oil painting on the pleasure of lively living titled "Gran Carnival". Cyprus provided a beige terra cotta vase made circa 600 B.C., and Egypt gave a 2,700-year old gilded bronze statuette of the ancient god Osiris. A hand-carved ivory obelisk constructed at about 327 A.D. in Aksum, the center of Ethiopia's government for the first nine centuries of the Christian era, stands on the second floor. A stainless steel sculpture celebrates the Finnish composer Jean Sibelius; a bronze sculpture of a standing male figure by Germany symbolizes "The Rise of Man"; the Vatican presented a ceramic "Embrace Of Peace"; Hungary, a porcelain vase; India, a statue of "Sun God Surya" and a portrait in crayon of its first Prime Minister; Iraq, a photographic album of antiquities; Kuwait, a teakwood model of a traditional ship, the *khow*; Mali, an ebony antelope headdress; Malta, an abstract painting; Mexico, a painting about brotherhood; Micronesia, a carved wooden eel; Mongolia, a golden plate from the period of Genghiz Khan that entitled the bearer to diplomatic immunity and privileges; Romania, a tapestry called "An Ode to Man"; Nicaragua, an old rifle on a wooden frame; Oman, a silver incense burner and coffee pot; Panama, a tapestry done in the *mola* style of the indigenous Kuna Indians; Peru, a ceremonial mantle representing the Paracas culture of 1,000 B.C.; and Portugal, a panel made of ceramic tiles depicting the city of Lisbon.

Saudi Arabia presented a black curtain from the door of the holy Kaaba in Mecca, a pure silk cloth with Koranic verses embroidered in gold and silver threads; it had originally hung for centuries at the site until changed in 1978. "Coco de Mar", held in storage, is one of six species of palm trees donated by the Seychelles. Syria presented an exquisite replica of an 1,800-year old sculptural relief of Ishtar, the Babylonian and Syrian goddess of love and fertility. Thailand gave "Suphannahong," an articulate replica of a royal barge carved out of a single trunk of teakwood; Tunisia, a 1,700-year old mosaic masterpiece showing the cycles of the year; and Turkey, a clay tablet replica of the oldest known peace treaty in the world, the Kadesh Peace Treaty, signed in 1269 B.C. between the King of the Hittites and the Pharaoh of Egypt.

Nowhere else does such a valuable collection of treasures from all cultures exist with the sort of care taken in its display. There is no alternative to a personal visit in order to feel the impact of a historic joint cultural commitment to international harmony. And an added attraction to visiting the international complex is an individualized, lively interpretation by a group of young men and women who guide visitors through this colorful maze of corridors, halls and conference rooms.

Older tour visitors, as previously mentioned, often wanted to see where Soviet leader Khrushchev banged his shoe. More currently favorite visitor highlights are the Japanese peace garden, the Chinese ivory carving on which a hundred men worked for two-and-half years, the giant Belgian tapestry which contains enough thread to wrap around the world twice, and the Norman Rockwell mosaic depicting people of every age, race and creed. Children have the most touching questions and answers. A guide who wanted to involve her young audience in front of a disarmament exhibit pointed to pictures of landmines and asked whether anyone knew their enormous expense. One responded: "They cost you your life." Another guide who asked about her group's array of nationalities was in turn asked about hers. "I am from the land of the giant panda," she answered. "You mean from the Washington Zoo?" yelled one child before another quickly shouted, "China, China!"

Confusion due to accents always abounds. An Italian guide reported that at the end of her route she made the ritual request: "For security reasons, please take your stickers off." She kept on counting people to make sure that everybody was there with her. It only took a couple of minutes, just enough to realize that two young visitors had taken off their sneakers instead of the stickers, showing them proudly and yet wondering what for!

In the 60 years since tours started in November 1953, the many guides have briefed 37 million visitors to the UN building, which is by now a predominant element of the New York City skyline. Immediately following September 11th., guides volunteered to staff information kiosks set up by the American Red Cross in order to help visitors and family members of the missing. This was part of a project, a partnership of Microsoft and Compaq, entitled "Register to let others know you are OK." Joining other staff, particularly while the UN was closed to visitors, they worked in 27 locations, mostly in Manhattan, but also in Brooklyn, the Bronx, Queens and Staten Island. Their ability to communicate in 38 languages proved to be of invaluable assistance.

May is usually the busiest month for school groups; the number of annual visitors has fluctuated between a peak of 1.2 million in 1964 to around 400,000 in lean years. Guides, who alternate between a sharp uniform and individual national costume, have comprised as many as 40 nationalities in a given year; most work in more than one language.

Officially named Public Information Assistants but usually called guides, they are the main contact for visitors. U Thant used to describe them as "our Ambassadors to the public," and one of his aides was so keen on following their performance that he ended up marrying one of them. Particularly during the time of the launching of the Guided Tours, they had a glamorous cachet. As the job provided a special visa to stay in New York, a select group of formidably talented people enjoyed the diplomatic atmosphere while displaying their multinational commitment to facilitate cultural understanding. Their annual talent show used to be a popular internal event. Some of them continued in other posts within the Organization, and others, such as Mrs. Elizabeth Dole, reached prominent office in their respective countries. And three of the rare male guides returned years later as ambassadors: the Permanent Representatives of Angola, Finland and Uganda. Two world-renowned jewelers - one in New York, another in Paris - who married guides still welcome their former colleagues annually at their seaside villas.

There was always a general frustration, however, of not quite climbing smoothly through the hierarchical ranks. For example, except for the most senior appointments, staff members are divided into Professional Officers and General Service Clerks. Only after five years of uninterrupted service could a Clerk be entitled to compete in an exam to break the barrier. Guides were excluded even from that competition. Their contracts were generally for only two years. Even if they somehow managed to stay longer, their training and background gave them an edge over others at the same clerical level, those who influenced personnel decisions as a pressure group. Having little taste for bureaucratic entanglement, most of the guides left. A shift in their contractual status in the late 1980s offered a limited number of them the option of longer career contracts. Sixty flexible posts were streamlined into about 15 permanent and 10 part-time assignments. A conceptual problem was that recycled political administrators keen on looking good as reformers who could cut the budget targeted that vulnerable area whose constituents - the general public - were not part of the power-brokering setup. Some even suggested cancelling the Service completely and replacing human warmth with recorded tapes "like in some museums." Delegates drew the line at this suggestion. At a time when the UN needed the most support, it seemed illogical to cut one of its main lifelines to the public. A display in different languages was not an expensive shortcoming but a unique qualification. Besides, the Visitors Service was one of the few revenue-generating operations in the building. U.N. guided tours are generally recognized as one of the ten most popular New York events for every visitor.

The UN reflects our world, and is always worth a visit. Even more valuable than the treasured international artworks are the UN's young believers who guide visitors through a Workshop for Peace. Many have foreign accents, but, as the saying goes, that cannot be helped at the United Nations. They speak in many tongues, yet they deliver a unified message.

ABOUT THE AUTHOR

SAMIR SANBAR

International Communications and Media

- Served at the United Nations for 33 years with five different Secretaries-General in various assignments and capacities including as United Nations Assistant Secretary-General and Head of the Department of Public Information, later elevated to Under-Secretary-General.

- Implemented the appointment of women in all senior Communications posts in that department, doubling their level of representation to exceed 50 per cent, the first by any UN department.

- Established United Nations presence on the Internet, with the launch of the UN Website (www.un.org) in June 1995. By February, 1998, more than five million accesses per month to the site had been registered. After retirement, launched in the year 2000 www.unforum.com , an informal participatory website reflecting feedback from diplomats and staff on pending U.N .issues.

- Organized and chaired the first and second UN World Television Forum (1997 and 1998) at UN Headquarters, an unprecedented gathering of prominent communications and personalities from all regions and cultures, with a balance between representatives of public and private broadcasting.

- Initiated "Voices for Life", involving a select number of creative and sports stars (starting with Maestro Luciano Pavarotti) to highlight issues like plight of children in conflict; anti-poverty and anti-drug campaigns; education; peace; development and human dignity.

- Special Representative of the Secretary-General to head the UN Observer Mission to Verify the Referendum and arrange for a peaceful political transition in Eritrea, which became a UN member state.

- Served as Director of the United Nations Information Centres (68 centres around the world) in the

Department of Public Information from 1987 to 1993. Chief, United Nations Centres Services from 1982 to 1987. Undertook special assignments for the Secretary-General.

- Served as Secretary of the Board of Trustees of the UN Institute of Training and Research (UNITAR).

- Before joining the UN, worked as a columnist and journalist in Lebanese, Arab and international media.

- Scriptwriter of television documentaries and radio programmes.

- Author of several publications in English, French and Arabic including two books of short stories and a booklet of inspirational hints entitled "Hold on to Your Dreams".

- Graduate of the America University of Beirut.

Board Memberships

- Member and Chairman, United Nations Appointment and Promotions Board, from September 1986 through May 1996.

- Chairman, United Nations Staff Recreation Council 1996 – 1998.

- Member, Board of Directors, UN International School 1994 – 1996.

- Member, Board of Directors, Dag Hammarskjold Tower.

- Member, Board of Directors, The International Council of the National Academy of Television Arts and Sciences (1996-1999)

INDEX

Baghdad, 50, 51, 53, 55,
65, 66, 126, 140, 157,
189, 192, 201, 203, 204,
205, 206, 208, 209, 211,
212, 215, 217, 219, 237,
239, 240, 241, 242, 243,
245, 246, 247, 248, 249,
250, 252, 316, 325, 329,
373

Bahrain, 207, 212, 299

Balkanization, 156

Balkans, 116, 264, 360,
364, 380, 385

Balliol, 40

Ban Ki-moon, 19, 20, 78,
79, 86, 107, 173, 177,
178, 181, 191, 192, 194,
195, 197, 255, 294, 297,
298, 327, 343, 378, 382

Banco de Santo Spirito, 75

Bangladesh, 75, 102, 187,
218, 257, 296

Bani-Sadr, 119

bank heist, 359

Banque Commerciale du
Congo, 362

Banque Commerciale du
Rwanda, 362

Banque de la Confiance
d'Or, 362

Banque du Commerce, du
Développement et
d'Industrie, 362

Bantenamo, 20

Barbara Hepworth, 390

Barbara Walters, 85

Barbra Streisand, 26, 83

Basra, 207, 340

Bataclan, 332

battle of Kerbala, 380

Bayer, 216

BBC, 57, 87, 104, 136, 140,
162, 163, 182, 347

BBC World Service, 57

beaches, 11

Beatles, 8, 83

Bechuanaland, 71

Becket, 139

Head of Department, 12

Head of Library, 147

Heads of State, 14, 16, 17, 29, 30, 31, 81, 87, 89, 151, 168, 187, 198, 347, 362, 368, 375, 378, 379, 396

Heathrow airport, 346

Hebrew, 63, 70

Hedi Annabi, 173, 298

Helen of Troy, 54

helicopter crash, 315

Helmut Kohl, 89

Helmut Newton, 36

Henri Matisse, 2, 396

Henry Cabot Lodge, 167

Henry Kissinger, 26, 48, 179, 211, 334, 335

Henry Moore, 2, 390

Herr Schroeder, 216

Herzegovina, 187, 361

Hezbollah, 50

Hicksville, Long Island, 4

High Commissioner for Human Rights, 243

High Representative for Elections, 295

hijack, 350

Hillary Clinton, 135, 173, 224, 225

Hiroshima, 393, 394, 395

historical artifacts, 385

HIV/AIDS, 256

Ho Chi Minh, 5

Hollywood, 83, 144, 169, 170, 187

Holy Family Church, 67, 153

Honduras, 262

Hong Kong, 11

Horace, 184

hostage crisis, 51, 162, 230, 263

hostages, 231

Indonesia, 37, 96, 172, 364

Indonesian Lounge, 12, 14, 97, 178, 285

inefficiency, 318

INF Treaty, 392

Information Assistants of the guided tours, 235

Inga-Britt Ahlenius, 316

Ingrid Laux, 27

institutional memory, 195, 197, 275, 308, 311, 314, 317, 345, 353, 378, 380, 381

integrity, 58, 100, 114, 126, 162, 196, 322, 323

Intercontinental Hotel, 75

International Civil Aviation Organization, 143, 258

International Court of Justice, 55, 120, 146

international crime, 366

International Criminal Court, 302

International Day for Women, 278

International Declaration of Human Rights, 367

International Herald Tribune, 128

International Institute for Peace, 299

International Institute of Strategic Studies, 78

International Labour Organization, 4, 258

International Monetary Fund, 37, 193

International peace, 143

International Peace Academy, 245

International Telecommunications Union, 143, 258

international think-tank, 318

International Women's Day, 101, 326

sexual exploitation, 295,
307, 312, 324

sexual harassment, 329

Seychelles "Coco de Mar",
398

Shabbiha, 337

Shah, 15, 29, 48, 59, 116,
117, 118, 119, 153, 207,
240, 262, 340

Shah of Iran, 15, 29, 48,
153

shaheed,, 51

Shakira, 198

Sham, 157, 287, 386

Sham Hotel, Damascus,
287

Shashi Tharoor, 194

Sheikh Abubakr El
Baghdadi, 386

Sheikh Hamad Bin
Khalifah, 376

Sheikh Khalifah, 126

Sheikh Muhamad, 333

Sheikh Rashed Al-
Maktoum, 333

Sheikh Sabah Al-Ahmad,
36

Sheikha Mozah, 376

Sheraton Hotel, 273

sherpa, 347

Shia, 384

Shiite, 51, 68, 157, 207,
211, 212

Shimon Peres, 299, 335

Siam, 71

Sidi Mohammed, 29

Sierra Leone, 31, 90, 296,
315

Silicon Valley, 197

Simeon Adebo, 4

Sinai, 260, 307

Singapore, 4, 32, 59, 343

Sir David Gore-Booth, 285

sitrep, 84, 266

www.ingramcontent.com/pod-product-compliance
Lightning Source LLC
Chambersburg PA
CBHW062149270326
41930CB00009B/1487